Start Drilling-the Year 2020 is Coming Fast

CRISES
OF THE
21st CENTURY

JOHN DURBIN HUSHER

INKS & BINDINGS

Crises of the 21st Century: Start Drilling-the Year 2020 is Coming Fast

© 2022 John Durbin Husher

ISBN:

Paperback   979-8-88615-095-7

E-book   979-8-88615-096-4

Inks and Bindings
888-290-5218
www.inksandbindings.com
orders@inksandbindings.com

CONTENTS

Crisis VIII:

Crisis IX:

Crisis X:

Crisis XI:

APPENDIX

Prelude

The sub title of this book relates to one of the findings in this book. Start drilling since it will take till the year 2020 for any of the oil to be produced from a drilling site that would start today. This finding in this book relates to one of several of the century's crises to be discussed and I wouldn't want the reader to have to reach the end of this book to realize that we need to start drilling right now to ensure an ample supply of energy by the year 2020 in the United States. This is not meant to take away from progressing rapidly on establishing renewable energy as is discussed as one of the crises. I am concerned if we don't start immediately on establishing the oil the United States needs by 2020, we may not have the energy to reach the required renewables in the third decade of this century to offset the loss of oil energy. We also need to be self sufficient by the 20's or find ourselves levered out as a super-power. Some think that the push for drilling offshore is to reduce the cost of gasoline today. Establishing the sites today will not have any effect on the price of gasoline in the next ten years or more; the drilling is to keep from being blackmailed in the third decade of this century (2020 -2030) by those that have this important entity.

As you read you will find this to be a short term solution for a much bigger problem and in fact relates to just one of the eleven major crises I will discuss. These are not fool hearty crises; these are real ones that will impact each and every one of us in this world during the next fifteen to fifty years. Too many people are looking at one problem, in this case global warming, and not looking at the total picture. I intend to provide a more complete picture for all of you in this one book and point out actions that can be taken to prevent or alleviate these crises. I would expect this book to provide a roadmap for the leaders of the countries of the world. I also want to relax you on the subject of the ice melting. It is supposed to do this; how do you think the ice came about to begin with?

It's interesting how I got started on this subject matter. I am an electrical engineer by education but spent about forty four years as a solid state physicist inventing integrated circuits and providing leadership in the production and engineering of those ubiquitous devices. Including in my patents are two for solar cells that sort of provided me a lead into the subjects of this book. I retired in February of 2002 and became interested in the topics through my interest and research on the subject of global warming.

For me, the twenty first century began with a few featured words or phrases in the newspapers about global warming that aroused the curiosity and a form of conflict within me about this subject matter. The phenomena these words represented were not common to me as the twentieth century ended but they soon became my center of interest in this new century. There were words or phrases like 'global warming', 'energy crisis', 'population growth', 'world famine' and 'international disputes over oil', or the cost of oil that represented the fears of many people as this century began and they aroused in me a form of fear, or at least a sensitivity, to the subject matter. On the other hand there were other words or phrases that were diametrically opposed to this feeling and represented the hope that might offset these fears. In fact, phrases such as, 'energy substitutes', 'reduction of fossil fuel consumption', 'reducing air contamination', renewable energy, 'biofuels', 'population control', 'gene therapy implementation', and 'stem cell implementation', each with their wonderful concepts, gave me reason for hope. Being an optimist by nature, these invoked a warm sensation of hope that, like always, things weren't as bad as they first appear. This brought a sense of hope that the others were not real and these represented the real world; the world where man always found a way to overcome the 'all encompassing' once they became known and accepted by man as real threats around the world. World-wide focus always seems to bring meaningful results to the most complex of issues here on earth.

However, in this case the issues and resolutions were like a play on words, since the issues appeared to be real and some progress was already making headway in the international community as the century began, but the resolutions were not as real and seemed to fall short. As I researched each of these I soon came to the conclusion that a review of one of the subjects and its possible solution came in direct conflict with one of the others in one way or another. The more I researched the various conflicts, the more people I found who didn't know what they were talking about, or at least they were in direct opposition to others that I tend to believe. Usually, they were the people who focused on one of these subjects without regard to how they might affect or be affected by other possible conflicts of interest. In several cases where a solution was espoused, not enough research had been done on the solution. It was taken for granted without regard to its authenticity. At the same time the phrases that brought hopes, in many cases, were not directly related to those that elicited fear.

Like two sides of a coin, where some issues brought fear the other side of the coin brought hope, but not always the hope to solve the fear problems.. This was no different than normal issues which raise fear and with focused work man has been able to belay those fears. As is normal, the fear always precedes the hope and usually the solution is forthcoming. With every major issue there is always the hope to resolve it. Meanwhile, if not the solutions to the problems, perhaps solutions to related problems which in turn would help resolve the original problems. In this case the problems were so globally encompassing that I was not sure there would be a consensus of opinion on the seriousness and therefore no forthcoming solutions. The large number of people in the world spread over many countries, each with their own agenda, provides a huge inertia to overcome and expect a consensus of opinion with an immediate solution. I set about understanding the details of the issues and the suggested solutions only to find there were new issues that were not being addressed; issues that were more serious. This book is about the eleven most serious interrelated issues and some recommendations to the solutions and the hope of providing a roadmap to the solutions. The quantifying of the renewable energies will provide visibility that is not apparent at this time.

Global warming was being blamed on an increase in the atmospheric carbon dioxide and the automobile and its exhaust was being mentioned as the main culprit. The energy crisis was less emphatic and was perhaps raised to a level of more importance with a book I had written, *Beyond Global Warming* which downplayed the global warming and emphasized the fact that the real problem that faced the world was the loss of gasoline and its capability for providing portable energy. Where was the world's solution to obtaining a portable energy as efficient as a gallon of gasoline when oil reserves are used up? This also raised questions concerning the world's stability as the oil reserves will continued to drop in the very near future. Would there be world wide conflicts caused by the shortage of oil and its by-products? If so; when? Countries without oil reserves and its derivatives would be pressing countries that held these capabilities more than they are presently being pressured. Would there be answers prior to the oil situation reaching an explosive nature? As the material reserves decreased and this material lost its commodity status there might be wars to obtain this scarce entity. Many wars in the past have been the result of a shortage of food or some other substance that a neighboring country had in its possession while a scarcity prevailed in the nearby country. Why not oil and its derivatives which are so vital to all countries? Surely there would be a problem as the demand kept increasing from the developing countries while the supply peaked and began to dwindle sometime in the near future. The near future wasn't that far away as some of the major suppliers of oil today will not be supplying it in the next ten years. I provide details concerning the shipping and using countries that will run out of oil in the next ten to twenty years. The lost of oil energy is closer than most think.

Oil and its derivatives are directly related to population; that is, as the population increases the demand increases no matter if it is in a developed, undeveloped or a developing country. We are now at 6.7 billion people worldwide and the population growth shows us reaching 8.7 billion people in the not too distant future if the growth continues as it has. So, population growth rears its ugly head to compound the problems. I thought this might be the major crisis; the one where the population outgrew the ability to supply food, especially if there is an energy crisis and no means of transporting enough food around the world. It soon became obvious that population growth, food demands and the ability to transport the food globally became crises in the same time span as the energy issues. Famine could be just around the corner for many places around the world that don't have the problem today. I list nineteen potential crises that are boiled down to really eleven major crises that contain portions of all the nineteen in some way; and point out the major conflict or dependence between each of them.

On the other hand there were the "warm fuzzy" subjects like the renewable energies. There were the biofuels, wind energy, ocean wave energy, solar energy, hydroelectric energy, geothermal energy, hydrogen energy and our earthborn radioactive materials to bring us some relief from energy problems. Although nuclear energy was not considered as renewable energy, I chose to accept it as such because of the parameters that came with it. Surely the American scientists and other world scientists would find a way to resolve this tremendously important issue of finding an efficient portable energy to replace gasoline among the various renewable energy sources. The world surely doesn't want coal's use to go up along with its environmental problems it brings as baggage, but I soon realized that coal might be needed. The reader can make his/her choice. There was also the hope of inventions that would bring other forms of energy to the forefront to offset the loss of oil. There were the other "warm fuzzy" subjects like the human genome with the defining of which genes related to which functions in the human body and stem cell research with its answers for those laid low by health issues. I had researched these and written a book *The Wonder of Life* covering these subjects and therefore felt, as important as those are, I needed to focus on the "crises" I saw coming and the possible solutions.

Being a scientist of sorts during my lifetime, I had begun my thinking of possible solutions to the energy issues in a previous book *Beyond Global Warming* and research on the other of the fuzzy warm hopes provided the basis for my book *The Wonder of Life* which covered such subjects as the human genome and the results of stem cell research to date. This research gave me high hope that our scientists already were approaching the state of solution on renewable energy as well as a resolution to possible food issues that I believe to be a major crisis. There is an immediate conflict between the need for food and the use of biofuels for energy. Here you will see one of the conflicts of the renewable energies. Surely there would be the same level of progress on reducing the contamination of the atmosphere through renewable energy. My research carried me in this direction.

With the research on these various phenomena, I began to take positions based on reasonable assumptions on each as well as my past experience in the technical world. Eight years of research on these various subjects began to show me where they were cross connected in many ways. In some cases, such as global warming, the mathematics just didn't work out and demonstrated what was being said as not being collaborated by data. I also found others that took similar positions and provided their inputs as reference. There will be an increase in Earth's temperature this century but not due to carbon dioxide. I found it to be a cyclic change in temperature, but if it is due to carbon dioxide it isn't due solely to automobile exhaust. You will see why I take that position.

The renewable energies, if successful, provide a new problem to solve that hasn't been discussed to date. I found there to be problems with obtaining the energy levels needed to replace the loss of oil and its derivatives and I found a logistic problem that hasn't been faced to date. Even if we find the solution to providing the quantity of renewable energy we would then be faced with the logistics of supplying it. This is not an insignificant problem since this supply is quite different than the infrastructure established for the supply of oil. This problem is real and planning must occur before the fact to make renewable energy the solution to the overall problem, the one of providing the renewable energies worldwide. This book discusses in detail each of the renewable energy sources and provides some direction to the logistic solutions, country by country.

This book quantifies how much energy we can expect from each of the renewable energy opportunities and where in the world these sources are located. It summarizes the cumulative total from all of these renewable sources and compares this total on an annualized basis to what is needed worldwide and especially in the United States. This book defines a new term, "energy neutral" as that amount of energy needed from renewable energy to replace the energy loss of oil and to prevent greater use of coal. It points out what fossil fuels could be used as a "carry over" to replace a deficit in the renewables until the oil deficiency can be overcome. The economic growth in the world is discussed and shows how this presents new issues that need to be recognized very early, if an early solution can be expected. The new logistic issues, as they relate to renewable energy, are pointed out and hopefully bring this problem into proper perspective if we are to expect an early solution. There are also logistic issues that relate to transportation and the supplying of food for the huge growth in population over the next thirty years. By the year 2037 there will be 8.7 billion people on Earth and we must provide them with food while at the same time providing the possibility of biofuels for our portable energy needs. This presents a conflict and one of the "crises" discussed. Finally it demonstrates where we could fail to meet these global requirements. A good example of population and food problems can be realized when you look at the United States compared to China. The U.S. is the third biggest country in area followed very closely by China. They have almost the same area, yet China's population is more than four times that of the U.S. and has one fifth the arable land of the U.S. They will have an energy issue along with a food issue that must be solved. They used a considerable amount of their land for dams and reservoirs to provide hydroelectric power, a renewable energy, but it only exacerbates the problem of population and food. In the end you will see how the United States makes out by 2037 versus how the World makes out by the year 2037 as the energy sources are detailed for the U.S. and the World. It's quite an eyeful for each of you readers. As I wrote, I realized several inspirations on how to provide the world its needed energy and the answer lies in the Arctic and Antarctic parts of the world.

Realizing the excitement of this subject matter and how little the average person was informed on most of this material, I decided to put it all together in one book. There are books or articles that contain a discussion on each of the subject matter, however there are no books that cover all these broad subjects under one cover and bring their relationships to the forefront and to a central theme. I felt compelled to write a book that covered each of these subjects in a novel like format that was easy to understand; showing their relationship to each other and presenting a picture that clarifies the priorities the world should be taking. Covering the present and extrapolated status of each of these major issues in a succinct and easy to understand presentation is the noble objective of this book. And so, I began.

John Durbin Husher

Introduction

Reviewing present day events and extrapolating them out over this century I see many crises occurring and most of them involving loss of life; loss of life excluding wars. These involve nature and nature's forces at work. They also involve decisions by each country concerning their own welfare as well as the welfare of the international community. They involve difficult decisions since taking a stand on one causes extreme difficulty on one or more of the others. The United States and the world have never entered a century with so much at stake. Where some think of one of the crises to be the most important, others think not. Where Al Gore thinks of global warming as one of the most serious of the crises, I for one disagree with this perspective on global warming since I believe it is a naïve look at what is in store for the world.

The purpose of this book is to introduce the crises I foresee and how they interact with each other. I will present a candid and open mind discussion about each and allow the reader to make his/her own decisions on which affect the world's population the most. One must consider all of them at one time and see how they affect each other. I will quantify each from my prospective as I proceed and summarize them at the conclusion. You may agree that Al Gore's focus on global warming may do more harm than good when you review the real problems that are on their way. Gore has blinders on and fails to see the other issues and how they interact with global warming. However, I do agree with the actions to be taken to reduce global contamination even though I consider it as a "non issue" as far as global warming is concerned and any affect man can have on it.

The crises I see, and there are probably more, are:

- Global warming – Not due to Carbon Dioxide, but it will be warming
- Climate cycles – The real world where we are on one of the warming cycles; never experienced by man over the last three hundred and fifty years.
- Fossil fuels – How we use them and which will disappear and which should be avoided
- The loss of Oil – Not many years left, the big crisis with no portable fuel to run our big earth movers that produce food and fly the airplanes.
- Portable/mobile energy – Nothing to replace oil and gasoline. How do we fly?
- Renewable Energy – Status and the future projections for replacing fossil fuels
- The energy crisis – What will we use to replace oil and not use coal and its contamination?
- Logistics – Why renewable energy is not there when you need it. It's a different world and the infrastructure is quite different than the one provided by the oil industry.
- Dislocation of energy sources – Some countries have the capability to supply renewable energy and some do not and there are logistic issues because of this disparity.
- Population growth – 8.7 billion by 2037; too many to feed, maybe? The conflict between food and fuel is real when reviewing the biofuels.
- Global transportation – Logistics again and how to provide enough food? The conflict between food and fuel is real. How do we fly airplanes?
- Food crisis – Population growth plus transportation issues causes this problem
- Famine – It's this way in many places because of population growth, the need for more food and logistics.
- Electricity – Renewables go this way, but not enough, but it will keep your home and industry moving in many ways.
- Air travel – What fuel for flying? If so, how much is there?
- Economics – It's in trouble too as a result of the other crises. Cost of energy and displacement of energy only amplifies the problems.
- Conflict of interest – To each his own; we hope not.

- International diplomacy – A basic requirement or what follows is not fun.
- International conflict – Hope not, but the world needs international diplomacy well ahead of time.

I have listed nineteen issues but they boil down to eleven basic and fundamental crises.

I will begin with global warming since that is the one most people have heard about and have begun to make decisions on. It is my hope that many will see global warming in its true perspective and place their priorities elsewhere. This book will provide the reader with information as to what we are seeing as being a typical temperature cycle or climate cycle that has been followed over several thousand years and is merely a continuation of these cycles. You will note that temperature cycle is one of my listings above. This subject is covered during the discussion of global warming since they are so closely related. As the above list is reviewed you will find this occurring several times where more than one subject is covered under one title due to their closely associated nature. There are really only eight major subjects.

Global warming will be followed by a discussion on what I believe is a more important issue; the one of an energy crisis. This chapter will cover the history of the source of earth's energy and how rapidly we are using up the oil reserves. It will detail how soon this will impact the economies of the world as well as the dramatic impact it will have on such things as transportation, the providing of the world's food supply, and possibly on the outbreak of several wars. Within this topic of energy one comes face to face with the population growth and the problems that reflect back on the energy crisis. One will recognize the conflict that has to erupt as a result of the relationship between energy and the number of people and animals on earth.

A detailed discussion will be presented on the various energy substitutes expected to replace those we presently enjoy. These are called the renewable energies since they are the direct or indirect result of our Sun and the energy it supplies to the world every second of every day. Their use is renewable from now till the Sun no longer exists. This will include the priorities that my technical analysis places on the use of each to replace the fossil fuels. It will bring to focus the various problems of logistics that these renewable energies present that have not existed before.

One might not believe it but food becomes one of the major issues as the population increases and we run into a different set of circumstances on how to supply food using the renewable energies and the logistics involved in these less global supplies of energy. We find that different foods affect our use of energy and may require the world to re-baseline what we eat.

The cross-coupling of these various issues becomes a major issue. There is not one of these issues that stands on its own as an issue. It is tied into all the others and requires a vision of all of them from an overall prospective.

Crisis I -
The increase in the global temperatures; climate cycles or global warming?

A subject that has swept around the world over the last few years is the subject of global warming. It has reached a level of importance among the leaders of the nations of the world and by many of the people the world over. It strikes a cord with the average person and their energies push it up to the levels of the tops of governments. It is difficult to ascertain where this subject began it rumbles. It may have begun with certain scientists that review nature or it may have begun with environmentalists who were pushing for "Green Peace" which is a way of saying "save the world", or "save the energy of the world" or "don't be wasteful", or "don't allow contaminants into the atmosphere that affect the lives of plants, animals and humans".

While the subject of global warming may have begun with one intention in mind, it broadened over the years. In the fifties it began with a war on reducing smog. Smog was a form of atmospheric cloud that consisted of smoke and fog which at times settled over parts of the country that were industrial sites. The outputs of these factories resulted in contaminated vapors escaping into the surrounding air and causing greenery to disappear. In these industrial sites like the steel mill cities of western Pennsylvania, there were large areas where trees didn't grow and grass was non-existent. There was no greenery to speak of. In addition the rivers and streams were contaminated such that they were void of fish and were unhealthy to intended swimmers. Then an even greater calamity befell these areas when the weather conditions were not satisfactory for these exhausts and an inversion layer would form over a city. This inversion layer was the result of warm weather and a fog like humidity that trapped the warm air and prevented natural air recirculation in the area; couple this with the contaminated smoke and exhaust belching out of the industrial mills and you have smog. Smog was the name given to this contaminated inversion layer. It resulted in the deaths of people in Donora, Pennsylvania. However, it wasn't about to stop there and soon it was recognized that Donora was just the unfortunate place that showed it first. Soon there were similar problems recognized across the United States and across the globe. This broad spread of the effects of smog began to make more and more people aware of the issue and soon there was a swelling of demand to rid the atmosphere of this problem. From this beginning there was a major push on eliminating these contaminants. It became recognized that there was smog in most of the large cities of the world and it was getting worse. The actions taken by industry the world over was to use such things as large electronic controlled precipitrons that charged the particles of contaminants of the outgoing exhausts and allowed the major contaminants to be captured electronically. Other actions were taken in these industrial sites to prevent the dumping of contaminants into the rivers and the actions moved on to the auto industry where automobile manufacturers were directed to reduce the contamination being emitted out of the exhausts of their autos. Thus, began a war on automobile generated contaminants.

In the late sixties and early seventies the engineers and scientists, supported by funding, focused on cars and taking steps to reduce the lead in gasoline and the nitrous oxides, carbon monoxides and other carbon related exhausts that came out of cars, machines and factories. All of these were based on the concept of keeping things green by reducing pollution and contamination. Some of the first steps included the elimination of leaded gasoline and other potential contaminants in the fuel. Soon catalytic converters were added to automobiles along with the injection of air into the exhausts that trapped the nitrous oxides, and eliminated the carbon monoxide and other carbon compounds. This resulted in the elimination of most of the harsh exhausts and left us with carbon dioxide being exhausted. However, at the time carbon dioxide was considered a non hazardous gas and was of little concern. So, by the late seventies the cleaning up of the smog over many of the cities became evident; although it wasn't gone, it sure looked a lot better. It was amazing that cars that used to whiz by with black smoke coming out of the tail end were no longer trailing this black smoke; in fact you couldn't see anything coming out of the exhausts. Cities like Pittsburgh, Pennsylvania that used to be considered "dirty" were now being championed as one of the clean cities. The rivers in western Pennsylvania now had fish; small mouth bass, large mouth bass, and many other types for the fishermen to now enjoy on their weekend fishing trips. Boating and water skiing now became popular activities on the rivers and lakes of Pennsylvania. These results showed that man could control his destiny; or at least it looked like he could. He at least could control the segments that he was causing. Smog days that used to be listed in abundance in California now were down to less than one could count on his fingers in northern California and there were now many days in Los Angeles where clouds did not hang over this large city. In fact the only major city with smog in evidence was the city of Los Angeles and this big metropolis reduced the days of smog to about a tenth of what it once was.

And then came "Global Warming", or so it is called. Here again, I cannot name the day the name of global warming was used. It may have been by a few as early as the seventies, but it didn't take hold until the change of the century, or just before. A lot of this notoriety was brought forth by presentations by Al Gore, the ex Vice President of The United States. Al Gore basically states that an increase in the atmosphere's carbon dioxide (CO_2) from approximately 280 parts per million increasing to 380 parts per million over the last hundred years is why there is global warming. He relates this increase in carbon dioxide to automobiles and other machines. In order to understand how he makes this relationship between carbon dioxide and the Earth warming one must step back and understand certain consistencies between the sun and earth and what controls our climate.

Understanding the wavelengths from the sun and from earth

In order to understand the concept of global warming one must understand the wavelengths we receive from the Sun and the wavelengths that Earth gives off. They are quite different in dimension and in the energy they entail.

The main factor that causes global warmth relates to this difference in the wavelengths of the Sun's solar energy that it radiates to Earth and the wavelengths that Earth radiates back toward space. It's a fundamental fact that the warmer the body, the shorter the wavelengths of heat that will be radiated from the body. The Sun, being very hot, radiates wavelengths which are much shorter than those emanating from Earth. Sun's peak energy is at a wavelength of 500 nanometers (billionth of a meter) or about half a micron, even though there are wavelengths that are both much shorter and much longer. The Sun's peak wavelengths are in the visible or near visible of our eyes, which peak at around 550 nanometers. The fact that our eyes see wavelengths that peak around the peak of the sun's sunshine is probably due to the evolution of man over time. This fact of our eyesight is a relative match to the sun's wavelengths was probably one of the first steps in the evolution of man's eyesight. However, there are wavelengths from the sun that we cannot see because they are shorter or longer than our eyes can perceive. Because a significant amount of the Sun's output is ultraviolet and much of it is captured by the ozone in the atmosphere, man's eyes are not able to see these very short wavelengths. The shortest wavelengths we can see are violet. Likewise there are wavelengths that are longer than our eyes can distinguish and these are called infrared wavelengths. The longest wavelength we can see is red and the infrared is longer than these and of a lower energy. We see the sunshine and all the waves that make up the sunshine. Man's eyes see wavelengths that are between 400 and 700 nanometers in length which makes up much of the spectrum provided by the Sun's light.

UV wavelengths that we cannot see have energies that are approximately 1000 times the energy of the light we can see. Fortunately most of the ultraviolet wavelengths are captured by the ozone layer in the upper atmosphere or we would have to live in a protected place from this wavelength. There is an amount of UV that makes it through our atmosphere and it is the wavelength that causes sunburn and man must limit his intake of this wavelength or suffer the possibilities of skin cancer. This is why doctors recommend we stay out of the sun's rays between approximately 11:00 am and 2:00 pm when the Sun is overhead and these wavelengths are more prevalent.

The colors we see are the result of the wavelengths that the object reflects. For example, when you see a green plant, it is absorbing light at all the wavelengths except the wavelengths of 570 to 590 nanometers. This wavelength is being reflected, and you are seeing that wavelength which is green. When a person sees white it is because all the wavelengths we are able to see are being reflected toward our eyes and they combine to appear white...When we see black it is because none of the wavelengths we can see are being reflected, they are being absorbed by the material.

And from Earth

Now that we have reviewed the wavelengths of the Sun and understand that they are very short wavelengths, we will review the radiation that Earth emits to outer space.

The Sun's radiation in short wavelengths is due to the temperature of the outside of the Sun which is approximately 5800 degrees Kelvin. Meanwhile the Earth's temperature is approximately 288 degrees Kelvin (15 degrees Celsius or 59 degrees Fahrenheit) and it will radiate heat of much longer wavelengths. Since the Earth is approximately twenty times cooler than the Sun it will radiate wavelengths that are approximately twenty times longer than those of the Sun and at much lower energies. In fact, the wavelengths being radiated by the Earth and everything on it are in the infrared wavelengths, which cannot be seen by the human eye. Some of you have seen night pictures on TV of the war in Iraq. It shows what the American soldiers see with special goggles at night. The heat being given off by the enemy or their own soldiers is in the infrared and with these special goggles they can see infrared radiation from the bodies during the nighttime. Some hunters hunt animals at night wearing these special goggles that allow them to see the animals at night.

These infrared wavelengths bring us to the main point of this discussion and how they relate to the potential of global warming. Remember I said that the wavelengths of the Sun peak at around 500 nanometers. The infrared of earth's radiation is about twenty times longer and is approximately 10,000 nanometers (10.0 microns or approximately 0.0004 inches). These wavelengths are of a much lower energy than the sunshine we see each day and the light that provides our plants their energy. However, it turns out that there are various gases in our atmosphere that vibrate and absorb energy from infrared wavelengths. They "like" these wavelengths and these gases are called the greenhouse gases. They consist **of water vapor, carbon dioxide, and methane** as the major greenhouse gases. There are several other gases but their contribution to this subject matter is insignificant compared to these three gases.

What is significant as far as these three greenhouse gases are concerned is the action that they cause with the Earth's radiation. Lets change the name of Earth's radiation to Earth's re-radiation because it is important to realize that this radiation is due primarily to the Suns radiation heating the Earth and causing the Earth to re-radiate the energy back toward space in a different wavelength as we discussed. Why is this important? It is important because if Earth didn't re-radiate the energy back toward space, Earth would continue to get hotter and hotter from the heat being supplied by the Sun. In fact, the Earth's re-radiation of energy via infrared radiation to outer space is equal to the radiation energy received from the Sun, therefore the planet is in heat balance and is stable. This stability, in general, has been maintained over the many thousands (and probably millions) of years. There have been times in Earth's history where an ice age existed for a number of centuries and then the Earth returned to this stable condition we are enjoying at this time. It turns out that it is rather easy to slip into an ice age and out of an ice age and I will discuss this in a later part of this subject of Global Warming.

The Good Global Warmth

Let's return to the subject of global warming. Scientists have reviewed the heat balance of Earth for many years and established that the Earth has gained its relative warmth from the greenhouse gases. Remember, I said its warmth, not its warming. Why do I state it in this manner? An investigation into this will also give you a picture of why Al Gore is claiming there will be Global Warming and why I call it Global Warmth. Remember those gases in the atmosphere that vibrate when heated by the infrared wavelengths being re-radiated from Earth; well these gases can't keep that heat. As they heat up they now begin to radiate their heat waves in all directions. For the sake of simplicity I will say they radiate over 50 percent to outer space and less than 50 percent toward earth, although it's probable that more than 80 percent is radiated into outer space because space is very cold and heat travels from hot to cold. This sort of places a "cap" on the temperature of the bottom of the clouds which are now warmer than the parts of the atmosphere that is above them due to the part of the heat that is sent out to space. This cap and this radiation of infrared wavelengths back toward earth have resulted in a sort of blanket for earth over many thousands of years and an average temperature maintained during these conditions. This blanket probably occurred when the earth began to develop clouds. This collection of infrared energy in the greenhouse gases and having less than fifty percent of it re-radiating back to Earth resulted in the **warming** of Earth. This blanket has provided the warmth we enjoy today.

It is estimated that the temperature of earth would be approximately minus one degree Fahrenheit without this blanket and the Earth would be unlivable; being covered with ice. As it is, with this blanket the temperature of earth is 57 degrees Fahrenheit (14 degrees Centigrade) and is quite enjoyable.

This brings us to the subject of why, if the carbon dioxide increases in the atmosphere, doesn't the Earth keep heating. I mentioned to you that the carbon dioxide has increased in the atmosphere over the last one hundred and fifty years by about 150 parts per million; from about 230 parts per million to 380 parts per million. This is the area that Al Gore is basing his assumptions from. After all, carbon dioxide is one of the greenhouse gases and since we have seen it increase; won't we have global warming? This is where the **error** begins. This, I believe is looking at only one element in the equation of what would cause global warming. Remember, I mentioned that water vapor and methane were two of the other greenhouse gases. The quantity of water vapor in the atmosphere is much higher than the carbon dioxide and absorbs infrared energy about an order of magnitude greater than the absorption rate of carbon dioxide. Methane is not as predominant as carbon dioxide in the atmosphere but it absorbs infrared energy at twenty times the rate of carbon dioxide. I will discuss later in this book how methane may be a problem more than carbon dioxide and will discuss its possible contributions toward global warming. Not only is Al Gore focusing his attention on one element that could cause the temperature of the Earth to rise, he is focusing on automobile exhaust as the major culprit for generating carbon dioxide; I find both of these premises to be incorrect and will explain why in the course of this discussion. You will see, if there is global warming due to carbon dioxide, that there are other contributors of carbon dioxide greater than automobiles (But we should reduce the carbon dioxide from our vehicles). There is one viable situation that probably exists and it relates to the point I made about these greenhouse gases being re-radiated from the clouds in all directions. I believe with the equilibrium condition that exists on Earth today relative to temperature, that very little of the heat energy captured by the clouds is transmitted back to Earth. I had mentioned in the example above that, for the sake of argument that less than 50 percent is transmitted back to Earth. I believe this to be a fact. These clouds exist with a temperature that is much warmer than outer space and of lower temperature and energy than the heat of Earth and the wavelengths being received by Earth from the Sun. Because of the lower energy infrared wavelengths and the stabilized temperature of Earth, there is probably less than five percent of this infrared heat energy being transmitted from the clouds toward Earth. In fact as we discuss this farther you will find that most of the infrared heat emanating from Earth really comes from evaporated water from the oceans that condense in the clouds and this condensation results in the heat being transmitted toward outer space and its cold temperature. The warmer Earth becomes the more energy that is transmitted outward towards these very cold space temperatures.

One of the purposes of this book is to provide you with information and to demonstrate the fallacies of focusing only on one factor that can cause a problem. Before pouncing on some of the other factors I thought I would digress a little and cover some other interesting subjects, all of which will come around to help close the subject on Global Warming. Of course one of the most important players in this subject of the Earth's warmth is the sun. So, we will review the sun and the part it plays in our everyday life and perhaps in any global warming.

The Sun, Earth's Constant Companion

Throughout time, the Sun has been Earth's constant companion and almost the sole source of Earth's energy. Radioactive material within our mantle since Earth's beginning provides energy, but it has reduced significantly over time. The only other sources of energy relates to a meteor that collided with Earth 65 million years ago. This, along with other material within Earth's bosom was converted to the fossil fuels we enjoy today.

The Sun is a gaseous star primarily composed of Hydrogen. It is a constant source of energy as it continues to manufacture energy via atomic reactions within its core. Due to the terrific internal pressure as a result of gravitational pull within this giant structure, its internal core is extremely hot. The heat within the core activates the hydrogen atoms and results in the fusing of four hydrogen atoms into one helium atom through nuclear fusion on a continuous basis. (1) Because the atomic mass of the helium is less than the combined mass of four hydrogen atoms, this loss of mass provides enormous amounts of energy via Einstein's equation, $E=mc^2$; where E is the energy, m is the mass loss in this reaction and c is the speed of light which is 3×10^8 meters a second (approximately 187,500 miles per hour) and c^2 is the speed of light squared or 9×10^{16} meters a second. So, without too much math or physics, the speed of light squared is such a big number that very little mass can be loss and still account for a great deal of energy given off as heat.

This energy release at the core of the huge Sun must make its way to the Sun's surface via countless absorptions and reemissions. The distance it must travel to reach the surface is enormous due to the Sun's size and the fact it makes this journey via a random route. It is estimated that it takes 65 million years to make it to the surface and appear as the sunshine we see. So the sunshine we see today was generated when the dinosaurs were roaming Earth approximately 65 million years ago. So, even if the Sun stopped generating the power internally, Earth would receive the power already generated for approximately 65 million years. It isn't about to stop now, so you don't have to worry.

The Sun is the heat engine that drives the circulation of our atmosphere. Although it has long been assumed to be a constant source of energy, recent measurements of this solar constant have shown that the Sun's base output can vary by up to 0.02 percent over the eleven-year solar cycle. Temporary decreases of up to 1.5 percent have been observed. (2) Scientists say this variation is significant and it can modify climate over time. Plant growth has been shown to vary over the eleven-year sunspot and twenty-two year magnetic cycles of the sun, as evidenced in records of tree rings.

But the temperature of Earth doesn't stay constant

As we got through the discussions on the Earth's temperature swings or climate swings, keep in mind a very important thing. The energy that earth receives from the sun on a second by second basis or a day by day basis, or a year by year basis or a century by century basis – can be considered as a constant. To date there has not been any correlation between the sun's slight variations and earth's variations. I consider the energy from the sun a constant in all my discussions and this being true, there is no reason for the earth to have any major changes in climate or temperature. With this said, let's review the graph below which shows the global temperature variation over the last 4,507 years. This graph is the work of Climatologist Cliff Harris, considered one of the world's top ten climatologists, and Meteorologist Randy Mann who is well recognized within his field. (3) If we assume that the only energy coming into earth is from the sun, and it is constant, then we need to determine what causes the variations in Earth's temperatures and more importantly, what causes Earth to cool over long periods of time. Why should Earth cool if the energy from the sun to Earth is constant? A review of the graph shows the temperature over the last 4507 years and there are some obvious trends. This chart and the trends provide a clue to what is happening to Earth's temperature today and why it is probably not global warming caused by atmospheric contamination. Note the length of each of these climate type changes. They are not short spells from a human's point of view, although they are rather short when one considers how long Earth has been around.

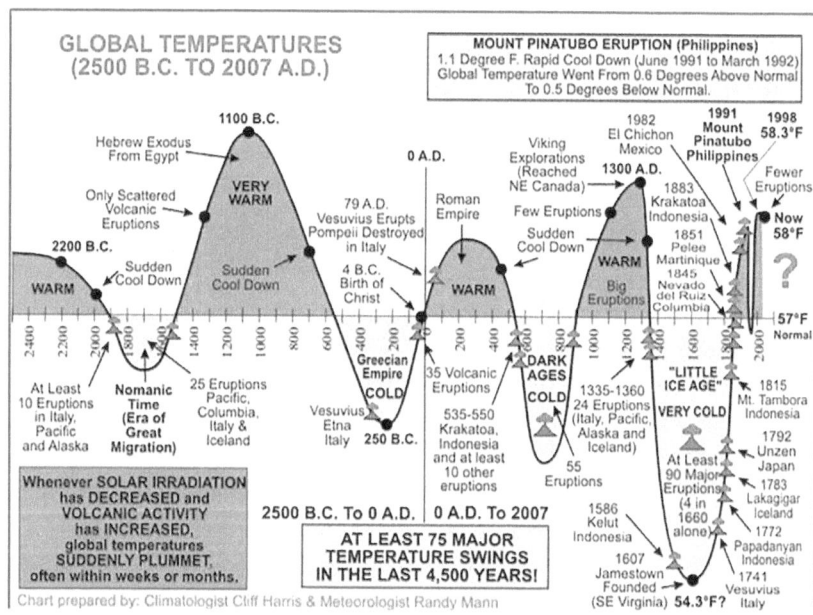

Chart #1 of Global Temperatures from 2500 B.C. to 2007 A.D.
The mean line temperature is 57 degrees Fahrenheit

Chart by Climatologist Cliff Harris and Meteorologist Randy Mann

Notice that there was a warm period from 2500 B.C. to 1900 B.C.; a period of 600 years followed by a cold spell to 1500 B.C., followed by another warm spell from 1500 B.C. to almost 500 B.C.; a period of almost 1000 years, and this was followed by a cold period from 550 B.C. to 0 A.D. This was followed by a warm period from 0A.D. to 550 A.D., which was followed by a cold period from 550 A.D. to 900 A.D. This was followed by a warm period from 500 A.D. to 1350 A.D. and this was followed by what is called the "Little Ice Age" (4) from 1350 A.D. to 1850 A.D. and this was followed by a warm period from 1850 to the present, although this warming trend started warming around 1650, just after the founding of Jamestown in the United States. There is significant information in these swings. The warmest period was the one from 1500 B.C. to 650 B.C when the temperature of Earth averaged approximately 60 degrees Fahrenheit. Notice the cold swings keep reaching deeper and colder and the most recent one was not long ago. It was the one from 1350 A.D. to 1850 A.D. Isn't that a coincidence, since this was the 1850 time used by Al Gore and others where they claim that the Global Warming started in 1850 and was due to the use of oil in industry, i.e. the Industrial Revolution and more recently to the exhaust of automobiles. However, looking at this chart it would appear that the swings occur whether there is any exhaust from cars or not. There is a very key point in these curves and it appears around 1650 A.D. when the temperature started this rise from the very coldest "Little Ice Age" period. In other words the world began to heat up around 1650. This was well before any industrial revolution or any oil being used in the world. So the "swing" from cold toward hot began at an early time of approximately 1650 A.D. and the claim that there has been a temperature rise since 1850 to the present of almost one degree centigrade (almost two degrees Fahrenheit) – and relating it to automobiles and the industrial revolution is **not a fact.** The rise has been from about 1650 to the present, from a "Little Ice Age" to the present and started well before automobiles and other machinery were in use. This temperature rise started over two hundred years before oil was commercialized; and it wasn't one degree Fahrenheit as many believe has been the temperature swing issued in by "global warming". The temperature has climbed approximately five degrees Fahrenheit (2.7 degrees Celsius) from 1650 to the present as it recovered from the Little Ice Age toward warmer temperature that we have enjoyed since.

Another important point to take from this graph is the very low average temperature around 1650. This is the lowest temperature in the last 4500 years. This low happened about the time that America was being colonized by England, France and others. Another trend that this graph shows is that the cycles from hot to cold show the cold excursions increasing in depth and length of time. A mathematician graphing this trend would state, if these continue to take lower and lower excursions that we may be in deep trouble relative to it being too cold to inhabit the planet in the not too distant future rather than the global warming scare being discussed. My review of the graph would indicate that we can expect the temperature to start toward the cold cycle at the end of this century.

Notice the very last warm period, prior to the one we are in, was from 900 A.D. to 1350 A.D.; but the important part of that curve shows that this is the fastest decrease in temperature in the last 4500 years; going from a warm high in 1300 A.D. (~ 59 degrees Fahrenheit) that was warmer than the present state of the earth's temperature (58.3 Fahrenheit), to the cold Ice Age in one hundred years. This is a faster rate than those that claim the present warming increase is obtaining. So, what's to keep the present trend toward warm temperatures from changing to very cold temperatures very rapidly? Incidentally, I would have called this chart "Climate Swings" since it is a change in temperature over extended periods of time that could constitute a change in climate. What causes them? Its not the CO_2 exhausts out of automobiles that some would like you to think. That's obviously one of the fallacies I want to bring to the readers attention. If we knew what phenomena causes the rapid drop in the global temperature over a short period of time it might help to determine what makes it go the other way as those advocates of global warming would have you think. I have some technical hypotheses that I will discuss as we go along.

Take another look at this chart and notice that it shows what is happening on a trend basis over 4500 years, but it has no temperatures shown on the vertical axis. I will make an assumption that the zero crossing point between warm trends and cold trends is the accepted standard global average temperature of 57 degrees Fahrenheit shown on the graph. Notice that the coldest time shown is during the Little Ice Age and there is a clue showing that the temperature around the time when Jamestown was founded in Virginia in 1607 was the low of 54.3 degrees Fahrenheit, or about 2.7 degrees ahrenheit colder than the 57 degrees considered as the average temperature of Earth over the last 4500 years.

If the reader were to go on the web and review the Earth's temperature you will find many articles on the subject matter. However there are several trends in those writings where they provide information that is misleading. There is a tendency to discuss how many glaciers have shrunk in size in the last 500 years or the last 150 years and relate it to global warming and discuss it as a tragedy. The articles all tend to discuss the 500 year period and show the great warming trend. The reason this is misleading is easily shown by again looking at the graph above. The little ice age began around 1350 and lasted until 1850. This is a period of 500 years during which time the glaciers and all ice on earth increased dramatically. There are several reports which show the following actions to have occurred during this Ice Age: (5)

- 1250 AD for when Atlantic pack ice began to grow
- 300 AD for when warm summers stopped being dependable in Northern Europe
- 1315 AD for the rains and Great Famine of Europe in 1315 – 1317
- 1550 AD for theorized beginning of worldwide glacial expansion
- 1650 AD for the first climatic minimum
- Generally thought that Little Ice Age concluded in 1850 AD; although the temperature started to turn up in 1650 and reached 57 degrees Fahrenheit in 1850..

So, in 1850 when Earth's temperature had already been increasing for two hundred years from the cold Little Ice Age, it reached what I will call a "normal" temperature of 57 degrees Fahrenheit and it's reasonable that the ice and glaciers will have a tendency to begin to melt. Keep in mind that the little ice age only lasted about five hundred years but during that time is when the ice thickness and volume grew to the tremendous amount that we became used to in 1650. Remember also that it only took the average temperature of Earth to change from a high of 59 degrees Fahrenheit to a low of 54.3 degrees Fahrenheit for this ice to form. I will discuss why such a small change could cause this kind of ice creation later in this book. We have gone through approximately 500 years where the temperature has been increasing from the low point of the "Little Ice Age" (LIA) and 150 years since we went above the temperature of 57 degrees Fahrenheit of warming and this certainly will result in a reduction of glaciers and ice in general. If it could be formed in such a small temperature change than it can also melt in a small global temperature change? But the chart indicates this has been a normal trend for the last 4500 years. In other words there must have been a building of glaciers in the three cold periods shown that preceded the LIA and a corresponding shrinking of the glaciers in the three warming periods shown on the graph. It shows that the warm trends last about 500 years but they peak in about 250 years before trending back down toward a cooling trend. So, when Al Gore and the others that are trying to scare people into thinking that we are having an unusual increase in temperature, they are tending to exaggerate or mislead the public (although I am for reducing the contamination of our atmosphere as much as he is). This is another oversight and indicates they did not look over the trend of the last 4500 years. If we go through this century to the year 2100 and increase one degree celsius the history has shown that this could be the peak and then the temperatures will drop toward a cooling and it's possible to have another "little Ice Age" starting in the year 2100, or earlier. Much depends on the ice in the world and I will discuss ice in a later part of this article on Global Warming and show why this is normal and easy to happen.

The average hot global temperature we are now sitting at, and considered global warming, is about 58.3 Fahrenheit as shown on the chart. The peak temperature is shown as occurring around 1000 B.C. when it is shown as approximately 60.5 degrees Fahrenheit. So, over the last one hundred and fifty years of warming we have not reached this past period and in fact are about like the previous warm periods. The slope gradient may be a little higher than some of the previous warm periods. Since we don't know what caused them, we may have a tendency to think the present CO_2 situation may take it higher. There are many scientists that believe this is the "chicken and egg" phenomenon; i.e., that it's the rise in temperature that causes the carbon dioxide to increase. It's a known fact that the higher the temperature the higher the activity of carbon dioxide. If we had the information about the carbon dioxide level in the atmosphere during the past hot and cold periods we might see that the carbon dioxide level in the atmosphere goes up during those hot periods and down during the cold periods. It's obvious that the automobiles didn't cause any of the rises in temperatures during the previous cycles. Incidentally, look close at the graph again. Notice the dramatic drop in temperature in 1991-92 from about 58.0 Fahrenheit to below the 57 degree Fahrenheit shown as normal (or average) on this graph. So, the temperature did not increase monotonically as discussed by the Global Warming experts. What caused that dip in that period of time just fifteen years ago? If we could answer that, we might be able to determine when the next dip will occur. Some of you may recall that when this occurred in 1991-92 that the media expressed grave concern that the world was going to go through a dramatic temperature drop and their terms related to freezing weather to be expected. Here we are a few years later and the media is playing the game the other way.

A little more discussion about the Little Ice Age so the reader will get a feel of what the temperature was like until 1850 and why there are alarmists that keep shouting out that the Earth is losing its ice and we are going to have global temperatures that are extremely warm. They also indicate that we will have ocean level increases of three hundred feet, to the point where the coastal cities will be wiped out. I believe we have enough history recorded to show that this didn't occur in the coastal cities in 1300 when the last peak temperature occurred.

Although the Little Ice Age affected the southern hemisphere, the impact was greater in the northern hemisphere. Even though the southern hemisphere may have seen the temperatures drift lower, it is so warm in many countries of the southern hemisphere that it was probably enjoyed. Meanwhile in the Europe and North America there were activities that are much different than today. In mid 1600's glaciers in the Swiss Alps advanced, gradually engulfing farms and crushing entire villages. (6) The River Thames and the canals and rivers of the Netherlands often froze over during the winter, and people skated and even held frost fairs on the ice. The first Thames frost fair was in 1607; the last in 1814. The winter of 1794/95 was particularly harsh when the French invasion army under Pichegru could march on the frozen rivers of the Netherlands, while the Dutch fleet was fixed in the ice in Den Helder harbour. In the winter of 1780, New York Harbor froze, allowing people to walk from Manhattan to Staten Island. Sea ice surrounding Iceland extended for miles in every direction, closing that island's harbors to shipping. The Viking colonies in Greenland died out in the 15th century because they could no longer grow enough food there. In the north and south temperate zones, snowlines were about 100 meters lower than they were in 1975 (6) In Ethiopia and Mauritania; permanent snow was reported on mountain peaks at levels where it does not occur today. Timbujktu, an important city on the trans-Saharan caravan route, was flooded at least 13 times by the Niger River; there are no records of similar flooding before or since. Early European settlers in America reported exceptionally severe winters and in 1607 – 1608 ice persisted on Lake Superior until June (6). Many famous paintings showing snow were done by European artists in the period from 1565 to 1665, indicating a relation with the weather at that time. These same cooling events are detected in sediments accumulating off Africa, where the cooling events for this Little Ice Age show that the temperatures may have dropped between 3 and 8 degrees C (6-14 degrees Fahrenheit). This is a dramatic swing downward in temperature, but as I mentioned, it was probably enjoyed.

The Little Ice Age by anthropology professor Brian Fagan of the University of California at Santa Barbara tells of the plight of European peasants during the 1300 to 1850 chill: famines, hypothermia, bread riots, and the rise of despotic leaders brutalizing an increasingly dispirited peasantry. In the late 17th century, writes Fagan, agriculture had dropped off so dramatically that "Alpine villagers lived on bread made from ground nutshells mixed with barley and oat flour." Finland lost perhaps a third of its population to starvation and disease.

This is a brief review of the LIA that occurred just 200 to 400 years ago. The thing that is shocking to me is that the average temperature for this LIA was only a few degrees below the normal on this graph. How do a few degrees from the normal and enjoyable temperature of earth result in such dynamic differences in select areas of earth. This is one of the things I will review. When you consider that only a few degrees below the normal can result in these kinds of swings in local temperature, you can imagine what may occur as the temperature swings up as it has been doing. Of course these chart curves show the average of the total global temperatures. So, if the average swing is not great, then it should satisfy in ones mind that any global warming or global cooling is not that great as to cause major problems in the world. Sure there will be local areas that will have hotter temperatures then they have seen in recent history but there will be other parts of Earth that will see no major shift. Remember, the sun is giving us constant energy. These curves indicate that any build up in temperature must be followed by a cooling trend if the sun's energy is constant upon earth and the average temperature of Earth is to remain constant over a long period of time. There must be an off swing to return Earth back to its apparent equilibrium point.

The graph above relates these excursions to volcanic activity which is another point of view. However, I have a problem understanding why the temperatures go up or down with these massive eruptions. I would assume the eruptions would result in particles in the air that would result in a one of two phenomenon happening; the dust in the atmosphere would shield off the sun's rays and there would be a cold period, or that the particles in the air form a blanket and the earth cannot re-radiate its temperature to outer space and the Earth would heat up. I believe it would relate to the temperature dropping due to the cut off of our major energy input from our Sun. You notice that eruptions are shown on the upswings of temperature and on the downswings of temperature. I will discuss in detail later where I believe the most recent increase may be coming from. However, it is important to recognize that volcanic eruptions are what provided Earth its three atmospheres and is still a major contributor to carbon dioxide in the atmosphere.

No matter; this graph prepared by Climatologist Cliff Harris & Meteorologist Randy Mann shows the temperature swings over this long period of 4500 years and indicates there is no relation between temperature or climate swings and human activity, otherwise one would think that the dramatic population growth of animals and people, as well as their related activities, would have kept this curve always going up. If due to CO_2 from human and animal activity, then it would have really been on a dramatic and steady climb, especially when the Industrial Revolution injected its vapors into the atmosphere along with these other enhancers such as these major eruptions. It is important for the reader to understand that there are many scientists that believe that global warming is due to the huge amount of CO_2 that volcanoes inject into the atmosphere on a regular basis. We sometimes have a tendency to forget that there are volcanoes all over the world and they erupt on a rather random basis. Many volcanoes are located in the ocean and since they are not visible to the average person on an every day basis, we tend to forget about them – although the oceans take up about 78 percent of Earth so there is much more area for volcanoes to be found. I am sure this is not true with the people that live near them. They know they exist and they create a level of concern for the local inhabitants. Many also exist above sea level. Remember Mt. St. Helens blowing a gasket in 1980. This could be why there was an effect on the cold temperature spike we saw in the graph around 1992? Bottom-line, volcanoes create much more carbon dioxide than humans and human activity. They have been blasting all over the place since the beginning of Earth. This is Earth's inborn energy leaving itself loose. It created our atmosphere, our oceans, and probably helped to create the nice climate we live in.

So, it would appear that there is something else controlling the swings and I believe I can relate to some answers as we proceed. In order to better understand where and how Earth receives and gives up its warmth each day, I need to provide the reader some background information on our Sun and its method of supplying Earth its energy and how the Earth relieves this energy.

First I want to cover how the Sun affects the climates and the weather and provides certain necessities for plants, animals and man. I believe it is important to convey some additional significant facts other than any global temperature change. There are several stories to be told concerning how earth receives its energy and how Mother Nature handles this energy, as well as the impact of man and other natural phenomena on temperature.

Solar Constant, the Sun's Energy to Earth

The solar constant, the amount of incoming solar electromagnetic radiation per unit area, is measured on the outer surface of Earth's atmosphere in a plane (not an airplane) that is perpendicular to the rays. It is called the solar constant because it provides this amount of energy constantly every second of the day. The solar constant includes all types of solar radiation, not just the visible light. Via satellite, the solar constant is measured to be roughly 1,366 watts per square meter. (7) It fluctuates by about 6.9 percent during a year, that is, it is 1,412 watts per square meter in early January and 1,321 watts per square meter in early July. It changes by a few parts per thousand from day to day. Keep in mind that this is the amount of energy per square meter is placed on the stratosphere and not on the land or water of Earth. Much of it never makes it to land or water due to reflections from the clouds, absorption by clouds of the infrared portion, and absorption of the UV by the ozone.

The Sun's light is radiant, meaning it is direct line of sight. If one were to take a picture of any sphere at a distance you would only see one fourth of the sphere at any given time. This is a fact of geometry. The same is true of the sun as it sends its rays directly to the exposed portion of the Earth at any one instance. At that given instant it can only see one fourth of our Earth. Fortunately, Earth is spinning or that one fourth would be intolerable with the amount of heat being received. Since Earth is spinning at 1000 miles an hour, the quarter of the Earth that is in the direct line of the Sun's rays is constantly changing. For you to have a better feeling of the amount of average energy that each part of Earth receives in a day; think about taking a snapshot of Earth as it revolves. This snapshot would essentially freeze Earth's rotation for an instant. In that instant, only one-fourth of Earth is visible to the Sun. The amount of energy that this snapshot of Earth's cross sectional area would receive is one-fourth of the total given to Earth in one complete rotation. During the snapshot, it would have received the full 1366 watts per square meter. But some would be reflected from the clouds, absorbed by the clouds, absorbed by terrestrial areas and some would be reflected from Earth, resulting in 51 percent, or 696 watts per square meter, being of use. Then, as Earth revolves during the other three-quarters of its rotation, it essentially receives no solar energy and is cooling and radiating heat energy away from Earth's surface to outer space. To simplify this, think of the sun hitting one fourth of the earth for six hours and then that portion of earth is out of the direct line of the sun and is goes into a semi dark area for six hours and then total night for six hours and then partial shade and sun for six more hours. That takes up the one twenty four hour rotation of Earth. During this time the Earth is radiating heat to outer space for twenty four hours; even during the dark. So, during the complete rotation, the energy per unit area provided by the sun averages out to 342 watts per square meter actually received if clouds do not block any solar energy. At any given location and time, the amount of this energy that is actually received at Earth's surface depends on the state of the atmosphere, mainly the clouds and their reflections of the Sun's ray to outer space. Now let's examine how that amount of energy is distributed across the globe.

Earth/Sun Energy Balance

By today's levels, I am assuming we reached a point in time where Earth's radiation levels that escape to space equals the incoming Sun's radiated energy to Earth's surface. With this balance, Earth essentially retained the stable temperature we enjoy today. This is energy in balance. To describe this status of energy neutral and give one a better understanding of my choice of words, see the following Figure 2. (8)

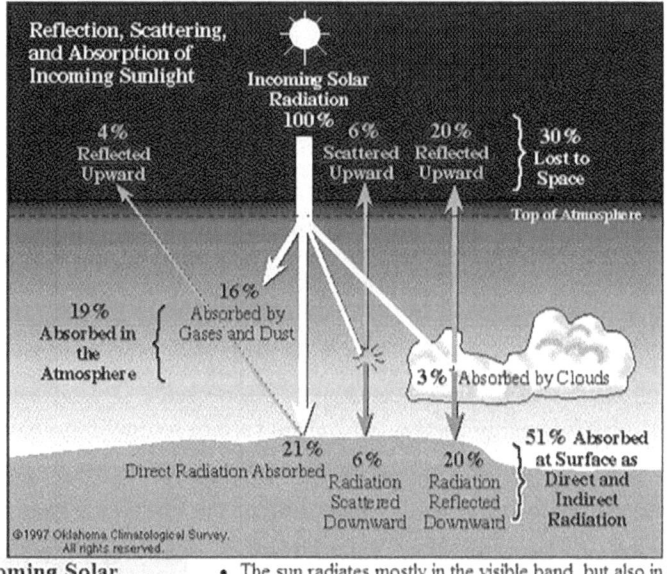

Incoming Solar
Radiation

• The sun radiates mostly in the visible band, but also in the ultraviolet (shorter wavelength).

Figure 2

The energy from the Sun is shown as being radiated with about 51 percent reaching the surface of Earth, 19 percent being absorbed in the atmosphere, and 30 percent lost to space via reflection from clouds.

Of the 51 percent that Earth's surface receives, 70 percent is reradiated back from the surface and clouds. It is lost to space or absorbed by the atmosphere, 23 percent is latent heat flux, and 7 percent is sensible heat flux that remains. The latent heat flux and sensible heat flux will be discussed. There is 21 percent of infrared from the surface that goes to the clouds or is absorbed by the water vapor or carbon dioxide in the atmosphere. This is not shown as staying on Earth because it is part of the infrared that is lost to space via clouds, water vapor, carbon dioxide, and methane after absorption by these medium. This is also the heat that warms the bottom of clouds in the atmosphere and provides each of us a relatively mild temperature.

This total amount of energy of the incoming and the outgoing energy is termed Earth's Energy Budget. This is the result of the Sun's radiation energy to

Earth and Earth's re-radiation back toward space. This balance results in Earth's Energy Budget which has been maintained over millions of years.

Earth's Energy Budget and the Atmosphere's Impact on Our Temperature

Absorption and reemission of radiation at Earth's surface is only one part of the intricate web of heat transfer in Earth's planetary domain. Equally important are selective absorption and emission of radiation from molecules in the atmosphere, as we discussed earlier when reviewing the greenhouse gases in the atmosphere. Keep in mind that Earth's plants receive the energy needed from the sunlight and in the wavelengths from 400 to 800 nanometers. Any infrared energy that is reflected and captured by the atmosphere has no relation on the wavelengths that plants use for their energy. The infrared wavelengths are essentially invisible to plants. They gain no energy from these wavelengths and there is no photosynthesis taking place as a result of the infrared wavelengths. Therefore, the greenhouse gases and any capture and readmission from the clouds to back to Earth should not have any effect on photosynthesis. There may be a secondary effect caused by any increase in temperature since some plants grow better in increased temperature but there are also some plants that can't survive in increased temperature.

The temperature of the lower part of the clouds provides the modest temperature to Earth. As one would travel vertically up toward space, the clouds bottoms have the highest temperature and then it decreases fairly rapidly as one proceeds beyond the clouds. Heat is released from the waters of earth and rises to the clouds and is eventually condensed to provide precipitation. During this condensation heat is transferred upward from the clouds toward space and represents the greatest relieve of heat from the earth. This causes the atmosphere just above the cloud level to be heated in this transfer of energy. However, the various levels of our atmosphere change to cooling as the vapors rise and then reach another level of warmth. This heating in the lower part of the stratosphere is due to the ultraviolet wavelengths being captured by the ozone layer, causing that particular volume of atmosphere to be heated. As one continues to rise toward the outer parts of our stratosphere and toward outer space the temperature drops dramatically. In outer space the temperature is approximately 4.5 degrees Kelvin above absolute zero (-269 degrees Celsius or close to absolute temperature of minus 450 degrees Fahrenheit). However, it is not quite that cold just outside our stratosphere since a certain amount of particle density still remains and retains some of the heat being released from Earth. It is approximately 40 degrees Kelvin above absolute zero (approximately -233 degrees Celsius). The clouds, and precipitation produced from the clouds, provide the toughest challenge for the scientists who model our atmosphere in order to determine the climate that is in store for us and everyday weather. This is a tough challenge that has been worked on for the past fifty years.

Water vapor in clouds is also an efficient absorber. It absorbs and radiates infrared radiation in all directions, about an order of magnitude better than carbon dioxide, and there is more of it. These clouds act similarly with their greenhouse gases to incoming radiation of the sun's rays. Water vapor and carbon dioxide in the atmosphere also absorb some of the Sun's incoming radiation. It is not a one-way street. So, if there is an increase in either one of these gases by any amount, it will increase the amount that the Sun's incoming infrared energy is absorbed and prevented from reaching earth as well as acting as greenhouse gases to Earth's re-radiation

Sensible Heat Flux, Latent Heat Flux, and Surface Heat Flux

The redistribution of energy across the Earth's surface is accomplished primarily through three processes:

1) Sensible heat flux (direct)
2) Latent heat flux (evaporation),
3) Surface heat flux (flow of currents in the ocean). (9)

Sensible heat (direct) flux is the process where heat energy is transferred from the Earth's surface to the atmosphere directly by conduction and convection. Keep in mind that most of earth's surface is water, so as the sun's energy heats the surface of the oceans much of it is transferred back directly by conduction and convection (sensible heat) into the atmosphere just as any other heat is transferred on Earth from the hot to the cold areas. Since the water is in direct contact with the atmosphere, if it is hotter than the atmosphere the heat will transfer by conduction from the water to the air.

This energy is then moved from the tropics to the poles by advection, creating atmospheric circulation. As a result, atmospheric circulation moves warm tropical air toward the Polar Regions and cold air from the poles toward the equator. Nations in the temperate zones, for example, the United States, benefit by this air movement from the equator and the poles by having a climate that is temperate and is not subject to extreme hot or cold weather. Much of the heat energy is in the infrared wavelengths. The oceans do absorb most of it; mainly at the surface of the water. As a result, Earth's oceans are warmer than the air above it by a little less than about 2 degrees Fahrenheit (1 degree Celsius). Direct heat transfer occurs from the water to the air by conduction, via infrared wavelengths;

Latent heat flux is associated with evaporation of water or ice at the surface, mainly by the oceans, the Arctic region and the Antarctic regions, and subsequent condensation of water vapor in the troposphere. It is an important component of Earth's surface energy budget. (9) This is a form of air-conditioning that Mother Nature provides. The heat from the Sun causes huge amounts of evaporation from the surface of the oceans, lakes, and rivers. Evaporation is always a cooling phenomenon and results in cooling the water surfaces.

This evaporation of water is taken into the clouds. The same process that creates winds and weather changes moves it. The subsequent movement of the clouds and condensation results in the water that was evaporated by the heat of the Sun in the oceans, to be carried to various locations in the world and dropped in the form of precipitation. As a result, three major phenomena occur:

- (1) The transfer of heat to the upper atmosphere and out to space as the water vapor in the clouds is condensed in the form of precipitation, thus transferring the heat removed from the waters back to outer space.
- (2) The transfer of potable water to all parts of Earth via the hydrological cycle. Through this mechanism, drinkable water is transferred in large quantities to various parts of the world. The evaporation of water from the oceans leaves the salt behind. It is Earth's desalination system. Our Earth can then provide freshwater from the resulting precipitation to oxygen-breathing animals, human beings, and to the growing plants.

- (3) Finally, large quantities of radiation energy are transferred into the Earth's tropical oceans along the equator. The energy enters these water bodies at the surface, where absorbed radiation heat energy is converted into the water's heat energy and, like the air, travels from the hot toward the cold waters north and south of the equatorial areas via water currents with a vector towards the North and South poles, but deviating from a true north and south direction due to the spinning of Earth.

Water currents

Heated water goes the same route as heated air. It moves from the warm waters to the colder waters. These water currents are another means that Mother Nature has provided to spread the sun's heat energy to the colder waters and thus warm the land that is adjacent to this flow of warm water. The Gulf Stream is a typical example of this means of ocean water transferring heat to the colder waters and to warm the countries such as the United Kingdom. The United Kingdom is a great benefactor of this warmth. The U.K. is at latitudes that relate to very cold areas in Canada that are much colder than the U.K and the U.K would have the cold climate of Canada if it weren't for the Gulf Stream and its warm waters crossing the Atlantic and moving northward toward the North Pole.

The percent absorption of the heat energy received from the sun onto the earth's oceans reduces dramatically with water depth: (10)

- 73 percent reach 1.0 centimeter (0.4 inches)
- 45 percent penetrate to 1.0 meter (39.4 inches)
- 22 percent penetrate to 10 meters (32.8 feet)
- 0.53 percent penetrates to 100 meters (328 feet) The shortest wavelengths with the greatest energy.
- 0.0062 percent penetrates to 200 meters (656 feet)

The minimum energy supply necessary to maintain photosynthesis is 0.003 cal cm^{-2}. Thus, photosynthesis is supported at 200 meters under optimum conditions and absolutely clear water and one would find many ocean plants growing at this depth under these conditions. This amount is available at 220 meters (722feet). (10) The Ocean's plant life provides almost half of Earth's oxygen via photosynthesis. This data relates to the suns direct rays. **Relative to the infrared wave lengths that are supposed to cause global warming; it is my opinion that these wavelengths, are of much lower energy, do not affect anything but the surface layer of the oceans, and in fact may just reflect off the surface; if so, they end up escaping to outer space and do not result in the global warmth that has been predicted. I have no direct knowledge or information concerning the absorption of infrared wavelengths but my engineering background tends to consider this to be the case. Low energy and long wavelengths would seem to react this way.**

Global Heat Balance

The equator receives much more heat than the North and South Poles due to its protrusion and therefore closeness to the sun. Because of this, there is a normal drive of wind to carry this extra heat from the equator to the North and South Poles. However, due to the earth's spin of one thousand miles an hour, the winds do not go directly North or South but are carried from the West to the East in the northern hemisphere (and the opposite in the southern hemisphere). This combination of vectors results in the winds general flow from the west toward the northeast. However, not all the heat absorbed by the area of the equator is transferred via the winds. Some is transferred by phenomena called heat fluxes, which I have discussed. These various methods of heat transfer result in temperatures settling out as shown in the graph below (Figure 4). This shows what happens to the heat being transferred from the equator to the various parts of the earth's temperate zones and polar zones in the north and south. (11) See how the graph shows the peak energy being received shown as the high arched curves and the flattened out curves that are the resultant heat energies after distribution by the heat distributors mentioned; because of this movement of heat via the winds, the precipitation, the water current flows and just plain heat transfer as a result of conduction and convection. Isn't Mother Nature wonderful? With this enormous transfer of energy via Mother Nature's forces, it is hard to believe that carbon dioxide's small increase (in the parts per million in the atmosphere) would have any major effect on Earth's climate.

If there were no energy transfer, the poles would be 77 degrees Fahrenheit (25 degrees Celsius) **cooler**, and the equator would be 57.2 degrees Fahrenheit (14 degrees Celsius) **warmer**. Obviously, these temperatures would have been uninhabitable at the equator and poles. This chart is another piece of evidence of how Mother Nature does her little tricks to keep things balanced on our Earth. It takes the extra heat shown in the graph and transfers it to the places where there is a deficiency of heat

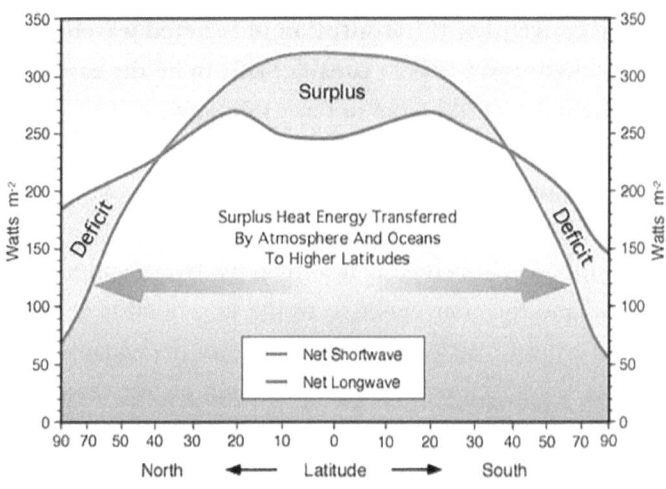

Figure 7j-1: Balance between average net shortwave and longwave radiation from 90° North to 90° South.

Figure 3. Balance between average net shortwave and longwave radiation from 90 degrees north to 90 degrees south. The surplus drops to approximately 250 watts per square meter at the equator and rises from 70 watts per square meter to almost 200 watts per square meter at the Poles. The temperate zone increases to approximately 235 watts per square meter.

Over the past several thousand years (and probably the last million or more) the sun has placed a constant amount of energy on the earth, year by year. At the same time the earth's ocean levels have remained fairly constant. So we have this constant energy and this constant large amount of water and a yearly rain fall that has remained constant over the world. To change this requires a huge action of nature to be able to overcome the large inertia provided by the world's large bodies of water. Global warming must overcome this to be a fact. So far, it hasn't.

What are the basics that determine Earth's climates?

Several major phenomena determine the climate and weather on Earth. The first is the Earth's tilt. The Earth is tilted approximately 23.44 degrees with respect to the plane of the solar orbit, therefore it is always pointing in the same direction while the Earth is spinning around the sun. This tilt results in the seasons as Earth circles the Sun. This is the major reason for the climates we experience. When the North Pole is tilted toward the Sun; the Northern Hemisphere will have summer and The Southern Hemisphere will have winter. This is the result of this half of Earth receiving warmer radiant heat as it is closer to the Sun due to its tilt and where we are in our circle of the Sun.

The opposite is true as the Earth is half way around its yearly orbit and the tilt of earth finds the South Pole is pointed toward the Sun. The Southern Hemisphere will have summer; the Northern Hemisphere will have winter. Between these two positions in its orbit around the Sun, neither the North Pole nor the South Pole is pointed toward the Sun. There will be spring or autumn, depending on which side of the Sun the Earth is located during its orbit.

A solstice is when Earth has its maximum tilt toward or away from the Sun. Winter solstice occurs around December 21 and Summer solstice is near June 21 for the Northern Hemisphere. An equinox is when the tilt is minimized. Spring equinox is around March 20 and the Autumnal equinox is around September 23 for the Northern Hemisphere. The Southern Hemisphere is the opposite. Thus, the seasonal effects in the south are reversed. Fortunately, Earth has this tilt. If it was perpendicular to the plane of its orbit around the Sun, Earth would get too hot for human life.

In modern times, Earth's perihelion (Earth's closest distance to the sun) occurs around January 3. The aphelion (Earth is the farthest away from the sun) occurs around July 4. Coincidentally, the Southern Hemisphere is tilted toward the Sun at about the same time that Earth reaches the closest approach to the Sun, that is, perihelion. This results in about a 6.9 percent increase in solar energy reaching the Southern Hemisphere at perihelion. However, this effect is much less significant than the total energy change due to the axial tilt. The higher proportion of water in the Southern Hemisphere absorbs most of the excess energy. So, Mother Nature has helped again by increasing the size of the oceans on that part of Earth to again provide us a balance.

The Earth's Balances and Man's influence

Up to this part of this book almost everything discussed related to energy and the transfer of energy. Initially the energy comes from the sun, but then the energy is transferred by the evaporation of water in the oceans, and then there is the precipitation that transfers energy to the clouds as condensation occurs to produce the precipitation. This relieves the heat that the oceans received and some of what the ground received. There are ocean currents that spread the sun's energy from the tropical waters of the oceans and seas toward the colder waters to blend out the heat of the equator waters and heat the northern waters to try to create parity of temperature. There is energy of the weather winds which, as I call it, "the great mixer," as it mixes and spreads the joy or harm around the world and evens out the temperature. There is the generation of water vapor, carbon dioxide, and the sun's light which brings together the working of photosynthesis and the production of plant life.

There are plants that store the sun's energy which is released through decay, or man's use of them for food or other conveniences. There are volcanic eruptions that generate water vapor and many different gases and this is not a direct result of the Sun's energy, this is an earthborn energy. This is more related to the energy Earth possessed from its birth and the early years of differentiation and the energy brought to earth via meteors. Remember the discussion about the outer core of earth being molten metal. Some heat is transferred from this to the surface via volcanoes. This heat is replaced in the Earth's outer core by the spinning of the earth which generates a certain energy taken up by this outer core. It is also related to the amount of energy being released by radioactive material in the Earth's mantel. These are all energies that happen as part of Mother Nature, and in general are fairly efficient and have nothing to do with man. They all work to balance the energy received and the energy released to space. We shall now visit man and the animals and show where their released heat is also taken to the atmosphere and eventually to outer space.

Distribution of the sun's energy

The amount of energy supplied to earth by the sun on a daily basis has been measured and it is equal to 1.5 x 10²² watts per day or 3.6 x 10¹⁸ Calories per day. (These are table Calories which are equal to a kilocalorie on the scientists measuring scheme. I use table Calories as designated by a capital "C" in all the energy calculations in this book. This is so the average person can relate to the Calories they eat or don't eat if on a diet.) It has been determined that: (12)

- approximately 23% or 8.28 x 10¹⁷ Calories of the suns energy are directed to the water cycle that provides fresh water to the world each day.
- Approximately 1.0 percent or 3.6 x 10¹⁶ calories of the sun's energy is directed toward the wind and ocean currents.
- Only 0.023 percent or 9.36 x 10¹⁵ Calories of the sun's energy is directed toward photosynthesis.
- Forty two percent or 1.512 x 10¹⁸ Calories are directed toward warming the land and the water on land.
- The remaining energy is reflected back toward space from the clouds, water, ice, and earth.

This daily energy distribution and how much reflects from the clouds, is absorbed by the clouds, or is reflected from earth in the form of infrared heat is just a look at the daily direct result of sun's energy. There are numerous indirect ways that the sun's energy is returned to space. Without all being returned in direct or indirect means, the Earth would heat up and history tells us that this has not been true. If it was true and the Earth had heated up, what mechanism caused the Earth to cool down? There is no direct way known for the earth to give up more heat than it receives and to cool. For Earth to cool it has to give up more energy than it receives. The Earth is a passive subject, meaning it can only put out energy it receives. The Sun is an active element putting out energy constantly. Since it receives no energy, the sun continually losses its energy and it is estimated it will run out of energy in a little over five billion years and will be a cold star; of course their will no longer be any life on Earth since we cannot exist without the sun's daily dose of energy.

I assume that man's entry onto earth would only have impacted the 42 percent or 1.512×10^{18} Calories of the sun's energy that is used to heat the land and water on land. I make this assumption based on the fact that this is the only energy from the sun that is not dedicated to the functions as mentioned. However, that is an over simplification since plants, animals and man consume the energy supplied for photosynthesis to provide them their daily needed energy. Now we will discuss how much energy man consumes or his daily activities. I want to see if they approach the energy partitioned off of the forty two percent of the sun's daily energy in addition to the 9.36×10^{15} (1000 trillion) Calories directed toward photosynthesis; which provides Earth the plants for the animals and people to eat and the meat we derive from eating the animals that eat the plants. I also want to bring into the discussion how much energy the various animals consume and how much carbon dioxide they generate each day.

Before proceeding on man's effect on earth I want to go back and provide some background I believe is important for the reader to understand in order to appreciate what came before man and how it ties into what may result in any increase in CO_2.

There is one over-riding issue that one has to keep in mind as you read this information and that is; the sun's energy is used primarily to provide weather, fresh water, and the growth of plants – and all other things depend on these three elements of nature.

Our three atmospheres

When earth was formed it initially had no atmosphere, but the earth was highly active with space substance pounding on our globe and with the earth trying to stabilize by being pulled together by its own gravity. There were eruptions from volcanoes all over the globe blasting out gases and the first atmosphere of earth was Hydrogen, Helium, Carbon Dioxide, Water vapor, Nitrogen, Sulfur Dioxide, and others, but no oxygen. After 65 million years or so the sun began to shine and it also generated Solar Winds. These winds blasted away at earth and tore off the Hydrogen and Helium atmosphere; as it did on the four planets closest to earth. Meanwhile, the earth had begun to stabilize through its gravitational pull toward its center core with the heavy elements such as iron and gold making up its core. The outer core was also made up of heavy elements such as iron but it did not solidify; it remained liquid while the mantle of earth was composed mostly of the lighter materials. As Earth spun around on its axis the spinning caused the liquid outer core to spin and generate electricity and provide a magnetic field. Now as the volcanoes belched out their gases, the ones that became dominant in this the second atmosphere of Earth were Nitrogen, Carbon Dioxide, Water Vapor and other elements to a much lesser extent. Oxygen did not take part in this atmosphere since all oxygen was tied up oxidizing much of the earth's surface including all the iron in rocks.

This second atmosphere was a miracle of sorts. With the combination of the sunlight, water vapor, and carbon dioxide, the stage was set for the process of photosynthesis to occur, as well as global warming. Fortunately, Earth contained several things required to establish a major change. Either as part of its original makeup or deposited by other space debris; it had RNA (ribonucleic acid) and DNA (deoxyribonucleic acid); and/or the equivalent of seeds that would produce the vegetation that became the next step in Earth's evolution.

Simply stated, photosynthesis is the conversion of light energy into chemical energy. It is the means of taking the light from the sun and producing plants. To do so, it must have carbon dioxide present. Photosynthesis occurs in plants in two stages. In the first phase, light-dependent reactions capture the energy of light and arguments for global warming? use it to make high-energy molecules. During the second phase, the light-independent reactions use the high-energy molecules **to capture carbon dioxide** and make the precursors of glucose. (13)

In the light-dependent reactions, one molecule of the pigment chlorophyll absorbs one photon of light and loses one electron The chlorophyll molecule regains the lost electron by taking one from a water molecule through a process called photoysis, which **releases oxygen gas** as a waste product. The Earth received a miracle. The process of photosynthesis begins to eliminate the atmosphere of its carbon dioxide, which was causing the greenhouse effect, while producing free oxygen to begin a change in the atmosphere's contents. Plants begin to grow in the solid Earth and sea kelp begins to grow in the oceans. Algae come in multiple forms from multicellular organisms like kelp, to microscopic, single-celled organisms. Photosynthetic bacteria do not have chloroplasts. Instead, photosynthesis takes place directly within the cell.

It is important to realize the other advantages of this phase of Earth's existence. Most plants are photoautotrophic, that is, they can synthesize food directly from inorganic compounds using light energy from the Sun, instead of eating other organisms or relying on nutrients derived from them. While performing this chemical marvel the plant itself retains its carbon and is organic. This is the first step toward providing food for the animals and man who will begin to inhabit the earth. The plants take in carbon dioxide and give off oxygen. The most important contributors of free oxygen into the Earth's atmosphere were cyanobacteria (blue-green algae). The oldest known fossils were found in rocks of Western Australia and were dated 3.5 billion years old. These were also photoautotrophic. Through photosynthesis, these bacteria convert carbon dioxide directly to oxygen through a chemical reaction. Another important aspect is the fact that plants take in nitrogen through their roots. Thus, the nitrogen becomes part of the plant's system. Human beings, even though they were not on Earth yet, need nitrogen, but they are unable to take in nitrogen from the air. We breathe it in, but it is expelled without being assimilated. To receive our needed nitrogen we eat plants or other animals that eat plants. So, photosynthesis brought many good aspects to the aging Earth in its early existence, and it still does.

While photosynthetic life reduced the carbon dioxide content of the atmosphere, it also started to produce significant amounts of oxygen. For a long period, the oxygen produced did not build up in the atmosphere. The oxygen oxidized rocks on the Earth's surface continuously for a significant amount of time. As recorded in banded iron formations and continental red bed formations, the rocks took it up. Only about a billion years ago (3.5 billion years from the beginning of earth and probably 3.0 billion after plants began to provide oxygen for earth's next atmosphere) did the reservoirs of oxidizable rock became saturated and the free oxygen begin to establish itself as a major player in our atmosphere. By this time, forests, oceans, and jungles throughout Earth were supplying large amounts of oxygen. Thus, the atmosphere evolved toward what is our present atmosphere as the oxygen increased and reached levels higher than today's 21-23 percent...

The Third Atmosphere

So, Mother Earth has accomplished several tricks, starting with differentiation to provide Earth with a magnetic field and generate heat that resulted in volcanoes belching out water vapor and carbon dioxide that supplemented the building up of the oceans and the second atmosphere. This atmosphere reacted with the sunlight to provide photosynthesis, which resulted in the beginning of the growth of plant life in the oceans and, eventually, on solid ground. While the oceanic plant life began the reduction of the carbon dioxide in the atmosphere, it also began to supply oxygen for the beginning of a new third atmosphere, one devoid of most of the carbon dioxide. With this last trick came the eventual elimination of the strong greenhouse effect. Well, not quite. We discussed earlier that we have a small greenhouse effect that provides us our present enjoyable temperature of 59 degrees Fahrenheit. It is probable that most of the greenhouse effect was caused by water vapor as there were heavy rains and high humidity at that time.

Meanwhile, this was the beginning of the growth of plant life on Earth, both on land and in the seas.

The combination of substances received began forming significant molecules, such as sugars, amino acids, and nucleotides, the building blocks of proteins and nucleic acids. Somewhere along the line, DNA and RNA entered into the scheme of things. DNA provides the instructions for the building blocks of nature's living organisms through the use of the RNA messenger. Some scientists believe that DNA was not present but RNA was and eventually there was a mutation that resulted in DNA. This started the chemistry working toward a future goal. It also gave us another surprise, single-celled microorganisms. Single-celled microbes have been identified in rocks that date back to 3.5 billion years, just a billion years after Earth's existence. (14) To date, we have only been able to identify multicellular organisms having existed a billion years ago.

The Earth, through photosynthesis, continued to reduce carbon dioxide and replace the atmosphere with oxygen. With the oxygen and nitrogen taking over a major role in the atmosphere, ultraviolet light from the Sun split the oxygen molecules in the atmosphere and produced an **ozone layer** in the upper part of the atmosphere. As this continued, an ozone ultraviolet shield was produced as a by-product. This shield prevented most of the harmful ultraviolet from reaching Earth. This occurred about a billion years ago and set the stage for oxygen-breathing life forms. Any life form of animals before the creation of the ozone layer would have found most, if not all, of that life form dying due to the ultraviolet rays from the sun. It has been recognized that living things as we know them can not take the ultraviolet rays and their extreme energy. The equivalent of skin cancer or other forms of cancer would have caused the death of any living organism before ozone was produced in the atmosphere. With the ozone layer formed, life of several forms appeared on earth around 540 million years ago, including what was to be the beginning of man as we know him today.

In summary: Preparing for Man

In summary, Earth had to go through several phases to allow man to exist on Earth.

- Earth's Magnetic Field had to be formed so that the Solar Wind could not eliminate our atmosphere.
- Earth's second atmosphere brought us global warming and photosynthesis so that plants could grow and provide the eventual nourishment for animals, including man.
- Earth's third atmosphere brought us oxygen and reduced the Ultraviolet radiation by producing the Ozone layer in the atmosphere.
- The sun's heating of the oceans freed up fresh water in the form of precipitation that provided fresh water for plants, animals and man.
- The climate of Earth stabilized with a certain level of global warmth that made the temperature swing around a nominal level of 57 - 59 degrees Fahrenheit (the chart I showed, 57 degrees Fahrenheit over the last 4507 years), thus providing a livable climate for plants, animals and man to prosper.

Now Man

Man, as we know him has been around for several tens of thousands years. It wasn't long ago that there were only a hundred million humans on the face of the earth (just before Christ) and now we have 6.7 billion. Each has a small effect on the Earth and perhaps its climate, but with 6.7 billion the effect can be large.

In addition to Man there is the infrastructure that is required to support man. It is important to analyze this infrastructure and see its impact on global warming or any other additional effects. This infrastructure includes all the animals and plants needed to keep man alive. This may sound as an inconsequential issue but when you look at the food crops and the number of cattle, sheep, pigs, chickens, Turkeys and other animals on Earth to support man's daily need of nutrients, it is a large number. Each of these animals takes in oxygen and expels carbon dioxide and methane and each requires more food energy per day than man to live. Let's look at how this number of people and this infrastructure can affect the balance of the constant energy provided by our Sun and whether global warming can emanate from this inclusion of man and the resources to support him.

Human energy and all energy measured in Calories; the same ones we eat

Let's look at one human first and understand his needs and what those needs entail. A human has an average temperature of 98.6 degrees F. (37 degrees C) and must maintain that temperature within + or – 2 degrees F (~1.1 degrees C) or he suffers from a sickness. Everything that man does while sleeping or awake requires energy. In order to survive he must take in nourishment in the form of food to replenish the amount of energy he burns off each day. The amount of nourishment required to maintain a given body weight (assuming it is a mature person) is approximately 2000 Calories for a man and 1500 Calories for a woman (some papers written on the subject claim its 2500 Calories for Man and 2000 Calories for a woman). A Calorie is a unit of energy. There are small calories that are equal to 4.184 joules (or its equivalent in watts of 4.184 watts per calorie) which are the International units of energy. In the United States we use the watt in place of the joule. The watt is equal to one joule per second, so a time element is involved with the watt compared to the lone joule. This has been accepted worldwide and watts are used in most countries. So, a small calorie is equal to 4.184 watts, a kilocalorie is equal to 4,184 watts and a table Calorie is equal to a kilocalorie, or 4,184 watts). Now that you know that, forget it.

The more familiar term used in most of the world is the Calorie that we use to measure the energy of table foods. This Calorie is called the large calorie and is equal to a kilocalorie and its 1000 small calories. It is denoted by a large C. The Calories needed by a person each day are these large Calories. Since it is equal to the kilocalorie, it is equal to 4,184 watts (small calorie) x 1000 (kilocalorie) or **4,184 watts per large Calorie**. This large Calorie is the energy required to raise the temperature of one kilogram (2.2 pounds) of water by one degree C. **I use the large Calorie** in all my discussions in the book. I will use Calories in place of watts in discussions of power where it makes sense. I will convert the sun's energy we receive each day to Calories. With these Calories being used throughout this book, it will easy for the average person to relate to this measure of energy. It relates to those of you that go on a diet to lose Calories, or go on a diet to gain Calories. When I write about the sun's energy in Calories you can relate to the food you eat and the energy a human dissipates each day. Now let's examine how that plays out in energy used by the average male or female, and what effect, if any, this has on the total incoming energy from the sun on a daily basis, or more specifically the energy for photosynthesis and to the 42 percent that is used to heat the land and the water on land.

Lets assume the average male burns off 2000 Calories of energy in a day This is equal to 2000 x 4,184 watts per table Calorie **= 8.4 million watts he burns off in a day.** This is listed as 8.4 megawatts or 8.4×10^6 W. This is approximately the amount of energy a man burns up during a day while breathing, walking, running, working and whatever other activities he engages in. It is higher in the US and is estimated between 3000 and 3500 C per day, but I will use this smaller amount since it relates more to the rest of the world's use of daily Calorie intake.

If man eats 2000 Calories during the day, his weight will remain constant. If he eats more than 2000 calories he will gain weight unless he exercises heavily so as to burn off more than 2000 calories per day. If he eats less than 2000

Calories in a day, on average, he will lose weight. If man is eating 2000 Calories of food each day he must make sure he uses up 2000 calories through his normal body functions and his activity level or he will gain weight on 2000 Calories per day. To lose a pound a man must burn off an extra 500 Calories per day for a week; or he must take in 500 less Calories a day than his normal diet over the course of a week. If he does this; i.e. if he takes in only 1500 Calories for 7 days he will lose a pound in a week if his normal diet of 2000 Calories a day allowed his weight to be stable. If he also exercises to burn off more Calories than he eats he will lose additional weight.

No matter what his normal diet, if he decides to reduce his intake by 500 less Calories a day he will lose weight at a rate of one pound a week. If his normal diet happens to be 2500 Calories per day and he drops his diet to 1500 Calories per day he will lose two pounds a week. This is an average person with a normal metabolism. So, it's important that the reader understands that we can convert all energy levels and express them in the same table Calories that we use for our daily diet. They are all energy and engineering and scientists just happen to use a different kind of calorie in their calculations; their calorie is one thousandth of our food Calorie and when they talk about kilocalories, they are the same as one table Calorie.

It is interesting to compare this to a common element used every day all over the world. Let's look at how man equates against the energy burned by a 100 watt light bulb. Remember I said that 2000 calories a day is equal to 8.4 million watt seconds; this is equal to 2,333 watt hours and since there are 24 hours in a day it is equal to a 97.2 watt day. So, this man will burn off about the same power as a 100 watt light bulb that stays on 24 hours a day. If the light bulb stays on 8 hours a day the man will consume about three times the amount of energy burned off by that 100 watt light bulb on that day. If a man in the U.S. consumes and burns off 3000 Calories per day it is equivalent to a 150 watt light bulb in this example. It's also equal to a one horsepower motor running for a little over three hours. We humans burn off a lot of energy in a day and in a lifetime.

A Female burns of about three quarters of the energy of a man, so she will burn off energy equivalent to a 75 watt bulb that burns for a full day. If the bulb is on for only eight hours of the day she will burn off thee times what that light bulb would burn off. The US woman consumes approximately 2500 Calories a day and her energy consumption must be raised accordingly to offset this larger amount of calories than other women of the world consume. To lose weight the woman must take in fewer Calories than she consumes.

These examples of how many Calories a male or female person burns in a day should provide one with an idea of energy consumption. Remember, we are trying to look at the energy the sun puts on earth each day and we are trying to determine if man's entry into the picture causes any problems with energy since we know that global warming requires additional energy.

So, let's look at the total population of 6.7 billion people and assume that each burns an average of 2000 Calories per day for a total of 1.34×10^{13} total Calories (or 13.4 trillion Calories) per day. This is a lot of energy. The sun supplies 3.58×10^{18} Calories per day and much of it is used to heat the oceans and provide evaporation so that man can have fresh water to drink. Man makes a big demand on the system of energy. Remember I mentioned that the sun provides 9.35×10^{15} Calories per day for photosynthesis which we can round off as 1×10^{16} Calories per day and man burns off approximately 1×10^3. This leaves only about a factor of 1×10^3 Sun/food Calories for other animals.

Remember, this is an approximation with man only eating plants and the assumption is that those plants grew in one day and the sun only had to provide them one days' worth of energy. Neither of these assumptions is true. It would normally take about four months to derive the plants we eat each day. This is about 120 days. So, this queue of plant food must always be there and growing and using the daily photosynthesis. There are no instant plants to eat (the closest is probably a mushroom). So, 120 days worth of photosynthesis energy must be provided on a daily basis to support the queue of food required for man if plants were all he ate. This adds up to approximately 120 times the daily Calories of 1.34×10^{13} calculated for the daily requirements by man. So, even if man only ate plants, we only have an excess of about ten times more Calories received each day from the sun's energy that is budgeted and supplied by photosynthesis because we have to keep the plants in the queue. This equates **to 1.608×10^{15}** Calories of energy used each day by plants to support man, if we include the queue of 120 days.

If these numbers remained and we now said we will determine how many Calories are required if the number of people increased by a factor of ten percent. We could run close to the daily sun's energy used for photosynthesis if the population rose to 7.37 billion people. Maybe the saving grace comes from the fact that we only partitioned out the 1×10^{16} Calories for photosynthesis because that happens to be all we thought (or I thought) is needed. For example we could be growing more plant food than is used in a day and is consumed over time. Let's go out on limb and say we are going to grow ten times man's daily need. If that many plants were growing, than more energy would be required from the sun's light to provide the photosynthesis needed for this extra growth. Since there is an over supply raining down on land, the added plant growth would be supplied by additional photosynthesis from this light energy. So, let's assume that instead of 1×10^{16} Calories for photosynthesis being consumed by the world's plants we will increase it to 1×10^{17} Calories per day for photosynthesis by adding ten times the amount of plants to provide the food for the growth in population. **If more plants are there, the sun's light will be there along with the carbon dioxide and more plants would be produced and more oxygen would be generated.** There really isn't any "magic number" of Calories partitioned off for plant growth. This is just a mathematical estimation. In fact, since many trees that were being supplied energy through photosynthesis are being cut down, this leaves more energy to be supplied to plants as the population grows. This will provide the extra energy needed for this extra population growth. It does reduce the amount of Caloric energy for any other use on Earth of Sun's constant energy. If the population grows by two billion over the next 20-25 years to approximately 8.7 billion, then additional Calories of plant food would be needed.

It's interesting to just think of carbon since that is the source of the carbon dioxide that the global warming advocates claim will cause global warming. Plants, as discussed are a marvel; they convert sunlight, water vapor and carbon dioxide into plants that are essentially a compound of carbon that provide the organic food for man and animals. They provide carbon via this food. At the same time the animals and man breathe out carbon dioxide which the plants take in during their photosynthesis act and convert into carbon for their growth. Therefore, there is a trading of carbon between plants and the animals including man. This carbon trade off not only satisfies the plants and their needs for carbon but it also provides man oxygen that he needs to breathe. This circle keeps growing since the population is growing, as well as the increase in animals and the amount of carbon dioxide being produced by the animals and man is increasing. We also have to consider the carbon dioxide being produced by the exhaust of automobiles which helps the plants to gain their needed carbon. Perhaps as the population grows and the number of cars increases it provides the carbon dioxide for the growing population.

Meanwhile, man has found ways to generate more plants through his ingenuity to keep up with the population growth. There are huge farms and their related farmland that are producing more plants each year, therefore increasing the ability to take in more and more carbon dioxide. So, it's possible that this increase in farm production is keeping up with the carbon dioxide man and animals are producing, and providing the increased oxygen needed for the animals and man. Perhaps there is a balance here. We haven't detected a change in the percentage of oxygen in the atmosphere, so its stability indicates that the increase in man and animals on Earth hasn't affected the amount of oxygen in the atmosphere. Has it affected the amount of carbon dioxide in the air?

What are the arguments for global warming?

Keep in mind that some of these are opinions as to what causes global warming and its effect. There are arguments that are contrary to these.

- Worldwide, 1995 was the warmest year since global temperatures were first kept in 1856. This supports the near consensus among climatologists that emissions of carbon dioxide and other gases are causing global warming. *(Chivilan and Epstein,* Boston Globe*) (15).* But don't forget the graph of temperature over the last 4507 years which showed the increase in average temperature began in 1650 before the big growth in population and before cars were invented, I therefore take issue with this article.
- On average, 16 million tons of carbon dioxide are emitted into the atmosphere every 24 hours by human use worldwide. *(U.S. Department of Energy) (16)*
- Carbon emissions in North America reached 1,760 million metric tons in 1998, a 38 percent increase since 1970. They are expected to grow

another 31 percent, to 2,314 million metric tons, by the year 2020. *(U.S. Department of Energy) (16)*

- The United States is the world's largest single emitter of carbon dioxide, accounting for 23 percent of energy-related carbon emissions worldwide. *(U.S. Department of Energy) (16)*
- An average of 23,000 pounds of carbon dioxide is emitted annually in each American home. *(U.S. Environmental Protection Agency) (17)*
- The transportation sector consumed 35% of the nation's energy in 1990; this sector is 97% dependent on petroleum. (17)
- Fossil fuels are depleted at a rate that is 100,000 times faster than they are formed. (This is the good news.) It takes about six million years for various materials to decay and be converted into oil.
- Another piece of good news is that, based on the programs to reduce carbon dioxide the United States will essential remain flat in its production of carbon dioxide by the year 2015.
- However, China's economic growth places it at the U.S level by the end of 2008 and they will be using more and more coal to support their economic growth which will generate more and more carbon dioxide. They will continue this trend for the foreseeable future. One of the main problems is that China has very little energy in the way of oil, but considerable energy in the form of coal. It has therefore began to establish more coal mines. It even is establishing coal mines to support it huge hydroelectric generation which is too variable. I will cover this in the hydroelectric section of this book.

Health

- Approximately 30,000 lives are cut short in the U.S. each year due to pollution from electricity production. *(ABT Associates study))(18)*
- About 81 tons of mercury are emitted into the atmosphere each year as a result of electric power generation. Mercury is the most toxic heavy metal in existence. *(U.S. Environmental Protection Agency) (19)*
- Burning fossil fuels to produce energy releases carbon dioxide and other global-warming-causing gases into the atmosphere. Global warming will increase the incidence of infectious diseases (including equine encephalitis and Lyme disease), death from heat waves, blizzards, and floods, and species loss. *(Chivilan and Epstein,* Boston Globe, *April 10, 1997) (20)*

Transportation

- The United States consumes 17 to 20 million barrels of oil per day, of which nearly two-thirds is used for transportation. We only produce approximately 8 million barrels a day.
- The United States imports more than seven to twelve million barrels of oil per day. while producing six to eight million barrels of oil per day.
- While the world's population doubled between 1950 and 1996, the number of cars increased tenfold. Automobile congestion in the United States alone accounts for $100 billion in wasted fuel, lost productivity, and rising health costs. Still, analysts project that the world's fleet of cars will double in a mere 25 years. *(Worldwatch Institute) (21)*
- Americans use a billion gallons of motor oil a year, 350 million gallons of which end up polluting the environment. *(Department of Energy and Maryland Energy Administration) (22)*
- A car that gets 20 miles per gallon (mpg) emits approximately 50 tons of global-warming-inducing carbon dioxide over its lifetime, while a 40-mpg car emits only 25 tons. Over the average lifetime of an American car (100,000 miles), a 40-mpg car will also save approximately $3,000 in fuel costs compared to a 20-mpg car. *(Natural Resources Defense Council) (23)*
- The cars and trucks reaching the junkyards this year have lower gasoline mileage, on average, than the new ones rolling off dealers' lots, for the first time on record. *(Matt Wald,* The New York Times, *August 11, 1997) (24)*

Renewables

- Only 7.5 percent of total U.S. energy consumption came from renewable sources in 1998. Renewable generate no carbon dioxide. Of that total, 94 percent was from hydropower and biomass (trash and wood incinerators). *(U.S. Energy Information Administration) (25)*
- For the 2 billion people without access to electricity, it would be cheaper to install solar panels than to extend the electrical grid. *(The Fund for Renewable Energy Everywhere) (26)*

- Within 15 years, renewable energy could be generating enough electricity to power 40 million homes and offset 70 days of oil imports. That is not where the problem lies as you will read.

Remember the affects of the famine in Europe

It's very interesting when one considers at one time there was a famine in Europe about three hundred years ago and the reason was that the population of Europe outgrew the ability of the land to produce the required food to sustain this population growth. Fortunately, the farms in the United States overproduced America's needs and a great deal of food was sold to the European countries. This could be an early example of where the world is heading now. I would expect there is a theoretical limit to the maximum population the world can sustain with the food that is produced. I don't know what that amount is but I will discuss a problem that any growth in population will cause further on in this book.

Remember, these calculations were made if man only eats plants. Essentially that is all he eats if you substitute the amount of plants an animal must eat to supply man his meat. We know that a huge part of the population eats meat of some sort instead of plants. Is that a good idea? We can calculate the energy required to supply the plants that are eaten by animals we eat, plus the animals on Earth that require nourishment and are not a source of our nourishment; wild animals fall into this category. In addition these animals, domestic and wild, all give off more carbon dioxide than man.

Determining the amount of Calories needed by the animals that support man's meat diet

Let's determine how many food Calories are needed for the animals that we eat for food. In addition to the food required by animals we need land to house them and water to supply them their everyday requirements. Using the United States as an example and the resources required, approximately half of the land in the US is required, along with approximately 75 – 80 % of the fresh water and approximately one fifth of the fossil fuel energy consumed in the US each year. (27) This is an enormous amount of land and energy required plus the huge amount of a scarcity such as water. But, this type of energy and resources must be directed to feed people and the animals that are consumed for food and other uses.

Calories from plants

Let's assume that half of man's daily requirements of Calories come from plants and the other half is through the consumption of meat. Let's assume that it takes at least that half of the calories to bring these plant foods to your table for consumption, so plants daily supply must equal to the numbers previously calculated if man only ate plants. This extra half is probably understated when you consider the energy used for fertilizers, water, and fuel to make it to man's table that have not been included in these numbers. Let's look at where the calories come from, besides the plants.

To provide some insight to this amount of energy and where the resources come from, the meat-based food requires more energy, land, and water than the vegetarian diet. A large amount of land is used up by the large number of food animals in the U.S. There are 9 billion animals including cattle, cows, pigs, sheep, chickens and other poultry maintained to supply the meat requirements that are consumed each year for food. (28) The queue for animals to grow and reach the level used for food is longer than the plant queue. Therefore, whatever meat Calories are eaten, there are eight times as many that are in the food chain taking on Calories, giving off carbon dioxide and being fattened up for future food. These Calories being consumed by these animals must be counted each day also since they are in the queue to insure that there is food in the supply chain available for food each day. This means when the Calories that are consumed using meat as the food you have to multiply that figure by eight to show the Calories being consumed on a daily basis by these animals to provide man's future consumption. This is not one of the places where "just in time" can be used. We can't grow them and consume them in the same day or same year; at least most of them can't reach that stage in a year. To sum this up, in order to supply the meat for man on a daily basis we must have approximately eight times as many animals in the energy queue to supply the daily meat requirements for man. When calculating the daily energy requirements required by the domesticated animals we have to take their daily Calories and multiply it by eight due to the queue that must exist to provide a continuous daily supply of those meat Calories. Another way of calculating the amount is to just take the total animals in the world and assume this number stays the same. In other words, as we consume them we replace them.

There is a rule I am going to quote at this time. There is no function in the world that is 100% efficient. There is always something loss in every transaction. Keeping this in mind, plants are the basic food in life and this is close to 100% efficient since it comes directly from the sun's light and photosynthesis and on to mans daily diet. When we eat meat from any animal we are taking our plant food via something that is not 100% efficient. There has to be a loss of energy when plant food goes to an animal to be consumed first and then to man. If animals were not around, man could survive on plants and water. If plants were not around, neither would there be animals nor man. So, by eating animals we are wasting the energy of the sun. As you will see in the section coming up, animals that we consume for food take more food than man, use up more energy than man, give off more carbon dioxide than man, are not even 50% efficient and by the time man eats meat the efficiency is down to less than 10%. This turns out to be a very inefficient use of the sun's energy. At the same time these animals are breathing out more carbon dioxide than man and give off a considerable amount of methane.

With that said, let's examine the animals and their contributions.

Meat Calories

In order to obtain meat for some of our Calories we must depend on cattle, sheep, pigs, chickens or turkeys or whatever form meat comes in. We also will include fish in this category and state that anything not a plant falls in this category to make the picture a little easier to comprehend. For information purposes there are 1.3 billion cattle in the world's queue that provide food for the given year, some of which end up as beef, milk, or cheese or some form of food Calories. (29) These cattle derive their energy from the vegetation they eat and we can again thank the Sun. Of course the vegetation comes in many forms for these animals, but most is through grazing of some form of grasses or it is provided directly by farmers in the form of hay, wheat, corn, foliage and other nutrients. Some critics say that it might be a better use of the food to provide it directly to man rather than through the indirect chain of the animals.

However, there are many nutrients supplied through the cattle chain that could not be supplied directly to humans. For example, man cannot digest cellulose and certain other carbohydrates that cattle and sheep are able to do because of their four stomachs and the ability to re-chew cud (a form that their food taken in one of their stomachs that they can re-eat and chew and eventually digest). In addition, man cannot take in Nitrogen directly into his system. It must come from the digestion of plants or animals that eat plants. Nitrogen and phosphorus are needed in some of the amino acids and other biological requirements for man. While supplying many Calories for man's consumption, cattle require a considerable amount of Calories each day to exist and this is the use of some of the Sun's provided energy. Meanwhile, cattle and sheep generate a considerable amount of methane mainly through burping. This methane is a "green house" gas that we must take into consideration when reviewing the sources of possible Global Warming.

Cattle Calories

Each of the 1.3 billion cattle requires approximately fifteen times the daily calories of a human; thirty thousand versus 2000 for man. So, the Calories add up to 1.3×10^9 (cattle) x 30,000 Calories per day for a total of **3.9×10^{13}** Calories per day;. These result in other food products besides beef such as milk, cheese, and hides.

Sheep Calories

There are approximately 1.8 billion sheep in the world and they require about half the daily calories of the cattle. So, the Calories add up to 1.8×10^9 sheep times 15,000 Calories per day for a total of **2.6×10^{13}** Calories per day. These provide the best wool clothing, sheep leather as well as their food.

Chickens are another major food crop for man. Each year there are approximately 60 billion chickens consumed for the production of food. (30) At any given time there are about 24 billion chickens alive and well. Chickens provide two main sources of food, their eggs and their bodies. When one considers there are four chickens to every human that is astounding. When one considers as those are consumed that more take their place and that 60 billion a year is almost ten times the human population. When one considers the amount of food they provide it is astounding. In some ways chickens are better food for man than what cattle provide. They have less fat and therefore allow for fairly fat free diets. I don't know what the world would do without eggs for breakfast – or for many supper meals. In addition chickens require much less food and care than do cattle. Many poor countries are able to maintain chickens because they take up less space and they require less food supplied daily. Chickens are able to survive on rather poor land. Many of the sources of chicken are raised in small pens or cages and allow for the efficient supply of food. The biggest countries in the production of chickens for food sources are the United States with 9 billion per year, Brazil with 7 billion per year and China with 5 billion a year. These are estimated numbers and they add up to 21 billion of the 60 billion a year consumed in one way or another. So, the other countries of the world provide the other 39 billion yearly. In addition, there were almost 15 million pounds of "other poultry" slaughtered for food. Chickens consume ground up corn, weed seeds, and many other foods of this nature. The chicken is highly active and burns calories rather profusely, especially the hen during her egg laying sessions. In general chickens are eaten completely from the top of their highest part of their body to the lowest part. In addition their eggs are eaten the world over for many meals and in many different forms. Chicken eggs are also used to culture flu vaccine. A chicken's daily intake of Calories is approximately 1890 per day. The total intake of calories per day worldwide is therefore $24 \times 10^9 \times 1890 = \mathbf{4.54 \times 10^{13}}$. For how small they are, the chicken provides the most food value for the world intake. I found this to be amazing but I think its probably because chickens are easy to take care of. Turkeys could be added to this list since they represent about the same scenario as the chicken.

Pigs (swine)

Pork is the number one meat in terms of global production, accounting for over 40 percent of all meat produced. The highest consumption is in Europe where approximately 50 kg (110 pounds) is consumed by each person in a year, which is about twice the amount consumed by each person in China and the United States. (31) Europeans enjoy the products that come from the swine such as bacon, ham, pork chops, pork roast, and sausages made from these meats as well as leather and other products.

The pig is a favorite due to the fact that it doesn't take up much space and eats select garbage of humans in many cases. Many farmers use their crops for food and the left over of the crops for the pigs. In addition, proper smoking of the slaughtered pig's meat results in long shelf life, so the food source can be spread out over time more efficiently than other forms of meat. There are approximately 2.4×10^9 pigs world wide. Besides their use as a food, their skin is used to make leather for various sporting events as well as other garments for man such as working gloves.

The calorie intake of a pig depends on the size of the pig before being slaughtered. Pigs fall into two main weight groups; those of approximately 5 to 30 kg (66 pounds) and pigs that are 30 to 100 kg (220 pounds). The smaller of these take in 6000 calories per day and the large ones take in 15000 calories per day. I will use 11,000 as the average number for the total of 2.4×10^9 pigs. This would be a daily intake of **2.64×10^{13} Calories** per day worldwide.

Fish

In 2003, the total world production of fisheries product was 132.2 million tons or approximately 2.64×10^{11} pounds. (32) This amounts to approximately 40 pounds per person in a year derived from the fisheries. This is an understatement for many of the countries of the world where fish is the main source of food and protein. This amount from fisheries is approximately one third of the total amount of fish consumed. The rest comes from the wild catch. This percentage has been growing as many new fisheries are started each year. Two thirds of the fish consumed are caught wild. This adds up to 8.0×10^{11} pounds of fish consumed, wild or farmed per year.

Efficiencies of fisheries has increased tremendously where at one time the food provided to each fish was two fish for each fish produced. This has been improved to one fish per fish produced. This may sound inefficient but the one fish supplied is of a nature that it is not high on the food chain for mankind's consumption. Essentially one fish that is not eatable by man is supplied to provide a fish that is eatable. Food for fish is also supplied in the form of ground up kelp or other ocean food. The source of wild fish has remained essentially constant over the past decade. This number must be doubled to account for the food the fish consumes of one fish per fish in the fish farms.

In the wild the numbers are an estimate of approximately the same amount consumed by man and animals. Keep in mind that fish that eat plants like kelp grow up and are eaten by bigger fish which do not live off of plants. This means 1.6×10^{12} pounds of fish are consumed to provide food for the fish for man's eventual consumption. However, at least 10 times that amount of fish are free and consuming food each day. So, the calories consumed by the fish eaten or the fish being maintained represent at least 1.6×10^{13} pounds of fish per year, for 365 days per year and approximately 365 calories per day consumed equals approximately **1.6×10^{13} calories per day** consumed by man or required in the queue. This is probably well understated as the amount of calories actually being consumed or swimming around in the wild, but I chose to use this number because it is relatively consistent with the other sources of food I reviewed. The fish is the hardest for which to make an accurate estimate, because if we knew where they all were we could catch more of them each day. China now produces 70% of the world's farmed fish.

In the US, approximately 90% of all shrimp consumed is farmed and imported. In recent years salmon aquaculture has become a major export of Chile, especially in Puerto Montt and Quellon.

Summary of Calorie energy

It is obvious that a significant portion of the world's energies are directed to providing the 1500 to 2000 Calories per day for man. In doing so, many calories are expended by the providers as they work to bring the food to others as well as themselves. We can't count their individual Calories because they are already included in the Calories determined for the 6.7 billion people on Earth of which they are a part. However, any energy provided by machinery used to provide these foods must be counted. In addition to the calories to keep these animals alive, there is also the potable water that is required for all of them except for the salt water fish. This water must be transported or pumped in most cases and even the fish that are in salt water fisheries must have their food and water transported. Note that most of the calories from meat sources derive their energies via the consumption of plants rather than other animals. Of course the energy of these plants was derived from the Sun. Consider all the fuel consumed to provide these foods for man. This is a terrific number of Calories.

To simplify the summary of calories required to keep people alive let's assume that all of their daily Calories are derived directly by eating the plants or indirectly by eating the animals that ate the plants. This means the Calories derived from the sun to raise the plants are only counted once with respect to providing man's daily requirement. However, the calories to keep the animals alive for whatever time they are eating plants and roaming around the fields or swimming in the water, or running around laying eggs represent Calories on a grand scale to support man. Let's add them up.

Cattle	3.9×10^{13}
Sheep	2.6×10^{13}
Chickens	4.54×10^{13}
Pigs	2.64×10^{13}
Fish	1.6×10^{13}
Total	1.53×10^{14} Calories daily supplied by plants for domestic animals and their food to support man.
120 day queue equals	1.83×10^{16} Plant Calories in queue plants consumed by man each 1.34×10^{13} day.
Plants in the 120 day queue	1.60×10^{15} Calories per day including the queue

Total Plants and Animals = 2.0×10^{16} Calories just in the food value to support man to replace the 1.34×10^{13} Calories he burns off. So it takes about one thousand times as many Calories to support man as he consumes in a day. This is largely affected by the 120 days in the queue for the growth of the plants to feed man and the animals that man consumes in his daily diet.

An interesting feature of these support Calories is the fact that one has to take the approximate one hundred and twenty days into account for the food to grow and be there for the taking each day by man and animals. Each day they eat something that was started one hundred and twenty days before, thus requiring the amount of Calories supplied by the sun to overdue the daily requirements by this factor. However, the carbon dioxide put out by man and the animals doesn't have this 120 day factor. Their carbon dioxide output is just what is put out on a daily basis. This means the plants are taking in the carbon dioxide and generating the oxygen for one hundred and twenty days for every day that man and the domestic animals breathes out their carbon dioxide. This is a plus when it comes to helping on both sides of that equation. Assuming the 120 days is the right amount to use for the growth of the plants to provide food, this remains as a "120 day float" that persists from day to day and year to year unless there is something that disrupts this cycle like an extended drought that deprives the man and animals their plant food and the Calories they need. Most of you readers have seen pictures of the deprived children of some poor country such as some of the countries in Africa.

These children are deprived and their bodies show it, but the 120 day factor still exists for them. When they finally get some food to eat it had to have been grown over time; there is no escaping this fact. Food has a time factor and it must be taken into account when analyzing the energy supplied for life's existence.

That number of 2×10^{16} daily Calories is approximately 1000 times the daily consumption of Calories required to feed the world's population and their 1×10^{13} Calorie requirements per day. That's probably a reasonable approximation; since it takes many of these plants and animals many days to be in the loop to be able to supply the daily requirements by man, plus each of them require more Calories per day than man requires to exist and **all of these Calories come from plants. If we didn't eat animals and stayed on a plant diet the Calorie demand would drop by a factor of one thousand times.** This doesn't take into account the wild animals that roam the Earth. There are more of them then the number of domesticated food providing animals.

This daily amount of 2×10^{16} Calories is compared to the sun's energy supplied to warm the land and water on the land of 1.512×10^{18} Calories per day. Therefore if man continues to eat animals for his daily food then man's consumption of food requires approximate one percent of sun's total energy that provides Calories to earths land and water on that land. At present the animals used for food consume approximately eight times as much grain as is consumed by man in the U.S.

Why go through this calculation of Calories? Remember, we are trying to determine if there is global warming. In order to have global warming one must find the energy to provide that warming. Keep in mind that the man and animals all put off infrared energy and it must go somewhere. Therefore we review the various energies being used each day and determine if they are done efficiently or inefficiently to provide extra energy for global warming. If we don't find the energy through this method then we must find where new energy is coming from to provide global warming. Since there is a large infrastructure to supply man I have reviewed it to see if we can find any clues. During my research on the food to support man I came to a conclusion that we may be faced with another problem bigger than global warming and more eminent. This is an important consideration and in a later discussion I will bring to the reader's attention how the demand for food and the ability to provide it worldwide creates a bigger concern than global warming and it relates to providing this food support for man as the population grows.

This indoctrination about the energy is meant to supply the reader a rough analysis of this energy to support man compared to the other uses of the sun's energy. When you consider that the main use of sun's daily energy is to supply energy to the oceans to provide fresh water for man, some energy to provide the weather that moves heat around to provide a livable temperature for man and almost all of the rest of it is used to handle the requirements for man's food and the other energy man dissipates; it provides a picture of a world made for man and consumed by man. It also places a limit on man's activities as we shall see.

In addition, the animals all breathe in oxygen and breath out carbon dioxide. Taken as a whole, animals put out approximately six times the carbon dioxide of man. In addition, the cattle and pigs put out a considerable amount of methane which is also a green house gas that has an effect greater than carbon dioxide when it comes to absorbing the infrared wavelengths given off by Earth. Methane absorbs infrared rays at a rate that is twenty three times that of carbon dioxide. Fortunately, the amount of Methane in the atmosphere is much less than the carbon dioxide. I am also interested in comparing these needs of man versus the problem of satisfying the basic requirements to keep Global Warming from being the major problem.

Do you know what's interesting about this number of Calories to support man? They are all supplied by the energy of the sun if you ignore the energy derived from fossil fuels to provide motion to vehicles that deliver the food. However, **man derives no direct energy from the sun.** **All the sun's energy is used to provide photosynthesis to provide the growth of plants for man to eat or to feed the live stock of the world for man to eat. Meanwhile the sun's energy provides the water cycle that provides plants, animals and man the fresh water to drink and the energy to keep the earth warm.** In other words man could live in a structure without any sun and if he had the food (It would have to contain vitamin D to substitute for the sun's providing it), and water brought in on a daily basis he would live a "normal" life and think he is making it without the sun. How wrong.

Maybe it's the queue?

But maybe the answer is in the queue I discussed. Remember the long time the plants have to be in the queue for man's food and the same goes for the plants for domesticated animals man takes in as food. The queue turns out to be between one hundred and one thousand times as much as is needed on a daily basis to ensure it is there when a person needs it. During this long queue the plants take in carbon dioxide and give off oxygen. Maybe that's our saving grace. As our population grows, the population of plants for food grows. As the population grows the demand for meat grows along with the plants to supply them their daily needs. So, maybe it's this long queue that compensates for any tendency for the carbon dioxide level to increase in the atmosphere?

So, the energy to support man in his food needs causes more carbon dioxide to be breathed into the atmosphere, but maybe it is offset by the extra long time it takes to grow the food and during this time there is an offsetting phenomenon. Maybe it isn't quite balanced, but it would be worth a study to determine the cause and effect.

Where does the energy of man go?

Man's everyday existence on earth requires that energy of his body that is used for some task, including staying alive, is replaced as I have discussed. Man requires energy for every breath he takes. Using this form of argument, man has taken several steps to remain atop the food chain. He has improvised since the time he came on earth to ensure he is able to acquire the needed food to keep him alive. Early in the life of man he only had plants that grew wild to feed, as well as wild animals. As time went on he learned how to plant large fields of plant food and he domesticated many docile animals to ensure a supply of food. As the population of the world grew, man took steps to increase this supply of plants and animals. Likewise as technology methods improved he found ways to increase the efficiencies of both the growth of huge fields of food and also the more efficient gain of weight of the animals he took in as nutrients. As the world's transportation systems improved, food began to be transported world wide to satisfy the needs of countries that had land that was non-productive in generating food. The plants and meat consumed each day add up to the Calories he needs to survive and live a useful life. As man consumes these foods and remains active he gives off heat in the form of infrared heat. This heat is provided to the atmosphere around him and becomes part of the heat that escapes to outer space. By this heat being exhausted to outer space it allows earth to remain at a constant temperature, and balancing the heat that is supplied by the Sun each day. In addition, man and the animals provide the perfect balance with the plant world by giving off carbon dioxide that is taken in by the plants. Here we are back at the balance between plants that take in carbon dioxide and give off oxygen and animals that take in oxygen and give off carbon dioxide. Keep in mind that for every human there are many animals that provide his food that are also expelling much more carbon dioxide than man.

Man burns up energy while moving around things that are an intrinsic part of Earth and are not relative to energy that the Sun provides. It is just part of the intrinsic energy of Earth that he moves around and man dissipates energy while doing this. His dissipation of energy results in heat given off to the atmosphere. When man takes cement from the ground that is part of the Earth, and fabricates concrete to make roads, he is giving up heat while just moving around a part of Earth that is here as the planet is here. He is taking mass energy from Earth and returning it to Earth in a new form. As a result, he is burning off a portion of his 2,000 Calories per day. So, in many cases, man's gained energy from eating plants or animals is used to take energy from Earth and put it into a different form on Earth at the expense of his energy and the gain of some of Earth's mass energy. For example, if a man lifts a boulder to a higher location, the boulder gains in potential energy at man's loss of energy. So, energy is conserved including the heat given off by man in this exercise. This heat rises and becomes part of the atmosphere to be eventually expelled. Each day around the world, this heat emission happens time after time by the 6.7 billion residents. If man did not eat his 2,000 Calories a day to replace the energy lost, he would lose weight. He soon would not have the energy to lift another boulder to the same height as the original one he moved.

As the population grows and man supports this growth by increasing the plants and animals needed for his maintenance the amount of sunlight required for plants increases. Fortunately, photosynthesis is a demand type exchange of energy, that is, the more plants the more photosynthesis occurs and the more carbon dioxide is consumed and oxygen generated. Man has been very creative in finding ways to capture the Sun's light energy. Before Man, the energy consumed by earth of the sun's rays was completely determined by nature and its demands on this energy. Man has a drive toward improving life on Earth. He moves dirt around, builds structures out of Earth's materials, works the land for food, provides means for moving food around, builds equipment for many applications including those required to provide heat or air conditioning, and participates in reproduction of his kind. The reproduction of his kind is an interesting variable in the equation of the use of Sun's energy.

But, has man impacted the climate?

Volcanoes deep in the ocean generate a tremendous amount of carbon dioxide into the atmosphere and we have discussed that man and the animals give off more carbon dioxide than the machines of man. At the same time the old forests of the world generate approximately ninety percent of the carbon dioxide generated. Trees, when young, take in carbon dioxide and give off oxygen. Trees that are old and in dense forests such as those that are in the northern part of Canada and Russia actually generate carbon dioxide due to their denseness not allowing the proper sun to reach their branches. If they could be thinned there would be a benefit. However, most of these forests are in areas that are not accessible, or at least are not easily accessible. But the machines of man which have been steadily growing since the industrial revolution add to this carbon dioxide total. So, with populations growing and generating increased amounts of carbon dioxide as well as the domesticated animals to supply man his food, volcanoes continuing to exhaust high levels of carbon dioxide, old forests generating large amounts of carbon dioxide and man's machines continuing to grow at a rapid pace, one would think there would be a huge increase in carbon dioxide.

With all this generation of carbon dioxide one would think there would have been a tremendous increase in the amount of carbon dioxide in the atmosphere over the last one hundred and fifty years. However, the increase has only been from 230 parts per million to 380 parts per million. This is a pittance compared to what one would expect. I have not found anything in these activities that results in an increase in global warming as a result of man himself, or his activities or the increase in animals to support man's daily needs. It would seem that, among plants, animals, and man, the carbon keeps making circles among them. This is the picture I see before the arrival of the industrial revolution and the entrance of oil into the picture, along with a huge increase of population.

Look back at the graph displayed in the beginning of the book of the global temperature over the last 4500 years. The temperature cycled with or without man and with or without the effects of man's machines. This is interesting since Man has been on Earth for a little over 30,000 years and only recently, has man brought up the subject of global warming; even though this temperature cycling has occurred over at least the last 4500 years. Man and animals did not give off enough carbon dioxide to impact the climate. This is at least true when the population was at the 1850 levels. The global temperature was already on its present slope recovering from the Little Ice Age from 1650 to the present. This is over 350 years and it is almost time for the cycle to turn the other way and start cooling off Earth. Over 95% of the total CO_2 emissions would occur even if humans were not present on Earth. For example, the natural decay of organic material in forest and grasslands, such as dead trees, results in the release of about 220 gigatonnes of carbon dioxide every year. This carbon dioxide alone is over 8 times the amount emitted by humans – but about equivalent to the amount emitted by the animals that support humans. These natural sources are balanced by natural sinks, which remove carbon dioxide from the atmosphere, with the biggest being the oceans of the world. The increase in carbon dioxide concentration may rise if the increase generated by man and his supporting cast is not offset by a balancing factor. It's possible that the huge CO_2 sinks can handle the increase that man supplies to the equation or the large queue of plant food being provided the world over along with its balancing effect.

Playing the devil's advocate

What if I play the devil's advocate and assume that carbon dioxide might be the culprit that causes an increase in temperature during this time period we are living in. Let's see what would cause it. Al Gore blames it on the industrial revolution and mainly automobiles. Let's see where the data takes us. Maybe, if the Earth is going through an unusual increase in temperature (which I don't believe) it's something besides the carbon dioxide and something besides the automobiles. Data indicates that automobiles generate about 10% of the total carbon dioxide generated by fossil fuels each year. Data has shown that automobiles, on average, generate somewhere between the same amount or twice as much carbon dioxide as man does in a year. This is based on the fact that automobiles put out one pound of carbon per day based on each automobile consuming one gallon of gas a day worldwide. When combined with air, it provides 19 pounds (8.6 kilograms) of carbon dioxide per gallon of gas burned. When this is extrapolated across the number of cars in the world of 650 million cars and multiplied times the number of days in the year, it arrives at a level of 4.5×10^{12} (4.5 trillion) pounds per year, which is two and a quarter billion tons a year..

Meanwhile a person generates approximately one to two pounds of carbon dioxide a day by breathing. Since there are 6.7 billion people in the world and 365 days in a year this equals between 2.45×10^{12} to 4.89×10^{12} (trillion) pounds of carbon dioxide per year. The higher number equals the output of the automobiles and the lower number approximately half the amount of automobiles. Either way, there is not much difference between what is generated by cars and man. So, if we are to believe that automobile generate 10% of the carbon dioxide of the fossil fuels than man must also generate about 10% of what fossil fuels generate. However, recall the data I derived about the total calories required to support man's food needs. This required ten times the amount of man's input per day. This is mainly due to the large amount of calories required by the animals in the food loop. These same animals breathe out carbon dioxide at a rate greater than man. Therefore, if you take the carbon dioxide that man puts out in a year and multiply it by ten, you will come close to the amount of carbon dioxide being **generated to support man**'s food needs from meat products. Man plus his support energy generates carbon dioxide at about the level generated by the total fossil fuel output. This makes man and his food support an equivalent generator of carbon dioxide to the fossil fuels at their present level of consumption. This turns out to be five to ten times the amount claimed for automobiles and doesn't count the wild animals roaming the Earth that are not used for food for man. They generate another ten times factor; so the automobile is not the culprit in generating enough carbon dioxide to create global warming; it happens to be one of the several and is not the biggest by far. This is another one of the **myths** being generated by the carbon dioxide/automobile advocates.

Keep in mind that I have not witnessed any increase in global warming other than the normal one that would be expected from the general temperature cycling of the world. I agree that Earth has benefited by global warmth, which has been around for several thousand years. Has Earth gained an increase in temperature in the last hundred years? It is not enough to be of major concern. It is not enough to call it global warming. It might be enough to make people aware of the possibility and take preventive measures to reduce the possibility. **I am in favor of reducing the use of the fossil fuels as much as possible. This is politically correct, economically correct, and environmentally correct. It is just plain good sense, but it is not an action required to prevent global warming, if global warming really exists.**

The problem is one of politics and economies. The people of the various countries, along with their leaders, gain economic power from their machine, and automobile production, no matter what they are producing. However, there can be no production without the use of fossil fuels at this time. We use hydroelectric power to produce electricity; and this adds little, if any, greenhouse gases to the atmosphere. But not everyone has the capability to have hydroelectric power. Meanwhile, there has been no major development of an energy source to take the place of fossil fuels. There has been a lot of talk about other renewable powers, like solar and wind, and Biofuels from sugar and corn to produce ethanol and methanol, but there has not been a real push that has provided any renewable energy of any major magnitude at this time, but it will come.

Other Possible Reasons for the Increase in Carbon Dioxide

On the other hand, looking at what may have occurred over the last fifty years and where there has been an increase in the carbon dioxide in the atmosphere; I find what may be a few major culprits that caused this recent increase. If we look at the time from about 1950 until the present, a couple of major events resulted in an increase in the amount of carbon dioxide created. One was caused by the worldwide actions taken to eliminate lead, carbon monoxide, nitrous oxide and others in gasoline. Starting in the 70's Catalytic converters were added to every car, and cars had to go through smog checks. This did a terrific job of reducing lead, nitrous oxides, carbon monoxide, hydrocarbons, and other gases that were dangerous to the health of humans and some animals. The catalytic converter significantly reduced these exhaust gases. Engineers also designed the cars to add oxygen to the exhaust stream, turning carbon monoxide to carbon dioxide in the exhaust. In addition, other chemical reactions, along with the oxygen addition to the exhaust, resulted in some unwanted, but less dangerous gases being reduced considerably. The recovery of some of the exhaust and routing it back through the combustion cycle to have it burned again has resulted in more efficient use of fuel and helped to reduce the hydrocarbons in the exhaust trail.

Before catalytic converters, cars had a trail of visible smoke. Now, this smoke has disappeared. Smog has been reduced in the United States. These catalytic converters and the change to unleaded gas had its good and bad points. **A bad result was a dramatic increase in the amount of carbon dioxide being exhausted.** The engineers who promoted this approach knew more carbon dioxide would be exhausted from the cars, but they weren't really concerned because this gas was friendly compared to nitrous oxide, carbon monoxide, hydrocarbons, and so forth. Here was an invisible gas that no one worried about. Clean air measurements in California demonstrated that the steps taken have improved the air quality by a dramatic amount. However, these reports on the improvement of air quality do not count carbon dioxide because it is not a listed as a dangerous gas. In fact, carbon dioxide is not considered a pollutant. There was never a drive to reduce carbon dioxide in the environment when the world was taking steps to reduce the lead content in gasoline as well as reducing carbon monoxide, and nitrous oxides coming out of the tailpipe of a car and other air pollutants. Carbon dioxide is still considered a reasonable gas if it doesn't result in global warming. Does it?

However, it is a new day. Now our focus has changed. Some of the scientists of the world consider carbon dioxide to be the culprit in global warming. One alarming figure relates to the increase in carbon dioxide since 1970. In 1968, there were around 70 million cars in the world. Today, that number is close to 650 million. This is an increase of almost a factor of ten. All have catalytic converters on them, and they are all pouring out carbon dioxide while reducing the other problem gases. So, this worldwide insertion of the catalytic converter, along with the huge increase in the number of cars on Earth, has resulted in a jump in the amount of carbon dioxide injected into the atmosphere. Perhaps the same engineers who developed the present methods that have shown a great improvement in air quality can now take a look at what it takes to reduce carbon dioxide exhaust being pumped into the air. Even though this should have shown a dramatic increase in the carbon dioxide in the atmosphere, it hasn't. This means the scientists of the world are missing something in their analysis.

Another major event that could be responsible for the increase in atmospheric carbon dioxide was the eruption of Mount Saint Helens on March 20, 1980. This eruption followed several earthquakes in the area. The initial eruption was mainly steam that added to the atmospheric water vapor. A couple of earthquakes followed. On May 18, the final blow came from another earthquake, which resulted in the biggest known debris avalanche in recorded history. This volcanic explosion eliminated vegetation and buildings over a huge area of approximately 240 square miles. For more than nine hours, a large plume of volcanic ash was ejected. It reached places as far away as Idaho, 300 miles away. The ash in Idaho was so dense that one could not take pictures. This ash fell for more than a week. The amount of dust put into the atmosphere must have created unfamiliar territory for our atmosphere and Sun to break through.

Ash in the atmosphere causes an accumulation of water droplets, which eventually had to result in abnormal weather. Cloud formation from Mount Saint Helens must have been extraordinary. I have not read any details on the amount of carbon dioxide put into the atmosphere, but it must have been a tremendous amount. However, carbon dioxide was not the big worry then. The bigger worry was if this large plume that eventually made its way around the world, although at a much reduced amount, would cause any global weather problems. The energy released was equivalent to 850 megatons of TNT, or 27,000 atomic blasts, like the ones dropped on Japan during World War II. Since that time, the volcano has been active, but it has been not like the May 18 eruption. From November 1990 to February 1991, there were large eruptions of ash. (Maybe this caused the cold spike in temperature that can be seen on the chart of Figure #1 that occurred around 1991 – 1992)

Wars

A few wars did happen in the meantime. There was World War II, Korea in 1950 followed by Viet Nam. The war in Vietnam was just before the 1970 period I have used as a reference, but a good bit of any gain in carbon dioxide may be due to this war. Considerable defoliants did strip the jungles of Vietnam to provide better targets. This huge amount of greenery lost resulted in a huge loss of plants that removed carbon dioxide from the atmosphere. This loss probably was in full effect in the early 1970s In addition, the chemical defoliant may have released considerable carbon dioxide to the atmosphere. It probably should be noted as a possible addition to the other one-time events I have mentioned followed by the first invasion of Iraq, which didn't last long, but the length of time it did occur resulted in numerous bombings by our aircraft. A considerable amount of firearm and tank weaponry created considerable extra energy to be exerted. The normal things of war polluted the air. Due to the desert, there was probably considerable dust in the air to attract water vapor. And water vapor is expounded to be a worse greenhouse gas than carbon dioxide.

The 911 terrorist attach on the two major buildings in New York created a fantastic amount of dust of all types. Next, American troops bombed and invaded Afghanistan as a result of the September 11 terrorist raid on New York City and the Pentagon. The fantastic bombing of key areas in Iraq followed.

We then invaded that country. This dramatic bombing and invasion released considerable energy and created a pollution of the air over and around Iraq. Various groups within Iraq attacked the oil supplies, resulting in fires and pollution of the atmosphere. These oil fires were of significance and probably added as much carbon dioxide to the atmosphere as all the other encounters in that region. Much of this internal war resulted in a tremendous amount of dust and pollution of the environment, which could add considerable water vapor in the air. I believe it added to the events occurring about that time to increase air pollution and the increase of carbon dioxide.

Temperature

There are many scientists that believe the carbon dioxide increase in the atmosphere is a normal function of the temperature of Earth. The temperature has been increasing since 1650 A.D. and this increase could be the cause of the increase in the atmosphere's carbon dioxide. There are two scenarios that could cause this increase. For one, it is possible that the increase of the atmosphere allows more carbon dioxide to remain in the clouded atmosphere. This would be a passive reason. It is possible that the increase in the average global temperature as shown in the earlier graph causes an increase in the generation of more carbon dioxide due to chemical reaction occurring at this higher temperature. It is possible that one thousand years ago when the temperature of the globe was at its highest that the carbon dioxide was also high back then.

Myth of how long carbon dioxide remains in the atmosphere?

Scientists have stated that carbon dioxide in the atmosphere will stay for at least 100 to 200 years. Maybe they are right. Maybe all we can expect is that any accumulative amount will have no increased effect related to the absorption of Earth's reradiation due to infrared wavelengths. Therefore, there will be no major effect on climate. If scientists are correct about the length of time that carbon dioxide remains in the atmosphere, then I would have expected there to be more than 380 parts per million. **These numbers do not add up**. It looks like another misdirected data. Of course they are incorrect. The amount of carbon dioxide that man, animals, cars and other machinery and human exploits have injected into the atmosphere have increased by a tremendous amount since the year 1850 and cannot be accounted for by this rather small increased amount of 100 to 150 parts per million in the atmosphere. What got rid of all that carbon dioxide over these past 150 years? There must be some other event that is taking place to neutralize the amount of carbon dioxide being generated. It may be that the Earth's precipitation has washed down a large amount into the ocean carbon sink. Or there must be some other act of nature that we haven't identified. There must be a balance between what's in the Earth's oceans and the atmosphere to maintain carbon dioxide equilibrium. Scientists have estimated a large increase in certain chemicals in the oceans if considerable carbon dioxide is taken in by the oceans. But, have we seen any change over the last 150 years that we have been generating huge amounts of carbon dioxide into the atmosphere? I haven't read or heard about any change in the acidic content of the oceans. Yet the change in carbon dioxide in the atmosphere is rather meager over the last one hundred and fifty years. Someone is wrong. Myths exist, or better still, a misunderstanding about where all the carbon dioxide generated over the years has been balanced by an offsetting phenomenon.

There was a recent article in the Wall Street Journal by Robert Lee Hotz and the subject was on tracking the carbon trail. This is an interesting article since there are several comments that support what I am saying. Comments include:

- Still, that reflects barely half of al the emissions from human activities. Some of it seeps into soil, vegetation and the oceans, where it can't affect climate so immediately.
- So far, scientists have no reliable way to measure all these fluctuation carbon emissions.
- quarter of all the CO2 that is emitted is gong somewhere, and we don't know where" said David Crisp at NASA's Jet Propulsion Laboratory, where he is senior scientist for the $270 million orbiting Carbon Observatory, set for launch next December 2008.
- The US, Mexico, and Canada together release about 2 billion tons of carbon as CO2 into the air every year – 85% from the U.S. alone – but only about a third of it typically is absorbed by so-called carbon sinks, such as new forest, grasslands, crops and soil. The rest is either in the air or unaccounted for. That is according to a new study of 38,000 measurements collected every week from 2000 through 2006 and

analyzed by the National Oceanic and Atmospheric Administration's online Carbon Tracker system.

- "Climate extremes can have a major effect on the amount of carbon dioxide in Earth's atmosphere," said NOAA atmospheric chemist Wouter Peters. (33)

The actual amount of carbon dioxide increase in the atmosphere has been small.

For all the carbon dioxide generated over the past fifty years, there is little evidence of it being in our atmosphere. There has been an increase, but it is little compared to the increase in people and machinery that generates it. We are missing something. Is Mother Nature playing with us again? It has been estimated, and maybe calculated that the plants on Earth take in 6×10^{14} pounds (2.73×10^{14} kilograms) of carbon dioxide per year. Maybe this has been enough to keep things balanced. Maybe the increase since 1970 is when Earth's carbon dioxide generators exceeded this balance with carbon dioxide consumption. Maybe that's Mother Nature's way of providing a correction factor. Maybe the rather small amount of carbon dioxide in the atmosphere is the answer to why we have not seen any large increase in the temperature? **The percent change has been significant, but the amount has not.** Maybe that's the answer. Based on these numbers, we definitely have not increased much carbon dioxide into the atmosphere. We definitely have not seen a significant increase in the temperature that relates. We have seen a normal weather pattern as shown on the graph of Global Temperatures over the last 4500 years.

There's another thing to consider relative to the effect that any additional carbon dioxide might have on the capture rate of infrared wavelengths; it relates to whether any increase in carbon dioxide would cause an increase in the amount of infrared heat waves being caught up in the atmosphere. The greenhouse gases supposedly create an opaque barrier to the infrared heat waves, but it may not double if the greenhouse gases in the atmosphere double. It may be a **non linear effect**. I have not seen any data on the percentage of capture as a function of the concentration. It may be that a doubling of the CO_2 will result in a capture rate of infrared energy that only increases by a few percent.

Another possibility relates to any effect an increase in temperature has on photosynthesis. Photosynthesis is a function of temperature and the rate increases as the temperature increases. This being the case, as the temperature tries to increase the increased rate of photosynthesis would cause an increase in the chemical reaction and more carbon dioxide would react and there would be an increase in the growth of plants which would pull the level of carbon dioxide down and increase the amount of oxygen being generated.

Another scenario relates to how much of the infrared capture returns to the Earth. The present understanding is that the infrared is captured by the CO_2 and other greenhouse gases in the atmosphere causing an increase in the cloud temperature. Then the cloud radiates in all directions, and it has been an assumption that 50% goes back toward earth and 50% goes to outer space. This assumption is based on the fact that the radiation from the heated up volume goes in all directions so they assume that 50% is down and 50% is up. However, it may be that the lateral portion that is radiated doesn't end up going toward earth. What if the radiation from these clouds end up with 10% going toward earth and 90% goes toward space because there is a greater temperature difference between the clouds and outer space than between the clouds and the temperature of the earth. In fact, it may be a "back pressure" set up by the heat radiating from the Earth that forces more of the captured heat to go towards the area of least resistance and this would be toward space.

This is a complicated issue and so far the increase in any CO_2 has not proven to increase the temperature at a rate that is significant. **There are some scientific studies that show that the weather changes first and then the carbon dioxide goes up or down if proceeded by the temperature going up or down. So, perhaps the increase in carbon dioxide is a reflection of the climate that occurred prior to the Little Ice Age?**

Water Vapor

Maybe we should be talking about the total percent of water vapor plus carbon dioxide that is in the air and if that total has changed. Water vapor causes 40 to 70 percent of the greenhouse effect on Earth. Carbon dioxide causes 10 to 26 percent. Because water vapor is the greater absorber of infrared wavelengths than carbon dioxide and there is more of it in the atmosphere (5,000 parts per million to 10,000 parts per million), this should be analyzed.

Let's assume that, in 1850, when the industrial revolution began and carbon dioxide was 200 parts per million in the atmosphere and water vapor was 2,000 parts per million. Now, when the carbon dioxide is 380 parts per million, the water vapor may be down by 500 parts per million. In this hypothetical example, the total of these two greenhouse gases would have gone from 2200 parts per million to the present value of 1880 parts per million. This would result in a decrease in the infrared absorbing gases in the atmosphere, ignoring methane and the other small contributors.

Let's take another hypothetical situation of the same sort. In 1850, the water vapor in the air was 5,000 parts per million and the carbon dioxide was 280 parts per million. Now let's assume the water vapor in the air remains the same and is now 5,000 parts per million and the carbon dioxide is 380 parts per million. There would no impact from the increase in the carbon dioxide by 100 parts per million. The carbon dioxide is insignificant in both cases. The water vapor is the controlling factor.

These are hypothetical examples, but it could explain why we have not shown even a minimal increase in temperature, that the combination of the two determines the overall effect. I have not seen any good comparisons of this total of infrared absorbing gases over the time period being mentioned. I have looked through the data and found no mention of the combination of the two constituents in the atmosphere. This may be due to the fact that the amount of water vapor in the atmosphere is changing all the time, making it very difficult to obtain real-time data. Reports say that water vapor varies from a level of approximately 500 parts per million to a little over 1 percent and could reach 5 percent on certain days. This is a rather large change. It is much more than the carbon dioxide varies and much more in absolute value. This somewhat reminds me of the light bulb not being able to last long because the tungsten filament burned up in the bulb. Then they added argon to the contained light bulb. It then lasted at least a year before the filament was consumed. Maybe a compensating element in Earth's atmosphere is doing something like this to compensate for the relatively small quantity increase in carbon dioxide. Maybe it is as simple as the precipitation that has been constant over many years and the precipitation is water vapor in its ultimate form. Precipitation can take carbon dioxide down to the waters of the oceans where it is a perfect sink. We have not seen any major increase in acid rain, have we?

Why the Concentration on Carbon Dioxide?

Without any evidence to the contrary, I believe that scientists have concentrated on the increase of carbon dioxide in the atmosphere and have not taken into account the water vapor in the atmosphere because they do not have models to show the water vapor percentage in the atmosphere at any given time. This is not an easy task to perform, even on a computer. Carbon dioxide in the atmosphere is easy to monitor because it stays constant over a period of time or changes in one direction slowly. It is easy to show that it has been increasing because it is a stable function. On the other hand, water vapor changes continually—daily, weekly, monthly, or yearly. And the change is not always in the same direction. However, one key factor is that no matter whether it is on the high or low side it is always a greater contributor to greenhouse effects than carbon dioxide. Water vapor is over ten times the greater factor when comparing its absorption effect against that of carbon dioxide. It can go up or down at any given time because it is a balancing parameter. It balances as a function of many variables. If the oceans are heated above a certain level for a few days, then the atmosphere responds through increases in evaporation, atmospheric water vapor, clouds, precipitation, and mixtures due to winds. These are real-time events, meaning they can take this form at any time and perhaps balance things. This is one of the reasons why there is a change in where precipitation takes place in the world at any given time. Various elements within Earth's weather system move the water that saturates the clouds. If the exact same amount of water vapor were to be released each day on Earth, do you think we could tell where the precipitation is going to occur on Earth? This is a very dynamic system. Just keeping one of the variables constant, like water vapor, would result in different amounts and different locations of precipitation in the world every day. When you think of all the clouds around Earth and one may be empty of water vapor, one may have 50 percent, and one may have another amount entirely, it makes determining their daily effect at the various locations almost impossible. Mother Nature does us a good turn again. I assume scientists have looked at the average water vapor in the atmosphere and therefore could combine this average with the 380 parts per million of carbon dioxide and determine if the increase of 100 parts per million in carbon dioxide makes a difference of note.

I recently watched a TV documentary about global warming and how it relates to carbon dioxide. This one very prominent bioscientist stated that Gore and the others that claim that carbon dioxide is the cause of an increase in temperature of the earth – has it backwards. He shows graphs that indicate that the climate change comes first and the carbon dioxide comes second.(24) In other words he shows that an increase in temperature causes the carbon dioxide to increase and when the temperature drops the carbon dioxide level in the atmosphere drops also. This would explain why the level of carbon dioxide shown in 1850 ice cores was much lower than today. In 1850, we were still recovering from the Little Ice Age. We should check the carbon dioxide level via the isotopes in ice cores that go back to 1650 or 1600 when the temperature has been the coldest in the last 4500 years. It is probably lower than the samples of 1850. I read somewhere that many plants can not grow and exist if the carbon dioxide level drops below 200 parts per million. Any lower than this and the world is in deep trouble. The ideal density is between 200 and 800 parts per million. Greenhouses keep their carbon dioxide level about in the middle of this level. It seems that with the present level of 380 parts per million we should be having wonderful growth around the globe on various plants that propagate well at this temperature.

Remember when I discussed Earth/Sun energy balance, earth's energy budget and the atmosphere, global heat balance, the ocean mass water balance, and nature's big circle? These all explain the major balances within Earth's structure. As much as I could explain many of these phenomena for which there have been many papers written, I could never explain or find enough clear data as to how the atmosphere, or water vapor, changes on a daily basis to accommodate many of these phenomena. The atmosphere responds to increases in evaporation of water, but it is not immediate. As Earth spins at 1,000 miles an hour, causing a vector that is from west to east and the heat transfer of Earth from the equator toward the poles results in vectors to the north and to the south away from the equator, these vectors combine to cause winds in directions that are the combination of these vectors. The poles also have an impact on the weather due to the jet stream. All play a part in the weather and the delay of the water evaporated to when it results in precipitation and where. In addition, cloud formations caused by increased evaporation impact reflections of the Sun back into space. I mentioned earlier that there are places just north and south of the equator where the highest amount of precipitation occurs. The scientists should measure the amount of carbon dioxide there and determine if it is significant.

Carbon generation

It is estimated that a car's exhaust of carbon dioxide results in 19 pounds of carbon dioxide for one gallon of gas. Assuming that all the drivers in the world with their 650 million cars use one gallon a day this would result in 1.235×10^{10} pounds per day or 4.5×10^{12} pounds per year. It is estimated that a normally active man expels the equivalent of 1.0 to 2.0 pounds of carbon dioxide per day. There are 6.7×10^9 people on earth at this time. This would result in their total exhaust being 6.7 to 13.4 billion pounds of carbon dioxide per day or 2.5 to 5.0×10^{12} pounds per year. So this would indicate that they are about equal with automobile exhausts. However, in order to feed man the cattle, swine, chickens and other foods require ten times the amount of expelled carbon dioxide as man; or 2.5×10^{13} pounds of carbon per year. This means that man and the food chain to supply his needs provides about ten times the carbon dioxide that car exhaust creates. So, if carbon dioxide is increasing in the atmosphere, it is more likely being caused by the fantastic increase in the population. But an increase of only 100 parts per million doesn't appear to be enough of an increase to cause a problem.

What about the ice melting?

I would say one thing about monitoring the earth's change in climate; the area to monitor is the ice of the world. The melting of ice is the most sensitive indicator of either climate or weather changes. When you consider that it only takes 80 Calories to melt one kilogram (2.2 pounds) of ice to water at 0 degrees C (32 degrees Fahrenheit), it shows how sensitive the melting of ice is to a small increase in energy with no increase in the temperature change in the resulting water. If 2.2 pounds of ice take on 80 Calories the ice melts but the water stays at 32 degrees Fahrenheit, but beyond that it only takes 1.0 additional Calorie to raise the temperature of the 2.2 pounds of water by one degree Fahrenheit. Ice has this fundamental characteristic of 2.2 pounds remaining at zero degrees

Centigrade while 80 Calories are being absorbed, before it melts and then begins a continuous slope up the temperature scale with each Calorie supplied after that. When you realize that a man has to take in 2000 Calories each day to exist and that those 2000 Calories can melt 25 kilograms (55 pounds) of ice, then you know how sensitive an indicator the melting of the ice is. For a world of people that numbers 6.7 billion then the Calories loss by them each day is 1.3×10^{13} Calories. This is enough to melt 368×10^9 (368 billion) pounds of ice per day to zero degrees Centigrade water. If you also take into account the factor of ten times this number of Calories for the other animals that supply food for man you are talking about 3.68 trillion (3.68×10^{12}) pounds of ice per day that could be converted to water. Over a year this would be equal to 1,343 trillion pounds of ice per year, or 671 billion tons being melted. I am using this as an example that would happen if the daily energy given off by man and animals were used solely to convert ice to water. When you consider that the energy consumed in this case is very insignificant compared to the amount of energy the sun puts on the Earth each day or each year, it provides the reader a feeling for the small amount of energy to melt ice and to relate it to how much heat is provided by the sun. This demonstrates how sensitive the melting of ice is to temperature changes, and this is without a resulting change in temperature of the water produced from that ice melting. These two things could occur and not show a change in temperature.

To understand this is to realize it takes that much energy just to melt the ice into water – with no observable change in temperature of the water. This is called the fusion temperature of ice to water. It takes this amount of energy to convert ice to water where both the ice and water were equal to zero degrees Centigrade and the water ends up at zero degrees Centigrade if no other energy is supplied. After ice melts it requires one additional Calorie to raise 1000 grams (2.2 pounds) of water for each degree after the melting. This is one of the miracles of water. It's probably the reason we see the ice melting at the Artic and Antarctic continents without noticing a change in the temperature. It won't show a change in temperature until all the ice is melted. The reason I can say this is that this has been occurring every day and we haven't seen any temperature changes. Of course, most of this melting will take place at the edge of the ice where it meets the water. I have read some articles that say the edge of Antarctica is melting but the center of the ice is actually increasing in thickness. If this is true, then there may not be an increase in the lost of ice, just a displacement. This would explain why scientists in one of the Scandinavian countries have not seen an increase in the water level of the ocean as the ice melts around the edges of the country.

It would be interesting to know whether there has been a decrease in the temperature of the earth's oceans due to any ice melting. Theoretically ice water and ice remain at the same temperature when they co-exist. So, I wouldn't expect any temperature change of the oceans that are up against the ice of the poles. In fact it wouldn't take much change in the other direction for this water to turn back into ice. It only has to lose 80 Calories for one kilogram (2.2 pounds) of water at zero degrees to turn back into ice. This is why it is so easy to go in and out of an ice age. It depends on how significant an ice age we are talking about. As witnessed in the years 1400 to 1850 there was the Little Ice Age. This type of ice age is tolerable. However, if this melting continues for any length of time the currents of the ocean would tend to mix their water with the ice water that is not at the edge of the ice and now the warmer water transfers its heat to this water and there should be a resultant cooling of the oceans as they lose their heat. This loss of heat is taken up in a temperature gain in the cold water and a drop of temperature in the warm ocean water. Overall, the oceans should show this cooling effect. At least it works that way when you melt ice cubes in a glass of water or any other beverage. That's how we cool our drinks. The result would depend on the volume of ice and the resultant increase within the volume of ocean water. Let's take this to the extreme where all the ice melts in the world and the temperature of the oceans drop by some amount. If this happens, the surface area would increase. An increase in surface area would result in more evaporation from the constant energy from the sun. However, if the temperature of the oceans should drop a slight amount as a result of this increased evaporation, the amount of evaporation of the cooler water would decrease, so between these two effects they may balance out and there will not be any increase in evaporation or precipitation. In fact if the evaporation were great enough to cause significant cooling and the transfer of heat to outer space, than we would have a cooling cycle and the ice would start to return.

The ice should be melting

Keep in mind that we are discussing the change from a Little Ice Age that occurred just before 1850 AD. During this ice age there was considerable build up of ice as previously discussed when reviewing this period of time and the global temperatures over the last 4500 years. We went from being able to walk across large bodies of ice during the Little Ice Age where water had frozen prior to the ice melting since 1650 when the temperature started to rise as a conclusion of the LIA. What we are seeing is just a continuation of this global cycling of temperature. We should be experiencing this phenomenon. It shouldn't be a mystery. The relation between this phenomenon and the term "Global Warming" is a **myth**. The key is how long will the present temperature cycle continue since it began this warming cycle in 1650 at the lowest temperature we have experienced over the last 4500 years? As mentioned, we have been warming up for over 350 years. It is almost time to start a cooling cycle.

I remember reading about earth's differentiation where it squeezed out much of the water that makes up our planet through volcano eruptions or by actually squeezing the water out of cracks in the earth's mantle. The report indicted that earth is still settling and it was possible that some water might actually return to the earth's mantle. If this were to be the case, it might offset any height to be gained by the oceans due to a large amount of ice melting. This might be Mother Nature's way of handling this problem. When you consider that the volcanoes on Earth continue to erupt and spill out water vapor it might be due to the extra water that is being returned to Earth's mantle and all we are seeing is a cycling of this water. Any change in the average temperature of the earth's oceans must result in some physical changes to our globe. This has been documented. When China and other countries build dams that provided large amounts of water reserves, it changed the center of inertia on Earth and slightly slowed the spin of Earth. This being the case, if there was significant melting of ice that resulted in increased water spread over a different area, and it might have some effect like this. Perhaps this is how those temperature cycles occur that we showed on Figure 2. When extra water is absorbed by Earth's mantle it causes a slight change in the spinning of Earth and this causes one effect and when there is an increase in volcanoes it causes a reversal of this effect.

We recently (third quarter of 2007) had a hurricane heading toward the Hawaiian Islands. At first they thought it was going to be a category 4 or 5 which is the highest levels. Then they changed that forecast and said the water temperature was too cool to sustain this hurricane at those levels. Eventually the hurricane was reduced to a category 2 and missed Hawaii altogether. The point I am making is that they indicated the water temperature was cooler than normal. Here is the place where the monitoring of the atmosphere's CO_2 level has shown it to be 380 parts per million. I would bet that they have not seen a climate change or temperature change in Hawaii. I would estimate that the water vapor level around the Hawaiian Islands is so high that it controls the temperature in that area and any rise in carbon dioxide is insignificant. When you realize that a change in carbon dioxide in the atmosphere around the Hawaiian Islands is only changing by approximately 100 parts per million over the last 50 years, it is probably insignificant relative to the water vapor in that area. It is definitely insignificant relative to the temperature of the oceans around the islands as reported.

While we are on the subject of ice melting, I would propose that the temperature cycling we have seen over the past 4500 years is due to changes in the amount of ice in the worlds oceans. As we have seen it didn't take much of a temperature change in the Little Ice Age, where the temperature went from a high of approximately 59 degrees Fahrenheit (15 degrees C) in 1300 A.D. to a low of 54.3 degrees Fahrenheit (12.4 degrees Centigrade) in 1607 A.D. to dramatically increase the ice in the world, only to see it start to erode from 1607 to the present global temperature of 58.5 degrees Fahrenheit (14.7 degrees Centigrade). We are only talking about a change of 2.6 degrees Centigrade from 1300 A.D. to 1607 A.D. to create a huge amount of global ice. I would expect it will take an increased change in time and temperature of the same amount to decrease the ice by the amount it built up during the Little Ice Age. Let's quantify that.

The time to build the ice up was 307 years as the temperature changed 2.6 degrees Centigrade, for a total of **798.2 years - Centigrade.** So far the time has gone from 1607 to 2007 which is 400 years and the temperature has gone from 12.4 degrees Centigrade to the present temperature of 14.7 degrees Centigrade for a change in temperature of 2.3 degrees Centigrade or a sum of **920 years - Centigrade.** This would indicate we have exceeded the time temperature sum of the build up of ice and it is about due to stop melting. There is one slight problem in that there was a cold spike in the temperature in 1992 that can be seen in the graph of Graph #1. This would increase the time temperature required to melt the same amount of ice as was built up, and would show a decrease in the 920 years - Centigrade calculated to the year 2007. How much that spike in cold temperature affected the "years Centigrade" is hard to calculate but I estimate it to be a sum of approximately 800 years - Centigrade; and would expect the melting to slow down in the next few years since that would make the time temperature about the same as the time temperature of the Little Ice Age.

Why the temperature cycling that we observed in the graph 1?

Keep in mind that I have not seen any description of why the temperature cycles of graph 1 occur. It shows four cycles of down temperature swings and four cycles of upward swings over the last 4500 years. Why there is this cycle over the last 4500 years would seem to relate to the most sensitive indicator on Earth and I would say this is the ice. The question is how do we get these swings in the hot temperatures to around 59 – 60 degrees Fahrenheit (15 -15.7 degrees Centigrade) to low temperatures that keep getting lower as we go from one cycle to the next? The chart #1 would indicate that the low temperatures keep getting lower, but as you look at the area under the curves for the warm cycles versus the cooler cycles, the areas are approximately equal. This would indicate there is a tendency for the temperature to stabilize around 57.0 degrees Fahrenheit (13.9 degrees Centigrade). Why this stabilization temperature, but more importantly, why the cycling?

One of my hypotheses for the Earth's temperature cycling.

What causes the Earth to cool if the sun constantly puts a given amount of energy to Earth? Is more energy lost due to some phenomenon as the temperature tries to increase above the 59 or 60 degree Fahrenheit temperature? Remember, Earth loses energy to the space adjacent to our planet dependent on the difference in temperature of Earth and the temperature of the space adjacent to Earth. As the temperature of Earth goes up there is more loss to space based on pure mathematics. Perhaps this dissipation to space only goes up slightly as Earth warms, but at some critical temperature difference between Earth's temperature and the space adjacent to Earth, a temperature is reached, perhaps 60 degrees Fahrenheit (~16 degrees Celsius) where there is a more dramatic increase in the transfer of heat energy transferred to adjacent space which would cause a **cooling of Earth**. With this transfer, over time, a condition is reached where the temperature of surrounding space is increased slightly, but enough to cut down on the transfer of heat from Earth to adjacent space and there is a warming of Earth, accounting for the **warming cycle**. This is one possible scenario and one of my hypotheses for these periods of cooling and periods of heating.

Another possible scenario relates to the sensitivity of the global ice. We have discussed how little energy loss is required for water at zero degrees Centigrade (32 degrees Fahrenheit) to freeze into ice. Let's assume the earth is in one of its warming cycles and something causes a dramatic shift in the winds in the Arctic and Antarctic regions. It's not unusual for a wind chill factor to cause the relative temperature to shift by fifteen to twenty degrees Fahrenheit (eight to eleven degrees Centigrade). In the Arctic or Antarctic, where the temperature of the water is near freezing, this will cause a build up of ice. Perhaps this shift in the winds comes from the first scenario I described where there is a rather sudden increase in the transfer of heat energy from Earth to adjacent space and this causes a sudden shift in wind speeds; enough to cause a wind chill factor and start the build up of ice on Earth in those areas most sensitive to any change in temperature. **It is a well known fact that the winds in these two areas are the greatest of any place on Earth.** So, these areas are already in a high wind mode and perhaps it only takes a small increase to cause the wind chill factor to cause a cooling of the water and the conversion of more water to ice. This would then start the cycle in the other direction.

Another scenario relates to the infrared heat energy given off by Earth and all things on Earth. Let's assume that the greenhouse gases of water vapor and carbon dioxide are responsible for a build up in temperature and tend to put a cap on Earth's atmosphere. Let's assume that this causes additional global warming towards the sixty degree Fahrenheit ambient temperature of Earth. As this blanket of greenhouse gases increases let's assume it now puts a blanket so great over the planet that the incoming infrared wave lengths are turned back into space and reduces the heating of Earth by only a couple of degrees as a result of this decrease in energy received by Earth. This may be enough to cause a cooling of Earth and we see the cycle proceeding in the other direction. Perhaps the dramatic shift of more of the incoming infrared to outer space causes a sort of vacuum effect, or heat transfer effect and this causes a certain amount of the other sunlight rays of energy to be pulled out toward space resulting in additional cooling of the planet. As this scenario fulfills its mission the blanket over the planet of water vapor and carbon dioxide is released to space, thus returning the earth to the more pleasant climate we enjoy.

These are three possible scenarios presented that may account for these temperature cycles. The key is to determine what causes the drop in temperature. This is more difficult to explain than the increase in temperature. It is harder to explain since the Sun continues to put the same amount of energy down on our stratosphere and we can determine how there can be an increase in the earth's temperature by not allowing the normal re-radiation from Earth to space.

There is another possible scenario that I find as a possibility. As the ice melts in the Artic it begins to change the flow two of the major oceans of the world. As more and more ice melts there is a channel opened between the upper part of the Atlantic Ocean that would allow this cold water to start flowing through this channel toward the northern Pacific Ocean. Their also would be a change in the flow of the water of the Gulf of Mexico that would find it flowing more to the direct North and this would result in a cooling period for the U.K and other countries in Western Europe. All these changes in the flow of these large bodies of water would result in changes in climate.

Population Growth during the time the carbon dioxide increased

Scientists are talking about the carbon dioxide increasing rapidly. The increase from 1850 to 2005 was from 250 parts per million to 380 parts per million in 2004. This is about a 36% increase in this time span but a rather small amount quantitatively.

If you think this is a major increase, look at mankind's increase over the same time span shown in the numbers listed below. Remember, each of these people walk around with a body temperature of 98.6 F and breathing out carbon dioxide. Also remember that the food to keep them alive requires significant numbers of animals and plants to keep them alive. So, the numbers of animals are increasing at a slightly greater rate than the population of man. See the data below for the people growth. I will start with 500BC where there were 100 million people on earth. The right hand column is the change in population over the number of years that the growth occurred. By dividing the population growth by the years you obtain the growth per year. This is very interesting since it shows a trend of an increased rate of population growth over time. Going from a growth of less than 10,000 per year in the time from 500 B.C. to 700 A.D it shows a population growth of much less than a million a year and remains at this low level until 1850 when the population grows at 6 million a year and by the year 2000 it grows at 104 million a year rate. It looks like it may be tapering off since the five years from 2000 to 2005 the rate was 40 million a year. This may be due to some countries limiting their population growth. This makes sense as you will see in my final conclusions of the problem faced by Earth. However, the main point is that there was a rather slow growth from hundreds of years and then the population boomed from 1850 till the present. More than this, the means of feeding that population growth has been maintained. This can be visualize when you think of the developments that hit the U.S. from the 1800's when the large cattle farms in the Midwest sprung up and then the huge farm growth in the Midwest. So, the means to support the large population growth began in this manner and then continued to grow as the use of gasoline and the industrial revolution began in full swing.

Year	Population in millions	Change Pop/years Millions	Rate per year
500 BC	100		
700 AD	200	100/1200	0.85
1500 AD	425	225/800	0.28
1800 AD	900	475/300	1.50
1850 AD	1200	300/50	6.0
1900	1625	425/50	8.5
1950	2500	875/50	17.5
1975	3900	1400/25	56.0
2000	6500	2600/25	104.0
2005	6700	200/5	40.0 so far

From 1850 to 2000 the population went from 1200 million people to 6500 million. This is a growth of 442%. This is a percentage growth that is **13.4 times the growth of carbon dioxide** during that period. Keep in mind that each person has a body temperature of 98.6 degrees Fahrenheit, and with 6.7 Billion walking around, this should cause the temperature of the earth to go up. Also keep in mind that the growth of domesticated animals has exceeded this growth of people. Let's review that the data. The Calories for man and to support man' food needs are 1015 Calories per day of the Sun's ~3 x 1018 per day. The Carbon released by man and the animals to feed him are a little over ten times the amount put out by the 650 million cars per day

Charging man, like charging a battery

Before man arrived on earth, the sun's light produced a certain amount of energy through photosynthesis, to allow plants to grow. At the time this was one of the few ways that Earth could retain some of the energy from the Sun. Many plants would die after a certain length of time and others would grow in their place plus some additional ones. So, if you were to look at Earth just before man appeared you would find that the only things that were storing some of the Sun's energy were the plants and the small animals at first and later by the larger animals.

When man arrived he ate the plants and the energy of the plants was transferred to him. What man ate he began to replace with his farms and the domestication of animals. As time went on, this transfer continued. It was essentially like taking one battery (plants) and charging another battery (man) where man took the energy from the plants and maintained it. Farther more, the number of these walking batteries continued to grow in number and take on more and more of the "charge". As the population grew the amount of charge taken on by this growth grew and held the charge. Let's say a man dies at the age of 70. It means he has carried 70 years worth of plant growth directly by consuming plants or indirectly by eating meat. Even though he was losing 2000 Calories a day, he was taking in enough Calories to offset this loss and gain in weight from a baby to a full grown man (and woman). As the population continued to grow, this charging of more walking batteries with the energy taken from plants continued. Now, some several tens of thousands of years later we have 6.7 billion people on earth, all charged with the food taken from plants or animals. Certainly most of the people have died that took on a considerable amount of this food in the early years. However, most of the increase in the population was over the last 150 years. How do you account for this; essentially going from zero to 6.7 billion people and the many Calories each carry with them? Whereas there was none of this energy walking around thirty thousand years ago, now there are 6.7 billion of them at 98.6 degrees Fahrenheit walking around. This is 6.6×10^{11} (.66 trillion) degrees Fahrenheit of thermal energy walking around where there was none not too long ago. Now if you take the energy of the animals that are domesticated and walking around compared to 150 years ago you would find another set of "batteries" walking around that got charged from the plant food they ate. So, many years ago there were plants and no man, now there are plants (more) and 6.7 billion people and their domesticated and wild animals carrying around many days and years of plant and animal food. So, there is this huge differential between what was here and what is here now. This is a huge amount of energy that didn't get sent back into space but got stored here in the bodies of man and animals. I will assume the number of wild animals stayed constant during this time. If you were to graph the number of people walking around as a function of time (years) it would show a steep climb in the past 150 years. This is the same 150 years that carbon dioxide advocates have been pointing to and saying the change in the atmospheric carbon dioxide is causing an increase in temperature. This curve doesn't even come close to the acceleration of the people curve, so if anything were to cause global warming it doesn't look like it is due to carbon dioxide from cars or anything that generates carbon dioxide. At the same time the domestic animal kingdom was force fed plants by man to grow and feed people. There was a huge increase in this domestic animal kingdom, plus the wild animals. Don't you believe these would have more effect on the increase of carbon dioxide as well as actually body heat being carried around and would be the reason for any increase in the temperature of the earth; if there really is an increase in temperature associated with carbon dioxide; which the curves of Figure 2 refute?

Most of that growth of walking temperature came in the past 150 years. This is heat that use to be in the form of plants with no exothermic production of heat and now it is stored in man and animals and there is exothermic production of heat. Let's take a fantasy as an example. What if the number of people went from zero in 30,000 B.C. to an infinite number in the year 2200 A.D.; wouldn't the temperature on earth go sky high? If it were due to these factors, it would certainly not be able to reach 2200 A.D. because of the great rise in temperature. This brings me to the subject of population growth and its effects, which I will soon discuss later in the book.

My conclusion on global Warming

The estimated use of fossil fuels in the year 2004 was 86% of the worlds total generated energy, which on average was 15×10^{12} (15 trillion) watts. This is 4.71×10^{20} joules per year or 1.125×10^{17} Calories per year. Eighty six percent of this is 9.7×10^{16} Calories for fossil fuels per year. The Sun supplies Earth 5.5×10^{24} Joules per year. This equals 1.314×10^{21} Calories per year. Therefore, the energy supplied by the Earth's fossil fuels equal 74×10^{-6} of the energy supplied by the sun or 74 parts per million. This is rather insignificant, being 74 parts per million if you count the total fossil fuels, and the carbon dioxide is much less than this total. How can anything so insignificant make a change in the temperature of Earth?

My conclusion on global warming is that there may be some but it looks like it is in the same form that occurred in the graphs shown earlier. Of course these graphs show that there is a normal swing of temperature every 500 years or so and it swings in one direction or the other with a change of a few degrees and then it swings back and goes in the other direction for its next cycle. This cycle seems independent of man, but may be misleading since most of the population growth came in the last 150 years, so it's influence may not be reflected in these curves as of yet. But, I bet it is. However, while this population growth was happening, the global temperature actually dropped form 1940 until 1980. In the meantime, man (and women) has handled these swings by taking certain steps to stay warm or to cool off. I believe the change in carbon dioxide in the atmosphere has been rather small over time compared to the amount of carbon dioxide being generated by the gain in population of both man and animals plus the machines. Therefore there is some offsetting phenomenon that is occurring to rid Earth of the carbon dioxide or it is being sunk in the oceans by a factor greater than scientists realize.

The growth of the population may have been offset by the tremendous amounts of plant food grown by man for his consumption. All this plant growth has produced increased oxygen and consumed a great amount of carbon dioxide. Keep in mind that most of that plant growth occurred in places where there wasn't much in the way of plants to begin with. The Midwest was really a sort of barren plane. Where we cut down trees for cities were in places where the foliage was not that great to begin with or the area consumed by these cities was insignificant compared to the large areas opened for growth of produce. It's possible that any increase in temperature results in an increased photosynthesis rate and plants take in more carbon dioxide, thus offsetting the generation of carbon dioxide.

It's interesting when you consider that there have been five cycles of global warmth over the past 4507 years (see the chart) including the one we are in now. **Excluding the one we are now experiencing, the United States and all of North and South America was not discovered and were essentially uninhabited in these large areas of land during the previous four temperature rises.** During the previous four elevated temperature cycles there were less than 100 million people in the world and no domesticated animals. So, what we are experiencing at this point in time is somewhat unique.

A small number of people experienced two warm cycles and two cold cycles. Many more experienced the cold cycle from 1350 A.D. to 1800 A.D. and therefore the present warming cycle is unique to the experience of man. When you consider that there were no books printed until around 600 A.D., the period of time before that found less than 100 million people inhabiting the Earth and no books were being printed about the temperatures hot or cold. It makes one step back and think about how little man has experienced the works of nature and how little we know about it. Most of the data is derived from men of science who look at tree rings, ice cores, isotopes, fossils and many other phenomena to determine the curves we see in the 4500 year charts. The present day population has never experienced even one of the cold cycles and most of them are just experiencing part of a warm cycle. It's no wonder there is much excitement about a minor warming cycle we are experiencing; the major growth of population has been since the "Little Ice Age" and since the United States has been populated so we have not been around long enough to realize this is the normal temperature history.

As I progress through this book there will be other crises that I will discuss that make this warm cycle seem insignificant. Even if the temperature goes up one or two degrees Fahrenheit during the 21st Century, the people on Earth would have experienced five generations of people. I believe they will handle this without much of a problem. We mutate too. It's not only the bacteria, and viruses that mutate; man mutates too. The change in temperature will be handled and then we will be seeing a temperature drop that might be more excruciating. The data I have covered shows that if anything would cause an increase in carbon dioxide in the world it would be due to the growth of human population and the domesticated animals that provide man with his food. As I mentioned, the curves may not have had time to respond to this increase and the last curve – the one we are on at this time – has not had time to run its cycle to date. There may be a time delay in the reflection of these curves relative to the growth of the population. The curve may reach the 59 – 60 degrees Fahrenheit upper temperature and curve right back down as it has in the past. Maybe if we could explain why there was the sharp drop off of the curve in the 1991-92 time period it would give us part of the answer as to what is controlling this ambient curve of our temperature on Earth. I have not seen any documentation of why we have had the temperature curves portrayed in this presentation, especially the drops in temperature over the last 4500 years, while the sun's energy has remained constant. It is my opinion that we will see the temperature curve bend over sometime in the next 100 years and the people living then will say we are going to freeze to death. Let's hope the drop in temperature is not as great as it was in the Little Ice Age that occurred only a few hundred years ago. I bet the people living in 1607 in Jamestown thought that their colony was living in a very cold piece of Earth. They would love the temperature that exists now. Remember in 1780 you could walk across New York harbor from Manhattan to Staten Island, just a little over 200 years ago. The forecasts by some that the temperature will go up by seven degrees Fahrenheit by the year 2100, based on carbon dioxide will probably be incorrect. Based on the curves I see it may go up by a half a degree Celsius. I guess I just don't believe that global warming is due to carbon dioxide buildup and what's more, I don't believe in global warming other than what we have seen in the distant past. History says we go through temperature cycles on Earth and they are not caused by carbon dioxide, or anything related to people. If it does go up then I would guess it will probably be due to the growth in the population. The people that tout global warming also estimate a huge increase in rain due to the increased temperature but there has been no increase in the world's rain, just its normal random process of raining hard in some places and raining less in others. The oceans evaporation rate is a function of temperature, but it also is a function of the energy rate of the wavelengths put out by the sun. This makes it a direct function of sunshine but not of infrared wavelengths. If there is global warming and it is due to infrared wavelengths being captured and re-radiated to Earth, the evaporation from the oceans would be a secondary effect at best.

If anything, an increase in carbon dioxide may be due to an increase in temperature. Some scientist's thing this is the case. Maybe the carbon dioxide level was even lower in 1607 during the colonization of Jamestown; when the temperature was at its lowest. Maybe if we had carbon dioxide measurements from the last high temperature cycle shown on the graph that occurred in 1300 AD we would find that the carbon dioxide level was high then. If we find that the carbon dioxide in the atmosphere followed the curves of the chart it shows several things:

1. The temperature is the driver, not the carbon dioxide.
2. Man has no effect on the carbon dioxide level in the atmosphere

3. We can expect this temperature increase we are seeing (if any) is part of the normal climate cycles of the past.
4. We can expect the temperature to turn colder near the end of this century.
5. The next low temperature cycle will be the coldest and is the one we should be more concerned about, especially if we lose our oil/gasoline energy and have problems with keeping warm.
6. Carbon dioxide is like water vapor, as the temperature increases clouds are able to carry more water vapor prior to precipitation. Perhaps the temperature increase allows more carbon dioxide to be held in the clouds and that's what we are experiencing compared to the Little Ice Age. The carbon dioxide level was lower then because the average temperature was lower. This also can explain why there was more ice generated during the little ice age.

However, my research convinced me that we will have bigger problems to worry about than temperature increases. I believe, even if carbon dioxide or the growth of the population were the cause for any temperature growth that it would be rather insignificant and I believe the hype about global warming is taking our attention away from a bigger problem; a problem that would make a half degree increase or a degree increase in temperature look subtle and benign.

Actions recommended for this increase in temperature

Let's assume that man and the food chain he requires is the potentially dangerous source of either carbon dioxide or the increase in temperature in any other way. If this is so, then the way to keep Earth's temperature in a controlled and desired level is to control the growth of the population of man and his animals. If people would change their diets to intake more plant food and very little of meat, this would result in a huge decrease in the domestic animal population and in carbon dioxide, and the heat created by the animals. The data indicates that this support of man is one of the major reasons for any increase in carbon dioxide and the major increase for the demand of energy via their food values.

Of course fossil fuels, and especially oil and oil derivatives account for some of the increasing amount of carbon dioxide and our scientists should work on methods to reduce the exhaust of cars and the exhaust of large factories. There should be a shift in transportation to electrical cars and liquefied natural gas for providing the fuel for large vehicles in industry. There is one major program that is being watched. It is the capture and storage of carbon dioxide to alleviate the amount of carbon dioxide being put into the atmosphere. It is called the carbon and carbon dioxide capture and storage programs.

Carbon and Carbon dioxide capture to reduce carbon dioxide.

For the 'global warming is due to carbon dioxide' advocates, there is some hope framed in the title of Carbon Dioxide Capture and Storage (CCS) projects. These projects are based on taking the carbon dioxide out of the exhausts of the large plants in the world and injecting this CO_2 into the ground or deep ocean areas for storage. This is a method believed to be fruitful in reducing the amount of carbon dioxide released to the atmosphere.

I have some problem with these programs although they are meant to be a method of reducing the atmospheric carbon dioxide it has other problems that may be more severe. This approach is fine for the advocates of global warming being due to carbon dioxide increasing in the atmosphere. The problem with this approach is that the cost of whatever the production plant is producing will go up by 10 to 20 percent to install, operate, transport the carbon, and maintain the system. Another problem with this approach is that a significant amount of energy must be used to capture, transport and inject the exhausts into the ground or into deep ocean water. This book is about how to reduce the cost of energy and how to reduce the inefficient use of our energy and how to save what little energy we have. This storage of carbon or carbon dioxide is diametrically opposed to my objectives. I present it for those who want to know about it and those that champion this cause. On the other hand as you read through the various projects using some form of capture, there are some that are pro active in that they take the carbon capture and turn it into a different product for sale. These programs stand on their own credentials and represent the free enterprise where ingenuity prevails. Several projects are being started or will start soon to capture CO_2 to sell to oil production plants. The CO2 is injected under pressure into the oil field and this added gaseous pressure forces more oil out of the ground. This is called enhanced oil recovery. This is a proactive program that may just break even on the costs versus the costs recovered. However, when one is trying to obtain a scarce entity these kinds of actions prove fruitful. There is some common sense to the operations in many cases since the pipeline used to transport the CO_2 are already in place to pipe the oil away and can be used to pipe in the CO_2.

Four sample sites

As of 2007, four industrial-scale storage projects are in operation. Sleipner is the oldest project (1996) and is located in the North Sea where Norway's StatoilHydro strips carbon dioxide from natural gas with amine solvents and disposes of this carbon dioxide in a deep saline aquifer. The carbon dioxide is a waste product of the field's natural gas production and the gas contains more (9% CO_2) than is allowed into the natural gas distribution network. Storing it underground avoids this problem and saves Statoil hundreds of millions of euro in avoided carbon taxes. Since 1996, Sleipner has stored about one million tonnes CO_2 a year. A second project in the Snøhvit gas field in the Barents Sea stores which is capturing 700,000 tonnes per year. (35)

The Weyburn project is currently the world's largest carbon capture and storage project. (35) Started in 2000, Weyburn is located on an oil reservoir discovered in 1954 in Weyburn, southeastern Saskatchewan, Canada. The CO_2 for this project is captured at the Great Plains Coal Gasification plant in Beulah, North Dakota which has produced methane from coal for more than 30 years. At Weyburn, the CO_2 will also be used for enhanced oil recovery with an injection rate of about 1.5 million tonnes per year. The first phase finished in 2004, and demonstrated that CO_2 can be stored underground at the site safely and indefinitely. The second phase, expected to last until 2009, is investigating how the technology can be expanded on a larger scale.[(35)]

The fourth site is In Salah, which like Sleipner and Snøhvit is a natural gas reservoir located in Salah, Algeria. The CO_2 will be separated from the natural gas and re-injected into the subsurface at a rate of about 1.2 million tonnes per year.

A major Canadian initiative called the Alberta Saline Aquifer Project (ASAP) is a consortium of 34 companies that are developing a pilot site for commercial scale carbon capture and storage in a saline aquifer. The initial pilot will sequester 1,000 tonnes per day in 2010, while the commercial phase could see 10,000 tonnes per day as soon as 2015. (36)

Another Canadian initiative called the Integrated CO_2 Network (ICO2N) is a proposed system for the capture, transport and storage of carbon dioxide (CO_2). ICO2N members represent a group of industry participants providing a framework for carbon capture and storage development in Canada.

In October 2007, the Bureau of Economic Geology at The University of Texas at Austin received a 10-year, $38 million subcontract to conduct the first intensively monitored, long-term project in the United States studying the feasibility of injecting a large volume of CO_2 for underground storage[18]. The project is a research program of the Southeast Regional Carbon Sequestration Partnership (SECARB), funded by the National Energy Technology Laboratory of the U.S. Department of Energy (DOE). The SECARB partnership will demonstrate CO_2 injection rate and storage capacity in the Tuscaloosa-Woodbine geologic system that stretches from Texas to Florida. The region has the potential to store more than 200 billion tons of CO_2 from major point sources in the region, equal to about 33 years of U.S. emissions overall at present rates. Beginning in fall 2007, the project will inject CO_2 at the rate of one million tons per year, for up to 1.5 years, into brine up to 10,000 feet (3,000 m) below the land surface near the Cranfield oil field about 15 miles (25 km) east of Natchez, Mississippi. Experimental equipment will measure the ability of the subsurface to accept and retain CO_2.

Currently, the United States government has approved the construction of what is touted as the world's first CCS power plant, FutureGen. On January 29, 2008, however, the Department of Energy announced it was withdrawing funding from FutureGen, as it had originally been proposed, casting considerable doubt on the future of the project and in the view of some, effectively terminating the project. I have not seen any action on this program to date (June 8 2008).

Examples of carbon sequestration at an existing US coal plant can be found at utility company Luminant's pilot version at its Big Brown Steam Electric Station in Fairfield, Texas. This system is converting carbon from smokestacks into baking soda. Skyonic plans to circumvent storage problems of liquid CO_2

by storing baking soda in mines, landfills, or simply to be sold as industrial or food grade baking soda. GreenFuel Technologies Corp. is piloting and implementing algae based carbon capture, circumventing storage issues by then converting algae into fuel or feed.

In the Netherlands, a 68 MW oxyfuel plant ("Zero Emission Power Plant") is being planned and is expected to be operational in 2009.

In the United States, four different synthetic fuels projects are moving forward which have publicly announced plans to incorporate carbon capture and storage.

American Clean Coal Fuels, in their Illinois Clean Fuels project, is developing a 30,000 Barrel Per Day Biomass and Coal to Liquids project in Oakland Illinois, which will market the CO_2 created at the plant for Enhanced Oil Recovery applications. The project is expected to come online in late 2012.

Baard Energy, in their Ohio River Clean Fuels project, are developing a 53,000 BPD Coal and Biomass to Liquids project, which has announced plans to market the plant's CO2 for Enhanced Oil Recovery.

Rentech is developing a 29,600 barrel per day coal and biomass to liquids plant in Natchez Mississippi which will market the plant's CO2 for enhanced oil recovery. The first phase of the project is expected in 2011.

DKRW is developing a 15,000-20,000 Barrel Per Day coal to liquids plant in Medicine Bow Wyoming, which will market it plant's CO2 for enhanced oil recovery. The project is expected to begin operation in 2013.

Germany

The German industrial area of Schwarze Pumpe, about 4 km south of the city of Spremberg, is home to the world's first CCS coal plant. The mini pilot plant is run by an Alstom-built oxy-fuel boiler and is also equipped with a flue gas cleaning facility to remove fly ash and sulphur dioxide. The Swedish company Vattenfall AB invested some 70 million Euros in the two year project which began operation September 9, 2008. The power plant, which is rated at 30-megawatts, is a pilot project to serve as a prototype for future full-scale power plants.[20][21] 240 tonnes a day of CO_2 are being trucked 350 kilometers (210 miles) where it will be injected into an empty gas field. Germany's BUND group called it a "fig leaf". For each ton of coal burned, 3.6 tonnes of carbon dioxide is produced. (36)

Australia

The federal Resources and Energy Minister Martin Ferguson has opened the first geosequestration project in the southern hemisphere. The demonstration plant is near Nirranda South in South Western Victoria. The plant is owned by the CO_2 Cooperative Research Centre. It is funded jointly by government and industry. It aims to store 100,000 tonnes of carbon dioxide extracted from a gas well. Carbon dioxide-rich gas is extracted from a reservoir via a well, compressed and piped 2.25km to a new well. There the gas is injected into a depleted natural gas reservoir approximately two kilometers below the surface. (36)] [24] This project is tiny by world standards as BP's Algerian plant is storing 1,000,000 tonnes each year.

This plant does not propose to capture CO_2 from coal fired power generation. There is no project anywhere in the world storing CO_2 stripped from the products of combustion of coal burnt for electricity generation at coal fired.

The share of fossil fuels in power generation decreases steadily and significantly. The use of CO2 capture and storage systems develops strongly; by 2050, more than 50% of thermal electricity production is from plants with CO2 capture and storage.

There are many articles on Carbon Capture and Storage to be found on the World Wide Web. This process is being reviewed and incorporated worldwide. All new plants being installed are incorporating some form of capture of the carbon emissions and storing them. It turns out that this is a very viable solution to reducing the carbon that escapes into our atmosphere. The interested reader is encouraged to find these articles by going to Carbon Capture and Storage on the internet. Wikipedia has a good article and good references for the interested reader.

Existing and Planned CCS Projects

PROJECT	CO$_2$ SOURCE	Country	Anticipated amount injected by:			
			START	2006	2010	2015
Sleipner	Gas Proc.	Norway	1996	9MT	13MT	18MT
Weyburn	Coal	Canada	2000	5MT	12MT	17MT
In Salah	Gas Proc.	Algeria	2004	2MT	7MT	12MT
Snohvit	Gas Proc.	Norway	2007	0	2MT	5MT
Gorgon	Gas Proc.	Australia	2010	0	0	12MT
DF- 1 Miller	Gas	U.K.	2009	0	1MT	8MT
DF-2 Carson	Pet Coke	U.S.	2011	0	0	16MT
Draugen	Gas	Norway	2012	0	0	7MT
FutureGen	Coal	U.S.	2012	0	0	2MT
Monash	Coal	Australia	NA	0	0	NA
Saskpower	Coal	Canada	NA	0	0	NA
Ketzin/CO2 STORE	NA	Germany	2007	0	50KT	50KT
Otway	Natural	Australia	2007	0	100KT	100KT
TOTALS				16MT	35MT	99MT

In addition to the possible contamination of our atmosphere by man and machines there is another problem that seems to be more of a major problem, and more imminent. This problem may actually truncate any temperature increase if it is due to man, his support system, and the use of oil; or didn't exist at all.

I will come back to the actions required for global warming, population growth and the supply of food, but first I must cover another crisis we will be hit with in this century and it affects the population and the food supply. This crisis is the one concerning energy for now and in the future.

Conclusion on Crisis I – The increase in the temperature of Earth

I have covered global warming and my conclusions on this phenomenon. Essentially I have taken a position that the temperature increase since the Little Ice Age has been a normal trend that Earth has followed for at least the last 4507 years and is not the global warming due to carbon dioxide or any man made function. It is part of a temperature cycling that Earth goes through every several hundred years where the temperature increases for several hundred years and then cools for several hundred years. We cannot blame this temperature increase on carbon dioxide; the temperature increase we have seen started in 1650 when there were no cars or abnormal carbon dioxide generators. The temperature trend has been increasing from 54.3 degrees Fahrenheit since 1650 and the trend curve has not changed during the past 357 years. If things go according to this recent history then by the end of this century or sometime in the next century the weather should start to drop down, and perhaps dramatically. However, since I am writing about crises of the 21st Century, let's assume the temperature doesn't start cooling during this century and the global temperature reaches a level we haven't witnessed in the last 4507 years. This would be a form of crisis. So, we have to keep our eyes on this phenomenon and hope I am right about the temperature cycles being normal and that we won't see any temperature that would much exceed 60 degrees Fahrenheit (15.6 Celsius). The good news is that the temperature extremes that have occurred during these cycles over the last 4507 years have not been dramatic enough to snuff out human life. It has caused some discomfort and a shifting on the way we live especially in Europe during the Little Ice Age. The message here is **to realize it is going to happen and prepare for it.** If nature follows course we will reach a temperature peak of 60 - 61degrees Fahrenheit (15.6 degrees Celsius) and start a cooling cycle.

The temperature in most places in the United States has been cooler than normal this past year. Here in California the temperature has been cooler and no rain at all during the summer which set a record. If we are to believe the advocates of Global Warming that not only will it warm but it will rain a lot more. It hasn't done either this year and not during my life time. It hasn't been a problem for anyone from age one to age eighty as far as I have been able to certify. I haven't read about any oceans rising as the advocates claim would happen. The constants have remained constant; i.e. the rain for the world hasn't changed, the Sun keeps putting out its normal amount, the temperature has been moderate, and the ice is melting as would be expected with the temperature rising from 54.3 degrees Fahrenheit to about 58.3 degrees over the last three hundred and fifty years since the Little Ice Age.

We may find the temperature is increasing due to the population growth of humans and domesticated animals. The temperatures they carry with them and the increasing population may be adding a form of stored energy here on Earth that is incrementally adding to the surrounding temperature as the population grows. How one determines this may be difficult to prove and should be a study by some university supported by a government program. If this proves to be the case steps need to be taken to reduce the population growth of both. Animals would be the start since they influence the Earth's temperature more than man. They consume more energy, burn off more energy, consume enormous amounts of water and some also provide methane which is a greenhouse gas.

The warming may not be due to carbon dioxide or related to humans, but it is a change. I believe it is part of the temperature cycling in the positive direction that few on Earth have experienced and we should consider it as happening **and take steps to be able to live with it.** Since it will be happening for about one hundred years if it is due to climate cycles, we will have five generations of families during that time and I believe each generation will become more accustomed to this temperature change. Humans mutate and become accustomed to temperatures as is witnessed by the people living in very hot temperature zones at present as compared to those living in the temperate or polar zones.

There will be the melting of much of the ice in the North and South Pole regions whether due to a climate cycle or global warming and this may even cause an increase in the depth of the oceans in some places. But I do not believe it will increase the ocean levels to the point being predicted by many of several hundred feet. I believe history will show that the ocean's waters were not this high during the last warming cycle which peaked at approximately 1250 A. D. just before the Little Ice Age started. Ice core samples taken in Greenland and other places around the world should prove this one way or another. However, we must be aware of the possibility and **take precautions to prepare for it if it were to happen**.

It's quite possible that physical changes in the Earth will stop the warming and cause a cooling trend. Some scientists believe as the North Pole ice shrinks it will reach a point where certain ocean straits will be opened that will allow a change in the flow of ocean water from the Northern Atlantic into the upper part of the Pacific Ocean. If this happens it is predicted that a cooling trend will begin. If one uses their imagination you might be able to consider that an opening in this northern route of the oceans waters will result in the Gulf Stream being steered away from the English coast and start the cooling of that part of Europe that is warmed by the Gulf Stream. Further cooling will result in the return of large increases in the ice mass of the Polar section of Earth. Remember what I discussed about how easy it is to go from water that is near freezing to ice just by releasing 82 Calories of energy to freeze 2.2 pounds (1 KGM) of ice. This is a very low energy release when you consider that a human loses 2000 Calories a day which would freeze about 25 pounds of ice. If this ice melt should result in a passage being opened between the Atlantic and Pacific **the world must plan for it and learn how to live with it till the next cold cycle freezes it shut.**

However, my research convinced me that we will have bigger problems to worry about than temperature increases. I believe, even if carbon dioxide or the growth of the population were the cause for any temperature increase, that it would be rather insignificant. I believe the hype about global warming is taking our attention away from bigger problems; problems that would make a half degree increase or a degree increase in temperature look subtle. I wrote about this a couple of years ago in a book *Beyond Global Warming* and related it to the loss of a certain energy that we may find quite difficult to replace. One of these losses relates to the energy of a gallon of gasoline or a gallon of diesel that will be loss in the near future.

Crisis II -
The beginning of oil and the end of oil

Up until now I have talked about the energy supplied by the Sun to Earth. This energy was in balance with the energy being radiated by Earth back into space. However, unknown until recently, a meteor had crashed into Earth 65 million years ago. This meteor strike brought a tremendous amount of energy to Earth and caused the elimination of the dinosaurs and almost all other animals. This collision with Earth resulted in much of the energy being sent back into space but it left a tremendous amount here on Earth. The kinetic energy of a huge mass striking another such as this struck Earth converts its mass and motion energy of $\frac{1}{2}$ mv^2 (where m is the mass of the meteor and v was it velocity) into a new energy received by the object, in this case Earth. This energy, less what was loss to space, was a huge amount of potential energy left here on Earth. The dinosaurs and many animals were covered with the dust that was created during this collision. This resulted in a tremendous amount of energy being stored in Earth that was not contributed by the Sun. Not realizing the source at the time, this energy was about to be relieved to the people of Earth.

In the mid centuries people in different parts of the world found oil on the surface of Earth and found that it could be ignited and used for heat. It was considered an oddity and nothing more. But it was recognized as something that was convenient to have around. This would soon change. Man was about to release this energy brought to Earth 65 million years ago.

Colonel Drake decided to drill for oil in the year 1859 with the intent of using it for commercial applications. He chose to do this in Titusville Pennsylvania. Thus began the most significant contribution to the industrial revolution the world was to realize. Prior to this commercial venture the fossil fuels, mainly coal, were used for heating homes and in generating steam with the burning of coal in steam engines. Natural gas had been used in small quantities. This drilling of oil was to find natural gas as a side benefit. With the coming of oil the world had found a major earthborn energy. I call it earthborn even though it was the result of the meteor collision with Earth some 65 million years prior to this commercial oil well. The oil didn't all come from that one meteor crash; it was generated by rotting greenery that lay beneath the earth's soil. This was the first commercial well drilled for the primary purpose of use in industry. This began a major source or energy that was separate from the daily energy of the Sun. Oil now entered the picture along with other fossil fuels being used at the time such as the coal and natural gas mentioned.

The drilling of the Titusville oil well was followed by a huge growth of oil wells across the United States. The good, adventurous, and ambitious Americans went to the Middle East and found oil there and this became the center of the oil industry. They eventually appeared in the Middle East, Russia, and parts of northern South America. More underground energy was put to use with the movement toward central heating that used natural gas. Previously, the main fossil fuel used was coal, but oil could be so easily obtained and transferred, and became relatively inexpensive; making it the major source of earthborn energy during the twentieth century and up to the present.. Oil and its derivatives provided capabilities that no other fossil fuel could provide, mainly it was portable. It was a mobile form of energy and provided more energy in a smaller volume than any of the other forms of energy. Before proceeding much father I will describe some units of energy to make it easier for the reader to follow the subject matter that will follow in this book. I provide it here but it is also provided in the Appendix of the book..

Energy and Power multiples
Energy units

Prior to proceeding I need to give the reader some information on energy and power multiples.
First it important to understand that energy is expressed in a basic unit by a joule of energy.
A calorie is equal to 4.186 joules.
A kilocalorie is equal to 1000 calories.

A kilocalorie is equal to 4,186 joules

A table Calorie is equal to the kilocalorie or 4,186 joules. (note the capital C in these Calories)

One table Calorie (which everyone who eats food or goes on a diet is familiar with) is equal to 1000 of the small calories used by scientists. I will use the table Calorie as shown with the capital C in denoting it. i.e., Calorie and it is equal to 4,186 joules. I will utilize the Calorie in describing much of the energy and power in the remainder of this book.

Power units

Energy expressed over time is power

The watt is the basic unit of expressing power.

One watt is equal to one joule per second. 1w = 1j/sec

One kilowatt is equal to 1000 watts = 1000 joules per second.

Multiples

Both energy and power are expressed in exponent values because of their enormous number values. This is to make it easier to work with these numbers. Since most people are familiar with watts as an expression of Power and Calories as an expression of Energy I will provide a chart to show the connection. This chart is shown here and is also shown in the Appendix V in the back of the book for easy reference.

Multiple ```Name in watts Symbol Calories

Multiple	Name in watts	Symbol	Calories
10	watt	w	.00040C
10^3	Kilowatts	kW	.240C
10^6	Megawatts	MW	2.4×10^2
10^9	Gigawatts	GW	2.4×10^5
10^{12}	Terawatts	TW	2.4×10^8
10^{15}	Petawatts	PW	2.4×10^{11}
10^{18}	Exawatts	EW	2.4×10^{14}
10^{21}	Zettawatts	ZW	2.4×10^{17}
10^{24}	Yottawatts	YW	2.4×10^{20}

It is very important to understand that when you are converting any power of watts into Calories that the Calories are an energy value and not related to time whereas watts are a power term and is expressed in joules per second. So when converting a watt minute to Calories you must multiply the normal watts listed by 60 seconds to express the total joules in that minute and then convert the joules to the Calories in that minute (both joules and calories are pure energy terms). Remember one Calorie equals 4,186 joules, so to convert from joules to Calories one must divide the joules by 4.186×10^3 joules per Calorie to obtain the energy in Calories.

If the watts are expressed in hours then you must multiply the watt hours by 3600 seconds to convert to the total joules in those watt hours and then convert the joules to Calories.

Convert the total joules to calories by dividing by 4,186 joules per Calorie. When expressing watts per day, then you must multiple the watts by 3600 (seconds per hour) x 24 (hours per day) to obtain the total joules per day before converting to Calories per day by dividing by 4,186 joules per Calorie. When the watts are expressed in a year then you must multiply the watts by 3600 seconds per minute x 24 hours per day x 365 days a year to get the joules per year. Divide these joules by 4,186 joules per Calorie to obtain the Calories.

Many people get confused by this since scientists are use to expressing energy in terms of joules (energy) and the commercial world is used to expressing things in watts (power); like your electric bill each month is expressed in Kilowatt hours.

Many times the terms used are in kilowatts, megawatts, gigawatts, etc. and you need to convert to energy terms of joules, kilojoules, megajoules etc. before converting into Calories. In these cases you must convert to joules by using the same rules as I just indicated, taking the exponents into account and then converting into joules first and then converting into Calories by dividing by 4,186 joules per Calorie.

It is a good practice to keep in mind that there are 3600 seconds in an hour and 86,400 seconds in a day (8.64 x 10^4) and 31,536,000 seconds in a year.

<u>I recommend the reader making a copy of above to use as reference as you rea</u>d

There is a copy of this in the appendix of this book, in the Terms Definition page.

The Twentieth Century began with a bang.

During the twentieth century, there was a major growth in industrial machines and vehicles that consumed gasoline, diesel, and eventually aircraft fuel. This century was witness to the major growth of the transportation industry. Inventions from the beginning of the presence of oil and gasoline were numerous and propelled the use of this new energy source. It was almost as if inventors were waiting for this missing link. Sure enough as soon as it became apparent that there was plenty of this form of energy in the world, man began to exploit its capability. It was a wonder and remains a wonder to this day.

The automobile was probably the prime example of the use of this new energy and it was soon followed by the Wright brothers and their invention of the airplane. Things wouldn't stop here. Anything that moved or could create some type of movement took advantage of gasoline. Machines were born and soon there was electricity beyond what had previously been available. Mobile generators of electricity powered by this marvelous gasoline and diesel fuel from oil became common place and with it the ability to provide power away from the city. The use of this energy was not relegated to the land as boats began to be propelled by this fuel. Big boats, speed boats, fishing boats were soon powered by this marvelous fuel. Then came war and the war machines propelled by gasoline or diesel fuel came with it. There were tanks, military vehicles, faster dual wing airplanes and the list grows. But the one common element during all this time was the automobile that now could be afforded by many based on production techniques brought on by Henry Ford and the Ford automobiles. Each year there were more and more automobiles built around the world. The only time cars weren't being built was during World War II when all the energy had to be directed toward the fighting of war. Now the use of the derivatives of oil became even more valuable as they fueled the machines of war on land, in the air, and on the seas. With the war over there was a new buildup of the automobile and its use. This time the build up was the world over; more so than any time before. Cars became a commodity that was built abroad, shipped, and sold the world over. What made it even better was the price of fuel dropped to the point where almost everyone could afford to drive the car for long distances. Where once the car was a source of transportation to work and locally, it now became the bearer of longer trips and along come the camper, the trailer, and the fun vehicles. The world was having fun with its toys and this inexpensive fuel.

There were an estimated 650 million automobiles or trucks in the world in the year 2004, or one for every 10 persons on Earth. The amount of energy consumed in the United States on 150 million cars was 4.65×10^{12} Calories per day or 4.65 trillion Calories per day if each car burned one gallon of gas on an average day for a total of 150 million gallons per day or 3.6 million barrels a day. The rest of the world had built up to 500 million automobiles. Assuming they each use one half of the fuel of a car driven in the United States on a daily basis, their consumption would be 7.75 trillion Calories per day or 6 million barrels a day. Including the US amount, the world consumption was 12.4

trillion Calories per day. On a yearly basis this consumption was **4,530 trillion Calories** during 2004, and this was growing at a rate of approximately 15.0 million cars each year that would be adding many more gallons of gasoline. The thing to keep in mind was the amount of energy being consumed as I mentioned in terms of Calories.

The daily energy consumption worldwide of man per day based on 2000 Calories is 1.34×10^{13} Calories (13.4 trillion Calories) and for a year is **4,900 trillion** Calories. I provide this number for a reference to show how the energy consumed by man each year compares to automobiles energy consumption. They are quite close when only considering the energy consumed by man alone and provided to man from his consumption of food alone. Keep in mind that the domestic animals that provide meat as man's food, consume about ten times the energy of man. Where man must replace his 2000 or so Calories, the animals must replace the greater number of Calories they use on a daily basis. Go back to the chart and see the listing of the various animal kingdoms and see how much they must replace in energy each and every day to stay alive. In many cases man over feeds the animals to fatten them up so as to provide a greater amount of food per animal. This is a normal routine. The point to make is that the energy consumed by man or by the animals to support his food requirements exceeds the energy consumed by the automobile by a factor of ten.

The above numbers for cars only considers the gasoline that the average person in the world uses for cars. There is also a tremendous use of gasoline to run tractors and bulldozers. Then there are the airplanes and their fuel requirements, which have a demand that is growing faster than car demands. The mass transit systems consume a significant amount of energy. There is the electricity that all the fossil fuels generate. Some generators are fueled with gasoline, some with diesel, some through the burning of coal and some from natural gas. There is a tremendous amount of energy supplied for the home heating and air-conditioning via the use of fossil fuels to be accounted for. Every act that is consumed in this world requires energy. These fuels did not come from the Sun's energy. They came from the earthborn energy discussed and continue to do soon an increased basis. In this case, when they are gone, they are gone. When you take these other consumers of oil and its derivatives it is about equal to the energy man's food support system supplies him. What would we do without this energy?

Remember when I covered the energy requirements to sustain man and his 2,000 table Calorie per day needs? As a result, he needed ten times this number of table Calories tied up in the animals needed for food and the entire loop to provide his daily need. This did not count the energy needed to bring this food to his table. It did not count the airplanes flying the food or the large transport tankers carrying food. It did not count the railroads and their part in the supply. It did not even count the small vehicles that deliver the food to the homes. They all take time to produce and deliver, so there is ten times the daily need for man in the loop at all times to be able to provide the daily needs. This long loop requires an enormous amount of energy. Forget about the energy that man needs per day to live; it is small in comparison to the amount of energy needed to provide this supporting infrastructure.

You now see what perhaps is more frightening than global warming. This crisis is what occurs when we run out of the energy of the crash of 65 million years ago; the earthborn energy of fossil fuels that came from that catastrophic meteor crash and other earthborn energy that lay in the ground for many years. This form of energy has afforded the world's people to live their life, reproduce, and still be able to supply the many that are not as fortunate to have the food at their fingertips. With this energy the food crops grown in the Midwest of the United States could be transported around the world as a commodity item. From this came trade the world over, not only on food but many other commodity items that would make the world a better place to live.

While the world's machines would grow in number so would the world's number of people and it would seem like a race to see which would reach its limit first. Fortunately this fuel allowed the world's population to grow since it became the vital element in transporting the food around the world. What we could do with a billion people on Earth years ago, we would not be able to do with today's 6.7 billion, let alone the 10 billion people, which is the expected growth not too distant in this century.

I am not trying to forecast doom. I am trying to figure out how to get around the problem. First one has to define a problem before it can be solved.

I am trying to define a problem that I see will happen in the not too distant future. The primary problem is running out of the portable/mobile fuel that is provided by gasoline and finding a way to replace it with some other energy source. There are other functions supplied by petroleum but there will be ready substitutes for most of them. Portability is the key function that will be the hardest to replace; portability and the necessary task of supplying food all over the world on a timely basis.

How long will the oil and its derivatives last? One of the biggest of the crises to solve.

Today, the world uses almost 100 million barrels of oil per day, or it will in the next few years. Some reports say there are a trillion (1×10^{12}) barrels of oil in the ground that is recoverable by today's methods. (37). (www.offshore-environment.com/facts.html134) Actually,100 million barrels a day is equal to 36.5 billion barrels of oil per year. At a recoverable amount of oil of a trillion barrels of oil estimated to be in reserves, this equals 27.4 years of oil left. Let's assume that the price of oil rises and this provides funds for finding additional recoverable oil. **Let's assume we are able to recover two trillion barrels of oil.** Then we would have 54 years of oil remaining, but this is only if the demand stays at 100 million barrels a day. With the population growth to 8.7 billion people in the next twenty to thirty years, the demand will increase by 50 percent to 150 million barrels a day or more; probably by the year 2020. Much of this increase will come from the accelerated use by China and India as they become more industrialized. This would reduce the above numbers to a range of 18.1 years and 36.2 years depending on whether there is one or two trillion barrels to be extracted. This is if there are the refineries to process this amount of oil to useable fuels. Keep in mind that oil refineries are expensive to build, about the same cost as nuclear atomic plants. Why would someone want to build additional refineries if they know that there will be limited return on their investment? I mention that the oil may run out in thirty or so years, but before the world runs out we face oil reaching a peak in as few as seven to ten years. So, if the people or countries that finance oil refineries realize that with a peak being reached, there is no need to build more refineries. If they thought it would only be about seven years to the peak of use they might not take the risk. But I believe the price of a barrel of oil will keep increasing as the demand goes up and the amount of oil available goes down after this peak is reached.

Also, because of the extra expense in extracting the oil that is in difficult places the suppliers will raise the price of a barrel of oil. Already there are companies drilling over 32,000 feet in the Gulf of Mexico for oil. As they go deeper for this black gold the cost will go up and the price will go up.

All of this is based on the assumption that no more than two trillion barrels of oil are available for extraction. This includes the shale oils. Shale oils are those oils that are integral with shale rock deep in the earth. In these cases both the shale rock and the oil are extracted and then there is the extra energy to separate out the useable oil. There are large deposits of shale oils in the United States and Canada and probably elsewhere in the world. However, taking all this into context, I believe we will be using one hundred and fifty million barrels of oil each day sometime in the 2020's. This being the case, I believe we will run out of oil around the year 2037. Even if we don't run completely out, there would be a limit to supply the world and it would be much smaller than the amount used today. You see the curves are going in the opposite directions; the population is going up, the demand for food is going up and the supply of oil will be going down. This portrays a terrible crisis.

Countries running out of oil

To give the reader a better feeling of how many years oil will be available, the following is a list of suppliers that will run out and the years they have left to supply the world. (146)

Supplier	Comment
Mexico	Less than ten years and this will hurt their economy
Russia	Seventeen to Twenty two years depending on shipments out
United States	Twelve years unless off shore drilling brings in more oil
Canada	Twenty three years
United Kingdom	Six years

Norway	Nine years
Nigeria	Twenty to forty since they are a small supplier
Libya	Small supplier could last thirty to forty years.

Summary – With these suppliers running out in a very short time it will leave the Middle East as the only supplier of volume for a time of over fifty years and possibly Venezuela who is a rather small supplier with a good volume of oil in their reserves. The reason for the broad range of years that these countries could supply the world is due to the unknown demand placed on each of them when the other countries I listed fall out of the supplier market. As the countries listed leave the market the market demand is still on the upswing. This will probably cause unusual pressure on the Middle East and Venezuela to increase their shipments. This will result in the price of oil increasing. This is probably the reason it showed a dramatic price increase in 2007 and 2008 as the non-OPEC countries' oil supplies have peaked and the demand continues to grow. The demand by the growing economy of China has placed an enormous pressure on the suppliers as their demand for oil has increased dramatically over the last several years. This demand from China will surpass that of the United States by the end of 2008 and by 2015 will have a demand that is probably equal to twenty five percent of the world's demand. This demand has distorted the cost versus oil supply in the world. You can imagine what will happen as the peak demand versus supply gets father distorted as the listed countries no longer supply the world. China doesn't supply the world with any of its oil reserves which are not great. It is estimated that China will run out of its reserves in eleven years. Another reason for the broad range of years of supplies by the Middle East is due to the lack of knowing the true amount of oil in the reserves of these countries. The factual data from the OPEC countries is unknown. There are some indications that the reserves of the Middle East are exaggerated by a significant amount. (147)

Now you know what **this crisis** is about. I have little doubt that the second scenario is the correct one of the population growth and the increased demand. Therefore, a thirty-year period is close to the one to worry about and that happens around the year 2037.

Scientists may be right that Earth's temperature might rise a degree or two in one hundred years. That is nothing compared to the loss of our extra earthborn energy we have been putting to use for the last 150 years. I doubt we can do anything about a change in climate and the temperature of Earth going up a degree in a century. But this would be a minor problem compared to what I am talking about here. Remember, I mentioned that the Earth going up a degree or so in a century is doing so with five generations of families being born during that time. I believe we people mutate and over five generations our bodies will be able to accustom itself to this temperature change. The loss of oil is a much greater problem than this; especially if the temperature follows the cycles previously discussed and will turn to colder temperatures in the not too distant future. We will be looking for something to keep us warm.

Let's review the meteor crash that hit earth 65 million years ago from an energy standpoint and determine how it compares to the amount of fossil fuel reserves we believe exists in the world and their energy. We will review the natural gas reserves, the petroleum reserves, the coal reserves, and compare them to the energy we receive from the Sun each day. Then compare the total fossil fuel reserves versus the amount of energy released from the formation of the Chicxulub Crater in the Yucatan Peninsula of Mexico. This will give the reader a broader picture of the situation that has and does exist. It's also another way of checking out how long the various fossil fuels will last. Keep in mind that any number raised to the 10^{18} power is equivalent to a million trillion when reviewing these numbers or a billion billion.

- 7.4×10^{21} Joules (235 trillion watts) the estimated energy contained in the world's **petroleum** reserves as of 2003 = **1.77 x 10^{18} Calories**
- 6.0×10^{21} Joules (190 trillion watts), the estimated energy contained in the world's **natural gas** reserves as of 2003 = **1.43 x 10^{18} Calories**
- 2.6×10^{22} Joules (824 trillion watts), the estimated energy contained in the world's **coal** reserves as of 2003 = **6.21 x 10^{18} Calories**
- 3.9×10^{22} Joules, (1,249 trillion watts) the estimated energy contained in the world's **fossil fuel** reserves as of 2003 = **9.32 x 10^{18} Calories (summary of the three above)**
- 5.0×10^{23} Joules, (15,855 trillion watts) the approximate energy released in the formation of the Chicxulub Crater in the Yucatán Peninsula [7]

when the **meteor crashed into Earth** some 65 million years ago. = **1.19 x 10²⁰ Calories**

- 1.5×10^{22} Joules, (422 trillion watts) the total energy from the **Sun** that strikes the face of the Earth each day [4] = **3.58 x 10¹⁸ Calories**

* 3.0×10^{31} Joules, (0.85 trillion trillion watts) is the estimated energy contained in the world's recoverable **Uranium – 238** reserves as of 2003 and equal to **7.17 x 10²⁷ Calories**. That's almost a billion times the fossil fuels and there would not be an energy problem (except for portable energy) for many thousands of years.

These are interesting numbers. The oil reserves and the natural gas reserves are about equal. If you total them they come to about the energy we get from the Sun **in a day**. However, the oil reserves are being used up more rapidly than those of the natural gas so the life expectancy of the natural gas is three or four times that of the oil energy, while the Sun's energy remains constant for billions of years. The energy of coal reserves is about five times higher than either the oil or natural gas reserves and is the key to the energy of the near future for fossil fuel energy (but it provides significantly more contaminants to the atmosphere and steps need to be taken to reduce this if we are to use it in the future). The total fossil fuel energy reserves equates to 9.32×10^{18} Calories which is about a tenth of the energy of the meteor crash of 1.19×10^{20} Calories. Remember a good bit of that energy was lost at the time of the impact on Earth. Look at the energy available from the world's U238 radioactive material that can be used for nuclear energy. It is so large a number that it could be considered an infinite source of energy compared to the fossil fuels. If we could use it all we would have enough energy to last ten billion years and Earth will not last that long.

I brought this one into the picture since we may choose to go in that direction for future energy needs. Also, because of the large amount of nuclear energy available I have used it as a renewable fuel in my calculations.

Note; that crash created a little more than ten times the energy left in all the fossil fuel reserves. Now you see how fortunate we were to receive this messenger from outer space. Also, consider that this crash doesn't count the fossil fuels that were also in the earth's body in addition to this crash. It is important to keep in mind that all the fossil fuels did not only come from that meteor of 65 million years ago. They came from much of Earth's decomposition of other animals and plant matter that was unused and covered over for at least six million years which is the time it takes to convert buried material to a fossil fuel. Some of it was derived from Sun's energy that was tied up many years ago in some form on Earth. Some fossil fuels such as peat bogs and coal were used as sources of fossil fuel energy much earlier than the oil derivatives. Extra energy above the normal Sun's energy is not easy to come by. It requires a special kind of event and a long time to nurture before it can be recognized as an unusable energy that became useful. This is what transpired from 65 million years ago to the present time.

We have been using up these coal for about two hundred and fifty years and the oil derivatives for approximately 150 years. Of course the amount used up in the last 50 years has been the big hit. We cannot continue to use this amount of energy per capita for the next thirty to fifty years. We will need to find a substitute energy source. More specifically we will need to find an energy source that is portable such as gasoline is portable and has the energy equivalent of gasoline per gallon used to meet our transportation needs for delivering food to the world; otherwise there is no way of providing the food for the general population.

To put this in prospective, at 100 million barrels of oil the world uses each day is equivalent to 7.3 million megawatts a day, day in and day out. At 150 million barrels a day, which is what I see in the future, it is equal to 11.0 million megawatts a day. This is equivalent to 33.2 years of reserves based on the numbers above for the oil reserves. However, if the use goes up to 150 million barrels a day by 2020 this equates to twenty two years. Remember, I was estimating that with the price of oil going up as it becomes more scare, that we will use extra resources to find double the amount shown above. The price of oil recently reached $150.00 a barrel but has settled down to around $100.00 a barrel as the economy slowed down. This would get us to forty four (44) years of oil left. I had estimated that it would fall somewhere between these extremes and would **last 30 years and the year 2037 would find us essentially out of oil. If not out, in low enough reserves that the price would increase and the use of gasoline and diesel would drop to a very low amount – almost like it was all gone, except for the countries that have it and use it for their own objectives.**

It's important for the United States to start setting up the drilling off shore. It will take till the year 2020 before these offshore drillings make contributions to our energy needs. The year 2020 comes fast and it will be about that time that the world's daily production will have a plateau of the supply for years while the demand goes up. We want to be sure of our supply and our energy independence. If we don't reach this level by the year 2020 we will lose our position in the world as the number one major power and along with that lose what leverage we have in the world. If America stays atop the world as its leader the world will be the same sane world it is today. As you will read later when I describe the renewable energy sources and the amount of effort it will take to equal 11.0 million megawatts a day that the oil would have been supplying and that the world will have to replace.

I hope this brings the message to you. We are using this energy up fast, and we are increasing its use. Whatever we replace this oil and its derivatives with, we must also provide the equipment to use it and the infrastructure to provide it worldwide. So, we don't have many years to invent and we better start immediately. I predict the world's oil derived fuels will essentially run out in thirty to forty years. It may take a little longer to completely run out, but what are available to be delivered in thirty to forty years will be from a greatly shrinking pool of these high energy fuels. The fuel needed to deliver them will be in short supply. It will be highly contested for. We will find the people that have what little fuel is left, keeping it for their own needs. This will completely crack the world trade we presently enjoy unless we can replace its capability with renewable energy.

Immediate actions to be taken.

There are some immediate actions to take concerning the oil's depleting reserves that will extend the time that oil and its derivatives are around.

1. Use less oil and its derivatives in our daily consumptions. Keep lower inventories.
2. Be efficient in our daily use by:

   A. Produce cars that use less fuel per mile. This includes smaller cars and hybrid cars that share gas and electricity

B. Use the cars only as needed. Conserve by not having each person in the family drive to an activity where more than one of the family is going.
C. Car pool
D. Take vacations that are not as far away.
E. The airplane industry needs to cut down on flights to some cities and reduce redundant flights such as those to deliver mail separate from passenger flights. They should concentrate on optimizing their flights for full loads.
F. Use diesel fuel which is easier to produce than gasoline.
G. Use commercial transportation to go to work in place of one's car.
H. For those that have trailers and drive to take vacations – drive to a nearer vacation site.
I. Industrial sites need to review their absolute requirements by shift for plants running on three shifts and decide if they can reduce to two shifts. This would allow one shifts use of oil, gasoline and other energy products to be eliminated and save that amount on a daily basis. The same is true for companies running on week ends. They need to determine whether week end shifts are practical. All of these moves, while practical, place a tremendous pressure on the working people in the areas of reduction of work force.
J. Replace oil burning furnaces with natural gas burning furnaces.
K. Use solar panels to provide electricity for the homes in place of electricity supplied from oil burning generators. Add to the power grid with solar energy.
L. Stop fighting a war in Iraq and Afghanistan where considerable gasoline and other fuel is used in land transportation and air transportation. Depend on the people of Iraq to produce more oil.
M. Replace gasoline engines for cars and other applications with electrical powered machinery or hybrids. This is easier to state then to accomplish.
N. Convert some public transportation to equipment powered by liquefied natural gas. This would be especially effective if used on large vehicles like buses and military vehicles.

O. Cut the lawn less frequently along with other chores that are similar.

P. Walk when the distance is less than a mile; or ride a bike, even if five miles.

Q. If you have more than one vehicle, drive the one that is more efficient if you have the choice.

R. Don't support the ocean going vacation cruise vessels for a vacation trip. The less of these large vessels that burn up lots of gasoline or diesel to take people on vacation cruises the greater the savings in fuels that are needed for more important functions.

S. Use solar power for heating hot water in homes.

T. Take the eventual loss of oil seriously by supporting the drive for renewable fuels

U. The media needs to understand the situation better and provide visibility to the average person.

V. Insulate homes and business building better to reduce the use of heating and cooling.

W. Stop using freezers and depend on the grocery stores to carry your food requirements. Stop using the second refrigerator in the garage.

X. Develop electric cars and better batteries to keep them going or fuel cells that produce electricity and are easy to replace.

Use less energy by eating fewer foods and make most of them vegetables and fruit and reduce the number of cattle and other domesticated animals on Earth. They consume a large amount of energy. Energy efficiency is a world wide issue but is more an issue at this time with the United States and China. The United States uses approximately 22% of the world's oil and China is growing and will pass the United States shortly.

- By taking appropriate energy-saving measures, by 2010 the United States can have an energy system that reduces costs by $530 per household per year and reduces global warming pollutant emissions to 10 percent below 1990 levels. *(Energy Innovations report) (37)*

- Just by using the "off the shelf" energy-efficient technologies available today, we could cut the cost of heating, cooling, and lighting our homes and workplaces by up to 80%. *(U.S. Department of Energy and Maryland Energy Administration) (38)*

- Replacing one incandescent light bulb with an energy-saving compact fluorescent bulb means 1,000 pounds less carbon dioxide is emitted to the atmosphere and $67 dollars is saved on energy costs over the bulb's lifetime. *(U.S. Environmental Protection Agency and Alliance to Save Energy) (39)*
- A decrease of only 1% in industrial energy use would save the equivalent of about 55 million barrels of oil per year, worth about $1 billion.

Conclusion on Crisis II – the loss of oil and its derivatives

It is important to understand that I am interested in the conservation of oil for several reasons

1. The reduction of carbon dioxide and other environment contaminants. Although I am not a believer of carbon dioxide being a cause of global warming, I am a believer that we should not contaminate our precious atmosphere. I am for the elimination of carbon dioxide in the atmosphere.

2. I also want to see our consumption of oil reduced to allow it to last longer. I wrote another book *Beyond Global Warming* where I expressed the dramatic effect the loss of oil would have on our means of living and how hard a substitute for gasoline would be.

3. There is no suitable replacement for gasoline or other oil derivatives. No portable energy equivalent. No energy equivalent in a gallon of anything to compare against gasoline. Biofuels are mentioned but the supply of this fuel is limited as will be discussed. We must find a suitable volume of portable fuel.

4. Even if we found something, do you understand the enormous task in building an infrastructure to provide it in the volumes that would be needed? Remember, we are talking about replacing 150 million barrels a day of oil by the 2020's. This is probably 300 million barrels a day required of an energy substitute of the same energy output and of the same weight. Weight is a major consideration when reviewing these needs. Airplanes cannot fly on nuclear energy because of the weight of the total system.

5. Develop renewable energy in a time period that is consistent with taking up where oil leaves off; i.e., when oil peaks renewable energy must be there. (Windmills, solar cells, biofuels, nuclear, hydroelectric, water power, geothermal, hydrogen power)

6. Use natural gas in place of oil or coal to power electrical generation. Natural gas is the cleanest of the fossil fuels. Use natural gas as the **cross-over supply** of fossil fuel when oil is gone to carry us to the renewable energy sources.

Crisis III -
Understanding the fossil fuels and their limitations

The third crisis relates to the present use of fossil fuels and what the priorities should be to reduce their use and replace them with renewable energy as soon as possible. To provide the reader with a **baseline** I will work with the amount of energy used in 2004 from the fossil fuels and renewable fuels. This will provide a good look at how each of the fossil fuels and the renewable energies compare. As you read through these I want you to keep in mind that I want to find a replacement for oil and its derivatives as a first priority for the use in transportation. This includes car, trucks, large vehicles, and airplanes.

The twentieth century saw a rapid twenty fold increase in the use of fossil fuels. Betweenas 2%. According to the US <u>Energy Information Administration</u>'s 2006 estimate, 15TW (15 x 10^{12} watts) total power consumption of 2004 was divided as follows, with fossil fuels supplying 86% of the world's energy:

Let's look at the various fuels and the energy they **supplied in 2004**

Fuel type	power (Millions of MW)	Energy in Exajoules	Calories
Oil	5.6	180	4.3×10^{16}
Natural Gas	3.5	110	2.63×10^{16}
Coal	3.8	120	2.87×10^{16}
Hydroelectric	0.9	30	0.717×10^{16}
Nuclear	0.9	30	0.717×10^{16}
Geothermal, wind, Solar, wood	0.13	4	0.096×10^{16}
Total	15	471	1.13×10^{17}

Remember Power in TW (1×10^{12}) or a more useable term - million MW shown in the 2nd column is the established power base and a watt is one joule per second. To convert this power in the second column to power in the third column, you multiply the 10^{12} joules per second times 3600 seconds per hour x 24 hours a day, x 365 days per year to get to the power in Exajoules or joules x 10^{18} (In general terms this is one million trillion joules) in a year; which is the energy shown in the third column. So, the third column is the power use per year. There are 4,186 joules per Calorie so you divide the third column by 4.186 x 10^3 to obtain the Calories (table Calories) per year. The fossil fuels are Oil, Gas, and Coal and add up to 12.9 TW (12.9 million MW) of the total shown. This is 86% of the energy used. The renewable energy is the Hydroelectric, the nuclear, the Geothermal, wind, solar, and wood biomass, which are 14% of the energy supplied and total approximately 2.0 terawatts or 2 million megawatts or a total of 1.13×10^{17} Calories per year.

Industrial users (agriculture, mining, manufacturing, and construction) consume about 37% of the total 15 million MW. Personal and commercial transportation consumes 20%; residential heating, lighting, and appliances use 11%; and commercial uses (lighting, heating and cooling of commercial buildings, and provision of water and sewer services) amount to 5% of the total. The remaining twenty seven percent of the world's energy is lost in energy transmission and generation. The new generation of natural gas-fired plants reaches a substantially higher efficiency of 55% versus the 38% efficiency when using coal. Coal is the most popular fuel for the world's electricity plants but doesn't have as high efficiency as natural gas fired power plants.

World Primary Energy Production Trends

Between 1995 and 2005, the world's total output of primary energy -- petroleum, natural gas, coal, and electric power (hydro, nuclear, geothermal, solar, wind, and wood and waste)--increased at an average annual rate of 2.4 percent (39). World production increased from 364 quadrillion Btu in 1995 to 460 quadrillion Btu in 2005.

In 2005, petroleum (crude oil and natural gas plant liquids) continued to be the world's most important primary energy source, accounting for 36.8 percent, or 169 quadrillion Btu, of world primary energy production Between 1995 and 2005, petroleum production increased by 13.4 million barrels per day, or 19.7 percent, rising from 68.0 to 81.4 million barrels per day. The **Middle East** had the largest production gain, followed by **Eurasia**, and **Africa**. Their combined gains over the period from 1995 to 2005 were 12.6 million barrels per day.

Petroleum

Global production of petroleum (crude oil and natural gas plant liquids) increased by 13.4 million barrels per day between 1995 and 2005, an average annual rate of growth of 1.8 percent (40). Saudi Arabia, Russia, and the United States were the three largest producers of petroleum in 2005. Together, they produced 33.6 percent of the world's petroleum. Production from Iran and Mexico accounted for an additional 9.8 percent. (40)

In 2005, the United States consumed 20.8 million barrels per day of petroleum--25 percent of world consumption. China and Japan ranked a distant second and third in consumption, with 6.7 and 5.4 million barrels per day, respectively, followed by Russia and Germany. (40)

Coal

Coal ranked second as a primary energy source in 2005, accounting for 26.6 percent of world primary energy production. World coal production totaled 6.5 billion short tons, or 122 quadrillion Btu, in 2005, and it increased by 27.1 percent from the 1995 level of 5.1 billion short tons. (40)

Natural Gas

Carbon dioxide emissions from the consumption and flaring of natural gas accounted for the remaining 20.7 percent of carbon dioxide emissions from the consumption and flaring of fossil fuels in 2005. Emissions from the consumption and flaring of natural gas increased from 4.5 billion metric tons of carbon dioxide in 1995 to 5.8 billion metric tons in 2005, or by 30.4 percent. The United States and Russia were the two largest producers of carbon dioxide from the consumption and flaring of natural gas in 2005 accounting for 21 and 15 percent, respectively, of the world total. Iran, the United Kingdom and Canada together accounted for an additional 10 percent.

World Energy Overview: 1995-2005

The International Energy Annual presents information and trends on world energy production and consumption for petroleum, natural gas, coal, and electricity. Production and consumption data are reported in standard United States physical units as well as British thermal units (Btu). Reserve estimates are shown for petroleum, natural gas, and coal and trade data are provided for these three fuels and for electricity. Data are provided on crude oil refining capacity and electricity installed capacity by type. Also available are estimates of carbon dioxide emissions from the consumption and flaring of fossil fuels. Prices are included for selected crude oils. Population data are also provided.

(**Note:** In the discussion that follows, the data for total **production** of primary energy in 1995 and 2005 include production in the United States of 2.6 and 2.5 quadrillion Btu, respectively, of renewable energy not used for electricity generation (40). This renewable energy production includes biomass (biofuels, wood, and waste), geothermal, and solar energy not used for electricity generation. Likewise, the data for total **consumption** of primary energy in 1995 and 2005 include consumption in the United States of 2.4 and 2.5 quadrillion Btu, respectively, of renewable energy not used for electricity generation and adjustment to remove the consumption of supplemental gaseous fuels.

Graph of trends in the buildup of the various energies used in 1965 to 2005

Let's look at the trends in energy use over twenty years. This shows the growth of each of the energy supplies. It gives one the feeling of how long it takes to build this capacity and the infrastructure for supplying the world's requirements. If we understand this, it should give us a good feel for how long it might take to build up the supply and infrastructure for renewable energy. It is not enough to state that we are going to replace our old energy system with a new system of renewable energy. It takes a world commitment. But, even with a world commitment, it takes planning and proper use of our resources to even come close to the curves you will witness that developed over those twenty years. Keep in mind that even as we build renewable energy sources these old sources will continue to be used for at least thirty years for oil and much longer for the other renewable energy to replace coal and eventually natural gas. This means the world's suppliers will be working on these two systems in parallel for some years to come.

We will review the various trends of supply of the fossil fuels and renewable energy. This will start to give one a feel for how slow the build up is for the renewable energy. The graphs will also show the various countries involved along with the economics.

Graph of the energy buildup for the various energy sources

The following graph displays the usage in energy in millions of megawatts of power going from 1965 to 2005. Millions of MW's of power is on the vertical axis on the following chart – representing from one to six million MW. (41) Notice, when you add the curves up there was a total of 5 million mega watts of power used in 1965 and oil alone exceeded that in 2005. The total for 2005 was 13.5 million megawatts or almost tripling the use with an increase of two hundred and seventy percent over this time span. The graph represents millions of megawatts on the left vertical column.

Green is oil, black is coal, red is natural gas, pink is nuclear, and blue is hydroelectric. Notice that all have shown an increase, with the growth rates of oil, coal and natural gas, the fossil fuels, being on an equal growth rate over the last few years. Notice that coal's slope is changing which is an indication that it will pass oil shortly. This is due to the immergence of China as a large energy user over the last decade and China's main source of energy is coal. At the rate China is increasing its industrial growth it will pass the United States in use and in atmosphere contamination in 2008 or 2009.

Figure 4 Energy buildup from 1965 go 2005
(millions of MW on vertical column)

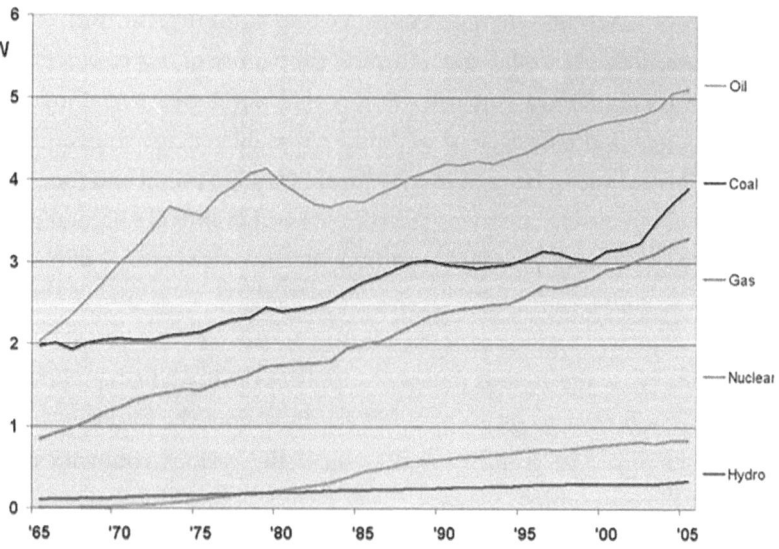

The mix of the various power sources is displayed. Oil is the highest followed by Coal. The use of oil will reach a peak in about five to ten years and coal will exceed oil in not too many years and will lead all sources unless the world decides to eliminate the use of coal due to its contamination of the atmosphere. However, this cannot happen until the renewable energy sources reach the levels of energy being consumed at that time. Keep in mind that the renewable energy sources is what this book is about; i.e., that is one of the big crises; trying to optimize the use of renewable energy to meet the total needs and eliminate contamination of the atmosphere. Also, keep in mind that this may not be achievable in time to take the place of the mobile energy of oil. I foresee this as being around the year 2037 when we will lose the use of our main source of mobile (or portable) energy. The use of coal will increase dramatically as China accelerates the use of coal in their big economy growth. The world needs to develop adequate renewable energy supplies to offset the use of coal and keep the atmosphere as clean as possible.

Bar graph of percentage of fossil versus renewable energy

The bar graph shown below is a good indication of where the renewable energy stands. (41) It is obvious that there is a long way to go to replace the fossil fuels. The world can live with natural gas as a fossil fuel supplier since it is available in large quantities and is the cleanest of the fossil fuels. Farther excavation for new natural gas deposits in the world continues with the hope of offsetting the dirty fossil fuels.

As you can see the nuclear energy leads the renewable energy sources. This is because the installation of these has been going on for approximately fifty years. I will cover how each country using nuclear energy considers this source for future growth. This energy source is in the greatest quantity available and would provide all the energy the world needs if it were installed. However, it is expensive to install. In addition, it is not popular with many people who were scared off when Three Mile Island had its limited problems but really scared off after the Chernobyl Nuclear Power Plant disaster in the Soviet Union. The good news is that once installed it is a rather inexpensive source of energy. It's only the initial installation costs that are high. The installation requires placement where there is sufficient water supplies to provide water cooling of the system. This would be around a river, lake or ocean. Biomass represents the burning of wood and other renewable materials used in this manner.

Figure 5 - Bar graph of percentage of various energies

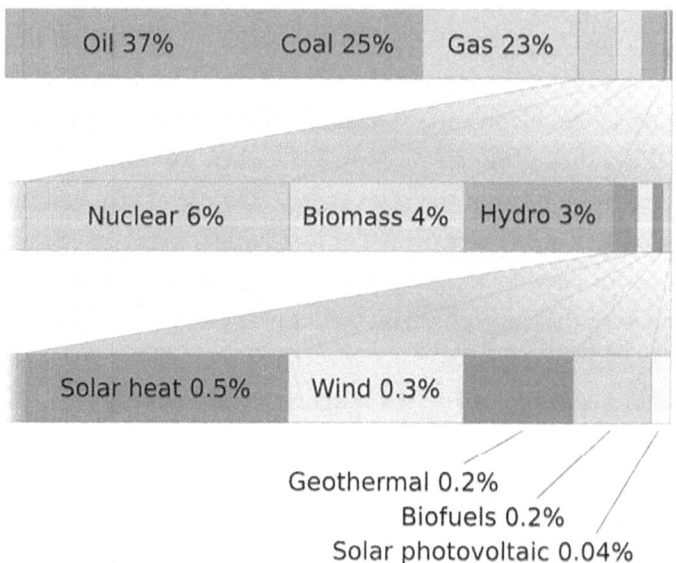

| Oil 37% | Coal 25% | Gas 23% |

| Nuclear 6% | Biomass 4% | Hydro 3% |

| Solar heat 0.5% | Wind 0.3% |

Geothermal 0.2%
Biofuels 0.2%
Solar photovoltaic 0.04%

Figure 6 - Chart of countries GNP versus their financial resources directed to renewable energy

While the chart above provides you a look at the various supplies it doesn't give one a feel for what each country is doing as far as directing their financial resources to provide renewable energy.

The chart below shows the various countries as a function of their GNP (Gross National Product) (Incidentally, the world is now using Gross Domestic Product as a better indicator of the country's internal health.) (41) You will note that Norway is leading the world in the percentage of their GNP being used toward gaining more renewable energy. This is no accident since Norway has had a program for several years on pushing for renewable energy. We will discuss some of these.

You will notice that Norway, Iran, and The Netherlands, are ahead of the United States; with the U.S ranking fourth of the nine countries listed. The U.S. is followed by China, Germany, Japan,

The United Kingdom and India. With the richness of the U.S. this chart is somewhat misleading since the 9.8 % of GNP of the United States means they are generating much more renewable energy than the three countries listed ahead of them because their GNP is much higher than the other countries. However, we need to do more. The same comments go for China, Germany, Japan, The UK and India. A somewhat misleading view would be given of Canada in this type of chart. Canada leads the world in hydroelectric power. This is a renewable power that has been installed for some time in Canada, so their spending for this power at present may seem low but they already are in good position with this hydroelectric power and a significant amount of natural gas resources. So, on a country basis and one with a rather small population (smaller than California), Canada is currently holding its own. However this is a place where much more can be done in the near future since they have natural resources in great quantities.

Figure 7 Graph of percent of GNP versus financial resources spent on renewable energy

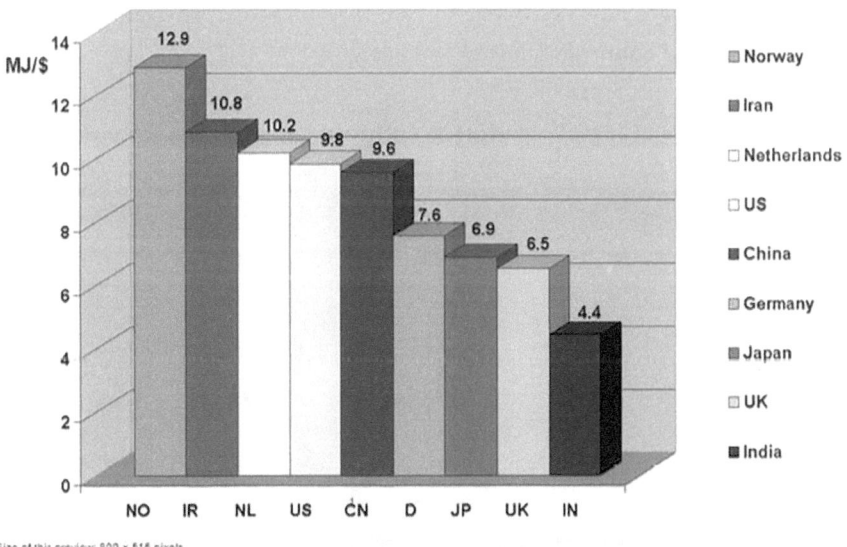

Figure 8 - Graph IV - per capita energy versus the per capita income

Review the graph shown below. This shows an interesting piece of information showing the per capita energy versus the per capital income for all countries with more than 20 million inhabitants. (41) These countries represent over ninety percent of the world's population, so it is a significant view of the world's use of its capital. As would be expected it shows the countries with the greatest wealth consume the highest amount of energy. This is to be expected relative to population since the use of energy is related to population. However, countries like India with their population being the second highest in the world, are not the wealthiest and this shows in this chart. The seven wealthiest are Japan, United States, United Kingdom, Canada, German, France and Australia in that order. The use of energy is highest in the wealthy countries of the United States and Canada. Japan is the wealthiest per capita but uses about half the energy of the United States and Canada. Saudi Arabia, Korea, and Russia use energy that is beyond their per capita wealth. This is a revealing chart. We know why Saudi Arabia uses considerable energy per capita. It has a great amount of the world's oil as its natural resource.

This chart is somewhat misleading for a country like China. Its population is so high that even though the per capita kW usage is low, when you take into account the large population the total kW usage overall is very high. However, this chart is quite revealing. It also gives one an overall feeling for the per capita income for many countries being so low. The undeveloped countries or the under-developed countries fall into this category.

Figure 9 - Graph V - per capita energy versus per capita income

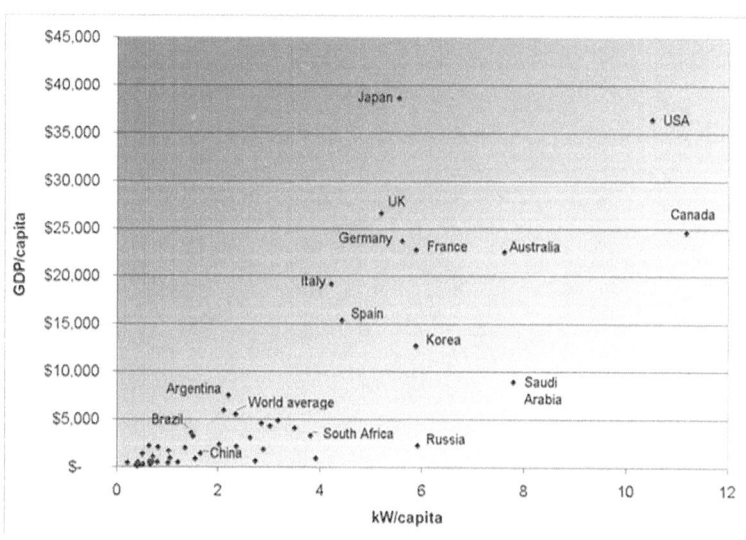

GDP and Energy consumption in Japan from 1958 – 2000

The data shows the strong correlation between GDP and energy use, however it also shows that this link can be broken. (41) After the oil shocks of 1973 and 1979 the energy use stagnated while Japan's GDP continued to grow, after 1985. With the price of oil per barrel going down dramatically Japan was able to grow dramatically in its GDP. However, notice how the curves start to coincide around 1998. The GDP is almost on a par with the energy being consumed. This bodes problems for the future unless Japan is able to develop some of its own renewable energy resources. The GNP may continue to grow but the GDP will be a function of the cost of oil and may continue to be as the price of oil will go up as I predict as this resource becomes more scarce. When the GNP grows much faster than the GDP it means the country is more and more dependent on outside resources. It also means the earnings on their efforts will be reduced much like a company that has high fixed costs and selling prices that have little margin. Until the present, Japan has had a large population in a small country and has been able to use their population resource and outside resources imported into the country to provide value added and sell their products at a profit. Their value added was in the productivity of their people and the rather low wages paid to their working population and this allowed them to sell their finished products at a good margin. When one of the resources being imported happens to be oil and it has a cost that is not in balance with the economies of some countries they will suffer this kind of fate. Hopefully the world's development of renewable resources at costs equivalent to the old prices of oil will be able to solve this problem for countries like Japan may continue to grow. However, this shows a tremendous issue that relates to the cost of oil. Over the last few years the cost of a barrel of oil has more than doubled. This spells trouble for Japan. Japan has very few natural resources. Its venture out into World War II was due partly to a lack of rice and it invaded China to be able to obtain the rich rice fields of China. This is a problem with small countries with big populations and rather scarce natural resources. This is the opposite phenomenon that Canada possesses. Canada has a small population and large natural resources which will stand them in good stead. The same is true of Saudi Arabia as with Japan, where it will become much more dependent on other countries for its energy. Its wealth is tied up in oil and this will be depleted over the coming thirty years.

Figure 10 - Graph VI - GDP and Energy consumption in Japan from 1958 -2000

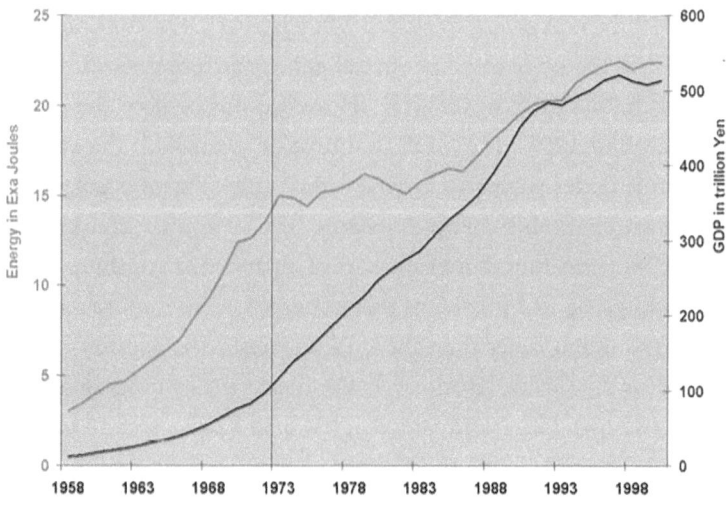

Figure 11 - Chart of the World's supply of energy

The worldwide energy supply in millions of megawatts is shown in a bar chart below. (41) As is expected oil energy is number one having 38% of the world's energy at about 5.6 terawatts. Coal and Natural Gas are next and not being too much different in quantity. I say this because the gas energy is much easier to excavate than that of coal. So, a certain amount of energy is loss in recovering coal. Coal is still a very inexpensive source of energy and the main user is China and they continue to increase their use of this energy source. I will discuss coal and what is being done to make it easier to use and to make it cleaner. As I will or have mentioned I would be happy if the world reached something I call Energy Neutral. This is where the renewable energy sources equal the oil shown in this bar chart and then it could use these renewable energy sources along with natural gas and have a clean source of energy for the world and not have to use the coal. Using the coal is sort of like destroying your planet to me. We would need to dig a huge hole in mother Earth to recover all the coal that is within its bosom. The hydroelectric source of renewable energy is real and will continue for ever. However, it will not grow very much. I will cover this later. The use of nuclear energy is one that is self retained at this level to date. There is enough nuclear energy available in raw resources to be able to handle the entire world's supply of electricity for the all the foreseeable future. People just have to make the decision to use it. It is expensive to install but becomes less expensive each year you use it. This will be covered in detail. You can see how small the efforts have been to date on the other renewable energy sources of wind, mass energy (burning of wood etc.), solar, and thermal. However, there is a great deal of effort worldwide on taking steps to bring those resources up. I will cover each of these as we proceed.

See how fairly insignificant the amount of the other renewable sources of energy are. However, as we proceed you will see how many countries are starting to install windmill farms and solar cells to overcome their local needs and hopefully put a dent in the worldwide energy needs. We will see how close we approach **Energy Neutral.**

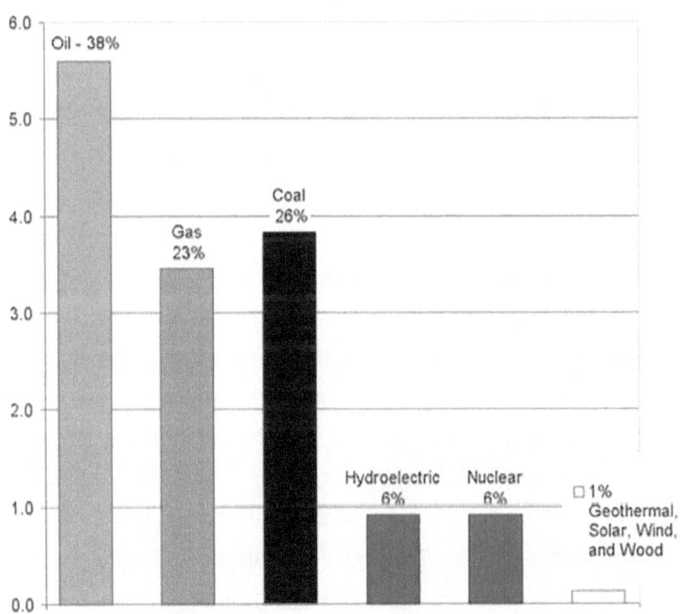

Terawatts of oil energy by type being used in today's economies.

Figure 12 - Pie chart on the various sources of oil in the world

The breakdown of the sources of oil in the world is shown below in the pie chart. (41) The total oil believed to exist in the world is 57 zettajoules (57 x 10^{21} joules or 1.36 x 10^{19} Calories). Of these there are twenty two (22) zettajoules that are unrecoverable at this point in time of technology. This leaves thirty five zettajoules of energy that are recoverable. However many of these are recoverable using extensive techniques that cost money. The oil shales of eleven zettajoules are tied up in rocks called shales. These will require new techniques to free up the oil at significant expense even if it is feasible. However, with the price of a barrel of oil going up it makes it more desirable to go after these types of oil reserves. Note that **only 8 zettajoules are proven reserves.** This is 1.8 x 10^{18} Calories. We will see how this extends out over the near future with the present use rate. We used 0.471 x 10^{21} joules in 2004 or 0.113 x 10^{18} Calories. This works out to a little over ten years if the world's demand remains the same as it was in 2004; however this is already being exceeded. The chart shows that there are 11 zettajoules of future additions. This could add up to another twenty two years based on 2004's consumption. So, the total between proved and future additions adds up to a little over thirty years of use based on 2004. China's use has increased dramatically and it is believed it will exceed that of the United States in the not too distant future. This also assumes this oil is still around by that time. Since the rate of use is increasing I had estimated that the world's supply will run out in about the 30 years. So, this pie chart and what is expected out of the world's reserves is very close to my projections. Even if it doesn't run out, it will be in scarce supply and very expensive. The cost may preclude many countries being able to afford oil and its derivatives. This would require a rebalancing of the world's economics unless renewable energy provides enough energy to overcome this situation.

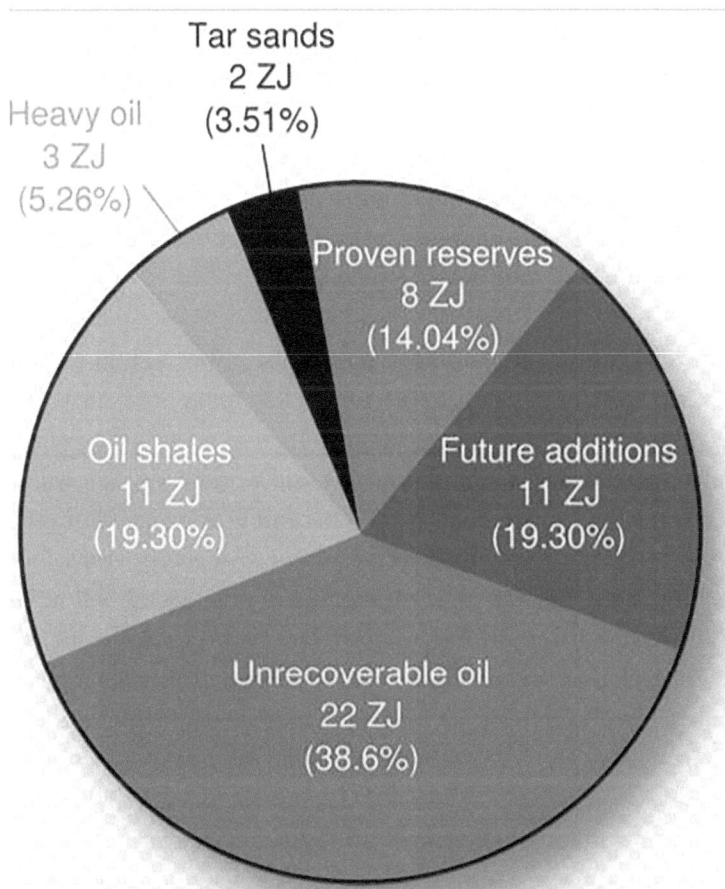

Now let's review the renewable energy as of the end of the year 2006 to see how we are doing in establishing these sources of energy. This will tell us where we are and how far we have to go.

Figure 13 - Pie chart showing the breakdown of the present renewable energy supplies

The pie chart shown below indicates the breakdown of the various renewable energy supplies. (41)

As previously indicated, hydroelectric power leads the group at 235 billion liters of supply each year.

This is followed by 105 liters a year of biomass energy. I haven't discussed much about biomass energy because it is not energy that I see growing. This biomass energy relates to things such as the use of wood to burn and other burnable entities. Materials like you burn in your fireplace. Remember there is still much of the world that depends on this type of heat to keep their homes warm. This will continue but will not grow. The one problem with using these energies is that they detract from entities that do other useful things that we do not want to see reduced; like building homes.

The next big one on the list is the use of solar power to heat hot water in homes. This is something that has been proceeding for at least thirty years and there has been very slow growth in that area. However, I will show that this is rapidly picking up as the solar industry picks up world wide. You will see the growth expected in the use of solar. Solar is becoming more practical as the cost of other sources go up. The cost phenomenon for solar energy versus fossil fuel energy is interesting. As time proceeds the cost of solar energy will be coming down while the cost of fossil fuels is going up. There is an immediate high cost for installation which many states are allowing tax breaks to alleviate this cost, but the cost after installation is rather insignificant other than maintenance. Most systems have twenty year warrantees. Meanwhile there are new systems called thermal solar that are now being installed. These direct the suns light using large parabola shaped reflectors to heat water to steam and the steam is used to turn the turbines of large generators. While the energy from hydropower will not increase much, there will be significant increases in solar power, wind power, water wave power, and nuclear power. This graph is somewhat misleading since it represents renewable power and understates the hydroelectric power since it was done before big hydroelectric power increases in China and the Yanze river project that I will discuss. There has been a significant increase in the use of renewable energy since 2006, mainly in hydroelectric power, biofuel, solar, windmill, geothermal and water wave/tide.

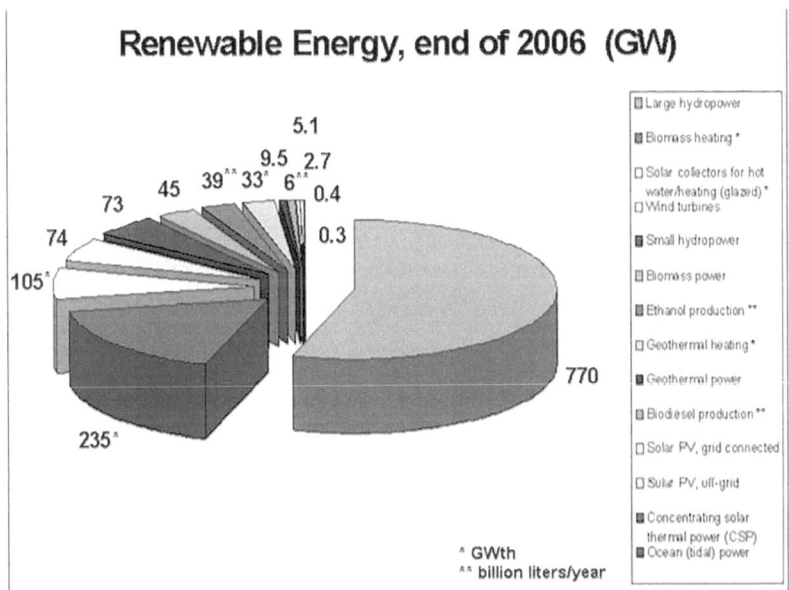

Renewable Energy, end of 2006 (GW)

Legend:
- Large hydropower
- Biomass heating *
- Solar collectors for hot water/heating (glazed) *
- Wind turbines
- Small hydropower
- Biomass power
- Ethanol production **
- Geothermal heating *
- Geothermal power
- Biodiesel production **
- Solar PV, grid connected
- Solar PV, off-grid
- Concentrating solar thermal power (CSP)
- Ocean (tidal) power

Values shown: 5.1, 9.5, 2.7, 45, 39 ^^, 33 ^, 6 ^^, 0.4, 73, 74, 0.3, 105 ^, 770, 235 ^

^ GWth
^^ billion liters/year

Keep in mind that one of the purposes of this book is to explain that the oil energy will be gone in 30 years and the coal and natural gas will be gone in approximately 100 years and we must replace these or life will be cut short for many of the world's population. The main purpose is to bring this to the forefront and suggest the approaches that will replace these fossil fuels. This will be done by showing where these renewable energies are presently being generated and how additional ones can be obtained. All of this will be quantified and shown in equivalent Calories. We must come up with unique means of supplying additional energy from the Sun's wasted energy and the use of nuclear and geothermal energy. Keep in mind that the renewable energy listed in the chart above, with the exception of nuclear energy and geothermal is all generated by the Sun. There are no other sources of energy that can be converted to useable energy for man's use. I have purposely left biomass heating off the renewable energy list because I believe it is saturated and will show no increase.

Energy Consumption

- Though accounting for only 5 percent of the world's population, Americans consume 26 percent of the world's energy. *(American Almanac) (42)*
- In 1997, U.S. residents consumed an average of 12,133 kilowatt-hours of electricity each, almost nine times greater than the average for the rest of the world. *(Grist Magazine) (43)*
- Worldwide, some 2 billion people are currently without electricity. *(U.S. Department of Energy) (44)*
- Among industrialized and developing countries, Canada consumes per capita the most energy in the world, the United Sates ranks second, and Italy consumes the least among industrialized countries.
- Developing countries use 30% of global energy. Rapid population growth, combined with economic growth, will rapidly increase that percentage in the next 10 years. China has already increased its use of global energy to a level almost matching the U.S. China is where the most carbon dioxide will be released into the atmosphere in the foreseeable future.
- The World Bank estimates that investments of $1 trillion will be needed in this decade and upwards of $4 trillion during the next 30 years to meet developing countries' electricity needs alone. (I believe this is not even close to the amount of money that must be spent and will show why as we proceed to detail the power sources.)
- America uses about 15 times more energy per person than does the typical developing country. Keep in mind my comment on Canada which uses more per capita than the U.S.
- Residential appliances, including heating and cooling equipment and water heaters, consume 90% of all energy used in the U.S. residential sector. This is to be expected for the residential section.
- The United States spends about $440 billion annually for energy. Energy costs U.S. consumers $200 billion and U.S. manufacturers $100 billion annually. These numbers will go up dramatically if the price of oil goes up as the world's capacity of oil goes down.

Remaining Fossil fuel reserves at best estimate

Fossil Fuel Energy Energy in Zj (10^{21} joules) Power (Million MW) Calories			
Coal	290.0	9,228	6.9×10^{19}
Oil	18.4	615	4.4×10^{18}
Natural Gas	15.7	498	3.75×10^{18}

Significant uncertainty exists for these numbers. However, if we use these as the probable figures the oil and its 18.4 zettajoules (4.4×10^{18} Calories) would show thirty nine years before we run out based on 2004 figures. Obviously the use since 2004 has increased and based on the growth in consumption the thirty nine years is an over estimation and we get back to my thirty years projection. The estimation of the remaining fossil fuels on the planet depends on a detailed understanding of the Earth's crust. This understanding is still less than perfect. While modern drilling technology makes it possible to drill wells in up to 3 km of water to verify the exact composition of the geology, one half of the ocean is deeper than 3 km, leaving about a third of the planet beyond the reach of detailed analysis. These figures may be too optimistic. Energy Watch Group reports show that we already cannot supply the demand for oil. (42) (44)

"Coal is the most abundant fossil fuel." According to the International Energy Agency the proven reserves of coal are around 909 billion tons, which could sustain at the current production rate for 155 years. (45) I believe this is an overstatement since China has its economy growing and using coal at a tremendous rate and this will increase resulting in the life span of coal as being much less. In addition, if oil runs out in thirty years as I project, there will be a shift to coal for many countries unless the growth of renewable energy exceeds projections. Coal was the fuel that launched the industrial revolution and has continued to grow in use; China, which already has many of the world's most polluted cities, (46) was in 2007 building about two coal fired power plants every week. Coal is the fastest growing fossil fuel and its large reserves would make it a popular candidate to meet the energy demand of the global community, short of global warming concerns and other pollutants. (44) Keep in mind that this could solve many energy problems while creating other problems. With the Fischer-Tropsch process it is possible to make liquid fuels such as diesel and jet fuel from coal. The Stop Coal campaign calls for a moratorium on the construction of any new coal plants and on the phase out of all existing plants, citing concern for global warming.(45) However, there has been no response to this campaign as far as I can determine. There are new coal plants being built all over the world. China is building new coal plants to supplement the huge hydroelectric dam project that has been proceeding for the past fifteen years. Germany is building new coal plants even thought they are one of the leaders in moving toward renewable energy. In the United States, 49% of electricity generation comes from burning coal. (47) The coal burning has an undesirable side issue since it contaminates the atmosphere locally so bad that people have to wear masks. A good example was during the Olympics and some of the towns near Beijing where the Chinese had to take extraordinary measures prior to the Olympics to reduce the visible contamination in the air. They did a good job of clearing the air in the short time they took.

Natural Gas

There is an abundance of natural gas in North America, but it is a non-renewable resource, the formation of which takes thousands and possibly millions of years. Therefore, understanding the availability of our supply of natural gas is important as we increase our use of this fossil fuel. This is especially important since it is the cleanest and can provide a clean crossover to renewable energy when oil is gone. This would hopefully truncate the use of coal and its very high contamination of the atmosphere.

As you read through my thoughts on energy you will see that I believe we should consider natural gas as the 'crossover' energy while we are installing renewable energy. The reason is rather simple; natural gas emits approximately fifty percent less carbon dioxide than coal and the pipe lines are already in place and in use so that decision is easy to make. Gas plants are also a well-known and well controlled source of energy with proven reliability. With these things going for it as a starter, the use of natural gas to heat water to steam in standard turbine generators that generate electricity results in and increase in efficiency that is about twice that of coal. Time and again with earthquakes occurring in California either the electrical power is on or the natural gas is on. It's rare that both go out during an earthquake. This is an example of its reliability and its cost is always less than that of electricity when used in residential heating of water, clothes driers, and home heating.. As the world strives to replace the fossil fuels with renewable energy this one fossil fuel can help carry us over the threshold. Present forecasts indicate that there is enough for one hundred years and that perhaps farther exploration can extend that time span. The renewable energy supplies we will be discussing are in some cases erratic in their continuous source of supply and need to be supplemented by something that is 'almost acceptable as natural gas is

Natural gas usage in Europe

The natural gas usage in Europe is projected to double between 2004 and 2037. This is a good indicator of the acceptability of this fossil fuel at the same time as there is a drive to rid their selves of fossil fuels. I present this with "tongue in cheek" so to speak since I have already indicated that there is a drive to build more coal plants. The present indicators of the use of natural gas in the United States are that it will grow by only about 25 percent over that same time frame. This is probably because of the large amount of coal that the U.S. has or it may be that there is a belief that the United States is in better position to supply renewable energy in a greater amount than Europe. Sometimes it depends on the overall area of a country and especially the overall open area, both of which the United States is in better shape than Europe and other countries; or its because no one in the U.S. has made the decision to use natural gas as the crossover energy as we pursue the renewable goals. One of my goals in writing this book is to provide our country at least my insight to the issues on energy. I am sure they are coming from all directions, but in this book I at least try to cover each of the possibilities. I have not seen this overview to be available to the general public of this country or any other country.

Although Europe will increase their demand for natural gas over the next twenty nine years the increase is not due to their own discoveries of new natural gas reserves. They intend to import much of their natural gas as their reserves dwindle. One must consider that the European economy has been using natural gas for many years and have depleted the fields found in that area of the world. It seems that much of the natural gas to be found will be found in large countries that are not heavily populated such as Russia and maybe places like Greenland, the Artic and the Antarctic. With Europe's domestic gas resources in decline, the region will become increasingly reliant on imports; there are several new pipelines in the works to deliver gas from Russia to the continent. It should come as little surprise that Germany is the largest customer for Russian gas and among the most import-dependent countries in the world. Germany seems to be ahead of most countries in its projections. They are probably projecting the loss of oil as I am in this book. Seems they are taking every avenue they can to bring in energy whether it be natural gas, coal, and oil while at the same time pushing hard on renewable energy.

To make matters worse, if Germany does decide to go ahead with the shutdown of its nuclear plants, gas import reliance will soar even more, as will emissions of carbon dioxide. Nuclear power accounts for around 27 percent of Germany's electricity supply and 19.5 percent of grid capacity. There's no way all that capacity can be replaced by alternatives without causing side issues such as contamination of the atmosphere since most of the alternatives contaminate more than nuclear.

Germany's current plan seems to be a phase out of its plants offset by an expansion of gas-fired power and, to a limited extent, alternatives. But Germany's main supplier of gas, Russia, is planning to greatly ramp up its reliance on nuclear power in order to free up more natural gas for export to the Europe. In an upcoming issue of *The Energy Letter*, I'll take a closer look at these key political relationships. There is one very important consideration that I must make; which is that we cannot consider the natural gas as the solution for the loss of oil or as a substitute for coal. We can consider it a cross-over energy source until the renewables reach a level of solution.

Overuse of natural gas will only cause an issue as great as the loss of oil if we overuse it.

As natural gas is essentially irreplaceable (at least with current technology), it is important to have an idea of how much natural gas is left in the ground for us to use. However, this becomes complicated by the fact that no one really knows exactly how much natural gas exists until it is extracted. Measuring natural gas in the ground is no easy job, and it involves a great deal of inference and estimation. With new technologies, these estimates are becoming more and more reliable; however, they are still subject to revision. As the ice melts on the poles there is investigation into the availability of natural gas from these areas that were too difficult to pursue with the large ice caps.

A common misconception about natural gas is that we are running out, and quickly. However, this couldn't be further from the truth. Many people believe that price spikes, seen in the 1970's, and more recently in the winter of 2000, indicate that we are running out of natural gas. The two aforementioned periods of high prices were not caused by waning natural gas resources - rather, there were other forces at work in the marketplace. In fact, there is a vast amount of natural gas estimated to still be in the ground. In order to understand exactly what these estimates mean, and their importance, it is useful first to learn a bit of industry terminology for the different types of estimates.

The EIA provides a classification system for natural gas resources.

U.S. Natural Gas Resource Estimates

There are a myriad of different industry participants that formulate their own estimates regarding natural gas supplies, such as production companies, independent geologists, the government, and environmental groups, to name a few. While this leads to a wealth of information, it also leads to a number of difficulties. Each estimate is based on a different set of assumptions, completed with different tools, and even referred to with different language. It is thus difficult to get a definitive answer to the question of how much natural gas exists. In addition, since these are all essentially educated guesses as to the amount of natural gas in the earth, there are constant revisions being made. New technology for finding large concentrations of natural gas keep improving and allowing more sites to be found. As I mentioned, the melting of the ice caps opens an area to be investigated. This new methods combined with increased knowledge of particular areas and reservoirs indicate different levels of estimates and the levels are in constant flux. Further complicating the scenario is the fact that there are no universally accepted definitions for describing the amounts. Different terminology is used by the scientists, engineers, bioscientists, and the various countries involved in the natural gas market.

Most of the natural gas that is found in North America is concentrated in relatively distinct geographical areas, or basins. Given this distribution of natural gas deposits, those states which are located on top of a major basin have the highest level of natural gas reserves. As can be seen from the map below, U.S. natural gas reserves are very concentrated around Texas and the Gulf of Mexico.

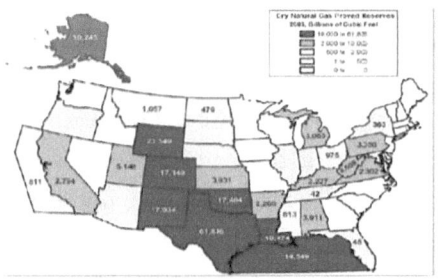

Dry Natural Gas Proved Reserves by Area - 2006
Source: EIA - Office of Oil and Gas

This map gives a general impression of where most of the proved natural gas resources are in the United States. Visit the EIA for more in-depth analysis into natural gas reserves across the country and to access geographical natural gas data. (48)

World Natural Gas Reserves

The EIA, in conjunction with the Oil and Gas Journal and World Oil publications, estimates world proved natural gas reserves to be around 5,210.8 Tcf. As can be seen from the graph, most of these reserves are located in the Middle East with 1,836.2 Tcf, or 34 percent of the world total, and Europe and the Former U.S.S.R. with 2158.7, or 42 percent of total world reserves. The United States, by this calculation, possesses 3 percent of the world's total natural gas reserves. (49)

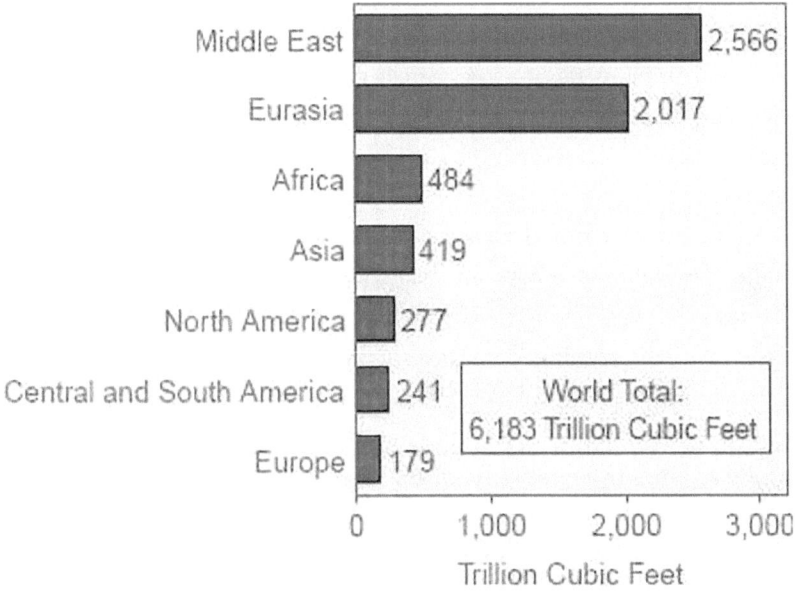

(49)

World Natural Gas Reserves by Region - Dec 2006
Source: Oil & Gas Journal 2006

World Energy Use Projected to Grow 57 Percent Between 2004 to 2030

World marketed energy consumption is projected to grow by 57 percent between 2004 and 2030, and I had only projected about a thirty percent increase in my calculations for the energy to be used in the year 2037. According to the reference case projection from the International Energy Outlook 2007 (IEO2007) (50) released today by the **Energy Information Administration** (EIA); the IEO2007 shows, "the most rapid growth in energy demand for nations outside the Organization for Economic Cooperation and Development (OECD), especially in non-OECD Asia, where strong projected economic growth drives Global energy demand grows despite the relatively high world oil and natural gas prices in the reference case." However, rising oil prices dampen growth in demand for petroleum and other liquids fuels as we have witnessed during 2008. This dampening of oil growth due to price per barrel can only go so far in reducing the demand for oil. At some point the demand has to fall back on the energy that is available and in this case it will be oil. What this increase in the cost of the use of oil does is accelerate the growth of the renewable energy sources. Therefore, some good many come from the petroleum suppliers raising their prices for a barrel of oil. We shall see. I will review the buildup of the renewable energy sources and one can take some solace in the fact that there is a buildup in a broad area of these renewables.

If anyone one thinks that political considerations over the security of supplies, environmental concerns related to global warming and sustainability will move the world's energy consumption away from fossil fuels, they have another thought coming. I believe this is a naïve look at the situation and understanding how the real world works. There are really no countries that have moved away from any of the fossil fuels to date as a result of any projection of global warming. If anything there are more coal plants being built now than probably any time in the last fifty years. This is because its an economical issue and that beats all other considerations. We are talking about an economical issue here and no one is going to shut down their growth that is needed for the growth in population and the growth in economical competition. The concept of peak oil shows that we have used about half of the available petroleum resources, and predicts a decrease of production in about seven to ten years. This is when the peak supply will occur. Some of the peak is not because of lack of oil but lack of refineries. There are not going to be many huge dollar amounts expended to add refineries if they believe there is a limit to the supply of oil. Refineries are expensive to build and in our United States businesses do not make rash decisions on adding capacity on something that has a limited life; at least that is my experience in the years I spent in industry.

A government led move away from fossil fuels would most likely create economic pressure in the countries concerned. Some countries are taking action as a result of the Kyoto Protocol, and further steps in this direction are proposed. For example, the European Commission has proposed that the energy policy of the European Union should set a binding target of increasing the level of renewable energy in the EU's overall mix from less than 7% today to 20% by 2020. (49) As good as this is, it must grow even faster to cover the loss of oil by 2037. Again, I believe that most of these projections are made by people that are naïve on the subject of energy and how long it will last with the fossil fuels. Many people believe that when oil is gone they will shift to coal. This may be a wild dream that will not come true because of various problems with supplying coal to the proper areas of the world on time for a cross over from oil. The transportation world has been set up for oil and it will be hard to reproduce with other means of energy supply.

Denmark and Germany have started to make investments in solar energy, despite their unfavorable geographic locations. Germany is now the largest consumer of photovoltaic cells in the world. Denmark and Germany have installed 3 GW and 17 GW of wind power respectively. In 2005, wind generated 18.5% of all the electricity in Denmark. (51) Brazil invests in ethanol production from sugar cane which is now a significant part of the transportation fuel in that country. Starting in 1965, France made large investments in nuclear power and to this date three quarters of its electricity comes from nuclear reactors. France is probably realistic and sees that they don't have the natural resources for renewable energy and are not in a good position for solar energy, they therefore made a conscious decision to go to nuclear. Switzerland is planning to cut its energy consumption by more than half to become a 2000-watt society by 2050 and the United Kingdom is working towards a zero energy building standard for all new housing by 2016. I don't think they will get there. In 2005, the Swedish government announced the oil phase-out in Sweden with the intention to become the first country to break its dependence on fossil fuel by 2020. I would not take this as a fact yet. Time will tell.

In the twenty first century, some of these different energy paths might become more main stream and start replacing the ubiquitous fossil fuels. It should be noted that between 1950 and 1984, as the Green Revolution transformed agriculture around the globe, world grain production increased by 250%. The energy for the Green Revolution was provided by fossil fuels in the form of fertilizers (natural gas), pesticides (oil), and hydrocarbon fueled irrigation. The derivatives from oil are throughout the world. Our roads, our farms, our chemical derivatives come from oil and this is only a small list of the plenty. Remember, with the loss of oil, these will not be available in the near future to help bolster production of vegetation through the use of fertilizers and control of pests through the use of pesticides unless some other suitable materials are found that do not use oil and its derivatives.

Renewable Solutions

Now that you have a good background on the fossil energies and the small amount of renewable energy used over the forty years from 1965 to 2005, we will now review the various drives to increase the renewable energy sources. There has been a dramatic pick up in the world to find additional supplies of these renewable energies. There are many long term and short term solutions to solve the loss of the fossil energies, especially the losses of oil, diesel, and gasoline that will be taking place over this century. Finding a solution to the portable fuels is being pressed, but this is a difficult task for a solution. It probably require invention as you will see. To date, the only solution that is seen to be reliable is to replace these fossil fuels with renewable energy from the Sun's supply that is lost or ill used. However, most renewable energy cannot be used portably as gas and diesel are, but all renewable energy is happily accepted since they provide alternatives. There are also other problems to be solved and they relate to how to provide any alternative energy worldwide. There must be solutions to the logistics of supplying whatever is available to other parts of the world that may not be as fortunate. But solutions to the logistics cannot precede the finding since each renewable energy requires a different solution. These solutions must be considered in concert with any findings by all countries. Some countries are prime candidates for certain renewable energy substitutions that other countries are not able to supply. As you will see this will cause a problem that I call dislocations. As we review these different sources of energy I will bring to your attention which countries may be prime candidates for a given type of energy potential. Although the most critical short term problems relate to solving the replacement for oil and its derivatives, we must also solve the problem for replacing the longer term energy of natural gas and coal with renewable energy. This is a longer term goal.

Of the fossil fuels, the one that is least invasive with placing carbon dioxide or other contaminants into the atmosphere is natural gas. For comparison, a combined cycle gas-fired power plant emits some 400 g/kWh (grams per kilowatt hour) and a coal-fired power plant 915 g/kWh and with carbon capture and storage some 200 g/kWh. Only nuclear power and wind are better than natural gas powered, emitting 6-25 g/kWh and 11 g/kWh respectively. There is also an advantage of natural gas over coal for providing the steam in large generators that supply electricity. The efficiency of natural gas is almost double that of coal for this application. As I progress through the renewable energy sources I almost consider natural gas as one of the "renewable sources" since it can be converted to liquid gas and be used in some vehicles as fuel to bridge our society over the hurdle as oil becomes more difficult to obtain.

Priorities

Therefore the emphasis will be to first replace oil as our number one priority because of its short term existence and then to replace coal because of its high carbon dioxide contamination of the atmosphere. **We can live with natural gas to supplement the drive to add renewable energy as a cross-over fuel** until it is deemed necessary to eventually replace the natural gas. This would seem to be a long term venture, but we must keep in mind that as the use of natural gas increases due to the demise of oil that the life time of natural gas will be truncated severely. There are no free lunches in the battle for energy and energy solutions. They are difficult battles to be won and there is always a side issue caused by a solution. Solutions like everything else have the good side and the bad side. We can only work toward the good side and then find solutions for the bad side. A perfect example that comes to mind was the placing of the catalytic converters in cars to eliminate the bad exhausts. This solution worked, but then we began to realize that this increased the exhaust of carbon dioxide from the automobiles. At the time we didn't feel concerned until someone started to say that an increase in temperature was being, or would begin to be, the cause of a climate change that they called global warming. Now we have to find out whether there is such an animal as 'global warming' caused by carbon dioxide, or if this is just another of the climate cycles Earth goes through.

Unlike the fossil fuels which are eventually depleted, renewable resources are available each year. A simple comparison is a coal mine and a forest. While the forest could be depleted, if managed properly it represents a continuous supply of trees and their biomass energy; versus the coal mine which, once it has been exhausted, is gone. Most of earth's available energy resources are renewable resources that are provided directly or indirectly from the Sun's energy. Renewable resources account for more than 93 percent of total U.S. energy reserves if I consider nuclear energy as renewable. I consider nuclear as a renewable source since the available energy from this source is sufficient to outlast the life of Earth. As we review the renewable sources of energy I believe you will see what is being done to bring these resources aboard and what the eventual capacity of these energy resources could be.

Energy neutral

Unlike replacing the portable energy function of oil, we will probably be able to handle the other functions of the loss of oil, such as for the heating of homes and the providing of electricity for all its functions through the use of renewables. You will witness the solutions to these problems. The world is in for a crash of some sort. This crash alone would reduce the problem of Earth's temperature rising if it is due to our use of oil and gasoline in automobiles and other machinery. With limited oil in several years, the amount used per day will remain constant for several years and then decrease beginning in twenty or so years and eliminate any problems that may be associated with a temperature rise due to the carbon dioxide generated via the use of oil and its derivatives, only to find coal is the next major contamination problem and a bigger one.

I would estimate that the use of oil will peak in about ten years. It is not because of demand, but because the ability to discover enough to meet the world's demands will self limit the world's use. Any global warming would be a "handled" problem by an act of nature in this scenario. Of course, some of the substitutes for the oil are dirtier than oil products and we might have to worry about their related pollution problems. It is better to have pollution problems to worry about that can be solved versus not having the transportation fuels that allow enough food to provide for the people of the world.

Limiting the atmospheric pollution

The more immediate problem for the world is to find other means of providing energy from renewable sources and their freedom from atmospheric pollution. In parallel we must continue to work on the pollution problems that can arrive due to the use of coal at a greater rate. Methods must be developed to reduce the carbon released through the added use of coal for our energy needs. Using coal in a liquid form will help somewhat. Progress is already being made on the capture of carbon that is being generated as discussed earlier in this book. Much progress is occurring and will continue to occur in this area.

One scenario would be to develop enough renewable energy by the time oil and its derivatives phase out to mitigate the need for coal to supply the energy lost by the lost of oil. With this scenario we would have renewable energy that is equal to the oil energy as well as not having to increase the use of coal to provide the world's need. If we can come close to that target we may be able to use natural gas and its cleaner approach to provide our remaining needs rather than relying on coal for this energy.

Energy neutral

Meanwhile we keep working on developing the renewable energy with a target to not ever have to increase the world's use of coal. **Let's call this energy neutral.** The energy use of oil in 2004 was 5.6 X 10^{12} watts or 5.6 million megawatts. Let's review the renewable energy sources and see how we can develop this amount of energy. Maybe to make it easy to calculate we will use millions of megawatts since they seem to rate all the sources of energy on the daily power of megawatts used in the world. To get to energy neutral – that is, replace all the MW of oil used with MW of renewable power, we need to get to 5.6 million of these megawatts just to replace what was being consumed in the year 2004. I would project that this will reach at least 10.0 million megawatt equivalents for oil by the year 2037 and that must be our minimum goal. As I review the various renewable energy sources and their megawatt output, I will keep an ongoing total to see how well we do against gaining 10 million of them and, where we fall short, what are other opportunities we might be missing. Let's see how close we can come to **Energy Neutral**. Keep in mind that this just replaces the energy required to replace the oil but doesn't yet overcome any increase in the use of coal, so with 10 million MW we will need to keep increasing to keep the coal use down.

Before we go any further it is important to get a handle on how this daily use of oil energy compares with the energy of people and their consumption of food. With 2000 Calories being consumed on average by the people in the world each day and there being 6.7 billion people on Earth, the daily consumption of food energy is 13.4 x 10^{12} Calories per day or 4.9 x 10^{15} Calories per year.

Remember that it takes about ten times this amount of Calories to keep the meat supply required for the world's consumption of meat in their diet.

This then totals 4.9×10^{16} Calories per year for the support of man's diet. This is a number that is almost the same energy that is derived from oil in the year of 2004 of 4.3×10^{16} Calories. This means the people of the world and their food consumption has equaled the energy output of all the oil energy used each day. I have estimated the population growth will be to 8.7 billion people by the year 2037. This will require 6.36×10^{16} Calories per year in the year 2037 and this will keep pace with the amount of energy needed to be supplied to replace oil that year. The two numbers have no direct meaning, but they show that as the population grows the food demand by people grows accordingly and this energy must be supplied by the Sun's energy and must be transported around the world with renewable energy to keep pace with the population growth.

Sooner or later this becomes an insurmountable task. By this I mean, the population can not just keep increasing because we run out of something in the meantime–food, or fuel, or energy means of handling all the issues that arise with a growing population. If global warming is real and caused by carbon dioxide or some other component, I believe it will be due to the increase in population. People generate significant carbon dioxide and they provide a constant temperature of 98.6 degrees walking around Fahrenheit for each one of them. As the population increases both of these phenomenon increase. This added temperature walking around on Earth can't go without some problematic issue.

All this energy to support man was supplied by the sun through photosynthesis. Remember the first crisis I covered in this book was the temperature cycling or global warming and I indicated it might be the number of people in the world that is causing a rise in today's temperature rather than from any carbon dioxide increase in the atmosphere. This is another indicator that this may be the culprit, if there is a culprit since I don't believe that there is global warming but just the normal climate cycling that Earth goes through every few hundred years. But, just in case I am proven wrong, this looks at the people as the major consumers of the world's energy, directly or indirectly. People consume food energy at the same rate as the present day oil energy supplies.

We then must look ahead and assume there will be 8.7 billion people in the world by the year 2037 or earlier. With 8.7 billion people we can assume this will require approximately thirty percent more food energy than the baseline of 2004 discussed. If we use 2000 Calories per person and 8.7 billion people we will consume and burn off 17.4 million megaCalories just by the people. If we continue to increase the number of animals to feed these people they will use up about ten times as much energy. Since I see the use of oil peaking in the next seven to ten years and then falling off to almost zero in thirty to fifty years, the energy dissipated by people and the food to support them will be much higher than the energy of oil. This will be much higher than the energy supplied by oil in the year 2037. The Sun's daily energy supplied for photosynthesis is 828 teraCalories (828 million megaCalories). This equates to 3,466,008 million Megawatts, or about 50 times the amount consumed by people but only about five times the amount consumed by people and the domesticated animals used for meat.

If we use **biofuels** to replace gasoline, this is the extra Sun energy needed to supply those plants that are used for biofuels. But we must keep in mind that there is much greenery in the world besides what people and animals eat. There is an interesting statistic I read recently that will give you an idea of how much greenery has not been touched by man. The statistic was that Africa has 28% of its land that has never been utilized by man and the United States has thirty eight percent of its land that has not been exploited. That's an amazing amount of land when you consider the amount of land that has been exploited by we humans in the United States. There is an interesting point of balance to be considered about all of this; the more people the more carbon dioxide and the more available for photosynthesis. The more plants there are, the more oxygen they provide for the extra people and animals on Earth by the year 2037. So, maybe the more plants for biofuel, the more the carbon dioxide is eliminated in the atmosphere and the more oxygen generated, but that's only if we grow extra plants to provide biofuel and food. **We wonder where all the carbon is going. Look at the large increase in people and animals on Earth over the last 150 years. People and animals are carbon walking around. So, while the carbon dioxide in the atmosphere has increased by 33%, the number of people has increased by 13.4 times the carbon dioxide increase. This is where all the carbon is coming from but no one can explain where its going since the atmosphere hasn't shown a big increase.**

Review of oil and its derivatives and determine which renewable should be prioritized

Now that I have base lined you on the energy of our fossil fuels, we have to review the renewable energies and compare them to the fossil fuels energies that will be replaced. Let's look at a barrel of oil and its derivatives. This seems like a good place to start and from this start we will review the various renewable sources of energy and their chances of replacing oil and its capability of being portable. This will be the first review of the renewable energy sources. I start here because I believe the loss of oil and its portability is the most critical crisis of the crises that we will have in this century.

Crisis IV -
The first priority is finding a replacement for the portability of oil

First, let's look at a barrel of oil and what is derived from it. See figure #14 below:

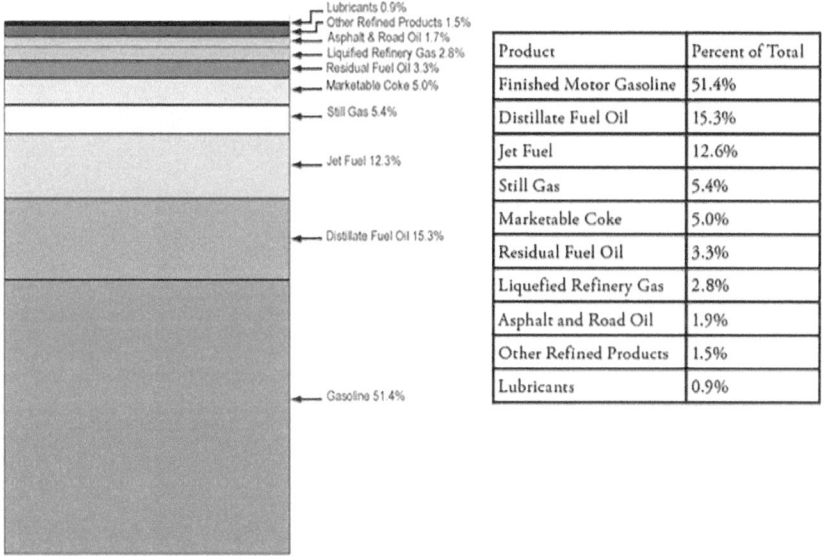

Product	Percent of Total
Finished Motor Gasoline	51.4%
Distillate Fuel Oil	15.3%
Jet Fuel	12.6%
Still Gas	5.4%
Marketable Coke	5.0%
Residual Fuel Oil	3.3%
Liquefied Refinery Gas	2.8%
Asphalt and Road Oil	1.9%
Other Refined Products	1.5%
Lubricants	0.9%

One barrel contains 42 gallons of crude oil. The total volume of products made from crude oil based origins is 48.43 gallons on average - 6.43 gallons greater than the original 42 gallons of crude oil. "This represents a "processing gain" due to the additional other petroleum products such as alkylates are added to the refining process to create the final products." (52)

"Additionally, California gasoline contains approximately 5.7 percent by volume of ethanol, a non-petroleum-based additive that brings the total processing gain to 7.59 gallons (or 49.59 total gallons)."

Source: California Energy Commission, Fuels Office, PIIRA database. Based on 2004 data. (52)

Commission Homepage | Site Index | Search Site | Glossary | Links | Contact Us
Page Updated: 07/19/2005 10:05:02 Unavailable

Here we have a barrel of oil and the various energy substances we achieve with this barrel of oil. It's interesting to see that you gain more than 42 gallons of gas from a barrel, especially in California where there are additives that bring the total up

Let's line up the renewables as we will be reviewing them.

1. Biofuels.
2. Hydrogen
3. Windmill farms
4. Hydroelectric energy
5. Solar energy
6. Water wave and surf energy
7. Nuclear
8. Geothermal

(1) Biofuels; the first of the renewable energies to be reviewed; a replacement for gasoline and diesel

Some believe that biofuels derived from various plants such as corn and sugar will be able to **replace the gasoline and diesel derivatives of oil.** These are called Biofuels. There are other energy masses that also can be converted to biofuels and we will review them also. At this point in history Brazil is converting much of its sugar to biofuels and using it in place of gasoline. They have converted their automobiles to be able to handle this fuel and seem to be successful so far. Meanwhile, in the United States, corn has been used to provide biofuels. A large portion of vehicles built over the last five to ten years in the United States are capable of running on biofuels at some percentage; for example many cars are able to run on gasoline with ten percent biofuel. There are many diesel cars that can run on biodiesel of certain percentages. Many of them can run on one hundred percent biodiesel. I think biofuels will not replace oil for worldwide use. In fact there are many strikes against it. I see it being a minor contributor in this function, but a very necessary one. There will be a time in this century where biofuels will be the only portable energy besides the oil products. I list below the reasons why I don't believe biofuels will be the replacement for oil and gasoline.

Biofuels as the nearest thing to replacing the portable energy of gasoline and diesel fuels

Without oil we have no positive substitute for gasoline and its portable qualities. The use of Biofuels has been suggested and has made some progress here in the United States and countries like Brazil have put their sugar crops to the use of biofuels. In the Midwest parts of the U.S. there has been a drive toward using corn to provide biofuels. In Europe where there are many diesel vehicles there is a better chance of using biofuels since diesel engines are able to run on many plant derivatives. I have reviewed the possibility of the use of biofuels to replace gasoline in cars and other vehicles. There may be some help in alleviating the shortage of oil and reduce the severity in the short run, however I see many problems in this use for gasoline. There is a better chance with biodiesel having a positive impact on vehicle travel. The problems I see are:

1. They do not put out the energy of a gallon of gasoline for the same size and weight. It's a little over half the energy capability of gasoline. In addition, notice in the chart above that there are other uses for the oil derivatives such as diesel fuel, jet fuel, lubricants, and the list goes on. This must be supplied by Biofuels or any substitute for oil. I don't see this as being an adequate solution but our scientists are great at using resources for inventing new things and perhaps this will apply in the use of biofuels. The chance in Europe is better since they have so many diesel vehicles and biodiesel is easier to produce. Keep in mind that if the world decided to go to diesel automobiles that it would take twenty years or more to make an impact on the auto industry because

of the large number of gasoline vehicles in the world and the amount of time it would take to produce large numbers of diesel automobiles and impact the world economy.

2. To date, producing biofuels in quantity requires sugar cane plants or corn plants in high volume above the demand for food for biofuels to replace gasoline at any large quantity. This is in conflict with our needs for food in the world. There are not many countries that have an abundance of either of these entities. I will cover the needs of food as a separate crisis in a later section of this book. Of these two uses of food plants the sugar biofuel is the better choice since it generates more energy per unit volume than corn sources.

3. The world presently use about 100 million barrels of oil per day and this will probably increase to a peak of 150 million barrels a day within ten to fifteen years. With the Biofuels capability of 50% of the energy of gasoline we would have to produce approximately 250 to 300 million **barrels a day** of these Biofuels by the year 2037 to replace the oil. There are estimates that a couple hundred million **gallons** a day of biofuel will be produced in thirty years. We talk about increasing the output "in gallons" per year rather than barrels used per year of oil. We should be talking about replacing the oil in barrels where there are 42 gallons per barrel to replace. When we arrive in gallons to the worlds needed supply in "barrels" we will be off by a large factor since this will supply about 2.4% of what is needed. This is a pittance of what is required. Of course some of the oil each day is not used for transportation, but transportation takes up about eighty percent of the use of oil and its derivatives. I don't see where the world can supply a ten percent of this with biofuels let alone the total amount while feeding the people of the world; maybe **only five percent if things fall into place.**

4. With no portable source of energy such as gasoline, I don't see how we can run the huge machinery used for growing food on the big farms in the Midwest, Florida, and California or anywhere else in the world. I don't see the Biofuels supplying the energy to run these large pieces of farm machinery while supplying the food needs of man. This is a major conflict that is fundamental. It's hard to conceive of running the large agricultural equipment with fuel that is derived from the food these machines are trying to generate. It appears to be counter-productive,

sometimes called "an oxymoron". I will discuss possible substitutes for running this big equipment.

5. Without the proper high energy fuel used for airplanes I see the possibility that there will be no airplanes flying after the year 2037; at least no jets. Jet fuel is of a higher energy and we may not be able to obtain it from Biofuels. The Biofuels would be too heavy in most cases and limit the cargo for the planes since one would have to use about twice as much of this fuel. Some of the Biofuels are **too corrosive for use in Jets**. This would mean that we would have to develop special engines for biofuels. While this is feasible, it takes many years to develop this capability in volume, along with the inventory of spare parts that need to be carried. Today's commercial aircraft are very reliable, but still require many expensive engine and mainframe checks to ensure this reliability. One would be concerned about the use of biofuels without much data for their reliability in the engines, the engines lifetime, and the amount of maintenance required.

6. With several of the points listed there would be a conflict between growing crops for food or for fuel. This conflict would become enormous if we were to allow the population to reach levels around 8.7 billion people by the year 2037. We need to take some steps to control population growth. I will discuss this as one of the crises of the 21st century. The addition of two billion people in the next thirty years sort of defeats the purpose of generating these biofuels from food sources. Some biofuel will be generated from wood chips and other discardible material. There is talk about supplying the biofuels using wood chips found in the southeast from years of lumber cuttings. I calculated all the wood chips they are talking about and it may supply several million gallons of biofuel and this would be a drop in the bucket of the worldly needs.

7. You have read about the energy needed to supply man his food including the plants and animals. As the population increases and this demand goes up, it is in conflict with the energy needed to produce the food and to transport it around the world as we do today. This would be especially taxing when one takes into account that there may not be enough fuel to fly airplanes while delivering the food that is produced all over the world today plus the amount for the population growth. There is a conflict between food, population, and transportation due

to the issue on gasoline. **Transportation will be under siege** with the elimination of oil and oil derivatives. This supply-demand criteria creates a logistic problem that I will cover.

8. We would have to develop an alternate fuel to provide the energy for equipment used to produce food and to transport it around. This would require the development of different equipment capable of using this biofuel energy source. The development of equipment for handling these requirements would take years to develop and produce in quantity; and be available to the entire world's people. If we could start now it might be possible. The problem with starting now is that we do not know which of the biofuels will be the mainstays. This will take time to determine and we don't have time.

9. We need to develop other sources of electricity and convert all the heavy equipment to all electric vehicles. Local atomic power plants situated close to the large farm lands such as the Midwest could supply electricity to the large earth moving equipment and their high demand of power. Special means of transmitting this electricity to these big pieces of equipment will need to be developed. Maybe we need the equivalent of large extension cords? I believe ac electricity can be supplied to moving vehicles by the same means of using 'slip rings' such as those that supply ac electricity to motors that continue to spin in the same direction like they are on dc..

10. We have to develop something I will call 'oil two' for the lack of another phrase (Oil II). This oil II (which we haven't found yet) would require the equipment to be designed to utilize it and be efficient. I doubt oil II would be capable of supplying the needs for flying jet planes. However, if oil II were developed it probably would require different equipment to use it and this would have to be in volume production near term.

11. I had a suggestion in the book "Beyond Global Warming" that we should find a way to capture the Ultraviolet rays that are making it through the hole in our atmosphere and hitting Antarctica. These rays have a thousand times more energy than the rays of sunshine. Perhaps we can harness this energy. Better still, if we could somehow establish vehicles that could hover in the part of the stratosphere where the ozone layer is located and capture half of the ultraviolet energy that strikes that ozone layer each day and find a way to wirelessly transfer that energy to earth, we wouldn't ever have to worry about running out

of energy. This probably shouldn't be listed with biofuels and probably should be listed with solar energy.

12. Biofuel derived from corn or sugar would seem to **deplete the soil** at a rate that would not allow it to be used for fear of not being able to use the land for food. This conflict seems to be a real one. Earth's soil can be overused to the point where we won't produce either the food or the fuel. This really needs a great deal of study before the people trying to make money off of Biofuel truncates the ability to provide the nutrients to the land. Presently most fertilizers are derived from oil. Depletion of soil is a real issue and it takes energy to provide the nutrients to replace loss nutrients in the soil. It seems we are going around in a circle on this subject since the nutrients need energy to produce them.

13. It's not clear yet whether the use of Biofuels will really result in a decrease in the production of carbon dioxide. I have read several reports that when you take all the steps into account the generation of Biofuels result in a greater amount of carbon being produced. So, from that standpoint, the only reason to push for Biofuels is to have a viable replacement for gasoline and other oil derivatives. If carbon dioxide really does affect the climate, then this is going in the wrong direction. However, if biofuels are able to replace oil then they take priority over the concern of how much carbon dioxide is generated. Solve one problem at a time. The solution for CO_2 may be near.

14. I have read articles by important sources that the U.S. is driving toward producing 35 billion gallons of Biofuels by the year 2020. 35 billion gallons is less than 1 Billion barrels a year and by 2020 the world's use of oil will be 55 billion barrels a year. So, this means we will produce less than 2% of the world's demand for oil energy, while depleting our farms soil and possibly reducing the amount of food being grown; at a time when the population will probably approach 8.7 billion people. Keep in mind that biofuel is about 50% the capability of oil; therefore this would amount to approximately 1% of the replacement value. The math doesn't work out well. Meanwhile, there are not many countries in the world that have the climates to grow large amounts of corn and sugar to produce Biofuels. I would guess if the world sources progressed as fast as the U.S.; by the year 2020 the world will produce a total of 2% of what's needed. Two billion barrel equivalents, at 6.1×10^9 joules per barrel of oil, equals **0.4 million megawatts of established power**

of the 10 - 20 million megawatts of power that may be needed by the year 2020. We probably should double the need by the year 2037 to 40.0 million megawatts of power since this energy is a variable which I will discuss later.

15. It is estimated that an acre of the proper land would produce approximately 1000 gallons of ethanol per year. Thirty five billion gallons of ethanol would require 35 million acres of land to produce the 1% level that the U.S. is setting their sights on by 2020. If the world matches these it would need another 35 million acres of arable land. That's a lot of land for producing 2% of the world's needs, while remaining as a viable supplier of food as well. Keep in mind that the biggest growth in population and the use of energy will be China and India. Neither of these have much arable land. This is a huge problem.

16. There is a problem with transporting ethanol or ethanol and gasoline mixtures and the Biofuels cannot use the present pipelines set up for gasoline or oil transport. There is a problem with water in the present lines that would cause the ethanol to separate out into two phases for the mix. It may be possible to eventually use the lines if no petroleum were in the lines. This may be the case in the future, but not now. At this time a completely new infrastructure would be required for Ethanol/Gasoline mixes, and Ethanol itself. A decision would have to be made by locale as to whether use the lines for oil or biofuels. There is no way that we will be able to shut off the pipes for gasoline and turn them all into pipes for carrying biofuels over a short time period. At best this will take significant planning and significant time in phasing in the biofuels.

17. There would be problems with using ethanol in airplanes and in colder climates of the world. Ethanol has a lower vapor pressure which would cause it to be difficult at best to ignite in cold climates. Airplanes used in the winter in the Eastern part of the U.S. would have a problem as would countries like Canada, Europe's countries and Russia and the countries that used to make up the Soviet Union. There are also problems with viscosity versus temperature which could affect the use in certain climates and/or vehicles.

18. Based on these various problems, I believe we will run out of oil in 2037 and it doesn't look like we will be able to replace 10% of it with Biofuels. We better start looking for a better source of power.

19. And here's the big kicker. We can see immediately that biofuels cannot handle the energy required. The total energy given to the plants by the sun each day is 8.64×10^{18} watts or 2.06×10^{15} Calories. The total energy derived from oil each day is 1.17×10^{15} Calories in 2006 and growing. Oil was therefore supplying about the same amount of energy per day as the sun supplied for photosynthesis. We would have to use almost all the energy required by the plants to supply the biofuel that replaces the gasoline. Of course not all the energy derived from oil is used for gasoline so we would be able to use some biofuels and help the portable picture on energy. Keep in mind that the conversion from plants to a biofuel requires energy. So by the time you are converting plants to biofuel you are using up all the energy the sun supplies for food. Eating is more fundamental than the other uses of energy..

20. Keep in mind that I used the amount of energy in joules and Calories stated for the year 2001. From this I derived the energy for photosynthesis based on the estimate in 2001 of 0.023 percent of the Suns energy being used for this. But I don't believe this is fundamental. I believe the more plants the greater the use of the Sun's energy for photosynthesis and less for other functions. I mentioned in the section on global climates that I believed that the combination of plants, people consuming them, the increase in the number of people and therefore the extra consumption will result on more of Sun's energy being kept on Earth and not being re-radiated out to space. This form of storage of the Sun's energy is an increase in Earth's energy and is probably the reason for an increase in Earth's temperature. The Sun puts out its energy and how much is consumed by plants is determined by the amount of plants that take in this energy. It is possible if we increase the amount of plants to support the use of plants for biofuels than the extra plants may suck up additional Calories and the above numbers will increase for photosynthesis and increase for biofuels.

21. World production of biofuel increased by 8% in 2005 to reach 33 billion litres (8.72 billion US gallons), with most of the increase in the United States, bringing its level to the levels of consumption in Brazil. Biofuel for use in diesel fuel increased by 85% to 3.9 billion litres (1.03 billion US gallons), making it the fastest growing renewable energy source in 2005. Over 50% is produced in Germany (53).

22. Biofuels from plant materials convert energy that was originally captured from solar energy via photosynthesis. A comparison of conversion efficiency from solar to usable energy (taking into account the whole energy budgets) shows that photovoltaics are 100 times more efficient than corn ethanol (54) and 10 times more efficient than the best biofuel.

23. Biodiesel. There is some hope for biodiesel which has been used in Europe for several years. In most cases the biodiesel is mixed with fossil diesel with a 20% mixture and is called B20. Recently there was a trial flight of an airplane from England to France using just straight biodiesel. The plane completed the flight but I don't know the results which would require the condition of the engine of the plane after the flight. Biodiesel is more popular in Europe because they have more diesel cars than any other country. There is concern about using biodiesel in airplanes because of its higher viscosity and inability to take low temperatures where it can jel and sieze up the engine. Experiments are ongoing to lower the temperature this material can be used. This is one hope for flight after the year 2037 and the end of fossil diesel. If the problems can be resolved we may see flights of diesel airplanes powered by biodiesel. The one problem with biodiesel is the shortage of it. Using it over from restaurants doesn't supplyi enough. Crops grown just for this fuel will not grow a consiserable amount at this point. Soy crops would be ideal but this will reduce the crops of food for humans and animals. There a good chance that once there is a shortage of standard fossil diesel and the price goes up that more biodiesel will be used. I wouldn't expect this before the year 2015 since the fossil diesel will be able to supply the needs till then and the price will not allow the growth of the biodiesel market till after 2015 is my opinion.

24. Economics And then there's the economics of all this. Many of the midwestern states started to generate biofuel from corn several years back. Then in the last couple of years as the price of oil increased this looked like a good time to generate more biofuels. Several things occurred; the price of corn went up as the price of oil went up. The people generating the biofuels looked like they were riding a winner and began producing more. But this whole scenario caused the price of corn for food to go up and people that depended on it for nurishment found that they couldn't afford it. The price of oil peaked to $150 a

barrel in about the first or second quarter of 2008. Then there was an economic disaster related to bank loans, house mortagages causing people to lose their homes and the price of oil started to drop. Recently it was down below sixty seven dollars a barrel. This drop caused corn to drop in price and the price of biofuel dropped. One of the biggest suppliers of biofuel and located in South Dakota, VeraSun, declared bankruptcy. This gives you a feeling of the battles that biofuels will have to fight. Unless this source of fuel is partially financed by the U.S. government, its possible that this form of energy will not get off the ground. The projections for the growth of biofuels as the one renewable energy that could provide propulsion for the world's equipment were never based on this kind of scenario. It was a clear blue sky look at an opportunity, but it forgot it had to battle the world's biggest energy supplier – the oil countries, the OPEC nations. This looks like it could be a continuous battle and fairly fragile balance of energy power for the years to come. It won't be a waltz.

Let's review Brazil and its energy sources since it is a leading producer and user of biofuels

Brazil has made great progress in the use of biofuels and this has resulted in a renewed look at how they should use their biomass. The growing demand for efficient and competitive biofuels to replace expensive gasoline and other oil derivatives has resulted in a great move in two directions. Besides the use of biofuels for use in vehicles and other portable energy requirements Brazil has an ambitious plan to focus the future of electricity generation in Brazil more on biomass. In this case biomass is any material that can be burned (such as paper and wood) or converted into a biofuel falls under the general category of biomass.

Sugarcane ethanol production yields a very large mass of waste, called bagasse, which is used to (co-)generate electricity. An initial step in the bio-electricity vision was the recent auction of 7,800 MW of biopower: more than 118 sugarcane factories capable of generating excess green electricity ready to be fed into the national grid, registered to participate.

According to the National Energy Evaluation, the current situation looks as follows: "ethanol and pulp accounted for 16 % of Brazil's total energy output in 2007, up from 14.5% the previous year. Hydroelectric power remained essentially stable at 14.7%, down 0.1 percentage points from 2006. Oil and derivatives retained the top spot with 36.7% of output, down from the 2006 level of 37.8%. Bioenergy has thus become Brazil's second largest primary energy source." (55):

"Overall, the Brazilian demand for all forms of energy grew 5.9% in 2007, totaling 239.4 million tons of oil equivalent, while he rate of growth for energy increased by 5.4%." (55) This is the "good news, bad news" sort of situation. It is important that the growth of energy sources increase greater than the growth of the population, but the bad news is it is that the demand keeps up with this growth. This just means that more and more energy is needed as the population grows. It is more important that the energy growth is greater than the population growth and the energy demand. This is a plus plus situation. This is not only important for Brazil but the world in general. As the oil is depleted and the renewables come on to supply the lost energy of the oil, it is very important that the total demand is less than the sum of whatever oil energy is available plus the renewable energy. This is a fundamental requirement.

Brazil's sustainable energy mix might hold the future for many African countries. (And perhaps the United States which has more virgin land than Africa) Not less than 25 countries there have a very large land and agroecological resource base that allows for the production of highly efficient energy crops, like sugarcane or sorghum as well as biomass in general. The present use of biomass is the main source of energy for some of the countries from time beginning. This is a potential for fuel replacement for vehicles while providing electricity for home and industrial use.

Brazil: sugarcane bioenergy bypasses hydroelectric power as primary energy source

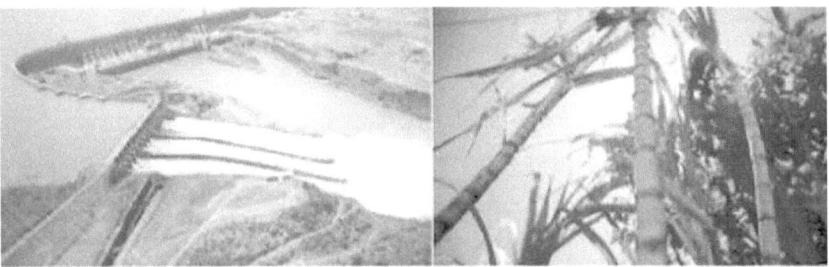

According to preliminary data from Brazil's annual National Energy Balance report produced by EPE (Empresa de Pesquisa Energética), "sugarcane ethanol and bagasse used for bioenergy became Brazil's second largest primary source of energy in 2007, bypassing the contribution of hydroelectric power." This doesn't mean that the hydroelectric supply or demand went down. It may have stayed constant with the previous period, but the total demand increased and much was supplied by bioenergy. So while the hydropower remained constant its percentage decreased. This will be the normal pattern around the world. Take Canada as an example. As great as Canada's use of hydroelectricity remains, as other forms of energy come on to use, the percentage of the hydroelectric will go down unless there are programs to increase the hydroelectricity as well.

Brazil is one of the fortunate countries that are near the border of the equator and as such has huge jungle growths and the growth of domestic products by producers using the huge vegetation that is available there. In addition, Brazil has the huge water source provided by the Amazon River and other natural waterfalls to provide natures form of energy. They are perfectly situated to apply the bioenergy with their jungle type forestry. Brazil is the fifth largest country in the world but has a population that doesn't meet that high level. It therefore has plenty of unoccupied land which is full of plants of wild growth. This is a country made for the expansion of bioenergy. "Bioenergy has become Brazil's fastest growing renewable energy source and is already generating more power than all non-oil fossil fuel sources combined. As a whole, the country now generates 46.4% of its energy from renewables." This compares very favorably with the primary energy mix of OECD countries, where renewables account for a mere 5.2%. Of course most of those countries do not have these natural resources of vegetation and hydropower. This is what

I call **displacement energy**; meaning the normal sources of energy will not be the big suppliers in the future but will be displaced by countries like Brazil with a different form of energy. The Mid Eastern countries will have a reverse problem as the oil supply lessens. They will be displaced.

Brazil is known for its large hydropower infrastructures, with more than 600 dams built on the country's many rivers. The largest dam, the Itaipu, has an installed capacity of 14,000 MW and provides some 20% of Brazil's electricity needs. However, erratic rainfall patterns over the past few years, combined with the fact that almost all large rivers have been dammed, have limited the prospects for any new large hydroelectric power projects. This is not an unusual result as we shall see as we review hydroelectric power generation later in this book. There were many countries that built dams and installed hydroelectric capability when the 20th century began and it was realized that electricity could be supplied via this method. Labor was cheap, water was available, and the installation of power stations using standard equipment developed at that time by companies like Westinghouse and General Electric was available. It was recognized that this was the way to go. Now a hundred years later, there are not many new places available for this type of power. China is the one remaining big country that has not saturated their natural resources relative to the use of hydroelectric energy, but it is on its way.

This covers the main contributors to biofuels in enough detail for the reader to gain somewhat of a grasp for the subject. It is obvious that in special cases this would provide a replacement for gasoline as it does in Brazil. Brazil is one place where it is working. It might be possible that the Hawaiian Islands might be a place where sugar could be used to provide the fuel just for use by these islands. As it stands now, oil is brought to the islands via tankers and when this oil becomes scarce sugar biofuel might be the way to go for the islands. Planning would be required to determine if the islands can provide the sugar they presently supply for the use in food and still be able to supply their energy needs with additional planning. It is interesting that when the sugar harvesting season is over in Hawaii that they burn the remaining vegetation to make the land ready for the following years of crops. It is possible that this should be rethought and instead of burning the stocks they should be used as biomass for the production of biofuel. There is significant land available in the Hawaiian Islands and there is enough of it that is arable. Many crops that use to be grown in Hawaii became too expensive to grow because of the lack of labor that was affordable. It may pay to review this situation. I have a home in Maui and would welcome the generation of electricity by biomass instead of expensive oil. Maui has installed a limited amount of windmills in their hills to assess their ability to supply energy. What is learned from that will provide some answers.

Alternative renewable Fuels to replace portable energy requirements

- Using biodiesel in a conventional diesel engine substantially reduces emissions of unburned hydrocarbons, carbon monoxide, sulfates, polycyclic aromatic hydrocarbons, nitrated polycyclic aromatic hydrocarbons, and particulate matter. This may induce private concerns to develop more pieces of equipment that work off of diesel. In addition:
- Biodiesel can be used at 100% levels or mixed in any proportion with No. 2 diesel or No. 1 diesel.
    - ° Contains no nitrogen or aromatics
    - ° Typically contains less than 15 ppm sulfur - Does not contribute to sulfur dioxide emissions
    - ° Has characteristically low carbon monoxide, particulate, soot and hydrocarbon emissions
    - ° Contains 11% oxygen by weight
    - ° Has the highest energy content (BTUs) of any alternative fuel (unless hydrogen fuel cells come into use) and is comparable to No. 1 diesel.
- Over 4,000 electric vehicles are operating throughout the United States (with the largest number in California and the western United States). This market is just beginning to come out of the woodwork. We shall see an increase in production each year but it is fairly insignificant compared to gas and diesel vehicles.
- More than 20,000 flexible-fuel vehicles are in operation. Still a pittance.
- Over 75,000 natural gas vehicles in U.S. and nearly 1 million worldwide. Mainly in large vehicles like buses that can carry around the heavy cylinders.

What's beyond biofuels to replace the portability of oil and its derivatives

Hydrogen

Hydrogen is a little farther out in time but it might be the key to resolving the portable energy loss of gasoline, diesel, and biofuels in the farther out future.

Hydrogen production and use

The use of hydrogen to provide fuel has been demonstrated as far back as the beginning of the nineteenth century. Of course the discovery that the Sun produces its energy from hydrogen was also an important finding that didn't happen till the early part of the twentieth century. The development of the atomic bomb and hydrogen bombs provided additional knowledge.

The projection of the production of hydrogen energy sources increases rapidly after 2030 and may play a role in relieving the possible shortage of energy with the loss of sufficient oil supplies. It is expected or hypothesized (by guess more than anything) that a method will be forthcoming and the world will reach significant quantities of energy supplied via the use of hydrogen but this depends on invention. There are even projections in Europe of how much energy will be supplied by Hydrogen in the middle of this century (later part of the middle). Scientists have been so vain as to actually place quantities for the amount to be supplied by year even though at this time not knowing how it will be accomplished. I assume they are just using "learning curve" methods to predict this. This is quite a teaser since with an inexpensive way to produce hydrogen electrically there will not be energy problems for many millenniums. However, I believe these are very optimistic projections.

If we can follow the example presented about Europe and its supply of hydrogen then we must believe that the problem will be solved here in the United States also. If this is the case, this book I am writing is worthless, since I am writing it to present the problems I see with supplying energy using a substitute for oil and its derivatives. Of course I only make that statement for effect. Even if today there were a means found for hydrogen to be provided as a fuel it would take many years to provide it. There would be an enormous amount of time for vehicles to be converted and for safety methods to be established. But there is no hydrogen today and it looks like it is fairly far off, but no one can predict invention. So, we keep looking. If there is a convenient and inexpensive way of producing and using hydrogen safely, then there will be no energy problem in the last half of this century. Maybe this book will provide an incentive to those brilliant scientists or bright people to come up with an ideal method of producing hydrogen without any carbon and with a method that is safe. Keep in mind that when something as volatile as hydrogen is present and used in great quantities there is always the enemy of this country that will try to get to its destructive power and cause destruction. At this time the methods conceived and used produce a great deal of carbon and the method that must be developed must be free of carbon and any health issues.

The free use of hydrogen would not only correct the energy situation, but it also would relieve the problems with global warming – if they are truly caused by water vapor, methane, or carbon dioxide. There will be many cheers for hydrogen!

The world must keep in mind the problems I spell out for logistics in all these energy subject matter. Oil, because of the huge quantities in specific locations in the world, allowed an infrastructure to be built up over many years to provide this consumable item's benefits. Although the use of hydrogen is not stuck with many of the logistics of the other renewable energy methods, it still has many that must be realized early in the game. I believe the solution to the problem of generating energy through the use of hydrogen would be an enormous step to providing energy the world over. If all it takes is water, there is plenty of water all over the world; therefore a solution allows energy to be produced all over the world without many of the problems that will be associated with renewable energy. It relieves many of the problems that oil had with transporting its sacred energy. With water all over the world, the energy can be produced at the place of use. This eliminates many transportation issues. However, it does bring into play other issues such as the explosive nature of hydrogen. Everyone of age knows about the **Hindenburg** blowing up in the air over New Jersey. This essentially eliminated the dirigibles as a means of travel. There are other infrastructure issues that I foresee. For example, if we use up water to free up hydrogen, do we run in a problem with not enough water in the world for the plants, animals and people? Possibly a good thing would come out of this besides the energy relief. In separating the hydrogen from the H_2O we end up with O_2 and water as by-products. Will the generation of additional oxygen in the atmosphere provide a better balance between the plants and their supplying the ever increasing demand of animals and people for oxygen? Will it help to balance out the added carbon dioxide generated by the increase in animals and people by the year of 2037 or 2050 or later in the century?

Even though one of its byproducts is water, it is always less water than it began with, so water shortage could be a problem. Keep in mind that salt water is not useable and to desalinate salt water is expensive and takes energy. As the ever increasing population makes demands on the supply of water for the plants, animals, and people will we run up against this problem? Perhaps the water we use for the hydrogen will come from the salty oceans by some method and therefore will not consume the fresh water. This freeing would increase the salinity of the oceans, but probably not enough to be noticed for thousands of years.

And then we come up with one of the big bonuses that the freeing up of hydrogen promises. This is the use of a fuel cell to use for propelling our vehicles.

Fuel Cell

A **fuel cell** is an interesting device that has been around since it was invented in 1838. This invention was improved upon by several GE chemical engineers with several iterations. The cell is basically a chemical cell that coverts chemicals to electricity. A simple version would be one where water is reacted by electricity to provide hydrogen and oxygen. The hydrogen is driven into one side of the cell called the anode and the oxygen is driven into the other side called the cathode. The anode side with its hydrogen is broken down to protons and electrons (hydrogen has an electron in its orbit and a proton in its nucleus). The cell has a membrane between the anode and cathode that is in an electrolyte fluid. The design is such that the proton can move through the membrane but the electrons can't. The electrons are diverted to go around the membrane and flow through circuitry which constitutes an electrical current that the cell is now providing and the circuitry provides this energy to the load and terminates in the cathode side of the cell. This provides electrons to the cathode side where the oxygen had been initially injected and the protons that made it through the membrane now exist. This combination of oxygen, the protons that went through the membrane, the electrons which have terminated their flow on the cathode side, results in a reaction to form water. So, the by-product of the complete reaction, besides the supplying of electricity, is water – which is what was used to begin with, but less of it.

The key thing about a fuel cell as I have described is that it uses water which is the most abundant material on Earth and it ends up expelling water. The wondrous thing about this type of cell is that it will continue working as long as the hydrogen fuel is supplied. It is unlike a battery, in that, its anode and cathode remain intact almost infinitum, as does the electrolyte. Where I mentioned that oxygen is driven into the cathode side it can actually be air that is driven in the cathode side. So the reaction is one of the hydrogen fuel on the anode side and an oxidant on the cathode side with the membrane allowing the protons to make it to the cathode side where reactions are set up to provide water that is discarded. I have described a basic function. In fact there are several fuels that could be used and several oxidants that can be used. I wonder if we could take all the free ions that are in the ocean and use them to form a similar cell. The ions in the ocean are due to the salt which disassociates to form the free ions of Cl^- and Na^+. I wrote up what I thought was a unique way of using the ions to provide us energy but after some thought decided I had not carried the idea far enough to be practical. Maybe some bright person will come up with a way to use the free ions of the oceans.

Advantages

There are several advantages for the use of the hydrogen fuel cell:

1. Very clean with no contamination of the atmosphere.
2. Very small for a given application
3. Cells can be placed in parallel to provide more current
4. Cells can be placed in series (totem pole arrangement) to provide higher voltage output. A cell normally is 0.6V to 0.7V which is too low for most applications
5. No moving parts therefore as long as fuel is supplied the cell will continue to produce ad infinitum and not wear out.

6. The fuel could be in high supply and very low cost.

7. Hydrogen in its natural form could be used in vehicles with the hydrogen provided in a sealed tank and therefore it is considered the key to finding the replacement for gasoline or diesel. In this approach you don't use the water in the car. The hydrogen is separated remotely and only the hydrogen is supplied. In this type of fuel cell it may be possible to use the electrons to supply current to the load and the protons could be used to supply circuitry in the opposite direction.

There are several disadvantages:

1. The need to increase the efficiency. The cells are running around 30% efficiency and it is believed it needs to be over 50%

2. The current flow from the cell is limited to the rate that the fuel can be injected into the cell and the reactions to take place. Under low power conditions this is no problem. But under high current draw, or the requirement for higher voltage, the drain on the cell's power can exceed the capability of the cell and it begins to loss the ability to supply the power needed. It will go into shutdown.

3. The anode and cathode are metallic and coated with a catalyst such as platinum. The platinum is expensive and the overall cost of a fuel cell is expensive. To date the main use has been to supply power for space vehicles and some applications in hospitals. However, catalytic converters have this same problem and it is overcome by economy of scale where the large volume would result in new practical ways to produce these coatings and the volumes that follow allow for automation and cost reduction.

4. The reaction has to be controlled very accurately since the production of too much water on the cathode side can result in "drowning" the cell. On the other hand if the cathode side reactions cause heat and the water is evaporated too rapidly it leaves the cathode side short of the needed oxidants and the system shuts down.

5. Danger of hydrogen and explosion if not properly constructed and monitored.

6. The flow of current from within the cell to the external circuitry through ohmic resistance constitutes a voltage drop and the voltage

will continue to drop under these conditions. However, this is no different than standard electrical issues.

Hydrogen future

With all the good and bad associated with the fuel cell it would take only a few creative inventions and it is believed the good will far outweighs the bad. Based on previous scenarios of this type it is believed that focused work on the development of the fuel cells will solve the problems associated with it and that it will be the fuel of the future. The fact that it can be produced from fuel sources that make even the petroleum used to date look scant ensures that there will be a continuous financial backing of these programs. Estimates are presently being made that by 2050 five to ten percent of cars will be fuel cell energized. The growth after that is dramatic. When the fuel cell is made as a commodity item in the later parts of this century, fuel will no longer be an issue unless they don't produce the instant power required by airplanes. The issues will be safety issues and how do you replace a billion automobiles in the world with new cars with these capabilities. Also, there are other vehicles and mechanical issues that have to be resolved to use this method efficiently and safely.

The Real World for Hydrogen (My estimation)

I believe that Hydrogen fuel cells and other approaches with the use of Hydrogen as the energy fuel will come about but I don't believe it will impact the world as most people predict. Mainly, I disagree with the timing. I do assume there will be dramatic inventions that will prove hydrogen as the savior sometime in the near future, however if we assume that there is a major breakthrough as many predict and that hydrogen is a ten to twenty percent source of our energy by the year 2050 then I have to believe someone is smoking something. The reason I express this opinion is that it will take many years to build the infrastructure and many years to spread it around the world. If hydrogen cells were available by the year 2040 and were to be used in cars it would take twenty years to build the infrastructure for providing this energy for cars. Then it would take many more years for a large number of cars to be built that would provide much of an impact on transportation in the world. Let's assume that fuel cells for cars come about in 2040 and the world starts to build cars to use this technology. Let's assume that they build 5 million cars a year (which is optimistic). In twenty years there are 100 million hydrogen fueled cars in the world and 1.2 billion cars that run on electricity, gasoline, biofuel, or diesel. By the year 2060 there are 10 billion people on earth and 20 million hydrogen fueled cars. This represents approximately 0.2 percent of the total. This may be so insignificant that the hydrogen car is too expensive at this low a volume for any but the richest to afford. It also is so small a volume that one would have a hard time finding the fuel stations to provide the fuel for these cars. Keep in mind I am talking about transportation of the world's workers, the world's thinkers, the world's rich, and the world's travelers. At this rate the vehicle world is essentially stonewalled from hydrogen as the fuel for their vehicles. It's an inertia type of scenario where it takes considerable energy to get the thing moving. Once it's moving at a level that is sustainable and growing it will grow rapidly. However, it will require significant momentum to be built up to allow this technology to take off. It will begin with large size units that are not easy to handle like gasoline or biofuels but it will eventually be trimmed down to a size that is marketable. There must be private enterprises or governments that recognize the upside on this approach and then it will start by building up service centers for supplying hydrogen. The whole thing would be a lot easier to sell if the supplies didn't begin with hydrogen but with water and the unit itself provides the separation into hydrogen and oxygen. This would be a safer solution and would eliminate the need for service centers that are very elegant. The vehicles would take on water, provide the separation and then the fuel cell would take over. The problem with this approach is that it is heavier because it must carry water as he source of energy. This approach may be good in large vehicles like farm vehicles and buses and military vehicles. Eventually, this approach will spill out the advantages and the fuel cell will take off in automobiles and the portable energy problem will be solved. The automobiles will use this form of portable energy and the biofuels will supply the energy for the chainsaws, lawnmowers and that class of equipment.

Let's take another tack at this hydrogen fuel cell and its potential growth. I see a chance if the creative people of the world find a way to produce a hydrogen fuel cell that can be placed in the standard gasoline engine and eliminate the need for gasoline or diesel or biofuel. At that time maybe there are enough electrical cars that we can take away the batteries and replace them with this fuel cell. One pays their money and the present engine is torn out of the present cars and this hydrogen replacement is stuffed into it and – it works; or one takes the batteries out of the electrical car and replaces it with the hydrogen fuel cell and it works. It not only works but it is inexpensive to run. This would be a dramatic event and a major turnaround in the world's transportation plans. This being the case the whole scheme would now be limited by how many fuel cells can be built each year and retrofitted into the old car, plus how many service centers could be installed around the world to provide the proper infrastructure, plus the cost to the consumer. You can imagine how big a worldwide business this would represent.

If this were to happen and by the year 2040 this was put into affect it would take another twenty years to make it practical and by the year 2070 there might be 100 million converted cars around the world and then it would at least represent a start. One hundred million hydrogen fueled cars out of 1.2 billion cars would represent eight percent of the world's cars. Now that's enough to give a boost to this market and to have service centers located in certain areas of the world. What would probably happen is that these hydrogen fueled cars would be located in about twenty big cities around the world where it was practical and efficient to build the service centers for these cars. These cities would have to set up the proper safety procedures for handling these vehicles to ensure we don't have another Hindenburg or Chernobyl (Russia).

How about fuel cells for agriculture use?

Another scenario would be that it is decided diplomatically and worldwide that the fuel cells would first be used to outfit the large machines used to provide the food of the world. At this time, with this large a population, it is important that the soil moving, harvesting, and other large agriculture machinery is made available with the power to do these big chores. The concentration in this area would require a significant commitment towards providing large fuel cells with energy enough to provide these tasks. There are other industries that may take a priority along with the agriculture industry. In fact, if it is proven that carbon dioxide is the cause of global warming by that time there may be a move toward replacing all the huge machinery of the world with hydrogen fuel cell energy capability. This all depends on the evolution of the fuel cell to a point where it can supply ample fuel out of a reasonably sized cell to a large load such as the large earth movers in the Midwest. Remember I mentioned that the cells to date don't supply large amounts of power. There has been one 5 KW tractor of sorts built. But 5KW is only 6.7 horsepower; not enough to do any major chores other than in one's back yard. You now begin to see the mountain that has to be climbed to put the world in a position to use a hydrogen fuel cell or some other invention using hydrogen. It's not a panacea at this point in time. We know it works, we know it's clean; we know the fuel is ubiquitous, we know some of the problems, but we don't know when someone is going to solve the mystery. When it comes, add twenty or forty years to when it becomes a major factor in the world. At this point in time I would be optimistic to believe it will provide ten percent of the world's power by the end of this century

Liquefied Natural gas can be used for heating homes and if liquefied could be used for bus transportation and other heavy vehicles. However this source has been proven to be an enormous expense to run buses using this fuel. The replacement parts are expensive and hard to come by as experienced here in California. There are other problems with the liquefied natural gas that I will cover. Automobiles could use the Biofuel but there may not be enough to go around. Countries like the U.S.A. could probably make out because they have large areas for growing plants, but other countries would be put in a useless situation. **A good example is China which has four times the population of the United States but only one fifth the arable land. India falls in the same category and it is only one third the size of the United States with a population about four times the U.S.** Keep in mind that the continuous growing of corn and sugar will deplete the land and eventually it will be useless unless there is some means developed to rebuild the soil or rotate crops that help to regenerate the soil. The southern hemisphere would probably function well because of their lack of need for heating fuel and their water supplies are ample for many of the countries in South America but not in Africa and India. The biggest population growth is expected in these two countries and they will not be in a position to supply their food needs and water needs. These countries must take steps to control their population growth.

You now know what the real problem is, and its not global warming. Even if there is global warming we can find ways to overcome these problems over the next one hundred years. This elimination of our major source of portable fuel – oil/gasoline – is the name of the game, and finding a way of delivering the food we produce. The only thing that comes close to its portability and energy is Biofuels at present and I have discussed the problems with the biofuels, which I do not believe is the solution. It may be part of the solution when we combine the various methods for obtaining energy together and see how each contributes to the whole need. We must look at the whole possible supplies and see how they fit and how they combine to overcome the total problem of energy independence from fossil fuels.

Technology must find other sources. Keep in mind that the use of plants for this substitute takes us back to the energy supplied by the sun and photosynthesis. It seems that we always get back to the sun as well as to the plants when looking to supply the energy of man or the energy needed to exist. There is no magic. The sun along with water vapor, carbon dioxide and the resultant photosynthesis are the only means of providing useful energy without consuming other energy. We need to find how to harness more of this energy. At present the sun's energy is used to provide us the weather we enjoy, the water we need and the light for the photosynthesis that provides the animals and man the plants we eat for food and very little other uses of its energy.

Much of the sun's energy is sent right back into space. The problem is, if we find a way to keep some of that energy from going out to space, it means we use it here on earth and any extra use of the sun's energy will result in an imbalance from our present state and will cause the earth to heat up. We just can't take more natural energy on without creating another problem. We need to find a way of utilizing more of the sun's energy while ridding Earth of some unwanted energy. This is a possible task since most of our Sun's energy is not put to effective use by man.

World Energy target for the future.

Here we are in the year 2008 and I don't have the latest figures on energy but it is much higher than the world's energy consumption in 2004 when it was approximately 1.13×10^{17} Calories or an increase of approximately eleven percent over 2001.

Energy consumption broadly tracks with gross national product, although there is a significant difference between the consumption levels of the United States with 11.4 kW per person and Japan and Germany with 6 kW per person.

In developing countries such as India the per person energy use is closer to 0.7 kW. Bangladesh has the lowest consumption with 0.2 kW per person.

The US consumes 25% of the world's energy (with a share of global productivity at 22% and a share of the world population at 5%). The most significant growth of energy consumption is currently taking place in China, which has been growing at 5.5% per year over the last 25 years. Its population of 1.3 billion people is currently consuming energy at a rate of 1.6 kW per person.

I have projected that the Earth's population will reach 8.7 billion by the year 2037. As I have shown previously, people are the biggest users of energy in the world and if the population goes up by approximately thirty percent (30%), then it is reasonable to assume the world's use of energy will go up by at least 30%. However, there is a limit for the use of oil and its derivatives. The supply of oil will not increase by this amount over this time span. The use will peak in about eight years at a level and reach a plateau and will start decreasing sometime in early or mid 2020's unless new reserves are found. This will require an increase in the use of natural gas, coal and renewable energy. Natural gas is the cleanest of the fossil fuels and the supplies should be available to approximately one hundred years. We can live with that. However, the use of coal to replace oil may not be acceptable due to its contamination of the atmosphere. This leads to the ideal scenario of renewable energy and natural gas being the prime suppliers of energy growth and the hope that we can keep the use of coal to plateau until we find a truly acceptable renewable energy source that allows renewable energy and natural gas to be the total suppliers of energy. This is probably not a valid assumption since China and India, the world's two biggest population countries have grown substantially from an economical standpoint with China's energy demand approaching the use by the United States and may exceed it by the end of 2008. This will find China increasing its use of its natural resource of coal and more atmospheric contamination. If there truly is global warming as a result of carbon dioxide's increase in the atmosphere, we will have it in spades due to the increased use of coal. If we take these economic growths of these two countries as well as the growth of other underdeveloped countries the use of energy in 2037 will probably be near double that of 2005 and we are already in trouble in reaching the energy that must be supplied to the world, especially in renewable energy sources. With this thought in mind, the use in the year 2037 will probably require more than double and exceed 31 TW (2.3 x 1017 Calories) in the near future. So, as I review the various means of providing renewable power and its conversion to electricity, I will use this figure of 31 TW of electricity as the reference target. This 31 TW must be supplied by renewable energy, natural gas, and coal. I will review the various renewable energy sources and establish targets for each of them so that when combined we reach the figure of 31 TW (31 million megawatts) of electricity power. Since the world uses megawatts of installed power as their reference we will do the same and the 31 terawatts becomes 31 million megawatts. So, as I go through the various energies I will show them as megawatts and see where we need to increase the supply. In order to do this the one source of energy that doesn't fit this pattern is the use of biofuels which is like the supply of oil or gasoline.

With this energy target in mind let's review the possible scenario by the world suppliers of energy. Let's take the various contributions each could be making using the renewable energy sources. You will find that each country has major advantages for the various means of supplying energy and we then must see if these could be optimized to provide the optimum amount of power. This is a scenario that is international in nature. It is one where a plan must be established as to what energy/power will be supplied by each large contributor and how it all comes together to supply the world. As we go from an oil rich world to one where oil is no longer the major player, many things will change with some countries falling from the lead where they were the oil countries to other providing the lead with their natural resources, their creative planning, and their world wide cooperation in supplying a fundamental need.

We have covered **Biofuels** and will come back to them and determine the amount of energy that they are able to supply, assuming this is a viable source. We will now cover Wind sources, hydroelectric sources, Solar sources, Water wave sources, Geothermal sources, and nuclear sources.

These renewables will be the ones that provide energy for functions using electricity and are not ideal for use as a replacement for gasoline and diesel. There is a good probability they will provide electricity for automobiles and other vehicles that run on electricity.

Crisis V -
Understanding the renewable energy sources to replace functions that do not use gasoline or diesel

In order to be free of fossil fuels which contaminate the atmosphere we must find ways to increase the use of the biofuel power, hydrogen power, wind power, hydro electric power, solar power, water wave and tidal power, geothermal power and nuclear power.. I will cover these as we progress. Keep in mind that I want to reach **Energy Neutral** as a first priority to offset the loss of oil. In this case it would require replacing the portable oil energy listed above first and follow this up with a renewable energy that provides no contamination of the atmosphere, while supplying the functions in the world that require energy that is not in the form of gasoline or diesel.. After that we will determine what it takes to replace all the fossil fuels in the next one hundred years with renewable energy. Chart IX on renewables will be repeated below to remind you of the renewable energy status in 2006 which showed we used 2.0 million megawatts of renewable power. This chart shows the sources.

Figure 16 - Renewable energy, end of 2006 (41)

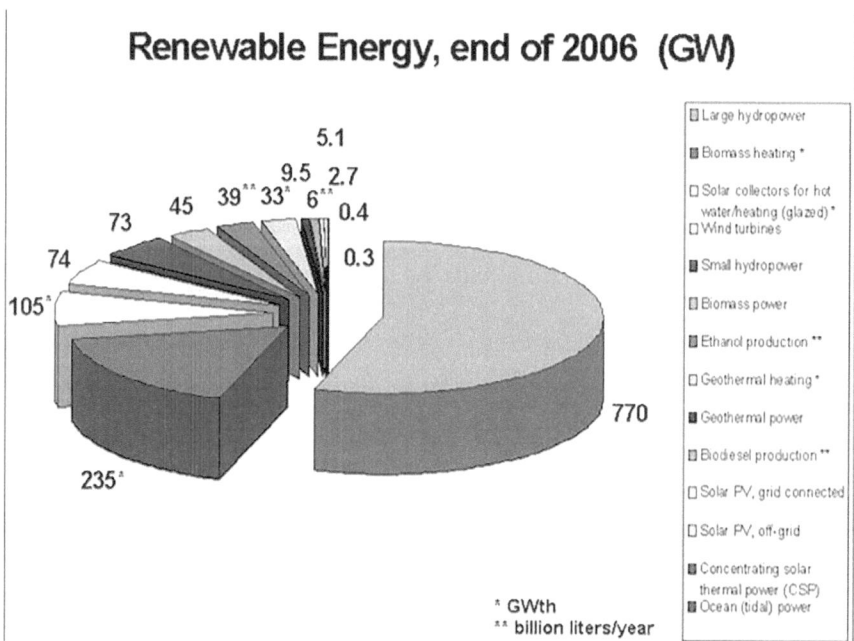

This chart doesn't include the nuclear power which I will consider a renewable energy in this book because of its vast amount of energy which should last the lifetime of Earth. The nuclear power use by the end of 2005 was 0.9 million megawatts. We need to make another 5.6 million megawatts of renewable power including any nuclear energy above the 0.9 million MW that will help to offset the 5.6 million MW of oil energy. By the year 2037; based on my calculations, we will be using the equivalent of 10 million megawatts of oil energy. This means with biofuels, hydroelectric, nuclear, solar, wind, geothermal, water energy and nuclear we need to increase these by 5.0 times the amount that we used in 2005. Let's see if we can do this. It will be difficult to reach the level of 10 million MW of energy supplied by renewable energy in the next twenty nine years. This will place an emphasis on increasing the use of Nuclear energy since we know this is a source we can rely on and even though the initial cost is expensive we would just have to make the decision to go that way. As we review the renewable fuels and how they will increase over the years we will find that the problem may be more difficult than just producing 10 million MW of renewable energy.

Because of the logistics I will cover, I believe we will have to provide a level over this 10 million MW. It is questionable at this time on how well we can use the Sun's energy to provide the other renewable energy in the short time we need to accomplish that task.

Why not use the Sun?

So, when all the fossil fuel is used up we have two inherently constant power; the Sun's contributions and that of the radioactive material inherent to Earth. The use of the radioactive material to provide nuclear energy power plants is obvious and I will cover this separately later in the book since it will serve as a makeup power to reach our goal.. So, let's look at how we can receive much more power than the 0.023 percent of the Sun's energy for photosynthesis and the food it brings and how it can provide additional captured energy to offset the loss of fossil fuels. Let's review again the amount of energy that comes from the sun and the amount we really put to use.

The amount of energy supplied to Earth by the Sun on a daily basis and its use is as follows:

Total energy	15 billion million **MW**	3.6×10^{18}	Calories
Water cycle Provides fresh water	3.45 billion million **MW**	8.28×10^{17}	Calories
Wind & Ocean Currents distribute	0.15 billion million **MW**	3.6×10^{16}	Calories
Warming the land and land water	6.3 billion million **MW**	1.512×10^{18}	Calories
Photosynthesis	3.45 million million **MW**	8.28×10^{14}	Calories

It is obvious that not much of the Sun's energy each day is used to provide the plants energy. We don't want to bother too much with the water cycle that provides us our drinking water. We might want to find ways to save it and use it for hydropower while it is making its rounds from ocean to clouds to precipitation and returning to the ocean. However, much has been done with the building of dams to provide hydropower and we are at the point of not seeing too many big new dams to provide significant hydropower. There has been a move toward micro hydropower generation and we will cover that.

The wind and ocean power is about fifty times greater than the Sun supplies for photosynthesis and provides us an opportunity to look at this energy for windmill farms. The big recipient of the Sun's energy is the Earth's land and water on land. Here's where we could pick up some huge increases in solar power, thermal power, and perhaps other means.

The amount of energy supplied by the sun to every square meter of our stratosphere is approximately 1350 watts per square meter (approximately 10.5 square feet). However, remember when we reviewed this and due to the spin of the Earth we get an average of about 350 watts per square meter at the equator and by the time the wind and ocean currents move the heat energy around we average between 250 and 200 watts per square meter depending on where we are located.

This ends up placing 3.6×10^{18} (a million trillion) Calories per day on Earth as a whole, as listed above or 15 billion million MW per day.

Keep in mind that only one thousandth of this energy is provided for photosynthesis. This means that only a small percentage of the Sun's energy is used each day to provide plant growth that provides food for all the people and animals in the world as well as supplying most of the forest's and tropical area's growth. If we had no fossil fuels to provide us our present earthborn energy, and no hydroelectric power, and no atomic power, and no solar power, and no wind power and no water wave power, then we would be receiving this rather small amount of the Sun's energy each day in the way of providing the food for the living creatures of the world. The only earthborn power we would possess would be that of the radioactive material born with Earth. This would be substantial if converted into nuclear power plants. But let's hold off the power plants till we can see what is to be gained by the other renewable sources.

But all renewable energy, except nuclear, hydrogen and geothermal, is provided by the sun.

The Sun does provide us power in other forms besides providing us food and the biofuels. This is called renewable energy or renewable power and is listed below:

1. There is solar power that can be picked up in solar cells and provide photovoltaic energy for man. This source of energy has a broad scope of use. It can be used domestically in homes with private owners paying for the systems with tax breaks. It also can be used in large industrial buildings and sites where a high percentage of the climate results in a large amount of sunshine and there is space for installation.

2. Solar thermal energy can be reflected from large mirrors and focused on water vessels to heat the water to steam and use the steam to provide energy for the turning of turbines for generating electricity. There is also solar thermal for heating water for home use.

3. There is wind energy that uses twenty percent of the Sun's daily energy that it provides Earth with wind and water currents and could be converted to wind energy for use by man. There is about 50 times more energy in the wind energy supplied by the Sun than that supplied for photosynthesis and man can capture a significant portion of this through the use of windmill farms.

4. There is hydroelectric power provided by the sun through the rains and the conversion to dams and waterfalls to provide us hydroelectric power. We could build more dams to supply us hydroelectric power. We might even make "man made" waterfalls to provide power. The use of large dams is under pressure by environmentalists because they result in the water eliminating certain fish and animals. Hydroelectric power at present supplies the same amount of energy as nuclear which is six percent for each or a total of twelve percent of the total energy of the world's use. This use of the Sun's energy is for water and water currents is a thousand times the energy of photosynthesis and about fifty times the energy used to create the winds.

5. There is water wave power provided by a combination of the Sun's wind and the spin of Earth. There is water tidal power due to the Sun's gravitational pull on Earth and the Moon's gravitation pull on Earth that cause the tides in the large water systems around the world. Each of these have a huge amount of energy.

6. There are biofuels which are produced from the plants on Earth. I have covered these under the **Crisis IV subject matter.** I will repeat them here as they may play other roles in the renewable energy picture. These are plants such as sugar and corn at present but there may be other biomass to provide a means of supplying biofuels. Going with

the strategy that natural gas could serve as a crossover fuel because of its lower contamination of the atmosphere. It may serve as part of the solution for fuel to replace the portable fuel of gasoline. Natural gas can be liquefied and used as a fuel until renewable sources are found. It is estimated that liquefied natural gas could replace approximately ten percent of portable fuel needs by the year 2037. Primary use would be in heavy vehicles such as buses, military vehicles and perhaps earth moving equipment in the Midwestern United States and other agricultural areas of the world.

7. Geothermal energy – this is energy derived from the earth; about 4 km to 20 km down in the earth. Some of it was supplied by the Sun but much of the geothermal energy is an earthborn energy since it was derived by the heat caused by compression from the gravitational pull toward the center of Earth (differentiation), by the molten outer core, or by radioactive material in the mantle of the Earth. Radioactive material has heated the internal parts of Earth since its initial existence. As you will learn there is considerable energy that could be acquired from this renewable source.

8. Nuclear power will be considered a renewable fuel even though it is finite in nature. It's such a large source of energy that it should outlast the life of Earth. It is also a non atmospheric contaminant and free of carbon dioxide generation. This is my opinion and this is how I handle nuclear power in this book.

9. Biomass – This is energy that was originally used in the world and is still used at many site of the world. This consists of burning wood and other natural materials to provide heat. It still is used to a great extent in countries that are undeveloped or underdeveloped.

Picking the winners

Assuming we have put pressure on supplying biofuels for the short term alleviation of the loss of gasoline and diesel for portable power, the next issue is to understand the various other renewable energy opportunities and picking the right ones. The picking of the right ones may be more a choice made by necessity brought on by what is available by country or by locales in the way of resources available for a given country or that covers many countries.

One of the key ingredients in the determination of choice, other than local resources is how to transport the energy to make it a world wide energy source. As you review the various renewables and where they are being used now, or will be available in the very near future, it will enlighten you on what's available and where. In order to provide it beyond a country's borders there has to be a universal method for this to happen. One obvious method would present itself if the energy was provided in electrical form. Many of the problems with supplying electricity world wide have been resolved. We have already covered biofuels and how they would be supplied. In this case it is to supply local electricity in automobiles and other remote pieces of equipment. We have discussed the eventual use of hydrogen and how it would be used to produce electricity. Now we will look at the following:

Wind and wind energies
Hydro electrical power
Solar power; photovoltaic and thermal
Water Power – tidal and wave
Geothermal power- from the center of the earth
Nuclear Power – I am assuming nuclear power as a renewable power because of its huge availability
Hydrogen power – fuel cells for the vehicles and perhaps for air flight
Another possibility is my personal suggested solution to renewable power which I will include.
Finally, the total power of the renewables by 2037.

Man's ingenuity must come to the rescue and convert the renewable energy to electricity

With the conflict of energy as described and the limitations on the use of biofuels to replace gasoline in automobiles and the length of time till we are able to use hydrogen power, we will have to find other means of developing energy. One plan would be to take all the means of supplying energy and converting it into electricity if in fact it isn't already derived in that state of energy. There will be means of supplying electricity for homes and natural gas for heating of homes when we analyze the various energy possibilities. We can even convert more of the natural gas to electricity if that becomes the obvious solution. We already have experienced that the use of natural gas in place of coal is almost twice as efficient as the use of coal, without the atmospheric contamination of coal. Therefore moving many of the large electrical generators in this direction would be a major savings in energy and a large reduction in contamination. At present natural gas is used to generate heat that turns the turbines of the world's large generators and supplies much of the world's power. However, even though it is more efficient than coal powered, natural gas conversion to electricity is a fairly inefficient process. We use about twice the fuel energy to heat the water to steam to turn the turbines and put out about half the energy in electricity. Perhaps we can find a way of making this more efficient for both coal and natural gas steam generation. It would save a significant amount of energy.

Electricity and the world's conversion

Electricity is not a direct generation of energy. Electricity is the conversion from one of the other forms of fossil energy or renewable energy to electricity which is a more fundamental means of supplying power around the world. Electricity is fundamental to solving the general problems to be discussed as we increase our renewable energy. It is in this form that most renewable energy will be supplied worldwide and in a format that is very efficient to transmit. It may not solve the loss of oil and its derivatives but that must be the goal. It may not solve the need for the portable power replacement for gasoline and diesel but a certain portion will. Many vehicles will be converted to electrical powering, while biofuels or some new approach will be directed to the replacement for gasoline and diesel for the portion that are not electrical and will help solve part of the transportation issues. That being said we shall direct our attention to using these other renewable energy sources to solving the non transportation problems. So, as I discuss the forms of generation of energy I will detail how it is converted into electricity. As we leave the 21st century most of the energy that is generated will be converted to electricity. This approach will allow us to solve some of the logistics which will be discussed.

Over the past four years, electricity consumption per capita in the U.S. has decreased about 1% per year between 2004 and 2008. Power consumption is projected to hit 4,333,631 million kilowatt hours by 2013, a growth of 1.93% over the next five years. Consumption increased from 3,715,949 in 2004 to an expected 3,937,879 million kilowatt hours per year in 2008; an increase of about 0.36% per year. U.S. population has been increasing about 1.3% per year, a total increase of about 6.7% over five years. (56) The decrease in general and per capita has been mostly due to efficiency increases. Some decrease in 2008 is due to higher prices for gasoline which may show even a bigger decrease versus the growth of population. Compact fluorescent bulbs, for example use about one third as much electricity as incandescents. LED bulbs, however, use about one tenth as much, and over their 50,000 to 100,000 hour lifetime are cheaper than compact fluorescents

There is one very important fundamental to keep in mind when we are covering electricity; if we were to be able to convert all the renewable energy sources to replace the electricity we presently use, it would not take care of supplying the electricity to offset the loss of other uses of gasoline and oil energy. There is one way of showing what I mean. The yearly consumption of electricity in the U.S. in 2001 was 1.34×10^{19} Joules. This equates to 3.2×10^{15} Calories. The yearly consumption of total energy in the U.S. in 2001 was 2.51×10^{16} Calories or approximately eight times the amount of energy used for electricity. **So, we would have to produce a factor of eight times as much electricity (or other forms of renewable energy) to support the total energy use in the United States if we were to replace all the fossil fuels.** I only use this as an example of what eventually would have to be provided when the world is out of all fossil energy forms in a future century..

Keep in mind that a significant amount of the electricity produced was not from oil but from natural gas and coal and this will continue for some time. Looking back on the chart of energy on page 78 where oil supplied 5.6 TW of power or 37% of the world's energy needs; these are the energy needs we would have to supply by renewable energy when oil is no longer available if the demand for oil remained the same as 2004. However, it is expected to increase to 150 to 200 percent of this level by 2037. Of course there won't be that much oil energy around then and the intention is to substitute with renewable energy. This I will call **Energy Neutral.** Energy neutral is when energy is supplied by renewable energy plus natural gas and coal energies and overcomes the loss of oil energy. At that point we at least pass the point of not needing oil and its derivatives. I hate to repeat this but this doesn't solve the transportation problem which stands alone. This brings another parameter into the equation; not only must we replace the energy of oil but also the ability of the transportation system to accept the form of energy that will take the place of oil and its derivatives. Cars and other vehicles must be able to run off electricity, biofuels, or some other developed source of energy. It's like the chicken and egg scenario – which comes first, the converted vehicles or the supply of the energy to power them? This takes advance notice and planning.

Review of renewable energy, not counting biofuels and hydrogen

(A)Wind energy; one of Mother Nature's renewable energy sources

Wind power is the fastest-growing energy source in the world. *(Worldwatch Institute).* **I disagree with this statement, but it does show the growth of wind energy is, and will be, great. As I review the various sources you will see that I believe the two solar methods of supplying electricity will grow faster than wind energy.**

- The wind in North Dakota alone could produce a third of America's electricity. *(The Official Earth Day Guide to Planet Repair) (56)* I believe this is an overstatement.
- Wind power has the potential to supply a large fraction--probably at least 20%--of U.S. electricity demand at an economical price.
- In 1990, California's wind power plants offset the emission of more than 2.5 billion pounds of carbon dioxide, and 15 million pounds of other pollutants that would have otherwise been produced. It is clean and can be inexpensive if available.
- Using 100 kWh of wind power each month is equivalent to: planting ½ acre of trees not driving 2,400 miles

These were the arguments for wind energy that have persisted in the U.S. since the late 80's and many countries in the world have increased their use of wind power. While there may not be ideal places to install windmill farms, why not the oceans? The oceans cover 78% of the planet and wind tends to blow stronger over open water because there are fewer obstructions. Of course this is a much more difficult area to establish windmill farms.

Windmill farms have an advantage over other renewable energy systems:

1. They generate no carbon dioxide or other environmental contaminants to the atmosphere.

2. They are rather inexpensive once in operation, being cost competitive with fossil fuel plants that run off of coal. This is a big plus.

3. Their present costs are between 5.5 and 8.0 cents per kilowatt hour based on inputs from FPL Energy builder from Texas and they are becoming more efficient with improved designs.

4. They cost more to construct than natural gas plants and coal burning plants, but they have no fuel costs, so as the years pass they reach levels that are very inexpensive. There are no transportation costs like those incurred with coal burning plants where the coal must be transported to the site. This is good news and bad news since it limits the use to the place of origin.

5. Their maintenance is believed to be much lower than the gas and coal burning systems.

6. In many cases they can be built where it is not practical to build other renewable energy plants or plants of other industrial types. Many other energy providing plants need facilities for providing water and providing sewers and systems for ridding their wastes. How about in the oceans? If oil rigs can be built there, why not wind mills?

7. Keep in mind that the power of the installations is what is designated when it comes to listing the windmill power. This is the power if the wind is blowing all the time. It isn't. A more definite rating would be how many megawatt hours of power were supplied by the windmills per year. There are limited places in the world where it would be feasible to install these systems. In many cases one or ten could be installed, but it is not normally economical to install a small windmill farm compared to the larger ones. For example Germany has more windmill farms than the United States but they don't produce the electricity that the U.S. windmills generate. This is because there is more wind where the U.S. windmills are located versus those locations of the German windmill farms.

8. Legendary oil man and wealthy industrialist T. Boone Pickens has an interesting plan. He believes we should free up all the natural gas supplying plants from their present duties of supplying homes with

natural gas or electricity from natural gas burning generators and divert this energy toward the energy of new fleets of trucks and government owned vehicles. Replace this application of natural gas with electricity supplied by windmill farms. This is a creative approach since the windmills electricity can not be supplied to vehicles but natural gas can be liquefied and used as fuel for buses and trucks and eventually cars. Pickens believes this will save the U.S. several hundred billion dollars a year in oil costs that we would defray using this approach. Of course Pickens has his hand in a company that supplies natural gas in this form and he recently purchased several hundred windmills from General Electric. This doesn't take away from the fact that it is an approach that I am looking for as I compare the various possible suppliers of energy.

There are several problems I envision with this conversion that I can see;

1. For one, although you get about the same energy value from liquefied natural gas and therefore can get equal miles per gallon out of this fluid on cars, the weight of the liquefied natural gas is much heavier due to the metal tanks that contain the fuel so they could only get half the fuel in the car and therefore the range would be cut in half.
2. This weight consideration will be a problem if we decide to use liquefied natural gas in cars or other means of transportation. This relegates its use to large vehicles like buses, trucks and heavy equipment.
3. There is another problem that is not obvious. Wind mills are located at remote places all over the world and their power is not easily obtainable to replace natural gas which is easily transported by pipelines that have been installed for years. There is what I call a "dislocation" when it comes to windmill farms and it is hard to amalgamate all these scattered windmills to replace a supply that is easily transported; even if by tanks for special cases.
4. If used in vehicles it requires a special infrastructure to provide the fuel easily and rapidly. The tankers that transport the supply to service stations will only be able to carry a limited amount due to weight.
5. Gasoline and diesel is stored at service stations in underground tanks. I believe liquid hydrogen tanks would take up much more room that gasoline and diesel storage. This will raise the cost.

6. It is inconvenient for the workers driving to work each day and for the suppliers delivering the tanks to the service stations.
7. Windmills supplying electricity to power generating stations would not be a good method due to the erratic nature of the windmill supplied electricity.

Windmills in the U.S. and Germany

Wind mills are being constructed in many places of the world. At this time Germany is probably the leader in installed wind energy, followed by the United States. However, the United States has produced more electricity from their installations due to better wind conditions in the U.S. locations. Meanwhile there has been high activity in the United States of installing more capacity. There have been a large number of windmills established in Texas and California and there continues to be activity in these states. There has been a big increase in the planning of windmills for the Midwestern parts of the United States. Germany has a larger installed capacity (57) than the United States but he U.S. has a greater amount of wind. At the end of 2007 Germany had established a capacity of 22,000 megawatts of windmills which could supply approximately 14.5 million homes if only used for domestic applications and assuming 1500 watts as the minimal amount a home could get along on. Of course if 2500 watts were required for each home then we are talking about 8.8 million homes. This is significant difference. Of course if it was used for industrial purposes it would not be very significant at this point in time, but like all good things, they take time. Germany plans to install about another1600 megawatts or is in the process of installing them which adds almost another ten percent to their power generation. If Germany keeps moving in this direction it would provide a significant amount of electricity to offset the loss of oil and gasoline.

These windmills must be established in places that have high winds and also be available space. Keep in mind that cities and agricultural areas are not candidates for windmills. High elevation land with access to wind and little use for agriculture or industry is ideal. Also, wind mills in the ocean could be a very acceptable place for installations. Germany is running out of places to establish additional windmill farms and has begun installations in the northern waters off Germany's shores. Ocean windmills have the direct wind and usually there is plenty of open ocean space to take advantage of their use. Germany is now reviewing the possibilities of installations in the North Sea and any other places that are available. It is probably more expensive to install windmills in the ocean and this must be taken into account. However, there are times when the cost considerations are of second priority since one needs power to function. No function is not an alternative and is the most expensive.

This year the United States is installing an additional 6,000 megawatts that will bring it past Germany and make the U.S. the largest installation of windmills. Keep in mind that installation is one thing but the more important consideration is the amount of power derived from them over a given time period. This relates to the efficiency. The installation power is what one would get out of the windmill under certain operating conditions. This depends on the wind at the location, the proper design for the wind at that location and the ability to produce at low wind velocity as well as under the design optimum condition. Evidently the designs in the U.S. and the wind conditions result in the higher output over a given time period. The U.S. has a better opportunity to find ideal locations since there is much open space in places like Texas and California where there are ideal winds available. Many companies outside the U.S. are courting us to install windmills here, including companies from Germany that have large manufactures that produce windmills. There are more companies in the business of installing windmills outside the U.S. than here and we need to take advantage of them, but probably more importantly, we need more U.S. companies involved in the business. This is a big business and will only grow over the years to come. It takes many windmills to put a dent in the energy demands of the world and here in the U.S. where we use twenty five percent of the world's energy, we should have numerous companies in this country involved.

With many businesses going out of the country, we need to take advantage of our technological skills and manufacturing skills in producing large windmills. We should have entrepreneurs providing start up companies in the U.S. to be the one supplying our country and other countries with this capability. General Electric is a major source in the U.S. for both the windmills and for any generators that go into windmills.

By the end of this year the US will have over 23,000 megawatts of installed windmill energy (with many supplied by international companies), but with a much higher output than the Germany installations due to the high winds. This would be enough to supply seven million homes if they were only used for domestic purposes. Keep in mind that the U.S. is much bigger than Germany and should be a leader in this field. (57)

China is growing in the establishment of windmill farms. They have a large amount of land that is *not* arable and ideal for this application. They are trying to reduce the air contamination in their country which is very high due to the high use of coal for supplying their energy needs.

Currently, windmills and their electrical generating capability will provide about one percent of the U.S. electricity. PG&E has 1,164 megawatts of wind energy in operation or under contract. A California company, Enxco is a windmill developer and manufacturer that believes California will be big in this technology and is vying for the installation of systems in the state and elsewhere. It is presently constructing a 150 megawatt system in Solano County of California near Rio Vista. (57) A system of this size is capable of supplying 35,000 to 45,000 homes. This is a city of several hundred thousand people. It is actively buying land in ideal locations for wind systems.

It is important to keep the target of energy required to replace oil's projected energy for the world in mind. The target of 20 million megawatts of power by the year 2037 is a huge number. Let's compare it to the amount we are presently talking about when we talk about Germany and the United States. Between them we might suggest they will have approximately 50,000 megawatts of energy supplied by windmill farms. This is rather small 50,000 divided by 20 million or 0.25 of one percent. So, you see how little we have scratched the surface of the energy needs to take the place of our present suppliers of energy. If Germany's and United States' wind farms consisted of one big windmill to represent each of their capacities (Which it isn't since each of these capacities are made up of multiple wind farms.), then we would have to produce approximately four hundred fifty times this amount of wind mills in the next 29 years. Of course, many countries are now beginning to ramp up their installations of windmill farms so it will be done on a mass country basis, but it is still a big chore. It can't be done and we will have to continue our quest of looking at other sources of power. The other problem I see is that this doesn't help reduce our dependence on fossil fuels. It just shifts the use around which might help for a certain length of time for transportation, however using this fuel for automobiles will reduce the time that natural gas will be available for use. We previously estimated that the use of natural gas will be around for about 100 years and will help supply homes for their heat as well as for electricity via the use of natural gas to heat water to provide energy for turning the blades of turbines.

Theoretically, wind could produce enough energy to meet global demand based on the fact that the Sun provides a significant amount of wind energy each and every day that is approximately fifty (50) times the amount used by photosynthesis to provide food. However, keep in mind that the energy supplied for wind by the sun has the oceans to cope with. They end up possessing a far greater amount of the wind energy than land does. In 2006, however, less than one percent of global electricity consumption came from wind. Why such an imbalance? There is not enough windmill farms and there is poor efficiency from those that are operating. Is the conversion of wind energy into a useful form, such as electricity, using wind turbines or are we doing something wrong? At the end of 2007, worldwide capacity of wind-powered generators was 94,100 MW (58). Although wind produces about 1% of world-wide electricity use, it accounts for approximately 19% of electricity production in Denmark, 9% in Spain and Portugal, and 6% in Germany and the Republic of Ireland (2007 data). Globally, wind power generation increased more than fivefold between 2000 and 2007 (59). Maybe I am looking at it too early in its history during this present build up of renewable power. It appears to have spurted up during the last few years and there are many plans on increasing this form of renewable energy wherever possible.

Most wind power is generated in the form of electricity. Large scale wind farms are connected to electrical grids. Individual turbines can provide electricity to isolated locations. In windmills, wind energy is used directly as mechanical energy for pumping water or grinding grain in many parts of the world. This is an effective way of using its energy. It need not be used in the electrical mode. It is just more difficult to account for these kinds of uses. Its obvious history that the land of Holland (or the Netherlands) used windmills to produce energy in forms other than electrical, and were very effective in its use at the time. Much of this occurred before electricity was discovered.

Wind energy is plentiful, renewable, widely distributed, clean, and reduces greenhouse gas emissions when it displaces fossil-fuel-derived electricity. Therefore, it is considered by experts to be more environmentally friendly than many other energy sources. The intermittency of wind seldom creates problems when using wind power to supply a low proportion of total demand. Where wind is to be used for a moderate fraction of demand, additional costs for compensation of intermittency are considered to be modest.

Global installed wind capacity in 2006 was around 74,000 MW, according to the World Wind Energy Association. This was more than one percent of global electricity consumption, but because installed capacity does not reflect actual production, its contributions to the global energy mix are less than that. Now we will compare this amount of windmill farm energy compared to our target of twenty million megawatts by the year 2037. It isn't even close to the target however we have to keep in mind that all the renewable power does not have to come from this one source. It is a contribution in the right direction that counts and then we add them up to determine how close we come. Of course, in the end, one doesn't have to add them up since they are either enough or not enough. As I previously mentioned, when big countries like China and India apply their resources in this direction it will be a big factor. The biggest technical problem is that wind energy cannot be produced just anywhere; average wind speeds must be good enough to make installing a turbine cost-effective. Germany, the world's largest wind energy producer, is already said to be approaching its potential for on-land wind production. As I indicated, they have installed many at sea and are now looking at the North Sea for farther installations. Investors feel that the requirements for windmills off shore are less difficult than the installation of oil rigs off shore.

The windmills do not have to have large equipment for drilling as the oil rigs do. The winds available off shore are higher than those on land and this should lead more installations in that direction. The countries in Europe are looking at big growth potential for offshore wind farms off the coasts of northern Europe and off the British Isles.

Windmill energy capacity is expected to more than double by 2010. Growth will be driven by rapidly developing countries, such as China and India. In terms of Megawatts, the biggest producers of wind energy are Germany, the United States, Spain, Portugal and India; together accounting for about 80 percent of global capacity. Norway produces the most wind energy per capita, and meets roughly 20 percent of its energy needs from wind energy. If Norway adds solar energy capacity to complement their windmill energy it will be approaching **Energy Neutral**. Keep in mind that other countries with rapidly growing wind power sectors include Canada, France, China, and the United Kingdom.

Keep in mind that we discussed Germany and its offshore windmill farms that are being planned in the North Sea and several other countries are reviewing the possible installation along their shores. Improving designs will improve the efficiency and there are improvements in the design of generators for use in windmill farms that will also result in reduced costs of turbine production. The competition among countries to supply these windmills will result in reduced costs to the customers. Windmill energy generation continues to drop in cost of megawatts supplied. Although the price may be competitive with fossil fuels, that is irrelevant since there will not be any fossil fuels to compete with these renewable energy supplies in the not too distant future. There will be no gasoline in the year 2037. It will be nice that the price will be better than that of gasoline by then, but gasoline will be gone. Let's face it, if the use of gasoline keeps following the present trend, there will be less and less of it to supply and the cost will go up and the price will go up. By the time 2037 rolls around the cost of gasoline will be out of sight. I wrote a book a couple of years ago when gasoline was about $1.50 per gallon and said that the price will go up as more of the oil supplying countries realize the obvious, that it is a scare entity with a high demand for it. Well, the price of gasoline has more than doubled since I wrote "Beyond Global Warming". It has been running $4.50 a gallon at many of the gas stations. It would seem that by the time the middle 20's are here that the price of a barrel of oil will be out of sight. It will probably be over one thousand dollars per barrel.

The price of producing utility-scale wind power have fallen by 90 percent in the last 20 years, and according to General Electric, the prices range between 3.5 and 4 cents per kilowatt hour, making wind competitive with the fossil fuels, nuclear energy, and natural gas energy. General Electric produces many of the generators that are installed in these windmill systems. With kind of pricing windmill farms will be installed wherever the location has the capability to meet the requirements.

The bad news

Sites convenient for wind power production are limited by factors such as land use for agriculture or living, distance to consumers, and technology. Experts from the Intergovernmental Panel on Climate Change estimate that only four to ten percent of given resources could be used economically. An entirely wind-powered economy is thus not yet possible. Global growth in wind power, however, is still tremendous. In 2005, markets grew by 41 percent. The value of new generating equipment installed in 2006 was about 18 billion euros or approximately twenty eight billion dollars. According to the Global Wind Energy Council, the installed capacity of wind power increased by 27% from the end of 2006 to the end of 2007 to total 94,100 MW, with over half the increase in the United States, Spain and China (60). Doubling of capacity took about three years. The total installed capacity is approximately three times that of the actual average power produced as the nominal capacity represents peak output; actual capacity is generally from 25-40% of the nominal capacity. (60) This is because the wind is not always blowing or is not blowing at optimum power output. Since the output varies there has to be ways to store the energy when it is peaking. This has not been an easy problem to resolve to the satisfaction of those countries involved.

The amount of wind energy generated depends mostly on the size, height, type, and location of a wind turbine. Some small turbines, such as those fixed on a sailboat, can generate as little as a few hundred watts - enough to power a few light bulbs. On the other side of the spectrum are the large, utility-scale turbines like the Vestas V90 that produces 3 MW. According to the manufacturer, these turbines produce in 2-3 hours the electricity that an average European family consumes in one year. The Enercon E126 turbines installed in Germany in late 2007 will produce 6MW each, making it the most powerful turbine on the market. Installation of more of this type will start to bite into the power needed, but that is easier stated than accomplished. Windmills have to be matched to the wind speeds it will be receiving. High speed winds are best served by large windmills with three large blades. However, these same windmills are not efficient when the wind is not blowing at rated speed. Windmills that are designed for lower wind velocity use windmills of a different design. They are shorter in structure and have more blades. These mills are efficient when located where the winds are not as powerful. These wind mills can be destructed under high wind conditions. So, what is the best wind mill for a given location? This is the type of questions that come up when these mills are considered for a given area. It is not enough to design and develop the highest megawatt generator since it may not be useful in many of the locations.

However, there is a very interesting discussion on the use of windmill farms in Germany that can prove to be a good example. Their installed capacity is worth noting, but as I mentioned the amount of power generated by the windmills depends on the true amount of wind that goes flying through these windmills. The installed capacity is lower in the U.S. but the wind is greater and more energy is being produced by the windmills in the U.S. than any other place on Earth. This leads me to an article about the German windmill farms by Elliot H Gue (148) and some of the comments made about the German installed capacity. In his article he discussed meetings he had with some of the business representatives of the European business leaders. The discussions centered on the various approaches being taken by each of the different countries. Spain and Portugal were going heavy in the solar area, mainly because of their location they have a high amount of sun per year with open skies which is ideal for solar and not for windmill farms. The discussions were not only on power but the advantages of the various sources relative to environmental issues and especially the subject of greenhouse gases and reducing carbon dioxide.

"Besides the European representatives there were those from the United States. I thought the theme of the meetings should have been; "How do we educate the heads of business and governments about the true value of each of the renewable energy sources?" The reason for this comment relates to the fact that too many leaders of the business community and governments don't know the true value of each of the renewable sources of power. When the installers of renewable power quote their products capability, they relate to the maximum power each can produce. This story is bought by the heads of businesses or governments without knowing the details. When someone says they will install a 20 MW system, whether it is in windmills, solar energy, or water power, the buyer believes that's what he is going to receive. Once installed and they don't reach this level they read the small print and see that what they bought was the peak value and what they are receiving is much lower than this because of being located in something besides ideal conditions. In many cases they have to use their old energy source (oil, gasoline, coal, natural gas) to support the system they purchased. This is the naïve nature of these new and upcoming technologies. This is not always the installers fault since it is new to his business also and he is on a learning curve." (Some of this is paraphrased)

But the fact is that most alternative power technologies aren't a true solution to the globe's energy problems. The best illustration of this is the long-time poster child of the alternative energy movement, wind power. Apart from hydropower, wind is the most economically viable, developed and feasible alternative energy source. But wind's contribution to the global electric grid is all too often overstated and under possessed. This sometimes reminds me of the air war in Vietnam. The U.S. took their best and fastest planes there to fight the war and eventually realized that the terrain was such that the planes were too fast to be functional in that terrain and they brought in the older slower airplanes to handle the missions. Its not always the fastest that's the best.

Germany has by far the largest base of installed wind power capacity in the world, with more than 20,622 megawatts of generating capacity. To put that figure into context, the runner-ups are Spain and the US with a little more than 16,000 megawatts of generating capacity each; Germany is far and away the undisputed leader; at least until 2008 when additional capacity being installed by the U.S. puts them in that position. However, they don't generate the power that the U.S. does without their additional installations this year. This has occurred even though Germany has pushed their windmill farms into the northern oceans to try and pick up the forecasted winds off the ocean. There are thousands of windmills that line the northern shore and out into the ocean.

The comment that strikes me the most of Elliot H. Gue was that "the windmill farms of Northern Germany have been subsidized by the government and although not so successful has been a profitable business for the people who build and install the windmills." This kind of reminds me of the situation in California and solar cells. These are subsidized by the state and federal governments and pay about twenty percent in rebates to the people who have solar cells installed in their homes and business. The solar cell people are making money. I guess that is the way of things when one buys a golden goose but it doesn't produce any golden eggs.

"To quantify the situation in Germany, installed windpower represents about 17 percent of the total electrical generated capacity that has been installed but it represents only five percent of the total power generated and used in 2006." according to Coe. This means the windmills are working at about thirty percent of the installed capacity. This is a perfect example of my comments on, "What are the real numbers?" When you buy a barrel of oil and it goes through a refinery you generally know within a few percent of what you are going to obtain out of this barrel of energy. Sure there are wastes and inefficiencies with oil but most of the learning curve has been obtained on this source of energy. We know that a certain automobile only gets 22 miles to the gallon on the highway. We know how inefficient certain operations are. But these newcomers to the energy field are strangers by comparison and learning at the expense of the buyer.

This lack of knowledge will be overcome with age. Some of it is already known. However, most of the known is disappointing. Germany can blame the problem on the North Sea and the winds that don't blow but in fact some of the problems relate to the transmission of the energy and the losses there. It's difficult to work with something that is varying like the wind and this is causing a variation in the power being received and there are not any ways (as of yet) of storing the energy like a capacitor can in fluctuating alternating current. The methods tried or conceived to date on the storage of power from windmill farms have not been successful. This is not to mean they won't be successful since there are bright minds around the world reviewing the possible ways of providing an answer.

"What may be worse is that once this commitment is made to install large windmill farms, they take up land or water that becomes fairly useless for anything else. So, they represent a footprint that is supposed to relieve the footprint of carbon dioxide or some other contaminant of the environment. But when the footprint fails to materialize one is still left with the footprint."

In some cases such as Germany they have foregone the use of nuclear power and placed their bet on windmills and solar energy and the possible use of more natural gas from Russia.. The decision was made by the German government to not install any additional nuclear power and perhaps power down the ones they have. The reasons are reasonable when one sits down and rationalizes the pros and cons of the nuclear power and the supply of energy by windmills and solar power. Both are clean when it comes to contaminating the atmosphere and one doesn't have to rid themselves of the left over waste such as needs to be done with nuclear fuel. One is safe and the other had one big, and one rather small incident with nuclear power. One is safe for eternity and nuclear power requires safety for eternity. There is a big difference between these two considerations. One is available for eternity and the other finds nuclear power only available for a few billion years. When you take these into consideration, plus the overstatements of the suppliers of the windpower and the naiveness of the people making the decisions, it's like flipping a coin. There are some people that believe the German decision was a political decision or a defensive decision. Germany receives much of its oil from Russia, or at least they could since Russia has an abundance of the world's oil reserves and has pipelines that could provide all the German needs. Germany would like to be free of this dependence on Russia. If the renewable energies could provide them what they need they would be happy to be free of any future pressure from Russia. The noble effort of using windmills is the reduction of carbon dioxide and this is in the favor of the countries that have taken this direction. Keep in mind that all the renewables are not available to all the countries of the world, therefore when a country does use the capability they have, we should all cheer for their effort to reduce environmental contaminants. This brings me back to my confusion relative to Germany's decision to drop the use of nuclear energy. This is a definite step in the wrong direction. Why drop any of the renewable fuels and I count nuclear energy as a renewable fuel since the abundance of it could provide energy for as long as Earth is inhabitable by human beings. Here is a strong industrial power that serves its own needs and the world's needs for its products. It has the technical capability to handle nuclear power. As I indicated, each country should provide any renewable energy that they have within their power to provide. Many of the countries are not so fortunate. But all is not lost. The windmills will keep generating whatever they are able to generate and will relieve the countries installing them of some level of their energy need. However, it doesn't look like the world can install enough windmills and if they ever come close the windmills will probably get in the way of doing something more valuable and more rewarding in reaching the power needs of the world.

Environmental Impact and Drawbacks of windmills

Wind turbines - large or small - are not always welcome additions to the landscape. Many people find them loud and unsightly, but I know of a farm town in Michigan that has them and they enjoy their company. They are also known to disrupt electro-magnetic communication signals. Others claim that turbines endanger wildlife, particularly birds, but this is not a proven fact. There are no large numbers of birds found at these windmill farms. I would think that birds would learn to avoid them. They are not like airplanes which are always changing their position. These are structures that remain in one place and birds don't take long to realize this. It's a fact of nature that some things that bother people soon go away as soon as they learn the alternatives. In this case the lack of energy for doing what man does in the various parts of the world would soon change the mind of the locals when they realize these are there to help them. Here's a picture of an installation in a Michigan town. They think they are beautiful and the sound is ok after a short while of adjusting. (51)

As I previously mentioned, people will get used to them, especially if the price of gasoline keeps escalating. As soon as it hits the consumer's pocket books, they change accordingly.

Windmill Efficiency

It is important to realize that windmills do not have to be part of a large windmill farm. Individual use of this type of equipment will be available and will be used by people to supply their own power just as they do now on solar panels for heating their homes, their hot water and their pools. Home owners require windmills that are higher efficiency with lower speeds and lower noise. At one time there were many of these types of windmills in the world. One major area was in Holland (The Netherlands) and some farms in the United States. They can be made much smaller, and able to run at slower speeds. When you compare the technology available today compared to one hundred years ago, you realize how well new windmills could operate compared to the old ones. Today we have metals that were not available back then. Aluminum was not available until World War II. Consider the lightness and strength of this metal and then think of other metals and technology that have come along since those of the past and you can visualize their ability to perform quite well. Individual windmills may still be better used in these small applications than other energy sources. They must be placed on the land in an area that is less of an eyesore than is acceptable. These windmills will not look like the ones on the windmill farms since they will be equipped with more blades and blades that are much shorter in radius. Efficiency is important for windmills, because the entire cost is in the technology, not the source of energy, which is wind. This is another reason why it is possible to install for individual use due to the fact that they don't require any fuels or cooling water, or drains and little maintenance. The most significant factor determining the efficiency of windmills is the number of blades. This is because more blades capture more energy, but more blades cannot be used where the winds are too high and will cause damage to the system.

But large windmills must use few blades due to stress on the metal. When the diameter of rotation is 300 ft (100 m), two blade systems must be used. When the diameter is 150 ft, three blade systems can be used and when the system is a home use one, the blades become quite small such as eight feet or so and many blades are used.

Government study on windmills

A large government study measured two blade systems only and showed moderate efficiency. Smaller, multi blades systems would have been much more efficient. They observed that the overall efficiency of a windmill has to be directly measured. It cannot be calculated, because there are too many interacting factors. A good guess at design efficiency can be made by direct observation. Only empirical measurements under operating conditions can provide accurate data.

For this reason, the US government spent a large amount of money (probably more than a billion dollars) during the late seventies and eighties creating experimental windmills for testing their practicality. But researchers only studied two blade systems. The results were worthless, in spite of having tested dozens of windmills. Maybe not worthless since they showed what not to use and probably promoted the three blade systems used today. None of the experimental windmills were designed for good overall efficiency, and the most important questions were not studied. The test designs were so large that the structures made them impractical, and such designs are never used. Three blade systems are used on wind farms; probably as a result of this study showing two blade systems as impractical. Two factors are important in determining overall efficiency of a windmill. One is its ability to use low velocity wind, and the other is its conversion efficiency. The ability to use low velocity wind determines whether the windmill is working or doing nothing while wind velocities are low, which can be a significant part of the time. For example, one site might have wind of 15 miles per hour (mph) or greater 20% of the time, and 10 mph or greater 40% of the time. A windmill that can use 10 mph wind is operating 40% of the time, while one requiring 15 mph wind is only operating 20% of the time. It is interesting that when considering today's materials that can be used there are a lot of places that could not get the energy they needed out of the old systems; probably because they didn't work at low speeds. With the lighter materials of today we may find that single windmills that have lower mass will work at lower wind speeds and be a big advantage on small farms.

I thought It might be interesting to have a study where both large three blade systems and small multiple blade are interspersed to make up the windmill farm; half being the small systems with small and a larger number of blades and the other half would be made up of large diameter with long three blades able to handle the higher velocity winds and not have to worry about the loss of the low velocity winds. The small and large windmills would be scattered throughout a windmill farm so that the one type picks up the high winds and the other type picks up the lower velocity winds. Using this approach a windmill farm may be very efficient for both high and low winds. It may even be possible to use on mast with the large blade system on the top and the smaller multiple blade system located closer to the ground. The outputs of the two would be multiplexed in a manner to provide a more constant output per mast. This would allow the design of the high speed windmills to be less critical since they would not have to provide output at low and high speeds. The low speed systems would be designed to cut off at high wind speeds to prevent damage. Their output would be high but the systems would have to be designed to be tolerant of the high speeds. This can be done with some of the newer high strength materials like carbon or titanium depending on the costs. Using computers the outputs of the high velocity and low velocity windmills would be combined to provide a smooth flow of electricity. The cost of the overall installation may be greatly reduced for a given power output. The maintenance issues would be less over time since the complexity of each of the types making up the total farm will be simplified. This is my suggestion for review. I would like feedback on this.

Homeowners who are considering using a windmill to provide their home energy versus the use of solar cells should use the web to find the manufacturers that provide an ideal system for their area. Many think that a windmill in the back yard adds a certain amount of charm and it is really charming if you don't receive a large electric bill because you chose to provide your own.

(B) Hydroelectric power

Worldwide hydroelectricity consumption reached 816,000 MW in 2005, consisting of 750,000 MW of large plants, and 66,000 MW of small hydro installations. Large hydro capacity totaling 10,900 MW was added by China, Brazil and India during the year, but there was a much faster growth (8%) in small hydro, with 5,000 MW added, mostly in China where some 58% of the world's small hydro plants are now located. (134)

In the Western world, although Canada is the largest producer of hydroelectricity in the world, the construction of large hydro plants has stagnated due to environmental concerns. The trend in both Canada and the United States has been to micro hydro because it has negligible environmental impacts and opens up many more locations for power generation. In British Columbia alone the estimates are that micro hydro will be able to more than double electricity production in the province.

In 2005, hydroelectric power supplied 16.4% of world electricity (53). Large dams are still being designed. Nevertheless, hydroelectric power is probably not a major option for the future of energy production in the developed nations because most major sites within these nations are either already being exploited or are unavailable for other reasons, such as environmental considerations. The biggest impact in hydropower will be in China and India as both are planning or already installing large systems. The Three Gorge Dam project in China has just completed the major part of this huge installation and results will show in the 2007 – 2008 summary of hydropower.

Hydro-Electric Power description

Hydro-electric power plants take the kinetic energy from falling water and convert it into electricity. The energy in water comes from the sun and so is always being renewed. The energy that is in the sun's rays evaporates water from rivers, lakes, streams and oceans and this falls on the land in the form of precipitation which eventually leads to water in the form of underground creeks, streams, rivers, lake filling, runoff and ice in parts of the world. Land elevations result in rainfall or melted snow runoff and allow the original solar energy to be used as hydro-electric power. (See 2 below)as the water falls from great heights to the rivers below.

Hydro power accounts for around 16.5 % of the world's electricity, and presently is the world's largest renewable energy source. In Canada, hydro supplies over 60% of the countries energy needs. Thought of as a clean, cheap source of energy, hydro plants being planned are coming up against great opposition from various environmental groups. This opposition relates to the dramatic change in the local environment when a river is dammed and flooding results. This flooding result in the loss of animal and plant life and the local population has to move their homes. This dislocation of the natural inhabitants of the land is opposed by environmentalists. Much of this opposition may disappear as they take on the global warming drive. They must choose since the hydropower is clean and there is no carbon dioxide released to the atmosphere and the prospect of global warming. The environmentalists have to consider this upside compared to the downsides of damming of rivers.

Early hydro power plants were much more efficient then the fossil fuel plants in the nineteenth century; and early in the twentieth century. For this reason, many small to medium sized hydro plants started to spring up anywhere there was a supply of moving water and a need for energy. As the demand for more and more energy soared in the twentieth century and the efficiency of fossil fuels grew, these small plants started to die out. Fossil energy became very economical in the middle of the twentieth century, mainly due to the demand for the growth of the automotive industry and other industrial endeavors. There was also the ease of obtaining the fossil fuels locally where no large hydroelectric plants existed. There was also the fact that the hydroelectric plants provided electricity and many of the industrial applications required gasoline or diesel to operate. Today, hydro power focuses on large mega-plants under government programs. Of course in countries like China where the people have less voice in the decisions made by government under a socialist system, large dams are being built. Small hydro systems, now called micro systems range in the 1 MW to under 30 MW are available in "ready to use" type packages where they are offered much like solar systems are offered. You purchase for a definite use and contract the work for its installation. Local governments are pursuing the micro dams mentioned where practical. We may find more of this as the cost of fossil fuels increase.

These hydroelectric plants involve the damming of water sources causing flooding of vast areas of land to provide water storage. Hydro-electric power plants take the energy from water falling through a vertical distance, and turn this energy into electricity. See figure two below that shows an outline of a typical system. The falling water is brought through a penstock (large tube that reduces the fluctuations of the water flow) to a turbine that converts the water's energy into mechanical power. The turning of the water turbines is transferred to a generator which makes the electricity. There are several factors that determine the amount of electricity that can be made at a hydro plant. The two primary factors relate to the height of the water falling (dam height) and the volume of water involved. The volume of water involved depends on the amount of water moving in the system toward the dam. The normal mode is to keep the height of the water constant near the top of the dam, but in some locations there are seasons where the water running is much lower than other seasons of the year. In many cases a system is composed of a series of smaller dams that help feed the major power supplying dam. In this way they can open and close or re-route water to keep the main dam at a desired level.

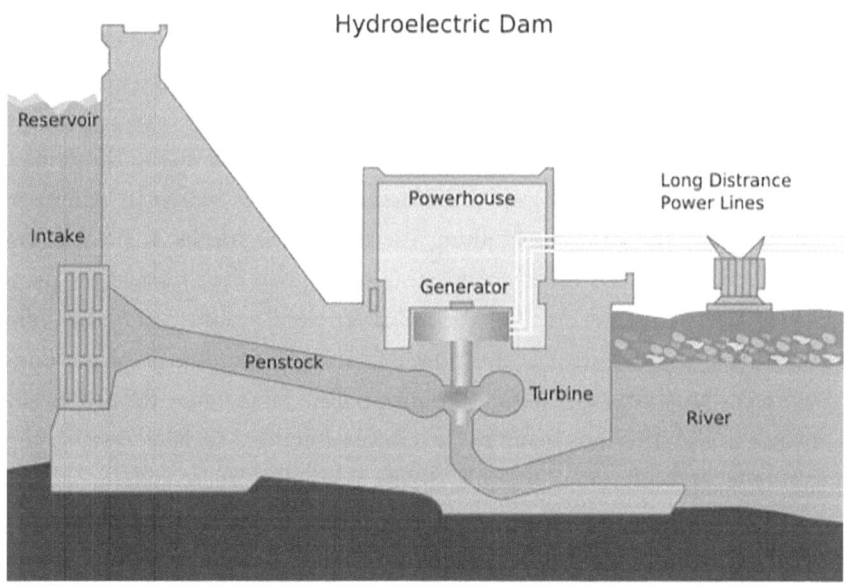

Figure 15 General view of a typical hydroelectric dam system (62)

Most hydroelectric power comes from the potential energy of dammed water driving a water turbine and generator. In this case the energy extracted from the water depends on the volume and on the difference in height between the source and the water's outflow. This height difference is called the head. The amount of potential energy in water is proportional to the head. To obtain very high head, water for a hydraulic turbine may be run through a large pipe called a penstock

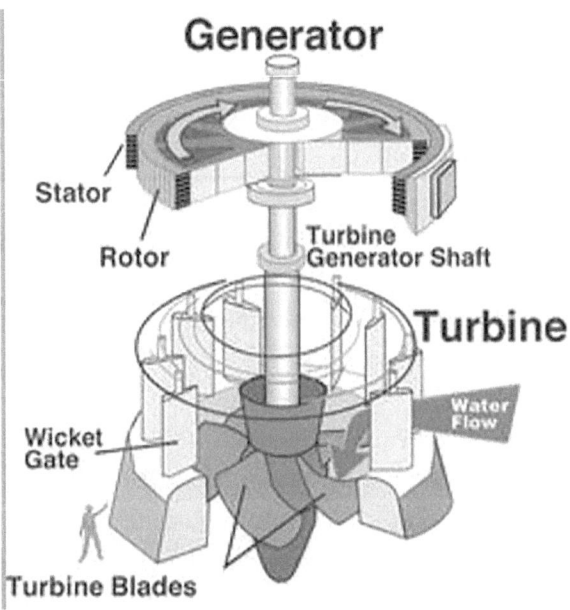

Typical turbine Figure 16

- The vertical distance through which the water falls. This is called the "head" and is measured in meters or feet.
- The flow rate, measured in volume per unit time which is related to the width of the dam. The volume is expressed in cubic meters per second or cubic feet per second.
- The controlled flow rate which is determined by the design of the dam. This is controlled by special weirs that are opened or closed by command to release more water to lower areas and prevent the overflow of the major dam.

Annual production of electricity depends on the available water supply. Most large systems do not have this problem but in some locations the water flow rate may vary by a ten to one factor depending on the time of the year.

Hydro power plants can be divided into three categories.

1. High head power plants. These are the large dam type structures such as the Hoover Dam which stores the water at a high elevation. Besides providing the power, the dam serves another major purpose of flood protection. The dam stores water during raining conditions and releases water as mentioned using weirs to release water upon command. Dams have been constructed with heads of over 1000 meters (over 3000 feet)

2. The other type is "low head" hydro plants that are constructed where the higher elevations are not available and the heads are usually less than 10 meters (33 feet). These types may use a low dam to retain or control water during heavy rainy seasons in the area.

3. No dam hydro systems that control of the direction of flow during certain heavy or light rainy seasons for the effect desired. This type of hydro power system can't store water since there really is no dam but a virtual dam exists. By directing the flow of rivers or stream by low lateral dams, this method can be used for electricity generation if the flow is considered to be high enough.

A large dam is one with a height of 15 meters or more from the foundation. If dams are between 5 and 15 meters high and have a reservoir volume of more than 3 million m³, they are also classified as large dams by the International Commission on Large Dams. In 2000, there were over 45 000 large dams around the world. (54)

Hydroelectricity at this time is the most widely used form of renewable energy. However this is about to change as there are pushes in other directions for renewable power. Hydroelectricity produces no waste, and does not produce carbon dioxide.. Hydroelectricity now supplies about 715,000 MW or 19% of world electricity, (16% in 2003) accounting for over 63% of the total electricity from renewable sources in 2005. The places where new dams can be constructed are very few in the industrial countries and most of the growth will be in the countries like China that is becoming an industrial power and is in the process of installling a large capacity of this form of renewable energy. They also have several large rivers.

Besides the normal amount of energy obtained from a system, some systems employ a pumped storage hydroelectricity system which produces electricity to supply high peak demands by moving water between reservoirs at different elevations. At times of low electrical demand (usually during the nightime), excess generation capacity from the low amount being supplied elsewhere is used to pump water into the higher reservoir. When there is higher demand, water is released back into the lower reservoir through a turbine pictured above in figure 3. Of course the energy to pump the water back up to the higher level during low demand is a waste of energy. However, there has been little success in finding other means of storing this large energy that would be wasted. This pumped storage does provide a more continuous output of electricity during demand that is high. Since the electricity produced is supplied mostly during the peak hours when the selling price is high it more than makes up for the cost of the pumping during the night. The pumping energy loss is about twenty percent of what is gained back in revenue. I believe it may be possible to produce manmade water falls using a technique like this. Water is pumped from a lower level to a higher level during the night and during the day the water falls toward the lower level. The efficiency is not as good as mother nature's but it is a means of using available water to provide economical energy (even if it isn't efficient).

There are many hydroelectric plants in the world that do not have a reservoir and capability to pump and they just depend on the flow of the river supplying the dam. The kinetic energy of the flow past waterwheels or other horizontal turbines provide energy from these plants. Annual electric energy production depends on the available water supply. In some installations the water flow rate can vary by a factor of ten to one over a year's time due to lack or rainfall during certain seasons. The annual supply also varies as a function of loading by the customers using this service.

However, Hydroelectric power systems provide a better constant flow that is better controlled then **windmill farms**. The reservoir and pumping into a higher reservoir allows computer control of the output. These systems are more dependable than those of windmills farms since they are able to predict in advance the amount of flow into the system and they control the output of the system to optimize fluctuations. This is not the case in windmill farms where the wind is less predictiable. Systems with computer controls can determine when water is or isn't going to be available and when to divert it and when not to.

Hydro plants producing up to 10 megawatts are considered small, although projects up to 30 megawatts in North America are considered small hydro and have the same regulations as the large systems. A small hydro plant may be connected to a distribution grid like the method used with solar cells to provide the grid with power that won't be used by the prime source or may provide power only to an isolated community or a single home. Many of these small hydro systems are installed for flood control as well as supplying power. Many are used in irrigation for large agricultural suppliers. This is done in places like California for example. Since the drive to increae renewable supplies of energy, many of the small sites that weren't being used are being redeveloped to provide local energy needs. Often the site can be redeveloped for electric power production, possibly eliminating the new environmental impact of any demolition operation. Likewise, since the capability is there and doesn't affect local environmental conditions, it faces less burecratic steps in going back into action.

Advantages and disadvantages of hydroelectric power

- One of the major advantages of the hydro systems is that no fuel is needed. The fuel is supplied by the Earth – Sun hydrological system.
- These systems have long lives and many are over one hundred years old. The systems require little maintenance and there are not many personnel involved in their operation.
- The systems are expensive to install but the payback can be under ten years. Additional money usually has to be spent to ensure the output of the systems especially during years where the rain fall is low.
- Energy derived is less expensive than most other forms of renewable energy
- It is not always easy to find an ideal location. The water may be there but it has to be fairly far from heavily populated cities. There are only a few places in the world that have the combination of land, water, open space,

and topilogical satisfactory terrain. And there are the enviromentalists that take issue with these large systems since they have environmental dislocations.

- There is dislocation of people when a new dam is to be built
- The water flowing out is warmer than normal and can cause a change in the kind of fish that inhabits the downstream areas. This also can change the other animals that reside in the downstream areas.
- Some dams have caused problems with fish spawning. In California the fish were not able to make it to their spawning areas in the upstream sites. Fish ladders have been installed which allow the fish to make their way up these ladders to their spawning grounds. This has worked with fairly good success.
- Some fish are caught in the turbines when they try to return to the oceans. Actions have been taken to transport the fish past these areas so they can make it to the sea. Having noted this the actions taken have procided the relief expected.
- The rush of water out the outlets has caused some erosion of the banks along the dowmstream areas. This pulsing of the output of the water has a much greater force than if the water flow was continuous and results in this grinding of the downstream areas. When installed in the proper location with the proper thought behind the system, this erosion has been taken into account with good results.
- Since damming and redirecting the waters of the Platte River in Nebraska for agricultural and energy use, many native and migratory birds such as the Piping Plover and Sandhill Crane have become increasingly endangered. Likewise, new creaters appear including new bird species.
- Some of the dams installed in areas of high vegetation has resulted in the vegetation residing at the bottom of the reservoir. This vegetation rots and decays and produces carbon dioxide and methane. Both are greenhouse gases. In many cases this provides electricity but at the price of generating more greenhouse gases than fossil fuels generate during their genertion of electricity. This is not true of the large dams and systems in Canada, United States, and Europe where the generation is much less than ten percent of the emisssions by oil burning systems. This has proved a problem in Brazil and other South American countries. This is expected to be a problem in China.

- There have been dam failures most of which are not major issues. The major issues are with large dams such as the Banquao Dam in Southern China that collapsed and over 170,000 people were killed and huge amounts of people were dislocated to parts of the country that were foreign to them.
- There is an interesting side effect that I read about a couple of years ago. The article related to the fact that all the large dams being built in the world have caused the Earth to have a slightly changed center of gravity or center of inertia. Supposedly this change has caused a slight change in the rotation of Earth. Although small, this change must be monitored to determine whether large dam should be built and if so, where?
- In the developed world, roughly 70% of hydroelectric power generation potential has already been developed; in the developing world, only about 10%. This means there will not be any huge investments in hydroelectric plants in most of the industrialized world. Most of the planned systems or systems under construction are in China where the demand for energy is increasing at a phenomenal rate. See the list of dams under construction or planned to be in the appendix in the back of the book.
- Hydroelectric power uses the greatest amount of land area to produce power. Approximately 220,000 acres are required to produce one million megawatts of electricity per year. Because of this constraint there are not many countries that have this much open land near large rivers. This limits the possible sites in the world. The cost is land and land is where food is grown or people live. The ideal locations are normally where water isn't available, such as the open areas of deserts. However, Arizona at one time was mostly deserts and the damming of water and the resulting irrigation has made many areas in Arizona quite beautiful and practical.
- A hydro-electric plant never operates at its full power rating. The power rating is determined by the power rating of the generatiors located at the site. The Load Factor is the ration of the actual annual power output of the system to the amount of the installed capacity. The actual output is in the KW hours achieved versus the KW hours available. The Systems listed below in figure 17 are the result of the BP Annual Report 2006 (55) List of the largest hydoelectric power stations

Figure 17 Countries with theLargest installed capacity and load factors (55)

Country	Installed Capacity (GW)	Load Factor
People's Republic of China(2007) [13]	145.26	0.37
Canada	88.974	0.59
Brazil	69.080	0.56
USA	79.511	0.42
Russia	45.000	0.42
Norway	27.528	0.49
India	33.600	0.43
Japan	27.229	0.37
Venezuela	-	-
Sweden	-	-
France	25.335	0.25

TOTAL – 541.517 GW installed capacity
TOTAL ACHIEVED – 242.24 GW
Or – 242,240 MW
Loading Factor average PERCENTAGE – 44.7 % OUTPUT
WITH Japan and China well below this load factor average

Although China has installed a significant amount of hydroelectric capacity, because of its low loading factor its output is about the same as that of Canada with a population that is about two percent of that of China.

This provides one with the expected output of the large hydroelectric systems. These are the load factors I will use as I project output capacities for the future growth of this renewable power. Remember to replace the oil energy output expected by the year 2037 we need to achieve renewable power of between 10 and 40 million MW of power not counting the amount that is already available. This is the present available amount and represents what is available as of 2006. The millions of MW of renewable power is what is needed above this to replace the oil energy that will be gone. So we can't count this but it gives you an idea of the tremendous amount of added energy that we must obtain from renewable sources and as big as this installed capacity is, we won't come close to this in installations of hydroelectric systems in the next thirty years.

I have listed in the Appendix II at the end of the book the present listing of the planned installations of hydroelectric systems some of which are already being installed. For those interested please check these numbers. This listing includes the power expected and the dates of completion. They will add up toward the power needs of the year 2037.

Worldwide hydropower.

Worldwide, hydropower plants produce about 24 percent of the world's electricity and supply more than 1 billion people with electrical power. The world's hydropower plants output a combined total of **776,000 megawatts** according to the National Renewable Energy Laboratory and the Union of Concerned Scientists in 2005. (56) Keep in mind that these 776,000 megawatts is the rating of the hydroelectric systems and the actual output is probably about 44% of this or approximately 350,000 megawatts due to the loading factor. This is already installed power and doesn't count toward the goal that must be achieved by 2037 by my calculations. We must not be fooled by numbers and we must make sure the people responsible are not being naïve. A review of Appendix II in the back of the book shows the hydropower systems in the works, in the planning, and proposed. These add up to approximately 250,000 MW. Combined with those in operation today the worlds total energy supplied by hydroelectric power will be approximately one million MW, a quarter of which will be new.

Global Hydropower Scenario

Hydropower constitutes 21% of the world's electricity generating capacity. The theoretical potential of worldwide hydropower is 2,800,000 MW, about four times greater than the 723,000 MW that has been exploited. Yet, the actual amount of electricity that will ever be generated by hydropower will be much lower than the theoretical potential due to the environmental concerns and economic constraints. About 44 % of the world's hydropower was generated in four countries in 2002, mostly large- and mid-scale plants. (57)

Asia accounted for 24% of the world's hydro generation, with 618,000MWh, followed by North America with 23% (595,000 MWh) and Europe with 20% (537,000 MWh).

Canada with 315,000 MWh is the largest producer of hydropower in the world followed by China with 309,000 MWh. Brazil with 282,000 MWh and the United States with 255,000 MWh comes after them. Even though Canadian hydro generation is growing, China will overtake Canada very soon, if it has not already done so, to become the largest hydro generator in the world. Keep in mind that China has forty times the number of people that live in Canada. In Western Europe and the United States, the scope for additional hydropower is limited, as the most economic sites have already been developed and further expansion is hindered by environmental concerns.

Hydropower accounts for 57% of the electricity generated in Canada, 7% in the US (the US uses hydropower for peaking not base load) and 12% in Mexico. Canada's economical hydropower potential is second only to that of Brazil in the Western Hemisphere. Canada still has several projects under either construction or planning, amounting to 6,600 MW.

Latin America has a very large hydropower potential. Many countries rely heavily on hydropower for their electricity supply. For instance, hydropower makes up 80% of Brazil's electricity generation.

Brazil has plentiful hydropower resources. Its installed hydropower capacity is 64,000 MW. The capacity under construction or planning is more than 25,000 MW. One of the hydropower plants under construction is the giant 1,118,000 MW Belo Monte power plant. Hydropower capacity under construction or planning in other South American countries, particularly Argentina, Bolivia, Chile, Colombia, Guyana, Peru, and Venezuela, amounts to 9,700 MW. Also, 4,400 MW of hydropower capacity is under construction or planning in Central American countries.

China has the largest hydropower resources in the world, with a huge territory and a host of rivers. Its installed hydropower capacity was at 83,000 MW by the end of 2002. A large number of hydropower plants are under construction or planning, amounting to 77,000 MW. The giant 18,200 MW Three Gorges Dam with a dam height of 181 m on the Yangtze River (the country's longest river) is the world's largest hydropower project under construction. Even though hydropower plants based on dams and reservoirs may require displacement and relocation of large numbers of people, China has one of the best resettlement programs in the world. (57)

Russia holds fifth place with 180,000 MWh and Norway in sixth with 125,000 MWh. Norway is regarded by many as having the best managed hydro system in the world, which accounts for 99.3% of the total power generated in that country.

Although there are hydroelectric power projects under construction in about 80 countries, the majority of the remaining hydro potential is found in developing countries particularly in South and Central Asia, Latin America and Africa. In most of the European countries the economically feasible hydro power potential has mostly been harnessed.

According to the United Nations, the total exploitable energy by hydroelectricity is 15 trillion kilowatt hours per year, but only about 15% of this energy has been developed so far (Union of Concerned Scientists, 2005 (57)

Dam builders have been busy beavers

United States

There are more than 2,000 hydropower plants operating in the United States, making hydropower the country's largest renewable energy source. The U.S was early in the establishment of hydropower and many dams and systems were started by President F.D. Roosevelt during the depression. Prior to nuclear reactors these systems supplied over forty percent of the electrical power. Systems have increased but other means of power generation have increased more rapidly. This is mainly the result of the constraint on the land needed to provide these systems. Hydropower still remains the least expensive way of providing electrical power. The systems presently supply energy that is approximately a half billion equivalent barrels of oil per year of renewable power. This saves this amount of oil year in and year out. There are approximately 80,000 dams in the United States and only three percent of them are used for hydropower. (58) This could be one direction to go and increase the hydropower by double without having to obtain permission for the land and to have to build a dam. Environmental factors are less of a problem with the smaller systems and they are easy to control. With these you don't have to acquire permission to build the dam and there would be a benefit to the local communities. To give you and idea of the value of these hydropower systems, the United States produced 3.6 trillion KWh of total energy and the hydroelectric plants produced 989,000 MWh or about 11% of this energy at a price lower than any other source of power.

Canada

- In 1999, the total electric power generated from hydro sources was 340 464 GWh, representing 60.4% of the total generated electricity in Canada. Over 45% of that electricity was produced in Quebec. (59)
- The largest hydroelectric power development in Canada is the James Bay project in Quebec, which started producing electricity in 1982; its eight dams and 198 dikes contain five reservoirs covering 11,900 square kilometers, half the size of Lake Ontario. The combined output of its generating stations is 15, 237 megawatts.
- Canada ranks as one of the world's top 10 dam builders. Although the Canadian Dam Association register of dams (2003) reports 933 large dams in the country, there are many thousands of smaller dams. Of these large dams, 596 are used primarily for hydroelectric power generation. Quebec has 333 large dams, more than any other province. Ontario and British Columbia are next with 149 and 131 dams respectively.
- The Daniel Johnson Dam on Quebec's Manicouagan River is the largest hollow-body multiple-arch-and-buttress dam in the world. It has a total of 12 generating units capable of producing 2,592 MW of hydroelectric power.

China – Three Gorges Dam; spanning the Yangtze

At a time when many countries are questioning the benefits of damming their rivers to harness electricity, China's government has announced it is almost finished building the World's largest dam. Called the Three Gorges Dam, it is a project 13 years in the making that began in 1993 and is just completed. It hasn't completed the installation of all the turbines yet, but they are scheduled to go in around 2012. The dam has taken 25,000 workers, and more than 16 million cubic meters of concrete to complete.

Spanning the mighty Yangtze, the world's third-largest river and the largest in China, the dam stretches 2,309 meters, and rises to a height of 185 meters. To take into consideration the size of the reservoir, the reservoir would stretch from San Francisco to Los Angeles in California - which would take in about half the length of California. Although this dam project will serve a huge purpose on supplying needed energy for the area the main reason the project was initiated was to reduce flooding With a total of 26 generators when the last six generators are installed it will have 18,200 MW of installed power. (60) When the project began it was based on the flooding issue but as time passed it became an issue as a major power supply for the needs of an economy growing like China's has. Without the benefit of this huge source of electrical power there would have been a truncation of China's economy growth. It now looks like it was good planning or serendipity.

HARNESSING THE YANGTZE

The Three Gorges Dam project involves harnessing the Yangtze River, Asia's longest, to generate prodigious amounts of electricity. Output should be close to one tenth of current Chinese electrical requirements. The dam also aims to end disastrous floods downstream, which have claimed hundreds of thousands of lives over the last fifty years.. Improved navigability on the river should also allow much larger ships to sail from Shanghai as far as Chongqing, upstream from the dam and 2,000km from the sea, to aid China's burgeoning domestic and export trade.

The project is located 44km (~26 miles) from the city of Yichang in Hubei province. This point is at the end of a series of steep canyons which will form a 630km reservoir, with an average width of 1.3km (~0.8 miles). The dam will reach 185m (~600 feet) in height As mentioned the lake formed will be about 350 miles long **Remember, China has 4 times more people than US and only has one-fifth US's arable land to feed its people. With this severe** resource constraint China could ill afford to use up so much land, but there were offsetting arguments that included the flooding issues and the need for renewable power.

Approximately two million people have or will have lost their homes and have to move to places above the water lines or to nearby cities. It is estimated that as many as five million people will be displaced by the year 2020 when the overall project is completed.

Other issues

While this is a major event relative to supplying China a significant increase in their generated electrical power there have been problems with achieving the desired outcome of the huge project. Because of several issues Chinese officials have decided to purchase several coal companies to augment the power output of the Three Gorges Dam. These issues relate to the lack of continuous output of the system. Most of this is due to the lack of rain in the area resulting in cycling of the system. Although there is an overall lack of rain the system was having problems prior to this due to the variability of rain during certain seasons of the year. This was expected prior to the building of this project but was not realized as to the amount of impact it would have on this huge system.

Remember my writing about the loading factors of these dams. This is always a point of issue; however China's large dam has a loading factor that is even below those of previously built hydroelectric systems. The coal systems will add a capacity that is approximately equal to the output of the Three Gorges Dam system. This initiation would offset the planned reduction of environmental waste gases that was one of the reasons for the building of this project. There were other issues that related to the transmission of the power over long distances from this inner part of China to the affluent large cities along the coast of China. These transmission lines would be costly and hurt a project that is not yet profitable. It has been recognized that there are also some safety issues for transmission over heavily populated areas to the coastal regions.

The planning of the coal plants plans included adding enough coal plants to essentially double the generating capacity and reduce its reliance on hydro by fifty percent. (60) Although this has its bad points related to the environmental contamination, the adding of these coal plants are needed by China to supplement their present capacity of power anyhow. They may use these comments to excuse the buying of the coal plants, but in the end they would have needed them anyhow. China is growing rapidly economically and this adds to their population which is the largest in the world with 1.3 billion people and growing. This combination makes demands on their need for added power. This combination is greater than probably any country due to the difference in growth of their economy versus the ability to supply this growth with required energy sources. China has the most coal in the world and they are short on renewable energy once they complete their hydroelectric projects. They have not planned on large windmill farms but there are large portions of non-arable land that could benefit from the use of solar power. This has always been the projection on China and its energy needs. With the oil cost to them increasing and the possibility of the oil supply running out this century (my projection), China has to find other available energy; hopefully renewable beyond hydroelectric.

Water diversion schemes are another threat to Yangtze Power's long-term earnings to ensure payback of their investment and loans. Prior to knowing the short coming of the Three Gorges Dam the central government had plans for multibillion-dollar investments for diverting water from the Yangtze to the heavily depleted Yellow River and to other sites. The diversion to the Yellow River got under way in December 2002. There are farther diversions of this type which will result in the Three Gorges Dam being depleted of water. This is probably the reason for some of those coal plants since it is recognized that these farther diversions will compromise the Yangtze's water to the Three Gorges Dam. The Three Gorge Dam is only part of a plan. This forms the basis for other huge dams along some of the other rivers; some of which tie into the Three Gorge system and may in fact cause it to run low on water at times if the total plan reaches fruition.

It was difficult to ascertain the problems that would arise at the Three Gorges Dam system such as drought and competing demands on hydro reservoirs. This has reduced the expected output of the large dams in China over the last few years. There have been severe power shortages in several of the country's large provinces, especially during the summer season when it is dry and the reservoirs are low and the demand is high. There are requirements for air conditioning and many of the large production facilities depend on heavy operations during this time period each year. This is a double hit when you consider this is also the highest demand for drinking water and water for agriculture. So, the shortage of water hits all these areas. Isn't it a shame that "Mother Nature" picks the worse times to make these moves and they are not predictable in advance – and they never are predictable.

Other issues

The dam and its large reservoir have other natural things playing with them and causing issues of another sort. This long stretch of water results in erosion of the sides along the length and the eventual scenarios that follow. This erosion results in many mudslides that create havoc for the people that have moved from the reservoir area and live adjacent to the banks of the reservoir, as well as causing the waters to be dirty. There are also landslides, silting, home loses, and closing of highways. There are also the problems that are associated with these type of phenomena such as sickness and mosquitoes for one. (61)

While this view had been forecasted by some scientists reviewing the planning over the years, the plan has continued and it was believed if these consequences were to occur that they would be handled as they happened. Many environmentalists had predicted some of these events, but many times these inputs are overlooked as being emotional rather than objective. This is the battle to be faced by any of these large projects. Beijing had suppressed domestic opposition to the project, focusing instead on the dam's capacity to control seasonal flooding and generate hydroelectric power. The building of the dam was supported by Japan since they wanted to reduce the acid rain that was being caused by the burning of coal in China and its affect on the atmosphere. The Three Gorges dam is now producing enough electricity each year to replace 50 million tons of polluting coal and reduce China's carbon emissions by 100m tons, but as indicated this will probably be offset by the addition of the coal plants over time.

While there are the problems as mentioned below the dam there are also problems in the area of the reservoir above the dam level. There are concerns with the human and toxic wastes that have built up over the reservoir portion. There are environmentalists that believe this is creating problems with the drinking water of large cities that receive their supplies of water from this reservoir. It would appear that additional water treatment plants will need to be built to provide cleaner water supplies from these reservoirs.

While they acknowledge hydroelectric dams in theory run cleaner than coal, which China relies heavily on, there are other polluting concerns. Scientists point out the reservoir created behind the dam has become a cesspool of human and toxic waste. Environmentalists like Dai believe it is threatening the drinking water of major cities like Chongqing. "The Yangtze used to be so clear, I could drop a pen and see it float to the bottom, but now it's a dirty muddy river, and the water is no longer good for drinking," says Dai. (72) The towns that were flooded over during the building of the dam were never cleaned of toxic waste, he says. "There was never a budget for clean-up. On the bottom of the reservoir, there is now hospital, factory, pig and animal waste. It will all be stirred up." This is a problem that should be cleared up on future installations.

Officially, the cost for the dam is $24 billion, but independent studies conducted by others suggest the real cost could be as high as $75 billion. While the government will subsidize the cost of electricity, many Chinese question the worth of such an expensive endeavor. Although flooding may be better controlled downstream, recent flooding and mudslides in areas above the dam have communities calling foul, saying the dam in fact has simply moved the problem elsewhere. The only consolation is that if the problems are no worse than those that were there before the dam, then the dam is worth the saving of the lives that would have occurred if the dam was not put there and the country would be very short of power. Remember what I said about energy, "The biggest cost is not having it."

Bottom-line on hydroelectric power

Even though large hydroelectric systems provide a huge answer to many country's energy needs, there are these side issues that make it difficult for large hydroelectric systems to be approved in many countries. Countries in the Southern Hemisphere that contain large jungles may not be good candidates for the dams since the flooded jungles will create environmental issues as the jungles decay beneath these waters and contaminate the environment with methane which has a much greater greenhouse gas effect than carbon dioxide. Solving the world's energy problems is not straight forward even when the supply comes from an unending source like the rains of the world and the Sun of the world.

(C) Solar power – the number one method of replacing oil's energy

Solar power falls into two major categories:

1. Photovoltaic
2. Thermal

(1) Photovoltaic (PV) solar power

Photovoltaic (PV) solar consists of elements that are reactive to the wavelengths and energy of the sunlight. One of the primary types uses silicon cells as the material. Sunlight hitting these cells results in hole - electron pairs of charge being generated in the material and these are converted into current and voltage. One of the primary uses of these types of cells is to provide power for the home. A matrix of these cells are placed on the roofs with the output being dc voltage and current that charges batteries for storage and this voltage is then converted into the ac voltage and current that the house normally uses as its ac power.

This type of installation is fairly expensive but most states are giving rebates for the installation as the power output of these installations are usually higher than the home needs and the power is then directed to the normally provided power matrix supplying homes. In this way the user of the installation has his power provided and also receives credit for the power it supplies to the normal supplier of power. The payback for these systems is approximately eight years, after which the power is being supplied at only the maintenance cost.

These types of installations are only viable in states where there is considerable sunlight for a significant part of the year. States that have gone heavily into this form of personal power are California, and the southwestern states of the U.S; Hawaii is expected to follow.

Advantages

- The 122,000 million megawatts of sunlight reaching the earth's surface each year is plentiful – more than 8,000 times more than the 15 million megawatts of average power consumed by humans, of which 38% is supplied by oil. Additionally, solar electric generation has the highest power density (global mean of 170 W/m^2) among renewable energies. [81] This makes it the prime candidate for the number one source of renewable energy. (62)

    ° Solar power is pollution free during use. Production end wastes and emissions are manageable using existing pollution controls. End-of-use recycling technologies are under development.

    ° Facilities can operate with little maintenance or intervention after initial setup.

    ° Solar electric generation is economically superior where grid connection or fuel transport is difficult, costly or impossible. Examples include satellites, island communities, remote locations and ocean vessels.

    ° When grid-connected, solar electric generation can displace the highest cost electricity during times of peak demand (in most climatic regions), can reduce grid loading, and can eliminate the need for local battery power for use in times of darkness and high local demand; such application is encouraged by net metering. Time-of-use net metering can be highly favorable to small photovoltaic systems.

    ° Grid-connected solar electricity can be used locally thus reducing transmission/distribution losses (transmission losses were approximately 7.2% in 1995).

    ° Once the initial capital cost of building a solar power plant has been spent, operating costs are extremely low compared to existing power technologies because of the continual free supply of the sun's energy.

    ° Compared to fossil and nuclear energy sources, very little government research-money has been invested in the development of solar cells, so there is much room for improvement in that direction. Much of the development has been born by private companies with hopes of increasing revenue. Nevertheless, experimental high efficiency solar cells already have efficiencies of over 40% and efficiencies are rapidly rising while mass production costs are rapidly falling.

° One issue relates to the fact that the sun only shines part of the day and the solar systems must be supplied with a means of storing the energy derived and be able to supply the energy during the night hours.

° Many areas of the world do not receive adequate sunlight to make solar systems viable. However, many of them will install a minimum amount of solar of one type or another so as to receive some energy even at a relatively high cost. That is what happens when oil is gone.

(2) Thermal Solar cells

There are two types of thermal cells and they provide their energy to a different market.

(A) Focus systems

Thermal cells are used like mirrors. They are made up of parabolic shaped reflective panels that focus the sunshine on receptors that can contain circulating water or a material such as oil and raise the temperature to approximately 600 C. Some of these receptors have salt or another material combined in them so the water or other fluid in the receptor circulation system heats this secondary material to provide heat storage. During the night the heat is delivered by this secondary material so that heated material is recirculating twenty four hours a day.

The heated fluid in these receptors is directed to a heat exchanger in large tanks of water and generates steam which is then used to power generators. These systems depend on the heat provided by the sun's rays and are used for large installations such as those that provide power for a city or large area. Like the photovoltaic approach the installation is expensive but there is no cost for fuel and there is no delivery system necessary, therefore the installation costs are recovered fairly rapidly and this method is inexpensive to maintain.

Many installations are installed that track the sun so as to be able to optimize the thermal power pickup for the full day of sun. These systems remind me of when I was a kid and used a magnifying glass to focus the sun on a piece of wood or paper and cause it to catch on fire. This just happens to be many times bigger. These systems are effective in areas where there is considerable sunlight for most of the year and for long times during the day such as the Mohave Dessert in Southern California. The same states that use the photovoltaic because of the availability of sunlight are using these types of systems for providing electricity for cities or to provide power to the power grid.

Trough Systems are specialized focus systems

A solar trough consists of a linear parabolic reflector that concentrates light onto a receiver positioned along the reflector's focal line. The reflector is made to follow the Sun during the daylight hours by tracking along a single axis. Trough systems provide the best land-use factor of any solar technology. The SEGS plants in California and Acciona's Nevada Solar One near Boulder City, Nevada are representatives of this technology.

A parabolic dish system consists of a stand-alone parabolic reflector that concentrates light onto a receiver positioned at the reflector's focal point. The reflector tracks the Sun along two axes. Parabolic dish systems give the highest efficiency among CSP technologies. (85) The 50 kW Big Dish in Canberra, Australia is an example of this technology.

A solar power tower uses an array of tracking reflectors (heliostats) to concentrate light on a central receiver atop a tower. Power towers are less advanced than trough systems but offer higher efficiency and better energy storage capability. The Solar Two in Barstow, California and the Planta Solar 10 in Sanlucar la Mayor, Spain are representatives of this technology.

Advantages of thermal solar systems

1. Do not require silicon solar cells and since silicon is one of the limiting factors in providing higher volumes of solar cells, thermal is not limited by this factor.
2. Ideal for higher energy levels required to provide power for a city or large area.
3. Cheaper per kilowatt hour of power than photovoltaic
4. Ideal for use in desert like atmospheres where there is plenty of land that is not arable and therefore is not good for most uses.
5. Can track the sun and provide higher efficiencies.
6. Used to heat water that turns a turbine in an electrical plant, therefore it is a known quantity and can use essentially the same systems as are presently used to produce electricity; conventional ac power which is easy to transmit; known capabilities.
7. It's possible that the Mojave desert in the United States and the territory around it in California, Nevada, Arizona, New Mexico, and Colorado can eventually produce all the required electricity for the United States. It definitely can handle the West and Southwest.
8. Clean power without environmental contamination during use. No carbon dioxide generated or other contaminating gases.

(B) **Hot water systems**

There are other thermal cells used for homes to heat the hot water and to heat pools. These systems are roof mounted and are fairly effective at providing the total hot water heating for a home and a separate system on the roof supplies hot water to the pool. These systems are less expensive to install than the others mentioned but they do not have the duties to carry out that the others do. Water is circulated up to the roofs by efficient pumps where they go through a maze of tubes within black panels that absorb the heat of the sun. The hot water systems are fed with this hot water reducing the amount of heat that would normally have to be provided by burning natural gas or using electric heaters to heat the hot water system of the home. These systems are fairly simple and the maintenance is fairly inexpensive. In parts of the world they supply more than enough heat for the hot water systems and the pool heating. The pay back on these systems is about five years.

The consumption of solar hot water and solar space heating was estimated at **88,000 MW** of thermal power in **2004.** The heating of water for unglazed swimming pools is excluded. (64)

Advantages of thermal hot water solar heaters

- Research shows that an average household with an electric water heater spends about 25% of its home energy costs on heating water. Solar water heaters offered the largest potential savings, with solar water-heater owners saving as much as 50% to 85% annually on their utility bills over the cost of electric water heating.
- Heating of pools. Thermal energy is used to heat pools and eliminates the cost of pool heating whether it is by an electric or natural gas heater.
- You can expect a simple payback of 4 to 8 years on a well-designed and properly installed solar water heater. (Simple payback is the length of time required to recover your investment through reduced or avoided energy costs.)
- Solar water heaters do not pollute. By investing in one, you will be avoiding carbon dioxide, nitrogen oxides, sulfur dioxide, and the other air pollution and wastes created when your utility generates power or you burn fuel to heat your household water. When a solar water heater replaces an electric water heater, the electricity displaced over 20 years represents more than 50 tons of avoided carbon dioxide emissions alone.
- * Solar hot water systems use sunlight to heat water. In low geographical latitudes (below 40 degrees) from 60 to 70% of the domestic hot water use with temperatures up to 60 °C can be provided by solar heating systems. (65) The most common types of solar water heaters are evacuated tube collectors (44%) and glazed flat plate collectors (34%) generally used for domestic hot water; and unglazed plastic collectors (21%) used mainly to heat swimming pools.
- As of 2007, the total installed capacity of solar hot water systems is approximately 154,000 MW (76).[36] China is the world leader in their deployment with 70,000 MW installed as of 2006 and a long term goal of 210,000 MW by 2020 (66). Israel is the per capita leader in the use of solar hot water systems with 90% of homes using them. In the United States, Canada and Australia heating swimming pools is the dominant

application of solar hot water with an installed capacity of approximately 20,000 MW.

Installation of Photovoltaic Systems

Between 1970 and 1983 photovoltaic installations grew rapidly, but falling oil prices in the early 1980s moderated the growth of PV from 1984 to 1996. Since 1997, PV development has accelerated due to supply issues with oil and natural gas, global warming concerns (see Kyoto Protocol), and the improving economic position of PV relative to other energy technologies. Photovoltaic production growth has averaged 40% per year since 2000 andinstalled capacity reached 10,600 MW at the end of 2007. (67) Since 2006 it has been economical for investors to install photovoltaics for free in return for a long term power purchase agreement. 50% of commercial systems were installed in this manner in 2007 and it is expected that 90% will by 2009.[124] Nellis Air Force Base is receiving.

Since the mid-1990s, leadership in the PV sector has shifted from the US to Japan and Germany. Between 1992 and 1994 Japan increased R&D funding, established net metering guidelines, and introduced a subsidy program to encourage the installation of residential PV systems. As a result, PV installations in the country climbed from 31.2 MW in 1994 to 318 MW in 1999,[74] and worldwide production growth increased to 30% in the late 1990s.[75]

Germany has become the leading PV market worldwide since revising its Feed-in tariff system as part of the Renewable Energy Sources Act. Installed PV capacity has risen from 100 MW in 2000 to approximately 4,150 MW at the end of 2007. (67) Spain has become the third largest PV market after adopting a similar feed-in tariff structure in 2004, while France, Italy, South Korea and the US have seen rapid growth recently due to various incentive programs and local market conditions.

Providing power for villages in developing countries is a fast-growing market for photovoltaics. The United Nations estimates that more than 2 million villages worldwide are without electric power for water supply, refrigeration, lighting, and other basic needs, and the cost of extending the utility grids is prohibitive, $23,000 to $46,000 per kilometer in 1988 and it is probably higher in 2008 – 2009. Interesting enough PV systems may follow the lead of what happened in India and China relative to telephone systems. Both of these countries were in poor shape when it came to telephones and it was going to take a lot of money and considerable time to install power lines and telephone lines in these countries. Then along came some dynamic inventions by Americans with the cell phone, the computer, the internet and even the camera. With the cell phone these countries could now forgo the large task of installing the power lines and all the paraphernalia required. With the cell phone they only had to supply terminal stations every 50 miles or so. Before you knew it both of these countries, as well as the rest of the world, had phone systems more flexible than the older systems. Then came the home computer and the internet and now the world was very small when it came to information. This is an example of technology advances that improves the lives of mankind. This example is given since the problem with supplying power to the many countries will be greatly reduced via the use of solar cells of the three kinds (PV, Thermal power, And Thermal Hot Water) of solar power.

A one kilowatt PV system receiving average sunlight each month provides some worthwhile environmental advantages:

- prevents 150 lbs. of coal from being mined
- prevents 300 lbs. of CO_2 from entering the atmosphere
- keeps 105 gallons of water from being consumed
- keeps NO and SO_2 from being released into the environment

A one kilowatt PV system in a place like Colorado provides even better results. When you see these numbers and the triple effect you receive (power while reducing contamination and reducing the use of water) it's a great momentum getter.

Production of PV cells for worldwide installation

In 2007 grid-connected photovoltaic electricity was the fastest growing energy source, with installations of all photovoltaics increasing by 83% in 2007 to bring the total installed capacity to **8,700 MW**. Nearly half of the increase was in Germany, now the world's largest consumer of photovoltaic electricity (followed by Japan). It's interesting that Germany has driven to the top on two of the renewable energy systems, the one of windmills and the other of solar power. Their plans include defocusing on nuclear power and emphasizing the use of natural gas much of which is piped in from Russia.

While this is promising it is not nearly enough to eventually replace the loss of oil energy.

Economics of solar power

See figure #6 below which shows the cost of the various renewable energy. It doesn't include nuclear since I am the only one (via this book) that is considering nuclear as a renewable energy. If someone showed this to you before you chose what type of renewable power you were going to install, you would see if you could install any of them besides solar since it is so expensive. All the other renewable energy systems are much lower and competitive to the grid electricity. However, this is deceiving because of the high initial costs of solar. However, if you review the choices it starts to direct one to solar. I will list each and give the reasons.

Small hydro – You might not have a water system available that provides more water than needed for other functions like drinking, irrigation (food), cooling of equipment and others.

Biomass – This is made up of burning of wood, paper and other disposable items. There is usually a shortage of this for present use at the location. It is very limited.

Geothermal – Probably not available. Geothermal is world location dependent and not much work has gone into this viable source of renewable energy for use around the world. It is a local choice

Wind – Wind is a selective world location source of energy and not available at many sites.

Nuclear – Very expensive installation costs but is viable if it serves a large area. Over time it has a payback and should always be considered especially in areas that cannot select one of the above

Figure 18 Cost competitiveness of selected renewable power technologies

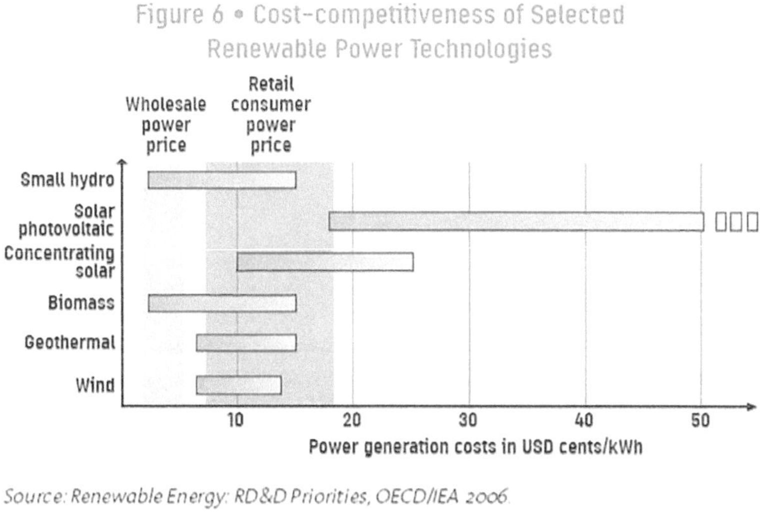

Figure 6 • Cost-competitiveness of Selected
Renewable Power Technologies

Source: Renewable Energy: RD&D Priorities, OECD/IEA 2006.

RenewableGeneratingCosts.jpg (33KB, MIME type: image/jpeg) (71)
http://www.wikinvest.com/image/RenewableGeneratingCosts.jpg (69)

The costs of renewable energy shown in the graph above are somewhat misleading. The wind costs do not take into account the facts I have discussed that this relates to installed power and one never seems to receive the installed power due to the variability of the winds and the fact that many of the wind mills do not produce energy at low wind velocity. The Geothermal is somewhat misleading since it is usually remotely located and cost money to activate it and it is only good for the local community and it not transmission able. The biomass is properly shown and is the way energy has been supplied since man found fire. The concentrating solar is not as costly as shown. It uses standard methods of delivering the energy through the use of heated water and turbines to provide standard electrical generation. It is usually a large installation that is costly for the reflecting panels but it requires no additional energy than the sun and except for maintenance costs is quite reasonable. I believe it will be competitive with oil in the not too distance future and will be the main growth area of supplying energy in the world. Solar voltaic is costly for installation but the cost is absorbed by the user and some federal assistance. IN approximately

233

eight years it pays for itself. Small hydro is properly shown and is ideal for small applications where there is water available.

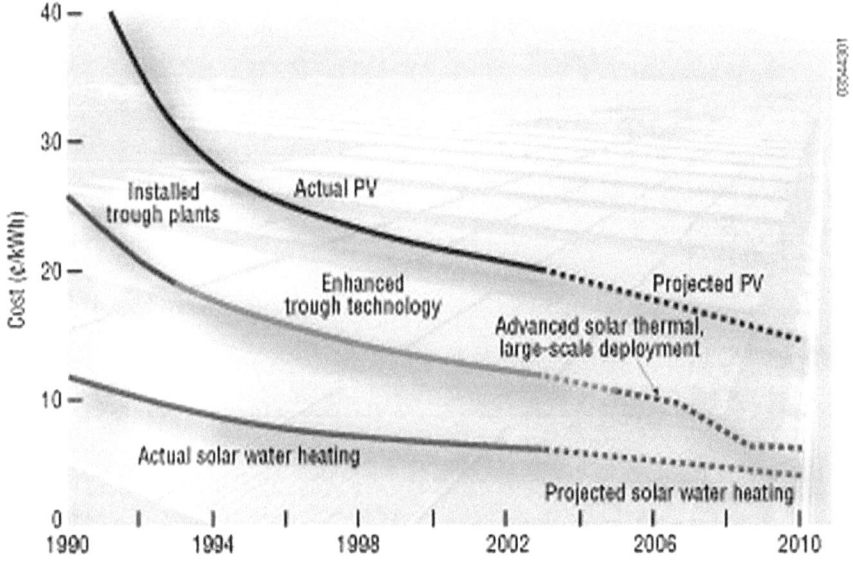

DecliningSolarCosts.gif http://www.wikinvest.com/industry/Solar_Power (72)

(69)

Declining Cost of Solar Energy

As you can see from the chart the cost of the various methods of applying solar power are all decreasing and are now reaching the costs of grid power or will in the very near future. This relates to my comments made on the cost of renewable and specifically on PV.

The use of trough energy is very important as it is the supplier of huge systems that are the kind of systems needed to provide grid power. The PV systems will continue to supply home systems and small factories and business buildings. The PV systems are becoming more efficient and this reduces the size of the system on the roofs for a given amount of energy being supplied. The "actual" water solar heaters have been less expensive since they are fairly straight forward and are used to heat water in the house hot water systems or swimming pools. At this point in time they are very competitive with grid hot water heaters and almost as inexpensive as natural gas hot water heaters.

Solar power generation has several unique features, one of them being that they are 'stand alone systems' and ideal for remote locations. Here again they remind me of the cellular phones and how they provided a function effectively. If located in a metropolitan area they can be tied to the grid and provide power to the grid when the system is underused in the home or office building. The major cost as I have mentioned is the initial cost and once that is amortized the system essentially provides energy free of charge. The only costs being the one of maintenance. One of the 'hindrances that never seem to be mentioned is the cost or one's own time required for cleaning the systems every so often so they stay efficient. Over time and weather they become dirty and are less able to absorb the suns rays effectively. There are cleaning services available if one doesn't accept the challenge to do it.

Like nuclear energy, the major driver of solar energy generating costs is the capital cost of installing the solar system. The good news is that the fuel (sun's rays) is always available; if not today then tomorrow. As can be seen on the graphs the costs are coming down and people buying, or businesses buying solar power will benefit by not installing until the volume is high such as is expected by the year 2009 – 2010 Cambridge Energy Research Associates estimates that every doubling in production capacity of PV modules should result in a 20% cost decline, prompting comparisons to personal computers and semiconductors, both of which have benefited from Moore's Law. In actual fact the law that will be followed is more like the book published by the Boston Consulting Group in 1967 which discusses "Experience Curves" and their findings is that most consumer products reduce in cost about 28% for each cumulative doubling of the volume. I believe the semiconductor industry is benefiting by this publication more than by Moore's Law. Texas Instruments lived by the Boston Consulting Group's estimated curves from 1967 through the 80's and may still be using them as their guide.

Governments of the various countries are aware of these learning curves based on volume and have pushed for reaching these volumes by subsidizing the initial costs of the building and installation of these systems. The whole integrated circuit market got its initial empathies from military funding by the U.S.Government back in 1959-60. The same procedures are being followed in the case of solar power. Many of the states in the U.S. and the Federal government is paying rebates on installation costs being incurred up through

2008 and will probably extend this. Germany, for example, has created a "feed-in" tariff system that requires utility companies to purchase solar energy from generators at the price of Euro 0.57/kwh (in 2004), or more than five times the maximum retail price for electricity in Germany. Essentially, this allows individuals and businesses to install solar systems and sell their solar energy back to the grid. U.S. encouragement for solar has been more subtle, focusing on tax breaks for the capital cost of installing solar systems and, in some states there are rebates to offset the high initial costs. The chart illustrates the battle that solar continues to face, especially in making inroads into the wholesale (i.e., on-grid) electrical market. However, the next chart illustrates the trend in solar pricing, and gives optimism to those making long term bets on the industry.

PV Solar, like all sources of energy other than perhaps wind, does require valuable raw materials, whose scarcity can often increase costs. In the case of solar, as I have previously mentioned, there is a direct battle with the integrated circuit market for the semiconductor material. Scarcity of silicon, which is also used to make wafers for microprocessors in your PC, has mitigated the downward spiral in the cost of solar systems. See, for example, the chart of the retail price of solar modules over the past six years. I personally believe this will change dramatically over the next two years because the economy is down and the demand for cars, computers and other semiconductor integrated circuits will be lower than normal while the demand for solar for energy is growing and it will take much of the silicon for the next few years. In the end this will help both markets as the semiconductor costs will come down because of the volume demand for solar material while the integrated circuit market is in a slow down.

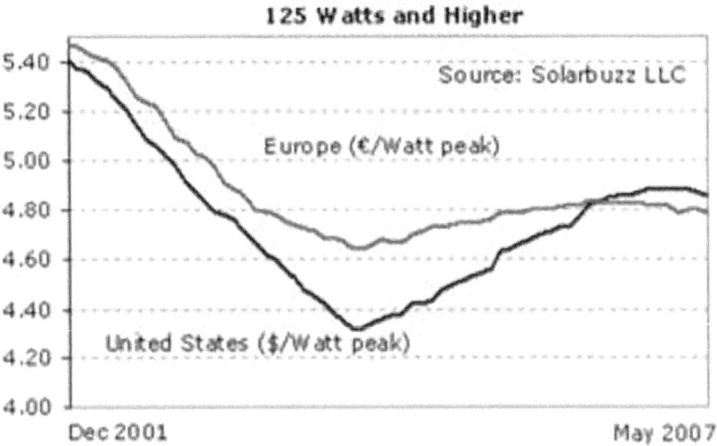

Figure 19 Scare silicon has caused retail prices of solar modules to rebound, but I believe this will change in 2008 and 2009.

It is worth reviewing the following list of conversion efficiencies provided by the various manufacturers. (72) Notice how efficient SunPower, with its polysilicon wafers, is well above the other suppliers in the industry. It is important for the purchaser to know this listing. With higher efficiencies less cells need to be placed on the roofs of homes or for a given number on the roof it supplies more power and much of it goes back to the grid to recapture some of the costs. The buyer should use this and the initial costs of the supplier for installation and figure out their return on investment. When all is said and done, once this payoff is made the units with the higher efficiency will allow the user to be less concerned about receiving power from a grid that is going to keep increasing in expense due to the loss of oil in the near future. That's one of the things this book is about. Notice that the thin film approaches are rather inefficient at this time. This should change in the next couple of years as the technologies developed will bring the efficiencies up. One thing to keep in mind other than the costs is there is no cost as high as not having energy. This will be here when oil isn't. **Figure 20 displays the various suppliers of PV Solar and their conversion efficiencies**

Industry Conversion Efficiencies	
Manufacturer	**Conversion Efficiency**
SunPower(Polysilicon)	23.4%[4]
Suntech Power Holdings(Polysilicon)	18%[5]
Sharp (Polysilicon)	13%[6]
Kyocera (Polysilicon)	18.5%[7]
Solarfun (Polysilicon)	17.2%[8]
JA Solar Holdings (Monosilicon)	17.7%[9]
Trina Solar(Mono & Polysilicon)	16.6%[10]
Evergreen Solar (String Ribbon)	15%[11]
EMCORE (GaAs Concentrated Solar System)	37%[12]
Energy Conversion Devices (Amorphous Silicon Thin Film)	8.5%[13]
First Solar (CdTe Thin Film)	10.5%[4]
DayStar Technologies(CIGS Thin Film)	14% [14]
Ascent Solar (CIGS Flexible Thin Film)	9.5% [15]

Concentrated Thermal Solar Is More Competitively Priced than PV Solar

Remember the discussion about the parabolic reflectors concentrating the suns power onto steam generators to produce power the conventional way of driving turbines. You can see in the curves that this cost is cheaper than PV and is mainly used for large systems that supply cities or large areas. This is less costly to install since it is like conventional machinery once the concentration of the solar energy has done its job; using existing generators, piping and mirrors, the production costs are much lower than PV solar and don't require special production facilities. The industry also does not use any rare or dangerous materials that have the potential to hinder production or face governmental restriction. Concentrated solar can also store the heat in salt or other materials to allow it to provide electricity twenty four hours a day. Most of this technology was developed by Sandia years back. Some systems are storing the heat in other material besides salt such as high temperature oils. This is much cheaper than storing energy in batteries that many PV systems use and windmill farms use. The cost and replacing of batteries is an expensive factor since it takes up so much labor time. I mentioned a system going into Spain that uses a version of this method. A Sandia National Laboratory study in 2008 projected that concentrated solar would reach the competitive level of 8-10 cents per kilowatt hour when international production reaches 3000 MW which is upon us now. The same study expects production to be double that by 2013, a full two years before DSTI expects to reach competitive pricing. The many advances made on this source of energy makes it very feasible to reach more than double the amount discussed I the study. I see this form of energy being employed more and more worldwide using the basic technology developed by Sandia of New Mexico.

Production of PV solar cells.

The production of PV Solar cells increased by 50% in 2007, to 3,800 megawatts, and has been doubling every two years. (73) This is a key and fundamental factor. Installations of these systems can never grow any faster than the production of the voltaic Solar cells. When one is trying to reach 40 million megawatts (40M MW) by the year of 2037 to offset the loss of oil's energy, we must be producing a significant amount of solar cell capacity each year. The installations can not move any faster than the production moves. This brings us to one of the possible limiting factors when we depend on silicon photovoltaic cells which are the number one source of PV cells. The amount of photovoltaic silicon solar cells depends on the supply of polysilicon. When you consider the amount of polysilicon that is devoted to the production of integrated circuits each year you understand the amount of polysilicon that must be manufactured. So far, the manufacturers of polysilicon are barely keeping up with today's demands. Unless some other method such as thin film photocells proves its capability and then increases its production, the demand for polysilicon may limit the production of silicon photovoltaic cells. As indicated above, the 2007 production of 3,800 megawatts of capability was a good start and if it is expected to double each year, it will be a help. If the rate of annual production stayed at 3800 it would take over ten thousand years to make enough of these types of cells to meet the energy target. If we continue to double this amount each year we will just make it by the year 2037. However, this means on the thirtieth year we would have to make one half of 40 million megawatts or 20 million megawatts of solar cell capability to meet the goal of displacing the lost of oil energy. This is unreasonable but this should be the goal in mind while summing the various methods of renewable energy. Keep in mind that there will be contributions by the other renewable energy sources that will reduce this goal. For example the thermal use of solar energy and the parabolic panels will be going in the same direction in parallel and may be able to cut the PV system requirements in half. Also we may become more efficient in the logistics that will be discussed and maybe only have to make 20 million megawatts to offset the loss of oil as an energy source by the year 2037. If this can be accomplished the PV and the Parabolic method each would have to reach approximately 10 million megawatts less whatever renewable power is supplied by the other methods discussed or to be discussed.

Cross over power - Natural Gas

Keep in mind that I have taken a stance that until reaching this goal of replacing the energy of oil we should be using **natural gas** in as many applications as possible to give us a cross-over source of fairly clean energy and to prevent the use of coal and its subsequent contamination of the atmosphere at a greater level than oil derivatives. Let's keep reviewing the other sources supplying renewable power that will relieve this total.

Keep in mind that this approach is very efficient on the use of land, especially versus the use of hydroelectric power. It would be interesting to determine how much energy could have been generated using photovoltaic cells in the area used for the Three Gorges Dam project if we would have been producing these high amounts of solar photovoltaic cells in 1993 till the present. We would have covered much less land with the solar cells than the land inefficient method of hydroelectric power. In those fifteen years we would have generated approximately the net loaded power generated by the hydroelectric system in approximately one third of the area. That was a huge area and used arable land that is needed to feed the people of China. But the real world is that you work with what you have. China had a large piece of land surrounded by huge cliffs and the Yanze River within reach. There were no large volumes of solar cells available at the time and they did a fantastic job with what they had. It didn't quite work out as well as they had planned due to unforeseen issues. Perhaps now they can review their plans to build other huge dams on the Yellow river and other rivers within reach of the Three Gorges Dam and see if an approach using photovoltaic cells or panorama thermal cells to reach their goals. They obviously will have the land and with this approach they would not need to move people away from their homes. In fact they could build the solar cells at a height that is above the villages and perhaps not move anyone; or very little. This would be cleaner than large dams and if they put their large population to work on making solar panels they would kill two birds with one stone.

The total solar energy absorbed by Earth's atmosphere, oceans and land masses is approximately 3,850 zettajoules (ZJ) per year. Which is equivalent to 1.2×10^5 million megawatts. (74) In 2002, this was more energy in one hour than the world used in a year

Photovoltaics (PV) is the field of technology and research related to the application of solar cells for energy by converting sunlight directly into electricity. Due to the growing need for solar energy, the manufacture of solar cells and photovoltaic arrays has expanded dramatically in recent years. (81) [2] [3] Photovoltaic production has been doubling every two years, increasing by an average of 48 percent each year since 2002, making it the world's fastest-growing energy technology. At the end of 2007, according to preliminary data, cumulative global production was 12,400 megawatts. (82)[4] Roughly 90% of this generating capacity consists of grid-tied electrical systems. Such installations may be ground-mounted (and sometimes integrated with farming and grazing) or built into the roof or walls of a building, known as Building Integrated Photovoltaic or BIPV for short (82).[6] Financial incentives, such as preferential feed-in tariffs for solar-generated electricity and net metering, have supported solar PV installations in many countries including Germany, Japan, and the United States.

See the figure 21 below which shows the areas of the United States having the most ideal locations for solar power. (75) This is based on the amount of yearly sun, clear skies and in some cases the average temperature. Although solar voltaic cells work off the Sun's wavelengths for its energy, there are also thermal solar cells that work off the Sun's heat and direct this heat to Earth applications. Therefore there may be parts of the United States that do not have a high temperature average but receive a great deal of sunshine which is ideal for solar voltaic cells. An example of this might be the high areas in Colorado where people like to ski. The average temperature is not high at these ski resorts in Colorado but the sunshine is bright and provides the wavelengths required for solar voltaic cells.

Places like California and Arizona have ideal climates for both thermal and voltaic applications and these states are moving rapidly to accommodate the energy needs of the local communities and the state's requirements. See figure 21

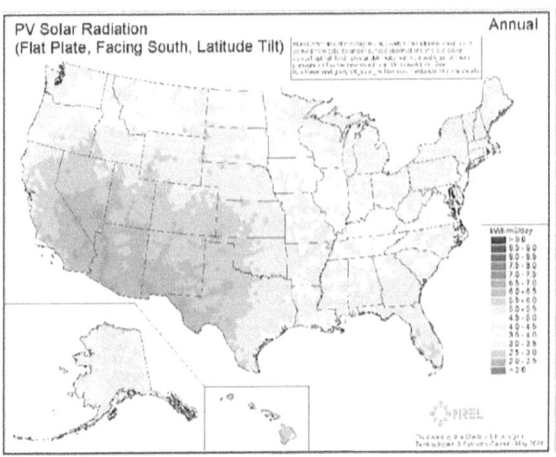

Figure 21 United States' optimum solar locations for photovoltaic cells

See the map of the world below in figure 22. It shows, using an average solar irradiance of 170 watts per square meter, where the optimum locations would be for photovoltaic solar cells. (75) Note that this is for a horizontal surface, whereas solar panels are normally propped up at an angle and receive more energy per unit area.

The dots and the related solar cells would add up to 18 million MW of energy. This is equal to 18 million megawatts of energy and is about the amount of renewable energy I feel is needed by the year 2037 to replace the loss of oil energy and to be able to handle the different logistics involved with this type of energy generation.. If oil is not lost by the year 2037, it won't be many years after that. This depends on the use of oil and its derivatives as countries like China build up their economy and the population of the world grows to 8.7 billion by then. The key is to convert many of the world's machinery that uses oil and its derivatives to electricity supplied by the renewable energy sources or with natural gas as the crossover energy until we are able to build up our renewable energy.

Figure 22 Ideal locations for PV solar in the world

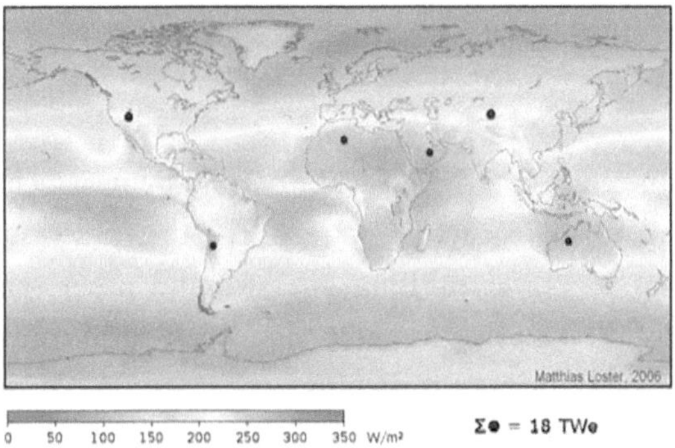

Matthias Loster, 2006

0   50   100 150 200 250 300 350 W/m²   Σ● = 18 TWe

Figure 23 - Ideal locations of Solar Photovoltaic in Europe

See the map below which shows the ideal locations of solar photovoltaic cells in Europe. (75)

The obvious locations are Portugal, Spain, Turkey, Greece and some very good locations in Italy, France, Romania, and the southern areas around the Mediterranean Sea. It's interesting that Germany is not ideally located for these installations, yet they lead the world in solar generation along with Spain and Portugal. Several islands in the Mediterranean could probably supply their total needs with photovoltaic solar cells. There has been a dramatic build up of cell matrixes in parts of Europe.

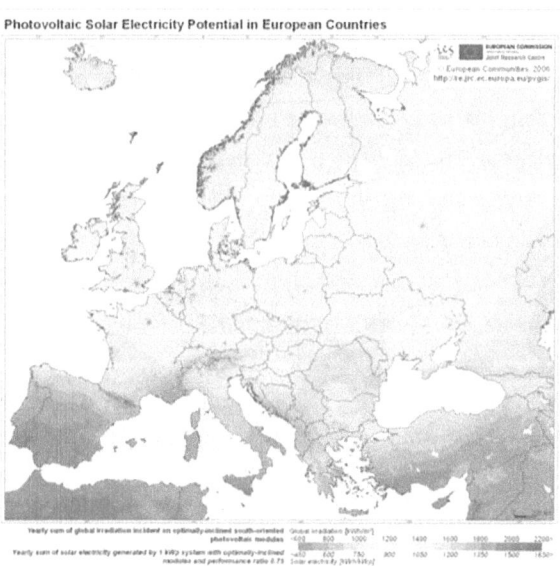

Photovoltaic Solar Electricity Potential in European Countries

Solar cells produce direct current electricity from light, which can be used to power equipment or to recharge a battery. The first practical application of photovoltaics was to power orbiting satellites and other spacecraft, but today the majority of photovoltaic modules are used for grid connected power generation. In this case an inverter is required to convert the DC to AC. There is a smaller market for off grid power for remote dwellings, roadside emergency telephones, remote sensing, and cathodic protection of pipelines. With the advent of the use of LED's as a light source and its low current draw and long life, it is ideally coupled with remote electrical stations for supplying light and electricity for other applications.

Cells require protection from the environment and are packaged usually behind a glass sheet. When more power is required than a single cell can deliver, cells are electrically connected together to form photovoltaic modules, or solar panels. A single module is enough to power an emergency telephone, but for a house or a power plant the modules must be arranged in arrays. Although the selling price of modules is still too high to compete with grid electricity in most places, significant financial incentives in Japan and then Germany triggered a huge growth in demand, followed quickly by production. Although the incentives were not as high in the United States and other countries, this is changing as the governments of the various countries realize the actions must start now to prepare for the not too distant future.

The most important issue with solar panels is capital cost (installation and materials). Newer alternatives to standard crystalline silicon modules including casting wafers instead of sawing, thin film, concentrator modules, 'Sliver' cells, and continuous printing processes. Due to economies of scale solar panels get less costly as people use and buy more — as manufacturers increase production to meet demand, the cost and price is expected to drop in the years to come. By early 2006, the average cost per installed watt for a residential sized system was about $7.50 to $9.50, including panels, inverters, mounts, and electrical items. (76) In 2006 investors began offering free solar panel installation in return for a 25 year contract, or Power Purchase Agreement, to purchase electricity at a fixed price, normally set at or below current electric rates. It is expected that by 2009 over 90% of commercial photovoltaics installed in the United States will be installed using a power purchase agreement. (135)

Life-cycle analyses show that the energy intensity of typical solar photovoltaic technologies is rapidly evolving. In 2000 the energy payback time was estimated as 8 to 11 years(76), but more recent studies suggest that technological progress has reduced this to 1.5 to 3.5 years for crystalline silicon PV systems. (136)

Thin film technologies now have energy pay-back times in the range of 1-1.5 years (S.Europe). With lifetimes of such systems of at least 30 years, the EROEI is in the range of 10 to 30. They thus generate enough energy over their lifetimes to reproduce themselves many times (6-31 reproductions, the EROEI is a bit lower) depending on what type of material, balance of system (or BOS), and the geographic location of the system. (77)

Disadvantages

- Solar electricity is often more expensive than electricity generated by other sources, in the initial installation but will pay back over time. The cost of no energy is much higher.
- Solar electricity is not available at night and is less available in cloudy weather conditions. Therefore, a storage or complementary power system is required. There have been major advancements in this area, mostly in the type of battery used to store the energy.
- Limited power density: Average daily insolation in the contiguous U.S. is 3-7 kW·h/m² (kilowatt hour per meter squared) (77) and on average lower in Europe.
- Solar cells produce DC which must be converted to AC (using a grid tie inverter) when used in currently existing distribution grids. This incurs an energy loss of 4-12%. This converter is included in the installation costs. The energy loss is included in the net solar power per meter squared.
- One may not have any other choice.

Major companies supplying photovoltaic solar cells and thermal solar cells

The major suppliers of photovoltaics PV cells through 2007 include BP Solar, Isofoton, Kyocera, Q-Cells, Sanyo, Sharp Solar, SolarWorld, SunPower, Suntech, and Yingli Green Energy (84).

BP has been involved in solar power since 1973 and its subsidiary, BP Solar, is now one of the world's largest solar power companies with production facilities in the United States, Spain, India and Australia, employing a workforce of over 2,000 people worldwide. BP Solar is a major worldwide manufacturer and installer of photovoltaic solar cells for electricity. The company has begun constructing two new solar photovoltaic (PV) solar cell manufacturing plants, one at its European headquarters in Tres Cantos, Madrid, and the second at its joint venture facility, Tata BP Solar, in Bangalore, India.

Isofoton is a Spanish company that designs and manufactures high-efficiency monocrystalline silicon cells and panels, as well as concentrated photovoltaics (CPV). Isofoton is present in over 60 countries, having subsidiaries in America, Africa, Asia, and Europe.

Kyocera Corporation has announced a plan to increase its solar cell production to 500 MW per year in 2010. 500 MW is about three times the current output of 180 MW, and the company will reinforce production bases in Japan, the US, Europe and China, investing a total of about ¥30 billion through FY2010. Through this production enhancement, Kyocera looks to meet increasing demand across the world for solar cells.

Nanosolar has been named Innovator of the Year for 2007 by Popular Science Magazine, in connection with its PowerSheet flexible solar film. Nanosolar manufactures PowerSheet by printing a solar-activated ink onto metal sheets in a low-cost, continuous process. Nanosolar is building a plant in San Jose, CA and one near Berlin, Germany. It promises to deliver solar film that will be low enough in cost to be at cost parity with power from the electrical grid.

Q-Cells is the world's second largest cell manufacturer, based in Thalheim, Germany. Q-Cells reached an agreement with the government of Mexico to build its new production complex for thin-film PV modules with an investment of U$3.5 billion in the mid-long term. With this, Q-Cells expect to achieve a better access to the growing Mexican and American markets.[94][95]

Renewable Energy Corporation (REC) is based in Norway, and was established in 1996. Over a relatively short period, REC has become the world's largest producer of polysilicon and wafers for PV applications. REC is involved in all steps of the value chain, from production of solar grade silicon to wafer, cell and module production. The company has customers all over the globe and seven production plants in three different countries. It operates on three different continents and has approximately 1,100 employees.

Sanyo Electric produced $213 million worth of solar cells at its plant in Hungary in 2006, and expects to triple its production capacity to 720,000 units in 2008.

Schott is one of the world largest producers of solar photovoltaic technologies. SCHOTT employs over 900 people and has worldwide production capacity of over 130 MW per year..

Sharp Solar is the world's largest photovoltaic module and cell manufacturer, which manufactures in Japan, and near Wrexham, UK. Sharp Solar produces both single and multi-crystalline solar cells which are used for many applications, from satellites to lighthouses, and industrial applications to residential use. Sharp began researching solar cells in 1959 with mass production first beginning in 1963. Production capacity amounted to 324 MW in 2004. (77)

SolarWorld is headquartered in Bonn, Germany, and purchased Shell Solar's crystalline silicon activities in 2006.

SunPower Corporation designs and manufactures high-efficiency silicon solar cells and solar panels based on an all-back-contact "All-Black" design. They install them through their subsidiary PowerLight. Recent projects include the Nellis Solar Power Plant, the largest PV installation in North America. SunPower's headquarters is in Sunnyvale California. The cells supplied have the highest conversion efficiency to date therefore providing more power per square meter than other methods of PV systems. This reduces the amount of panels needed on a roof for a given power required by the home owner. This can be a critical consideration. Much of the silicon is probably supplied by the parent company of SunPower which is Cypress Semiconductor located in Silicon Valley.

Suntech Power is based in Wuxi, China, where construction of a 1 GW module plant has begun. Year-end production capacity for 2007 is expected to be 480 MW. (77) per year.

Yingli Green Energy is currently one of the largest manufacturers of PV products in China, with an annual production capacity of 200 megawatts of polysilicon ingots and wafers, cells and PV modules, as of July 2007. Yingli Green Energy sells PV modules under its own brand name, Yingli Solar, to PV system integrators and distributors located in various markets around the world, including Germany, Spain, China and the United States.

Many new companies have entered the solar production area. They produce solar cells for other companies who install them on home roofs, business roofs and over parking lots. Japan used to be the biggest supplier and owned over 50% of the PVC market. However, this has changed as many new companies have entered the market as suppliers. Most of them use the approach of a silicon cell for the PVC market. There is at least one major United States supplier, CdTe, using a thin film approach, but there are more expected to enter this market in the next year. With companies entering the market from China, Taiwan, Australia and more from The United States, Japan's share of market has dropped to approximately twenty percent. However, even this will probably change within the next year as many of the Japanese suppliers are planning on placing higher quantities on the market.

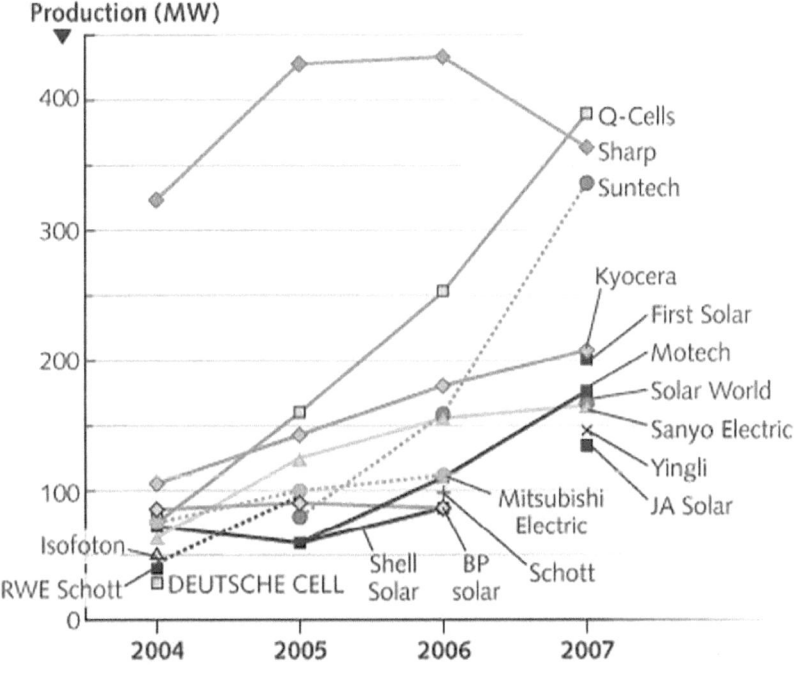

Figure 24 Graph of the growth of suppliers to the market and added new suppliers.

Source (78) Nomura Securities, Nikkei Microdevices as displayed in Solid State Technology magazine of October 08

See the chart above and notice the large increase in the volume of the suppliers. Where suppliers used to supply capacity up to a MW, this shows that many companies are now supplying hundreds of Megawatts per year and this will continue to grow. Keep in mind the objective would be to supply approximately ten million megawatts of renewable power (including nuclear) by the year 2037. With these companies supplying PV cells in the hundreds of megawatts per year there is a chance of making the 2037 objective. Note that the curve summation is just over 2000 MW per year, entering the year 2008. In twenty nine years, if the supply quantities by each of these companies remained at the peak points on the chart we would fall quite short of what is needed. If this supply stayed flat it would only provide approximately 60,000 MW (or 60 GW) of the 10,000,000 MW (or 10,000 GW) needed. This is **only 0.006 of what is needed according to my projections**, being a tenth of one percent of the target. This indicates there is still a lot of room in this market for new suppliers and for growth by these suppliers.

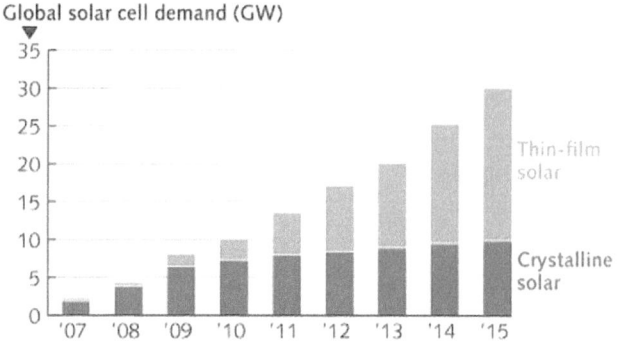

Global solar cell demand (GW)

Figure 25 Chart of buildup of supplies of crystalline and thin film (Source Nomura Securities, Nikkei Microdevices) as displayed in Solid State Technology magazine (78)

A farther review of the build up shows that in the next seven years the volumes that will be supplied are listed in the GW (gigawatt) range instead of the MW (megawatt) range. This is a big step forward with the year 2015 supplying thirty GW of crystalline and thin film photovoltaic cells. Notice the big increase in the thin film portion of the supply. This large increase in the thin film portion is based on new thin film approaches that are expected to advance over the next several years. To date the thin film has not grown at the rate of the crystalline approach because of its lower efficiency. Many of these approaches are running at six percent efficiency. However, there have been some breakthroughs in the crystalline with efficiencies of eighteen percent. This major thrust in the thin film is also being generated due to the inability of the silicon suppliers to supply the polysilicon in volume great enough to provide the needs of both the solar cell and the integrated circuit needs.

If this amount stayed constant from 2015 to 2037 at a 30,000 MW rate per year it would provide a cumulative amount of 660,000 MW versus the goal of 10,000,000 MW or 6.6 percent of the need. This is meant to show that even with this build up the supply is not close to what is needed by 2037. However, if the supply curve keeps increasing at the rate shown on the chart it would reach a yearly supply of 60 to 70,000W per year by the year 2037 and a cumulative amount of approximately 1,100,000 MW or about eleven percent of what is needed. However, this doesn't include the thermal solar cell approach which is the approach used for large facilities or to supply a complete town or a large metropolitan area. I believe this method will be in a position to supply much greater quantities of total solar power and bring the total from solar to close to the need for 2037.

The key in reaching the needed amount is fivefold:

1. Keep the growth curve of the Photovoltaic cells increasing at the rate shown (or slight above) what is shown in the chart.
2. Keep the thermal solar supply increasing using the solar reflectors to heat water to steam that turns the turbines of the large electrical generator plants. This is the commercial side of the solar market that doesn't require PV cells.
3. Invention of improved thin film PV approaches with greater efficiency.
4. Maintain the supply of polysilicon required to support the PV approach.
5. Reducing the cost per kilowatt of power to a level approaching that of present electrical costs from the power generating stations to induce more people to convert to this form of energy.

I believe these are all real and reachable goals. There is no blue sky in them. They are factual and determined by proper planning and the available economics in the world over these twenty nine years.

World solar photovoltaic (PV) market installations reached a record high of 2,800 MW in 2007. (136)

The three leading countries (Germany, Japan and the USA) represent nearly 89% of the total worldwide PV installed capacity. On Wed 1 August 2007, word was published of construction of a production facility in China, which is projected to be one of the largest wafer factories in the world, with a peak capacity of around 1,500MW. (79))

Germany was the fastest growing major PV market in the world during 2006 and 2007. In 2007, over 1300 MW of PV was installed. The German PV industry generates over 10,000 jobs in production, distribution and installation. By the end of 2006, nearly 88% of all solar PV installations in the EU were in grid-tied applications in Germany. The balance is off-grid (or stand alone) systems.(85) Photovoltaic power capacity is measured as maximum power output under standardized test conditions

Photovoltaic solar panels on a house roof.

Building-integrated photovoltaics (BIPV) are increasingly incorporated into new domestic and industrial buildings as a principal or ancillary source of electrical power, (80) and are one of the fastest growing segments of the photovoltaic industry. Typically, an array is incorporated into the roof or walls of a building and roof tiles with integrated PV cells can now be purchased. Arrays can also be retrofitted into existing buildings; in this case they are usually fitted on top of the existing roof structure. Alternatively, an array can be located separately from the building but connected by cable to supply power for the building.

Where a building is at a considerable distance from the public electricity supply (or grid) - in remote or mountainous areas – PV may be the preferred possibility for generating electricity, or PV may be used together with wind, diesel generators and/or hydroelectric power. In such off-grid circumstances batteries are usually used to store the electric power.

PV has traditionally been used for auxiliary power in space and the space programs can probably be credited for bringing solar to where it is today. PV is rarely used to provide motive power in transport applications because it doesn't have enough power, but is being used increasingly to provide auxiliary power in boats and cars. Recent advances in solar cell technology, however, have shown the cell's ability to administer significant hydrogen production, making it one of the top prospects for alternative energy for automobiles.

PV in standalone devices

Solar parking meter.

PV has been used for many years to power calculators and novelty devices. Improvements in integrated circuits and low power LCD displays make it possible to power a calculator for several years between battery changes, making solar calculators less common. In contrast, solar powered remote fixed devices have seen increasing use recently, due to increasing cost of labor for connection of mains electricity or a regular maintenance program. In particular, parking meters, emergency telephones, and temporary traffic signs are using solar.

Solar systems are beginning to displace such things as night lights surrounding homes. They charge during the day and come on during the night. They charge rechargeable batteries.

With increased usage of LED arrays for lighting, especially in remote areas, solar systems are ideal for charging the systems and eliminating the need for power being supplied to remote places. LED systems use low power to supply significant lighting and the LED lifetimes are extremely long. More recently traffic light systems have gone to LED's use to reduce power and these are supplied by solar systems in many locations. The combination of LED's and solar systems will find many uses for [edit] Economics of PV

Grid parity

Grid parity, the point at which photovoltaic electricity is equal to or cheaper than grid power, is achieved first in areas with abundant sun and high costs for electricity such as in California and Japan and probably Spain. If not now, it will be within ten years for those locations.

Grid parity has been reached in Hawaii and other islands that otherwise use diesel fuel to produce electricity.

George W. Bush has set 2015 as the date for grid parity in the USA. General Electric's Chief Engineer predicts grid parity without subsidies in sunny parts of the United States by around 2015. Other companies predict an earlier date.

Financial incentives

The political purpose of incentive policies for PV is to grow the industry even where the cost of PV is significantly above grid parity, to allow it to achieve the economies of scale necessary to reach grid parity. The policies are implemented to promote national energy independence, high tech job creation and reduction of CO_2 emissions.

Three incentive mechanisms are used (often in combination):

- Investment subsidies: the authorities refund part of the cost of installation of the system,
- Feed-in Tariffs (**FIT**)/Net metering: the electricity utility buys PV electricity from the producer under a multiyear contract at a guaranteed rate.
- Renewable Energy Certificates (**"RECs"**)

With investment subsidies, the financial burden falls upon the taxpayer to make the initial investment and this is supported by state and federal programs. With feed-in tariffs the extra cost is distributed across the utilities' customer bases. While the investment subsidy may be simpler to administer, the main argument in favor of feed-in tariffs is the encouragement of quality rather than personal satisfaction. It's quality for the investment. Investment subsidies are paid out as a function of the nameplate capacity of the installed system and are independent of its actual power yield over time, thus rewarding the overstatement of power and tolerating poor durability and maintenance. Some electric companies offer rebates to their customers, such as Austin Energy in Texas, which offers $4.50/watt installed up to $13,500. (81)

With feed-in tariffs (FIT), the financial burden falls upon the consumer Normally with net metering deficits are billed each month, while surpluses are rolled over to the following month and paid annually.

Where price setting by supply and demand is preferred, RECs can be used. In this mechanism, a renewable energy production or consumption target is set, and the consumer or producer is obliged to purchase renewable energy from whoever provides it the most competitively. The producer is paid via an REC. In principle this system delivers the cheapest renewable energy, since the lowest bidder will win. However, uncertainties about the future value of energy produced seem to apply a negative break to people taking the risk. They keep thinking it will not be cheaper than they are paying now and they may think they will be gone when it gets cheaper. The Japanese government through its Ministry of International Trade and Industry ran a successful program of subsidies from 1994 to 2003. By the end of 2004, Japan led the world in installed PV capacity with over 1,100 MW.

In 2004, the German government introduced the first large-scale feed-in tariff system, under a law known as the 'EEG' (Erneuerbare Energien Gesetz) which resulted in explosive growth of PV installations in Germany. At the outset the FIT was over 3x the retail price or 8x the industrial price. The principle behind the German system is a 20 year flat rate contract. The value of new contracts is programmed to decrease each year, in order to encourage the industry to pass on lower costs to the end users. The program has been more successful than expected with over 1,000 MW installed in 2006, and political pressure is mounting to decrease the tariff to lessen the future burden on consumers.

Subsequently Spain, Italy, Greece and France introduced feed-in tariffs. None have replicated the programmed decrease of FIT in new contracts though, making the German incentive relatively less and less attractive compared to other countries. The French FIT offers a uniquely high premium (EUR 0.55/ kWh) for building integrated systems. California, Greece, France and Italy have 30-50% more insolation than Germany making them financially more attractive.

In 2006 California approved the 'California Solar Initiative', offering a choice of investment subsidies or FIT for small and medium systems and a FIT for large systems. The small-system FIT of $0.39 per kWh (far less than EU countries) expires in just 5 years, and the alternate "EPBB" residential investment incentive is modest, averaging perhaps 20% of cost. All California incentives are scheduled to decrease in the future depending as a function of the amount of PV capacity installed.

At the end of 2006, the Ontario Power Authority (Canada) began its Standard Offer Program, the first in North America for small renewable projects (10MW or less). This guarantees a fixed price of $0.42 CDN per kWh over a period of twenty years. Unlike net metering, all the electricity produced is sold to the OPA at the SOP rate. The generator then purchases any needed electricity at the current prevailing rate (e.g., $0.055 per kWh).

The difference should cover all the costs of installation and operation over the life of the contract.

The price per kilowatt hour or per peak kilowatt of the FIT or investment subsidies is only one of three factors that stimulate the installation of PV. The other two factors are insolation (the more sunshine, the less capital is needed for a given power output) and administrative ease of obtaining permits and contracts.

Unfortunately the complexity of approvals in California, Spain and Italy has prevented comparable growth to Germany even though the return on investment is better.

Environmental impacts

Unlike fossil fuel based technologies, solar power does not lead to any harmful emissions during operation, but the production of the panels leads to some amount of pollution. This is often referred to as the energy input to output ratio. In some analysis, if the energy input to produce it is higher than the output it produces it can be considered environmentally more harmful than beneficial. Also, placement of photovoltaics affects the environment. If they are located where photosynthesizing plants would normally grow, they simply substitute one potentially renewable resource (biomass) for another. It should be noted, however, that the biomass cycle converts solar radiation energy to electrical energy with significantly less efficiency than photovoltaic cells alone. And if they are placed on the sides of buildings (such as in Manchester) or fences, or rooftops (as long as plants would not normally be placed there), or in the desert they are purely additive to the renewable power base.

Large installations in the Mojave Desert

The Mojave Desert in southwestern United States has proven to be a great place to install thermal solar systems. The installations are large and it is possible that the Mojave Desert locations in Southern California, Arizona, Nevada and Utah may eventually be able to supply the power requirements for most of the southwestern part of the United States, including parts of California..

Mojave Desert (82) http://upload.wikimedia.org/wikipedia/en/c/c9/Usgs_
mojave_desert.jpg

Figure 26 Extent of Mojave Desert. Green square is the area of a survey made by the USGS which covers 25,000 square miles (65,000 km2)

There are several **solar power plants in the Mojave Desert** which supply power to the electricity grid. **Solar Energy Generating Systems (SEGS)** is the name given to nine solar power plants in the Mojave Desert which were built in the 1980s. These plants have a combined capacity of 354 megawatts (MW) of thermal solar power, making them the largest solar power installation in the world. (83)

Nevada Solar One is a new solar thermal plant with a 64-MW generating capacity, located near Boulder City, NV. (137) There are also plans to build other large solar plants in the Mojave Desert. The Mojave Solar Park will deliver **553 MW of solar thermal power** when fully operational in 2011.

Insolation (solar radiation) in the Mojave Desert is among the best available in the United States, and some significant population centers are located in the area. This makes the Mojave Desert particularly suitable for solar power plants. These plants can generally be built in a few years because solar plants are built almost entirely with modular, readily available materials. There have been innovations to the type of systems used and they came from Sandia and are now being installed in other locations such as in Spain. These innovations provide a greater power output for the amount of land area used. See the section on Spain.

Overview

The southwestern United States is one of the world's best areas for insolation, and the Mojave Desert receives up to twice the sunlight received in other regions of the country. This abundance of solar energy makes solar power plants an attractive alternative to traditional power plants which burn polluting fossil fuels such as oil and coal. Unlike traditional power plants, solar power stations provide an environmentally benign source of energy, produce virtually no emissions, and consume no fuel other than sunlight. (84) The only thing negative about them is they use land and that is not always available in places where sun is available.

Currently, the cost of solar thermal produced energy can be close to 12 cents (US) per kilowatt-hour (kWh). However, many economists predict that this price will gradually drop over the next ten years to 6 cents per kWh, as a result of economies of scale and technological improvements. This is extremely important since the cost of the grid power will be increasing due to the cost of oil, natural gas, and coal and normal inflation economics.

While many of the costs of fossil fuels are well known, others (pollution related health problems, environmental degradation, the impact on national security from relying on foreign energy sources) are indirect and difficult to calculate. These are traditionally external to the pricing system, and are thus often referred to as externalities. A corrective pricing mechanism, such as a carbon tax, could lead to renewable energy, such as solar thermal power, becoming cheaper to the consumer than fossil fuel based energy within a few years. (85).

Solar thermal power plants can generally be built in a few years because solar plants are built almost entirely with modular, readily available materials. In contrast, many types of conventional power projects, especially coal and nuclear plants, require long lead times.

Solar One and Solar Two

Aerial view of the Solar Two facility, showing the power tower (left) surrounded by the sun-tracking mirrors (138)

Solar power towers use thousands of individual sun-tracking mirrors (called heliostats) to reflect solar energy onto a central receiver located on top of a tall tower. The receiver collects the sun's heat in a heat-transfer fluid that flows through the receiver. The U.S. Department of Energy, and a consortium of U.S. utilities and industry, built the first two large-scale, demonstration solar power towers in the desert near **Barstow, CA**. in the 1980s.

Solar One operated successfully from 1982 to 1988, proving that power towers work efficiently to produce utility-scale power from sunlight. The Solar One plant used water/steam as the heat-transfer fluid in the receiver; this presented several problems in terms of storage and continuous turbine operation. To address these problems, Solar One was upgraded to Solar Two, which operated from 1996 to 1999. Both systems had the capacity to produce 10 MW of power. The unique feature of Solar Two was its use of molten salt to capture and store the sun's heat. The very hot salt was stored and used when needed to produce steam to drive a turbine/generator that produces electricity. The system operated smoothly through intermittent clouds and continued generating electricity long into the night. (85)

Solar Two was decommissioned in 1999, and was converted by the University of California, Davis, into an Air Cherenkov Telescope in 2001, measuring gamma rays hitting the atmosphere.

Trough systems predominate among today's commercial solar power plants. Nine trough power plants, called Solar Energy Generating Systems (SEGS), were built in the 1980s in the Mojave Desert near Barstow. These plants have a combined capacity of 354 MW making them the largest solar power installation in the world. Today they generate enough electricity to meet the power needs of approximately 500,000 people (86).

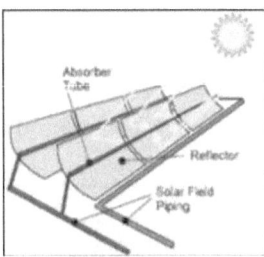

Figure 27 Sketch of a Parabolic Trough Collector system

Trough systems convert the heat from the sun into electricity. Because of their parabolical shape, trough collectors can focus the sun at 30-60 times its normal intensity on a receiver pipe located along the focal line of the trough. Synthetic oil circulates through the pipe and captures this heat, reaching temperatures of 390 °C (735 °F). The hot oil is pumped to a generating station and routed through a heat exchanger to produce steam. Finally, electricity is produced in a conventional steam turbine. (149) The SEGS plants are configured as hybrids to operate on natural gas on cloudy days or after dark, and natural gas provides 25% of the total output.

Nevada Solar One – United States

Nevada Solar One has a 64-MW generating capacity and is located in Boulder City, Nevada. It was built by the U.S. Department of Energy, National Renewable Energy Laboratory, and Acciona Solar Power, Inc. formerly known as Solargenix Energy, Inc. (150)

Nevada Solar One uses parabolic troughs as thermal solar concentrators, heating tubes of liquid which act as solar receivers. These solar receivers are specially coated tubes made of glass and steel, and about 19,300 of these four meter long tubes are used in the newly built power plant. Nevada Solar One also uses a technology that collects extra heat by putting it into phase-changing molten salts. This energy can then be drawn at night.

Solar thermal power plants designed for solar-only generation are ideally matched to summer noon peak loads in prosperous areas with significant cooling demands, such as the south-western United States. Using thermal energy storage systems such as those using salts or flowing oil the days heat can be stored and provides energy at night by heating water for turbine generators. These solar thermal operating periods can then be extended to provide power during the night and meet base-load needs. The cost of Nevada Solar One is in the range of $220-250 million. The power produced is slightly more expensive than wind power, but less than photovoltaic (PV) power.

Nellis Solar Power Plant – United States

In December 2007, the U.S. Air Force announced the completion of a solar photovoltaic (PV) system at Nellis Air Force Base in Clark County, NV. Occupying 140 acres (57) of land leased from the Air Force at the western edge of the base, this ground-mounted photovoltaic system employs an advanced sun tracking system, designed and deployed by PowerLight subsidiary of SunPower. Tilted toward the south, each set of solar panels rotates around a central bar to track the sun from east to west. The 14-megawatt (MW) system will generate more than 30 million kilowatt-hours of electricity each year and supply approximately 25 percent of the total power used at the base. The Nellis Solar Power Plant is the largest solar photovoltaic system in North America.

Mojave Solar Park – United States

Solel has signed a contract with Pacific Gas and Electric (PG&E) to build the world's largest solar plant in the Mojave Desert. When fully operational in 2011, the Mojave Solar Park will deliver 553 megawatts of solar power, the equivalent of powering 400,000 homes, to PG&E's customers in northern and central California. The plant will cover up to 6,000 acres (24 km²) of land. (151)

Stirling Solar Dish

Shown is a parabolic solar dish concentrating the sun's rays on the heating element of a Stirling engine. The entire unit acts as a solar tracker (139)

Stirling Energy Systems under an agreement with utility company Southern California Edison is planning to erect a 500-megawatt, 4,600 acre (19 km²), solar power plant to open some time after 2009. This will be the first commercial application of the Stirling Solar Dish which concentrates solar energy by the use of reflective surfaces and uses a Stirling heat engine to convert the heat into electricity.

Stirling Energy Systems have announced another agreement with San Diego Gas & Electric to provide between **300 and 900 megawatts** of electricity. This is a huge contract and brings aboard considerable electricity into California using thermal solar systems. Here we have a large utility company driving the business unlike many countries.

Land use issues

Solar thermal power plants are large and seem to use a lot of land, but when looking at electricity output versus total size, they use less land than hydroelectric dams (including the size of the lake behind the dam) or coal plants (including the amount of land required for mining and excavation of the coal). There is plenty of land available like in the Mojave Desert and the various deserts the world over. While all power plants require land and have an environmental impact, the best locations for solar power plants are deserts or other land for which there might be few other human uses. Besides deserts I believe they could be used effectively in the North and South Pole regions. It's interesting that the place that has the most oil; the middle east, has the deserts to provide this type of solar in the future.

Renewable energy sources are even larger than the traditional fossil fuels and in theory can easily supply the world's energy needs. **89 million MW of solar power fall on the planet's surface**. (87) While it is not possible to capture all, or even most, of this energy, capturing less than 0.02% would be enough to meet the current energy needs but to replace oil it would require approximately ten percent of this power. Barriers to further solar generation include the high price of silicon used to make solar cells, reliance on weather patterns to generate electricity and a lack of space for solar cells in areas of high demand, such as cities. Also, solar generation does not produce electricity at night, which is a particular problem in high northern and southern latitude countries; energy demand is highest in winter, while availability of solar energy is lowest. Globally, solar generation is the fastest growing source of energy, seeing an annual average growth of 35% over the past few years. Japan, Europe, China, U.S. and India are the major growing investors in the building of solar panels which are required to generate solar energy. Advances in technology and economies of scale, along with demand for solutions to global warming, have led photovoltaics and thermal solar to become the most likely candidate to replace fossil fuels.

For comparison with solar photovoltaics, see **the world's 13 biggest photovoltaic solar energy projects**.

World's Largest Photovoltaic (PV) Solar Power Plants (Proposed and Operational)

Gavin Hudson summary on website
http://ecoworldly.com/2008/03/05/worlds-7-biggest-solar-energy-plants/
(88) shows the following information about the largest solar plants.

By 2011**, Deming, New Mexico, USA**
300 MW

Deming will be the home of the world's largest solar power plant. This 300 Megawatt solar facility will be 15 times the size of the current largest solar plant on the planet (but these keep happening each month in the year of 2008 and there seems to always be a new "largest in the world".). New Solar Ventures and Solar Torx are the companies behind the project. The solar energy plant will cover as many as 1,300 hectares and employ between 300 and 400 people. The project's planners estimate that the plant will supply enough energy to power 240,000 homes.

The Solana solar plant Gila Bend, Arizona, USA 280 MW

Located 70 miles from Phoenix, near **Gila Bend, Arizona, USA**, will compliment the Deming plant when both begin operations in **2011**. It will produce 280 megawatts of energy, provide 1,500 jobs, and cover an area of 769 hectares. The solar power facility will be the child of Abengoa Solar and Arizona Public Service Company. However, the project depends on the United States Congress to renew clean energy tax credits, which would otherwise expire at the end of 2008. (Photo: APS. Source: Newlaunches via EcoFuss.)

Fresno, California, USA
80MW

The Fresno installation will be completed by **2011**. Cleantech, together with the California Construction Authority, will be responsible for construction. When finished, the plant will occupy about 260 hectares. It will be called the Kings River Conservation

District Farm. In addition to this solar farm, Cleantech is in the preparing stage to develop several other facilities of a similar size also in California. In addition to these centralized solar energy plants, California's Governor Scharzenegger pushed through legislation by the name SB1 with which

California will add **solar panels to one million roofs throughout the state by 2018**.

Mojave Desert, USA.
500 MW, with plans to expand to 900 MW.

Solar Company & Electric Utility: BrightSource Energy and Pacific Gas & Electric.

Status: Will begin operating as early as 2011.

More: To date, this field of power towers is the largest planned Concentrated Solar project in the world. Meanwhile, through contracts with a number of other solar companies, PG&E will soon be operating over 2,000 MW of solar energy. California state law requires each investor-owned utility to supply at least 20% of their grid with renewable energy. Source: PG&E [PDF]. Photo: Pictured here is Solar Two, also in the Mojave Desert, which has a similar design to the upcoming plant;

Mojave Desert, USA.
500 MW, with possible expansion to 850 MW.

Solar Company & Electric Utility: Stirling Energy Systems and San Diego Gas & Electric.

Status: Will begin operating in **2011.**

More: 20,000 parabolic dishes will be spread over 4,500 acres of desert. The dishes are each 40 feet tall and capable of producing 2.5 KW. Source: Foreign Policy. Photo: Stirling Energy Systems.

Mojave Desert, USA.

553 MW.

Solar Company & Electric Utility: Solel and Pacific Gas & Electric.

Status: Will begin operating in **2011.**

Solel, an Israeli company, will use 1.2 million mirrors and 317 miles of vacuum tubing for the project. When complete, the solar field will cover 6,000 acres and bring power to 400,000 homes. Source: Ynet news; Solel [PDF]. Photo: WikiMedia.

California, USA.
400 MW.
Solar Company: Solar Partners
Status: Scheduled to begin operating in **2012.**

Ivanpah Solar Electric Generating System (ISEGS) (152) will consist of three power towers, connected at a central point. The heliostats being considered are just over 7 feet tall and 10.5 feet wide. Construction will take place in three phases, beginning with two 100 MW towers and finishing with one 200 MW tower. Plants will use a gas boiler only during morning times while the towers are warming to start the day's operating more quickly. Source, photo: The California Energy Commission.

Mojave Desert, USA.
310 MW.
Solar Company & Electric Utility: Florida Power & Light and Southern California Edison.
Status: Operating.

More: Known as the Solar Energy Generating Systems (SEGS) this is a group of nine concentrated solar plants. It's currently the largest single source of solar energy in the world. By comparison, the largest operating photovoltaic solar plant to date, which is in Spain, produces 20 MW. The site has 400,000 mirrors laid over an area of 1,000 acres. The mirrors were built between 1984 and 1991.

Mojave Desert, USA.
250 MW.
Solar Company & Electric Utility: Florida Power & Light.
Status: Scheduled to begin operating in **2011.**

More: The Beacon Solar Energy project will use 500,000 parabolic troughs over an area of 2,012 acres. Once in operation, the plant will employ roughly 1,000 workers. Sources: Green Wombat; Florida Power & Light. Photo:(153)

Florida, USA
Megawatts: 300 MW.
Solar Company & Electric Utility: Florida Power & Light.
Status: Scheduled to begin operating in **2011.**

More: This project, which will utilize Fresnel reflectors, will help Florida to meet its goal of 20% wind and solar energy. Currently, the state of Florida receives half of its power from natural gas and another 20% from nuclear. Florida Power and Light has already identified the location of 1,100 MW of new solar plants. Sources: St. Petersburg Times; Energy Business Review. Photo: WikiMedia.

Arizona, USA.
280 MW.
Solar Company & Electric Utility: Abengoa Solar and Arizona Public Service Co.
Status: Scheduled to begin operating in **2011.**

More: The plant, being built by Spanish solar company Abengoa, will cover 1,800 acres and offer 1,500 jobs. The solar field will power an estimated 70,000 homes and keep about 400,000 tons of CO_2 out of the atmosphere. Source, photo: Abengoa.

California, USA.
177 MW.
Solar Company & Electric Utility: Ausra and Pacific Gas & Electric.
Status: Scheduled to begin operating **in 2010.**

More: Using Fresnel reflectors, Ausra will supply roughly 60,000 homes with renewable solar power. In contrast with parabolic troughs, Fresnel reflectors are series of flat mirrors that reflect light onto a thermal conducting rod. Ausra's client, Pacific Gas & Electric currently fulfills 12% of its energy needs with renewable energy. Source: News.com. Photo: Ausra.

Las Vegas, Nevada, USA
14.2 MW
Operated by SunPower.

Located at the Nellis Air Force Base, which it powers. This saves the Air Force base an estimated $1 million USD annually in energy costs. The solar array covers an area of over 56 hectares and comprises 70,000 PV panels.)

Seville, Spain.
11 MW currently, planned increase to 300 MW.
Solar Company and Electric Utility: Mirrors by Abengoa and power tower by ALTAC.
Status: Operating. Scheduled 300 MW production **by 2013.**

More: With the completion of other solar energy plants in the same area, the total energy production will be about 300 MW. The current power tower stands 115 meters above the surrounding sunflower fields. 624 heliostat mirrors focus sunlight on the tower. Source: Environment News Service; BBC.

Jumilla, Murcia, Spain
20 MW

Currently one of the two largest solar energy plants in the world. It produces 20 megawatts with 120,000 PV panels. The panels are spread over an area of 100 hectares and provide enough electricity for the equivalent of about 20,000 houses. With construction recently **finished,** the plant is expected to generate $28 million USD. The project was completed by Luzentia Group with help from Elecnor's solar industry Atersa. The solar plant was built over 11 months with 400 people in an area that locals

Beneixama, Alicante, Spain.
20MW
Opened in summer of 2007
Perfect location since it receives about 300 days of sun a year
It produces 20 megawatts with 100,000 polycrystalline City-Solar-Modules, City Solar's own version of PV panels.

Salamanca, Spain. Another accolade for big solar in Spain goes to the plant 12 miles outside of **Salamanca**
13.8 MW

The solar field incorporates 70,000 PV panels from the Japanese Kyocera Corporation into three separate 36-hectare arrays. The plant opened in **September, 2007**, with a grand inauguration in Salamanca. It's been powering roughly 5,000 homes ever since. (Photo: Kyocera. Source: Kyocera via PV Resources Sunny Spain captures another solar opportunity in the PV plant at **Lobosillo, Murcia, Spain**. The PV plant has a 12.7 megawatt output. The solar project is currently in operation, and is also being expanded from 80,000 PV panels to 80,808. The plant uses PV panels from Ecostream. (Photo: Ecostream. Source Ecostream via PV Resources.)

Mildura, Australia.
154 MW.
Solar Company & Electric Utility: Solar Systems and TRUenergy.
Status: Plant will begin operating in 2010 and reach full capacity **by 2013.**

More: When fully completed, the solar field will power about 45,000 homes in Australia. By 2030, Mildura may be producing as much as 5,000 MW of solar energy. Source: EcoWorldly via Foreign Policy. Photo: Solar Systems.

Brandis, Rhineland-Palatinate, Germany, The Waldpolenz Solar **Park 40MW**

Near Leipzig. It's located on the site of a former military airfield. Talk about swords to plowshares. Now that the PV plant has received building approval, its construction is underway. Juwi Solar, the company spearheading the construction, has set a goal of completion of the plant for **2009.** At that time, the facility will be able to generate 40 megawatts.

Arnstein, Bavaria, Germany
12 MW
This system went into full scale operation in **2006.**

It features over 1,400 PV solar panels that can move with the angle of the sun to capture maximum light energy. This design allows the panels to capture up to 35% more energy. The plant, which took 14 months to build, currently produces 12 megawatts of energy. The solar power company involved with this plant is Solon AG. Germany is also a leader in renewable energy. The country increased its stock in renewables from 6.3% in 2000 to 12% in 2006. With this in mind, some **predict 40% renewables by 2020.**

Sinan, Jeollanam-do, South Korea
20MW
Expected to be operational by end of **2008**

109,000 solar panels are expected to by installed. Working with SunTechnics, the solar project is part of South Korea's Act on Climate Change. The country currently generates electricity with about 50% Middle Eastern oil, 25% coal, 22% nuclear, natural gas, and hydroelectric, and just 2.3% renewable. The goal is 9% by 2030. News of the solar farm coincides with South Koreas announcement that they will also be building one of the world's largest tidal energy plants by 2014.

Serpa, Alentejo, Portugal
11 MW

The sunny southern coast, helps make Portugal the renewable energy leader it is. The location is ideal as the area receives 3,300 hours of sunlight a year. The 11 megawatt power plant opened in March of **2007.** Its 52,000 PV modules span over 60 hectares. They produce enough energy for about 8,000 homes. PowerLight, the company that operates the solar farm, estimate that energy produced by their panels prevents 30,000 tons of greenhouse gas emissions each year from burning fossil fuels for energy. In addition to this plant, **Portugal will invest $10.8 billion USD in renewable energy**

Mildura, Victoria, Australia.
270MW

It will go into operation in **2010** and continue to grow in size until its completion in **2013**. A project of TRUenergy and Solar Systems, the plant will generate 154 Megawatts of solar energy. With the Mildura plant complete, Solar Systems will continue to expand in Australia with the goal of 270,000 megawatts of output from a number of plants. Australia's renewable energy goal is 20% by 2020.

Negev Desert, Israel.
250 MW.
Status: Government is seeking bids from thermal solar companies.

More: Israel's solar goal is 5% by **2016**. Already, more than 1 million homes in a country of 7.1 million have rooftop solar water heaters. Source: Economic Times

Upington, South Africa.
0100 MW
This is a pilot with the possibility of expansion to 600 MW.
Solar Company & Electric Utility: Eskom.
Status: Eskom is currently considering whether to continue with plans for the project.
More: This project has been on the drawing board now for several years. If it gets the green light and is completed, it will drop South Africa from the 15th biggest CO_2 emitter to the 25th.

The project relies on the power tower method of production. In this solar thermal variation, a circle of moving mirrors, or heliostats, track the Sun as it moves across the sky. The mirrors focus light on a central tower. Heat from this concentrated light can reach up to 600°C. These rays heat molten salt, which is used to generate steam and power a turbine. Source: Engineering News; Eskom via Solar4Africa.

Total commercial solar power installed or will be installed within five years based on the listing above is 6,500 MW

As big as this number is, we would need one thousand times that amount to reach a level that would replace oil if it is gone by the year 2037. This would require 216,450 MW of capacity each year between the year 2007 and 2037. This gives one the idea of how much of a task this is to replace oil. Even if this is done, it doesn't provide us a portable fuel to replace gasoline and diesel.

Additional Solar power in planning or beginning installation

These facilities are shown in the Appendix III at the end of this book under Solar Power build up.

World's largest photovoltaic (PV) systems

See the listing of the world's top 500 PV systems in the Appendix III in the back of this book.

The top fifty of the five hundred are displayed in the digest along with the power, the location, and the amount of carbon dioxide emissions that are reduced by each. The remaining four hundred and fifty can be reviewed by going on the web site (89) - http://www.pvresources.com/en/top50pv.php

It is important to know that the top 500 systems result in Photovoltaic power (PV) in excess of one million megawatts against the goal of establishing ten million megawatts of renewable power by the year 2037 to replace the loss of oil energy. This is an extremely important step towards reaching the goal in the next twenty nine years. The bulk of the 1 million MW were attained over the last ten years. If we were to continue at this rate we would reach approximately three million additional megawatts (MW) for a total of 4 million MW against the goal of 10 million MW by the year 2037. This means we have to add PV energy at a greater rate than we have over the past ten years. Keep in mind that during these past ten years we have had a shot at some of the best places to install this energy of one million MW. There are still ideal places like the Mojave Dessert and the southwestern part of the U.S. to continue this expansion. There are also many places that are shown on the world map on page 144 to install this type of renewable energy and the map for Europe.

Unique system in Spain

The following article was in my ieee Spectrum in this past month and describes a large solar system that uses a combination of solar power that may be unique in that it takes several of the previously proven solar technologies and applies them together. During the day it uses the parabolic mirrors to focus the heat on a steam generation system that turns the turbines of an electrical generator. However, because of the location in Spain, the heat is so great that they have to divert much of it during the hot parts of the day and it is stored in a large salt storage plant. During the night when there is no sun the heat is released from the molten salt to continue to heat the steam generating system and turn the turbines of the generator. This supplies electricity for 24 hours a day using this combination system. This is a unique system devised from previous experience from the United States and Spain on using salt to store the heat. This is the largest thermal storage plant and Spain and other countries that have good sun hours are reviewing this system.

Largest Solar Thermal Storage Plant to Start Up By Peter Fairley
First Published October 2008 - http://spectrum.ieee.org/oct08/6851
(90)

Spanish solar power station will produce 50 MW in the dark

PHOTO: SOLAR MILLENNIUM

"1 October 2008—A few weeks from now, the Andasol 1 solar thermal power plant in Andalucía, Spain, will begin charging the largest installation built expressly for storing renewable energy (other than the tried-and-true hydroelectric dam, of course). Heat from the solar thermal power station's 510 000-square-meter field of solar collectors will be stored in 28 500 tons of molten salt—enough to run the plant's 50-megawatt steam turbine for up to 7.5 hours after dark.

It's pretty strange for solar power to generate electricity in the dark. Stranger still for a renewable-energy project is the fact that Andasol 1's developers— German renewable-energy firm Solar Millennium and Madrid-based engineering and construction firm ACS/Cobra—believe the energy storage that makes the plant's output more predictable will also make it more affordable. The developers say Andasol 1's electricity will cost 11 percent less to produce than a similar plant without energy storage—dropping from 303 euros per megawatt-hour to 271 euros per MWh.

The lower cost of production is actually a by-product of Andasol 1's energy-storage system, according to Paul Nava, a managing director of Flagsol GmbH, the Cologne, Germany–based engineering subsidiary of Solar Millennium that designed the plant. Nava says storage is a means of maximizing the net energy production from each plant and thus maximizes the revenues paid under Spain's generous incentive program for renewable-energy generation. A feed-in tariff for solar thermal power pays 2.5 to 3 times the average power price for every MWh of energy generated for 25 years (though new rules will reduce the rate for future projects) but limits the capacity of qualifying facilities to 50 MW. Storage enables Andasol 1 to run its 50-MW turbine for more hours.

Nava estimates that Andasol 1 will generate 178 000 MWh of renewable electricity per year, whereas the same field of solar collectors and turbine would turn out just 117 000 MWh sans storage—a difference worth more than 24 million euros per year (US $36 million) at today's power prices.

At Andasol 1, generating this clean energy surplus starts with 24 kilometers of trough-shaped mirrors concentrating sunlight on solar collector tubes and heating the synthetic oil flowing within as high as 400 degrees Celsius (the safety and durability limit for the oil). To put power on the grid, hot oil is circulated to the plant's "power block," where the heat is converted to steam and drives the turbine. However, when the sun is strongest, Andasol 1's oversized collector field should gather almost twice as much heat as the turbine can handle. This extra heat will be dumped into the storage system: a heat exchanger connecting two insulated storage tanks, each 14 meters high and 36 meters in diameter, holding molten potassium and sodium nitrate salt.

The tanks are kept at different temperatures. Molten salt pumped from the "cold" tank (maintained at a not-so-chilly 260 °C to keep the salt molten) into the heat exchanger picks up heat from the oil and then flows into the hot tank (which will reach 400 °C when fully charged). To discharge the stored energy, the process is reversed, with molten salt pumped from the hot tank to the cold tank to reheat the oil.

One problem with running a molten-salt storage system is that the salt could freeze during cold snaps, necessitating an injection of heat that reduces the plant's power output. But Nava says Andasol 1 has some improvements over earlier experimental designs to minimize the need to warm the salt.

Andasol 1's valves are fewer in number, and both the valves and the heat exchanger are designed to drain when not in use, eliminating the need to keep them hot. The pumps, which cannot be drained regularly, sit submerged within the tanks instead of outside the tanks, where they would have to be heated separately. Nava estimates that, overall, annual energy losses from the storage system will be just 5 percent.

Plans are for more of this type of plant to be installed in Spain. Solar Millennium and its Spanish partner expect to start up a twin plant, Andasol 2, next spring and plan to begin building a third 50-MW plant early next year.

Spain's Abengoa Solar and Sener, meanwhile, are each testing solar thermal plants with integrated molten-salt storage. Both use a "power tower" configuration in which arrays of mirrors direct sunlight onto a central solar receiver where the light directly heats a molten salt. This configuration matches that of Solar Two, a 10-MW solar thermal demonstration plant at Sandia National Laboratories, in New Mexico, built in the 1990s. The power-tower design makes energy storage cheaper and more compact because the salts can be safely heated well beyond the limit of the synthetic oils. The problems with cold weather never bothered the Sandia installation since it was installed in the warm part of the United States.

"Using the molten salt as both the working and storage fluid gave us high heat capacity," says Sandia concentrating solar-power program manager Thomas Mancini. "Instead of 260 °C to 390 °C, you're going from 260 °C to 560 °C. It's a bigger temperature difference, so you need less salt to store the same amount of energy." (I would mention that the molten salt was installed in several of the Mojave Desert installations during the past fifteen years to prove its functionality)

At present, most of the anticipated U.S. solar thermal projects, which are driven by state-level renewable-energy mandates rather than a rich feed-in tariff, are focused on minimizing upfront costs, and few projects plan to integrate energy storage. But Mancini and Nava say that may change as utilities adopt time-of-day electricity pricing.

Nava says a pricing scheme already introduced by Southern California Edison should encourage what he calls a "solar booster" thermal power plant.

The California utility pays 3.28 times its base rate for electricity delivered between noon and 6 p.m. on summer weekdays. A solar booster would use an undersized collector field and storage to focus generation on that sweet spot. "In the morning, you use the solar field only to charge the storage, and then from noon on, when you have that factor of three for the electricity rate, you discharge the storage and use the field in parallel to drive the steam turbine," says Nava."

About the Author

Contributing Editor Peter Fairley has reported for IEEE Spectrum from Bolivia, Beijing, and Paris

(D)Wave and tidal power

Tidal energy

At the end of 2005, 300 MW of electricity was produced by tidal power. (91) Due to the tidal forces created by the Moon (68%) and the Sun (32%), and the Earth's relative rotation with respect to Moon and Sun, there are fluctuating tides So, several million MW of tidal energy can be produced without having a significant effect on celestial mechanics. However there is a limit to tidal power to twenty percent of the amount available and not cause a dissipation factor. This limits the tidal source to about 1 million megawatts. Since I say the goal for renewable energy should be in the 10 to 20 million this would be capable of supplying about ten percent of that need. It therefore is significant.

Water Wave Energy refers to the energy of ocean surface waves and the capture of that energy to do useful work — including electricity generation, desalination, and the pumping of water (into reservoirs). Wave power is a form of renewable energy. The waves are primarily the result of wind energy. Wave power generation is not currently a widely employed commercial technology since we are learning more about it and more about how to capture that energy. Various experiments have been carried out with widely different methods.

On December 18, 2007, Pacific Gas and Electric Company announced its support for plans to build America's first commercial wave power plant off the coast of Northern California. The plant will consist of eight buoys, 2 1/2 miles offshore; each buoy generating electricity as it rises and falls with the waves. The plant is scheduled to begin operating in 2012, generating a maximum of 2 megawatt of electricity. Each megawatt can power about 750 homes.

The world's first commercial wave farm is based in Portugal, at the Aguçadora Wave Park, which consists of three 750 kilowatt Pelamis devices. Other plans for wave farms include a 3 megawatt array of four 750 kilowatt Pelamis devices in the Orkneys, off northern Scotland, and the 20MW Wave hub development off the north coast of Cornwall, England. (140)

The north and south temperate zones have the best sites for capturing wave power. The prevailing westerlies in these zones blow strongest in winter.

Modern Water Power Technology

Wave power devices are generally categorized by the method used to capture the energy of the waves. They can also be categorized by location and power take-off system Locations are shoreline related and are near shore or off shore. Types of power take-off for these systems are quite varied and I can not cover the various methods within the scope of this book.

These are descriptions of some wave power systems:

• In the United States, the Pacific Northwest Generating Cooperative (92) is funding the building of a commercial wave-power park at Reedsport, Oregon. The project will utilize the **PowerBuoy** technology which consists of modular, ocean-going buoys. The rising and falling of the waves moves the buoy-like structure creating mechanical energy which is converted into electricity and transmitted to shore over a submerged transmission line. A 40 kW buoy has a diameter of 12 feet (4 m) and is 52 feet (16 m) long, with approximately 13 feet of the unit rising above the ocean surface. Using the three-point mooring system, they are designed to be installed one to five miles (8 km) offshore in water 100 to 200 feet (60 m) deep.

- A floating near shore device called the **Energen Wave Power** device has floating pontoons and multiple pivot arms. (93) This device converts ocean wave energy over a large surface area and utilizes each wave repetitively until it passes through the device.
- An example of a surface following device is the **Pelamis Wave Energy Converter**. The sections of the device articulate with the movement of the waves, each resisting motion between it and the next section, creating pressurized oil to drive a hydraulic ram which drives a hydraulic motor. Two commercial projects utilizing Pelamis technology are under construction, one in Portugal the Aguçadora Wave Park near Póvoa de Varzim which will initially use three Pelamis P-750 machines generating 2.25 MW. (94) Funding for a 3 MW wave farm in Scotland was announced on February 20, 2007 and is projected to use four Pelamis machines.
- With the **Wave Dragon** wave energy converter large "arms" focus waves up a ramp into an offshore reservoir. The water returns to the ocean by the force of gravity via hydroelectric generators.
- The **AquaBuOY**, made by Finavera Renewables Inc., wave energy device: Energy transfer takes place by converting the vertical component of wave kinetic energy into pressurized seawater by means of two-stroke hose pumps. Pressurized seawater is directed into a conversion system consisting of a turbine driving an electrical generator. The power is transmitted to shore by means of a secure, undersea transmission line. A commercial wave power production facility utilizing the AquaBuOY technology is beginning initial construction in Portugal (95). The company has 250 MW of projects planned or under development on the west coast of North America.
- A device called **CETO,** currently being tested off Fremantle, Western Australia, consists of a single piston pump attached to the sea floor, with a float tethered to the piston. Waves cause the float to rise and fall, generating pressurized water, which is piped to an onshore facility to drive hydraulic generators or run reverse osmosis desalination
- A device called **Neo-AeroDynamic**: It is an airfoil base design to harness kinetic power of the fluid flow via an artificial current around its center. The device differentiates from others by its capability to directly transfer wave power into rotational torque to drive a generator without any moving parts. As the result of its high efficiency; it's not only applicable to wind but also to the variety of hydro electric including **free-flow**

(rivers, creeks), tidal, oceanic currents and wave via ocean wave surface currents.

- A point attenuating device called the **Aegir Dynamo**, currently being developed by a UK based company called Ocean Navitas uses a direct mechanical conversion technique to produce rotational energy that can be converted to electricity in a similar way to wind turbine technology, and has a mechanical efficiency of 93%.

Challenges

These are some of the challenges to deploying wave power devices:

- Efficiently converting wave motion into electricity; generally speaking, wave power is available in low-speed, high forces, and the motion of forces is not in a single direction. Most readily-available electric generators operate at higher speeds, and most readily-available turbines require a constant, steady flow.
- Constructing devices that can survive storm damage and saltwater corrosion; likely sources of failure include seized bearings, broken welds, and snapped mooring lines. Knowing this, designers may create prototypes that are so overbuilt that materials costs prohibit affordable production.
- High total cost of electricity; wave power will only be competitive when the total cost of generation is reduced. The total cost includes the primary converter, the power takeoff system, the mooring system, installation & maintenance cost, and electricity delivery costs.

Portugal has built the world's first commercial wave farm, the Aguçadora Wave Park near Póvoa de Varzim, installing three Pelamis P-750 machines generating 2.25 MW. Subject to successful operation, a further 70 million euro is likely to be invested before 2009 on a further 28 machines to generate 72.5 MW. (140)

Funding for a wave farm in Scotland was announced on February 20, 2007 by the Scottish Executive, at a cost of over 4 million pounds, as part of a £13 million funding packages for marine power in Scotland. The farm will be the world's largest with a capacity of 3MW generated by four Pelamis machines. (96)

Funding has also been announced for the development of a Wave hub off the north coast of Cornwall, England. The Wave hub will act as giant extension cable, allowing arrays of wave energy generating devices to be connected to the electricity grid. The Wave hub will initially allow 20MW of capacity to be connected with potential expansion to 40MW. Four device manufacturers have so far expressed interest in connecting to the Wave hub.

The scientists have calculated that wave energy gathered by this generator will be enough to power up to 7,500 households. Savings that the Cornwall wave power generator will bring are significant: about 300,000 tons of carbon dioxide in the next 25 years.

Potential

Good wave power locations have a flux of about 50 kilowatts per meter of shoreline. Capturing 20 percent of this, or 10 kilowatts per meter, is plausible. Assuming very large scale deployment of (and investment in) wave power technology; coverage of 5000 kilometers of shoreline (worldwide) is plausible. Therefore, the potential for shoreline-based wave power is about 50,000 MW. Deep water wave power resources are truly enormous, but perhaps impractical to capture

Summary of water energy

Taking the various approaches into account and with proper financial support, I believe that water energy could provide 1 million MWe of electrical energy by the year 2050. This is significant and would represent about ten percent of the goal. This is completely an individual power source only capable of supplying power to the local communities. However for each significant amount of energy that can be supplied locally it reduces the worldwide total needed. The world is made up of local needs and worldwide needs that total around 10 to 20 million MW by mid century to offset the loss of oil energy. Every little bit helps reach that goal.

(E) Biomass and biofuels

Until the end of the nineteenth century biomass was the predominant fuel, today it has only a small share of the overall energy supply. Many of the readers will not be familiar with the term 'biomass' since it is the latest term to describe what we used to call it "burning wood and other things'. Electricity produced from biomass sources was estimated at 44,000 MW for 2005. Biomass electricity generation increased by over 100% in Germany, Hungary, the Netherlands, Poland and Spain. A further 220,000 MW was used for heating (in 2004), bringing the total energy consumed from biomass to around 264,000 MW. The use of biomass fires for cooking is excluded. (97)

Production of biomass and biofuels are growing industries as interest in sustainable fuel sources is growing. Utilizing waste products avoids a food versus fuel trade-off, and burning methane gas reduces greenhouse gas emissions, because even though it releases carbon dioxide, carbon dioxide is 23 times less of a greenhouse gas than is methane. Biofuels represent a sustainable partial replacement for fossil fuels, but their net impact on greenhouse gas emissions depends on the agricultural practices used to grow the plants used as feedstock to create the fuels. While it is widely believed that biofuels can be carbon-neutral, there is evidence that biofuels produced by current farming methods are substantial net carbon emitters. Geothermal and biomass are the only two renewable energy sources which require careful management to avoid local depletion.

(E) Geothermal energy

"Geothermal" can generally refer to any heat contained in the ground that could be released on a controlled basis and provide a large source of energy to supply heat energy where needed and to provide a portion of heat needed for an electrical generation plant.

History.

Geothermal steam and hot springs have been used for centuries for bathing and heating, but it wasn't until the 20th century that geothermal power started being used to make electricity.

Prince Piero Ginori Conti tested the first geothermal power generator on 4 July 1904, at the Larderello dry steam field in Italy. It was a small generator that lit four light bulbs. (98) Later, in 1911, the world's first geothermal power plant was built there. It was the world's only industrial producer of geothermal electricity until 1958, when New Zealand built a plant of its own.

The first Geothermal power plant in the United States was made in 1922 by John D. Grant at The Geysers Resort Hotel. After drilling for more steam, he was able to generate enough electricity to light the entire resort. Eventually the power plant fell into disuse, as it was not competitive with other methods of energy production. (99)

In 1960, Pacific Gas and Electric began operation of the first successful geothermal power plant in the United States at The Geysers. The original turbine installed lasted for more than 30 years and produced 11 MW net power. The Geysers are currently owned by the Calpine corporation and the Northern California Power agency; and it currently produces over 750 MW of power.

Worldwide use of geothermal energy

Geothermal energy is used commercially in over 70 countries.[32] By the end of 2005 worldwide use for electricity had reached **9,300 MW**, with an additional **28,000 MW** used directly for heating. (141) If heat recovered by ground source heat pumps is included, the non-electric use of geothermal energy is estimated at more than **100,000 MW**.

Potential

If heat recovered by ground source heat pumps is included, the non-electric generating capacity of geothermal energy is estimated at more than 100,000 MW (megawatts of thermal power) and is used commercially in over 70 countries. This is a significant amount of heat that can be provided for other than electrical generation such as the heating of homes. During 2005, contracts were placed for an additional 500 MW of capacity in the United States, while there were also plants under construction in 11 other countries. (100)

Estimates of exploitable worldwide geothermal energy resources vary considerably. According to a 1999 study, it was thought that this might amount to between 65,000 and 138,000 MW of electrical generation capacity 'using enhanced technology'

MIT report on Geothermal energy

A 2006 report by MIT, that took into account the use of Enhanced Geothermal Systems (EGS), concluded that it would be affordable to generate 100,000 MW (electricity) or more by 2050 in the United States alone, for a maximum investment of 1 billion US dollars in research and development over 15 years. I would be inclined to push for this to happen by 2037.

The MIT report calculated the world's total EGS resources to be over 41,222 million MW, of which over **6,345 million MW would be extractable, with the potential to increase this to over 63,419 million MW with technology improvements - sufficient to provide all the world's energy needs for several millennia. (101)** This is a very significant input from MIT. Yet, this information seems to sit in the background when discussing renewable power. I would have to assume this is because it is more difficult to come by than the other sources of renewable energy. I believe it may be due to the nature of the product; that is, it is hard to market. It is not like oil with a huge amount in several locations all over the world, whereby the countries that have it do not need it for their own use at the large quantities available and where an infrastructure has emerged over many years for shipping it all over the world at good profits. Geothermal is not transportable and has no infrastructure. It's like having individual energy sources at various locations in the world and those locations can use the energy but it falls short of being transferable. Another major weakness in geothermal energy is the lack of knowing how much energy one will obtain from a given source and how long it will last. This area of uncertainty results in little progress in this field that may be the answer to many of the energy problems.

The key characteristic of an EGS (also called a Hot Dry Rock system), is that it reaches at least 10 km down into hard rock. At a typical site two holes would be bored and the deep rock between them fractured. Water would be pumped down one and steam would come up the other. The MIT report estimated that there was enough energy in hard rocks 10 km below the United States to supply all the world's current needs for 30,000 years. This must be the limitation of the EGS systems, i.e., the ability to go 10 km (3.85 miles) deep to reach this level. This is the same problem that prevales in obtaining more oil energy; the need to be able to drill deeper successfully. However, this problem seems to be overcome in today's oil production with some oil drills going over 10 km. I would assume that eventually this technology will be transferred to the Geothermal field when it becomes impractical to go deeper for oil wells. As the price of oil increases and it becomes harder to find there will be a shift to geothermal drilling, probably using the second hand oil drilling equipment.

Drilling at this depth is now possible in the petroleum industry, albeit expensive. (Exxon announced an 11 km hole at the Chayvo field, Sakhalin. Lloyds List 1/5/07 p 6) Wells drilled to depths greater than 4000 meters generally incur drilling costs in the tens of millions of dollars. The technological challenges are to drill wide bores at low cost and to break rock over larger volumes. Apart from the energy used to make the bores, the process releases no greenhouse gases.

Other important countries considered high in potential for development are the People's Republic of China, Hungary, Mexico, Iceland, and New Zealand. There are a number of potential sites being developed or evaluated in South Australia that are several kilometres in depth. Favorable locations for EGS (eg in central Australia) may only require wells 4 km deep

Advantages

Geothermal energy offers a number of advantages over traditional fossil fuel based sources;

1. Primarily that the heat source requires no purchase of fuel.
2. From an environmental standpoint, emissions of undesirable substances are small and easy to handle.
3. It is also nearly sustainable because the heat extraction is small compared to the size of the heat reservoir, which may also receive some heat replenishment from greater depths.

4. Geothermal power plants are unaffected by changing weather conditions.[5]
5. Geothermal power plants work continuously, day and night, making them base load power plants.
6. From an economic view, geothermal energy is extremely price competitive in some areas and reduces reliance on fossil fuels and their inherent price unpredictability.
7. It also offers a degree of scalability; a large geothermal plant can power entire cities while smaller power plants can supply more remote sites such as rural villages.
8. An MIT report states that the total world needs of energy can be handled by Geothermal power. This is an awsome declaration by noted scientists.
9. It can be found all over the world and provide local areas all the power they need for their economy to operate. (155)

"Among them are these desert geologists. Employed by the Navy, they are responsible for one of the largest geothermal power plants in the United States, a 270-megawatt generation facility at Coso Hot Springs, at China Lake. In the next few years, these scientists hope to figure prominently in a Department of Defense plan to generate 25 percent of its electricity from renewable sources by 2025.

For an organization that spent $13 billion on energy in 2007 and has a War on Terror to finance, whittling away at domestic electricity bills, which account for only one-fourth of that figure, may seem like a silly exercise. The scale of the projects and the savings, though, prove that the military is not merely indulging in a public-relations ploy. Not counting the geothermal power plant, the Defense Department says that in fiscal year 2007 it had produced or bought enough renewable energy to cover 11.9 percent of its electricity needs, which amounts to about 1.3 trillion kilojoules a year." (155)

Disadvantages

From an engineering perspective, the geothermal fluid is corrosive, and worse, is at a relatively low temperature (compared to steam from boilers), which by the laws of thermodynamics limits the efficiency of heat engines in extracting useful energy as in the generation of electricity. Of course it could provide the first stage of a heat cycle where additional heat is supplied to bring it up to the level needed for the generation of electricity. This approach would lower its efficiency but I believe people will overlook this issue as energy becomes more scarce. Much of the heat energy is lost, unless there is also a local use for low-temperature heat, such as greenhouses or timber mills or district heating, etc. This relates to the lower energy geothermal sites. Since the heat produced is not high enough to generate steam perhaps it could go through a heat exchanger and heat water enough to heat a home. This would be very valuable in reducing the amount of energy needed for other home applications. It might be useful in a clothes drier. Hot water systems in a house do not need steam and this could be used to heat water to a desirable temperature for use in bathing etc.

There are several environmental concerns behind geothermal energy. Construction of the power plants can adversely affect land stability in the surrounding region. This is mainly a concern with Enhanced Geothermal Systems, where water is injected into hot dry rock where no water was before. (102) Dry steam and flash steam power plants also emit low levels of carbon dioxide, nitric oxide, and sulfur, although at roughly 5% of the levels emitted by fossil fuel power plants.[7] However, geothermal plants **can be built with emissions-controlling systems that can inject these substances back into the earth, thereby reducing carbon emissions to less than 0.1% of those from fossil fuel power** plants. Hot water from geothermal sources will contain trace amounts of dangerous elements such as mercury, arsenic, antimony, etc. which if disposed of into rivers can render their water unsafe to drink. This has been proven to be handled rather easily at health sites using geothermal.

Although geothermal sites are capable of providing heat for many decades, eventually specific locations may cool down. It is likely that these locations was poorly designed for the applications at those sites. Engineering learning curves have brought this natural technology to the level of being used with only a percent of the safety issues with several of the other renewable energy sources. Some interpret this as meaning a specific geothermal location can undergo depletion, and question whether geothermal energy is truly renewable. For example, the world's second-oldest geothermal generator at Wairakei has reduced production.

An assessment of the total potential for electricity production from the high-temperature geothermal fields in **Iceland** gives a value of about 1500 million MWh (total) or 15 million megawatt hours per year over a 100 year period. (154) The electricity production capacity from geothermal fields is now only 1.3 million MWh per year, indicating a significant amount that could be achieved if so directed. This study in Iceland was an ideal study for understanding the advantages and limits of georthermal with the information provided to be used by other potential sites in the world. This is like a controlled experiment since the site of Iceland is remote and there are not many other choices for energy. It provides untarnished data.

(F) Nuclear power

In 2005 nuclear energy accounted for 6.3% of world's total primary energy supply. (103) The nuclear power production in 2006 accounted 2,658 TWh (303,424 MWe), which was 16% of world's total electricity production. In November 2007, there were 439 operational nuclear reactors worldwide, with total capacity of 372,002 MWe. **See the chart** below which shows the reactors located by country, along with the capacity, those under construction, those planned, and those proposed. It shows 36 reactors under construction with a capacity of 29,848 MWe. There are 97 reactors planned for 105,075 MWe. There are another 221 reactors proposed. for 198,575 MWe. This would provide 793 reactors when completed (if all follow through on plans) for a total of **706,745 MWe.** This is an average of 891 MW per reactor. If the proposed and planned are to actual be installed it would be about ten percent of what is needed to be added by the year 2037, including the ones already in operation. This amount will be considered renewable energy since nuclear energy is almost an infinite supply and will not be consumed during the life of Earth.

Nuclear power will have to supply much of this energy by the present methods of supplying electricity. We would have to start immediately to plan for their installation in order to avoid a crisis in the early 2020's when the demand for oil is higher than the supply is capable of reaching. Solar power will help homes but be of no use for large farm equipment. You can't get the horsepower out of Solar cells that is needed for many applications. For example, a solar cell of 100 square yards would only be able to supply approximately 3.3 horsepower. This is about enough for a small riding lawn mower. So, if we increase this in size by a factor of ten to 1000 square yards (or meters) we would get to 33 horsepower. Can you see one of these with that big of a solar cell above it? It is obvious it can't be used to power the large farm equipment. We have reviewed solar power and its uses in a previous section of this book and solar has its place but not in large machinery unless it is run by electricity. Hydroelectric power is probably the best source of electricity for many applications but we are out of places to generate hydroelectric power. We would have to examine the possibilities of building additional dams in the world to supply hydroelectric power. If we started now it might help in ten to fifteen years. I have even been thinking about the way we might build manmade water falls to supply considerable electricity. As you will see there is a great amount of energy being put into windmill farms all over the world. It would take an enormous amount of windmill sources to provide the needed energy for homes and industry electricity. Nuclear power is going to have to supplement the renewable energy sources for the world to remain stable. This **706,745 MWe** of nuclear energy would be added to the energy of Solar Power, Wind Power, Biofuel power, Hydroelectric power, Hydrogen power, Geothermal power, and Water wave power to determine if we would reach the approximate 10 million MW of renewable power to replace the loss of oil by 2037 or until the natural gas energy can bridge the world over and not have to rely on coal as the power to be used.

Among the nations listed there are nine without reactors and they all have reactors in their plans. There are another 6 countries without reactors and do not have them planned A few nations have announced plans to phase out nuclear power altogether, but to date only Italy has done so (though Italy continues to import electricity from nations with active nuclear power plants). (104) In addition, while Austria, the Philippines and North Korea (not North Korea) have built nuclear power stations, these nations abandoned them before they could be fueled and operated. You have probably seen the odd shaped towers if you have had the opportunity to witness a reactor station.

These are the cooling towers. The heat generated by the nuclear reaction is used to heat water to provide steam to turn the turbines that generate the electricity. This steam must be cooled and those cooling towers are used to condense the steam back to cool water. Many of the reactor stations are located near the ocean to use that water for cooling. This has aroused the environmentalists since they feel this warming of the ocean water would cause a displacement of some of the sea creatures. However, it has been witnessed that the sea creatures seem to enjoy the warmer water.

Besides environmentalists there are others who are against nuclear reactors. They fear a tragic accident from the radioactive material in the reactors plus they are concerned with the disposition of the nuclear waste which is radioactive. For the reader's information, as of the beginning of 2006 the total electrical production since the initial system was activated in 1951 was 52, 470 billion kWh. This cumulative operating experience amounted to 12,193 years by the end of 2005. During this time there were only two major breakdowns, the one in United States at Three Mile Island in Pennsylvania which occurred with no fatalities and the worse breakdown was the one in Chernobyl in Russia with significant damage and deaths. Both facilities have remained closed due to radiation concerns. These two breakdowns in 12,193 operating years is a failure rate of 0.0164 percent per year or 164 parts per million. This is a very low failure rate and only one of the two was a true catastrophe. The new systems have fewer parts and much better controls and the failure rate is considered by scientists to be much less than has been experienced. The key is not to have a catastrophic failure such as occurred at Chernobyl. It is believed, based on statistics that we can, prevent another Chernobyl with the risk being very low for any major incident. The world should be building more of these nuclear systems to ensure a long and dependable supply of energy via the use of these systems. They are very consistent in their power output and control and provide an energy source that is only second to the Sun's source in amount and in cleanliness. It is kind of ridiculous for countries to be scared away from using nuclear energy when the world is surrounded by nuclear reactors and the military has an enormous amount of reactors. Adding reactors to this significant list should be of little concern.

Supply of material

Uranium is a fairly common element in the Earth's crust. Uranium is approximately as common as tin or germanium in Earth's crust, and is about 35 times more common than silver. Uranium is a constituent of most rocks, dirt, and of the oceans. The world's present measured resources of uranium, economically recoverable at a price of $130/kg, are enough to last for "at least a century" at current consumption rates. (105) This represents a higher level of assured resources than is normal for most minerals. On the basis of analogies with other metallic minerals, a doubling of price from present levels could be expected to create about a tenfold increase in measured resources, over time. The fuel's contribution to the overall cost of the electricity produced is relatively small, so even a large fuel price escalation will have relatively little effect on final price. For instance, typically a doubling of the uranium market price would increase the fuel cost for a light water reactor by 26% and the electricity cost about 7%, whereas doubling the price of natural gas would typically add 70% to the price of electricity from that source. At high enough prices, eventually extraction from sources such as granite and seawater become economically feasible.

The International Atomic Energy Agency estimates the remaining uranium resources to be equal to 2500 ZJ (2500 x 10^{21}J) which is approximately 1000 times the natural gas reserves. This assumes the use of Breeder reactors which are able to create more fissile material (one capable of sustaining a chain reaction) than they consume (see the section on breeder reactors below). IPCC estimated the ultimately recoverable uranium to be 17 ZJ for once-through reactors and 1000 ZJ with reprocessing and fast breeder reactors. (103) This combination would approximate five times the natural gas available. These figures are based on uranium and would not result in any constraints on power during this century if this capability were to be employed However, political and environmental concerns about nuclear safety and radioactive waste started to limit the growth of this energy supply at the end of the past century, particularly due to a number of nuclear accidents or possible accidents. Concerns about nuclear proliferation (especially with Plutonium produced by breeder reactors) mean that the development of nuclear power by countries such as Iran and Syria is being actively discouraged by the international community. (142)

Conventional thermal power plants all have a fuel source to provide heat. Examples are gas, coal, or oil. For a nuclear power plant, this heat is provided by nuclear fission inside the nuclear reactor's core. When a relatively large fissile atomic nucleus is struck by a neutron it forms two or more smaller nuclei as fission products, releasing energy and neutrons in a process called nuclear fission (or a chain reaction); (155) the neutrons then trigger further fission, and so on. When this nuclear chain reaction is controlled, the energy released can be used to heat water, produce steam and drive a turbine that generates electricity. While a nuclear power plant uses the same fuel, uranium-235 or plutonium-239, that is contained in a nuclear explosive (which involves an uncontrolled chain reaction) the rate of fission in a reactor is not capable of reaching sufficient levels to trigger a nuclear explosion because commercial reactor grade nuclear fuel is not enriched to a high enough level. Naturally found uranium contains 0.711% U-235 by mass, the rest being U-238 and trace amounts of other isotopes. (155) Most reactor fuel is enriched to only 3–4%, but some designs use natural uranium or highly enriched uranium. Reactors for nuclear submarines and large naval surface ships, such as aircraft carriers, commonly use highly enriched uranium. Although highly enriched uranium is more expensive, it reduces the frequency of refueling, which is very useful for military vessels. The chain reaction is controlled through the use of materials that absorb and moderate neutrons. Light water reactors use ordinary water to moderate and cool the reactors. When operating, if the temperature of the water increases, its density drops, and fewer neutrons passing through it are slowed enough to trigger further reactions. That negative feedback stabilizes the reaction rate.

A **breeder reactor** is a nuclear reactor that generates new fissile or fissionable material at a greater rate than it consumes such material. (156) These reactors were initially (1950s and 1960s) considered appealing due to their superior fuel economy; a normal reactor can consume less than 1% of the natural uranium that begins the fuel cycle, whereas a breeder can utilize a much greater percentage of the initial fissionable material, and with re-processing, can use almost all of the initial fissionable material. Also, breeders can be designed to utilize thorium, which is more abundant than uranium. Renewed interest is also due to the dramatic reduction in waste they can produce and especially long-lived radioactive waste components. In normal operation, most large commercial reactors experience some degree of fuel breeding. All commercial light water reactors breed fuel, but they have breeding ratios that are very low (though still very significant) compared to machines traditionally considered "breeders." In recent years, the commercial power industry has been emphasizing high-burnup fuels, which are typically enriched to higher percentages of U-235 than standard reactor fuels so that they last longer in the reactor core. As burnup increases, a higher percentage of the total power produced in a reactor is due to the fuel bred inside the reactor, so all reactors breed but those specified as "Breed System" are designed to increase the total amount of additional fuel.

At a burnup of 30 gigawatt-days per metric ton of uranium (GWd/MTU), about thirty percent of the total energy released comes from bred plutonium. At 40 GWd/MTU, that percentage increases to about forty percent. This corresponds to a breeding ratio for these reactors of about 0.4 to 0.5. That is to say, about half of the fuel in these reactors is bred there. (106) Correspondingly, this effect extends the cycle life for such fuels to sometimes nearly twice what it would be otherwise. This is of interest largely because next-generation reactors such as the European Pressurized Reactor, AP1000 and pebble bed reactor are designed to achieve very high burnup. This directly translates to higher breeding ratios. Current commercial power reactors have achieved breeding ratios of roughly 0.55, and next-generation designs like the AP1000 and EPR should have breeding ratios of 0.7 to 0.8, meaning that they produce 70 to 80 percent as much fuel as they consume, improving their fuel economy compared to current high-burnup reactors. Up to a third of all electricity produced in the current US reactor fleet comes from bred fuel, and the industry is working steadily to increase that percentage as time goes on.

As well as their thermal breeder program, India is also developing Fast Breeder Reactor (FBR) technology, using both uranium and thorium as the feedstock. India is also considering what is known as an Advanced Heavy Water Reactor (AHWR) since it uses thorium. They are motivated by their country's heavy thorium reserves which are about a third of the world's supply and they essentially have no uranium. Thorium reserves are about three times those of uranium in the world which will probably find many other countries following India's lead if they are successful. India's stated intention is to use both fast and thermal breeder reactors to supply both their own fuel and a surplus for non-breeding thermal power reactors. Another alternative would be to use uranium-233 bred from thorium as fission fuel in the thorium fuel cycle. Thorium is about 3.5 times as common as uranium in the Earth's crust, and has different geographic characteristics. This would extend the total practical fissionable resource base by 450%.(107) Unlike the breeding of U-238 into plutonium, fast breeder reactors are not necessary — it can be performed satisfactorily in more conventional plants. India has looked into this technology, as it has proponents of nuclear energy that argue that nuclear power is a sustainable energy source that reduces carbon emissions and increases energy security by decreasing dependence on foreign oil. (107) Proponents also claim that the risks of storing waste are small and can be further reduced by the technology in the new reactors and the operational safety record is already good when compared to the other major kinds of power plants.

Generation five (IV) of the nuclear reactor systems

(Gen IV) are a set of theoretical nuclear reactor designs currently being researched. Most of the current reactors in operation around the world are generally considered second- or third-generation systems, with the first-generation systems having been retired some time ago. Gen IV designs are generally not expected to be available for commercial construction before 2030. (157) The innovative nuclear systems considered within Generation IV require new tools for their economic assessment, since their characteristics differ significantly from those of current generation II and III nuclear power plants. The current economic models were not designed to compare alternative nuclear technologies or systems but rather to compare nuclear energy with fossil alternatives. It should be noted that such Generation IV reactors are not necessarily fueled by uranium but by thorium, a more abundant fertile material that decays into U233 after being exposed to neutrons. Such reactors use about 1/300 the amount of fuel to power them. This would provide the reactor material needed to carry us well into the future.

Next Generation Nuclear Plant (NGNP) is to be completed by 2021. (158) Research into these reactor types was officially started by the Generation IV International Forum (GIF) based on eight technology goals. The primary goals being to improve nuclear safety, improve proliferation resistance, minimize waste and natural resource utilization, and to decrease the cost to build and run such plants.

France is one of the world's most densely populated countries. According to a 2007 story broadcast on *60 Minutes*, nuclear power gives France the cleanest air of any industrialized country, and the cheapest electricity in all of Europe. (108) France reprocesses its nuclear waste to reduce its mass and make more energy. However, the article continues, "Today we stock containers of waste because currently scientists don't know how to reduce or eliminate the toxicity, but maybe in 100 years perhaps scientists will.

In countries with nuclear power, radioactive wastes comprise less than 1% of total industrial toxic wastes, which remain hazardous indefinitely unless they decompose or are treated so that they are less toxic or, ideally, completely non-toxic. Overall, nuclear power produces far less waste material than fossil-fuel based power plants. Coal-burning plants are particularly noted for producing large amounts of toxic and mildly radioactive ash due to concentrating naturally occurring metals and radioactive material from the coal. Contrary to popular belief, coal power actually results in more radioactive waste being released into the environment than nuclear power. The population effective dose equivalent from radiation from coal plants is 100 times as much as nuclear plants. (143)

Embalse nuclear power plant in Argentina uses a fission reactor to generate 2109 MW of heat, which creates steam to drive a turbine, which generates 648 MW_e of electricity. The difference is heat lost to the surroundings. Remember our discussions on solar power using the thermal type systems. This system has the same type parameters as to how it relates to electrical power supplied as a percentage of the total generation of solar power heating.

The last U.S. commercial nuclear reactor to go on-line was February 7 1996. This is often quoted as evidence of a successful worldwide campaign for nuclear power phase-out. However, political resistance to nuclear power has only ever been successful in New Zealand, and parts of Europe and the Philippines. Even in the U.S. and throughout Europe, investment in research and in the nuclear fuel cycle has continued, and some experts (109) predict that electricity shortages, fossil fuel price increases, global warming and heavy metal emissions from fossil fuel use, new technology such as passively safe plants, and national energy security will renew the demand for nuclear power plants.

According to the World Nuclear Association, globally during the 1980s one new nuclear reactor started up every 17 days on average, and by the year 2015 this rate could increase to one every 5 days.

Many countries remain active in developing nuclear power, including Japan, China and India, all actively developing both fast and thermal technology, South Korea and the United States, developing thermal technology only, and South Africa and China, developing versions of the Pebble Bed Modular Reactor (PBMR). (159) Several EU member states actively pursue nuclear programs, while some other member states continue to have a ban for the nuclear energy use. Japan has an active nuclear construction program with new units brought on-line in 2005. In the U.S., three consortia responded in 2004 to the U.S. Department of Energy's solicitation under the Nuclear Power 2010 Program and were awarded matching funds—the Energy Policy Act of 2005 authorized loan guarantees for up to six new reactors, and authorized the Department of Energy to build a reactor based on the Generation IV Very-High-Temperature Reactor concept to produce both electricity and hydrogen. As of the early 21st century, nuclear power is of particular interest to both China and India to serve their rapidly growing economies—both are developing fast breeder reactors. In the energy policy of the United Kingdom it is recognized that there is a likely future energy supply shortfall, which may have to be filled by either new nuclear plant construction or maintaining existing plants beyond their programmed lifetime. I recently read a newspaper article that recommended the United States review their present reactors and determine if they are technically expandable. Their suggestion was based on the fact that when these reactors were built the sites were approved for doubling the energy output over time if the extra energy was required. This is interesting from the standpoint that it already has approval for the extra capacity on those sites and this would provide an opportunity to increase the US supply of nuclear energy without having to find new sites and obtaining approval.

Fusion Reactors

Fusion reactors, which may be viable in the future, have no risk of explosive radiation-releasing accidents, and even smaller risks than the already extremely small risks associated with nuclear fission. Fusion power reactors will produce a very small amount of reasonably short lived, intermediate-level radioactive waste at decommissioning time, as a result of neutron activation of the reactor vessel, they will not produce any high-level, long-lived materials comparable to those produced in a fission reactor. (110) Even this small radioactive waste aspect can be mitigated through the use of low-activation steel alloys for the storage containers.

There is a possible impediment to production of nuclear power plants, due to a backlog at Japan Steel Works, the only factory in the world able to manufacture the central part of a nuclear reactor's containment vessel in a single piece, which reduces the risk of a radiation leak. (143) The company can only make four per year of the steel forgings. It will double its capacity in the next two years, but still will not be able to meet current global demand alone. Utilities across the world are submitting orders years in advance of any actual need. Other manufacturers are examining various options, including making the component themselves, or finding ways to make a similar item using alternate methods. (110) Other solutions include using designs that do not require single piece forged pressure vessels such as Canada's Advanced CANDU Reactors or Sodium-cooled Fast Reactors.

Other companies able to make the large forgings required for reactor pressure vessels include: Russia's OMZ, which is upgrading to be able to manufacture three or four pressure vessels per year;[31] South Korea's Doosan Heavy Industries; and Mitsubishi Heavy Industries, which is doubling capacity for reactor pressure vessels and other large nuclear components. The UK's Sheffield Forgemasters is evaluating the benefit of tooling-up for nuclear forging work.

Figure 28 Listing of countries and their nuclear reactor status

I am listing the various countries and their status as taken from the chart below which displays the various countries and their use of nuclear power, those under construction, those planned, and those proposed. The biggest users are United States, France and Japan. However, this is about to change as listed: (111) (160) The **United States** has one hundred and four systems, none under construction, twelve planned, and twenty proposed for a total **of one hundred and thirty six** systems.

China will be adding significant capacity that will take their present capacity from eleven, plus seven being constructed, twenty six in planning, and seventy six proposed. This would bring them to **one hundred and twenty systems** if all of these are installed.

Japan has fifty five systems with two under construction, eleven planned and one proposed for a total of **sixty nine**.

Russia has thirty one with seven under construction, twelve planned and twenty five proposed for a total of **sixty**

France with fifty nine systems only has one under construction, none planned, and one proposed for a total of **sixty**; so they are essentially standing pat

India has seventeen with six in construction, ten planned, and nine proposed for a total of **forty two**.

The **Ukraine** has fifteen, with two planned and twenty proposed for a total of thirty **seven.**

Canada has eighteen systems with two under construction, three planned, and four proposed for a total of **twenty seven.**

A recent newspaper release• Higher fossil fuel prices, energy security concerns, improved reactor designs, and environmental considerations are expected to improve prospects for nuclear power capacity in many parts of the world, and a number of countries are expected to build new nuclear power plants. World nuclear capacity is projected to rise from 368,000 MW in 2004 to **481,000 MW in 2030**. Declines in nuclear capacity are projected only in OECD (Organization for Economic Cooperation and Development) Europe, where several countries (including Germany and Belgium) have either plans or mandates to phase out nuclear power, and where some old reactors are expected to be retired and not replaced. I don't believe these numbers of 481,000 MW in 2030 unless there are many to be built starting just before that time and will be completed by 2037. Eventually the world is going to realize that there are not many alternatives to their energy needs and they will turn to nuclear. I would expect nuclear to rise to close to one million megawatts by 2037. This will have nuclear at about fifteen percent of the electrical power by that time.

Definitions of status
See the Chart below with the following directions (160)

Operating = Connected to the grid;
Building/Construction = first concrete for reactor poured, or major refurbishment under way;

Planned = Approvals, funding or major commitment in place, mostly expected in operation within 8 years, or construction well advanced but suspended indefinitely;

Proposed = clear intention or proposal but still without firm commitment. Planned and Proposed are generally gross MWe;

TWh = Terawatt-hours (million MW hours), MWe = Megawatt net (electrical as distinct from thermal)

64,615 tU (tons of uranium) = 76,200 t U_3O_8

* In Canada, 'construction' figure is 2 laid-up Bruce A reactors.

**The world total includes 6 reactors operating in Taiwan with a combined capacity of 4,916 MWe, which generated a total of 39 million MWh in 2007 (accounting for 19.3% of Taiwan's total electricity generation). Taiwan has two reactors under construction with a combined capacity of 2600 MWe.

http://www.world-nuclear.org/info/reactors.html (160)

Figure 28 World Nuclear Power Reactors 2007-08 and Uranium Requirements 1 September 2008

	NUCLEAR ELECTRICITY GENERATION 2007		REACTORS OPERABLE Sept 2008		REACTORS UNDER CONSTRUCTION Sept 2008		REACTORS PLANNED Sept 2008		REACTORS PROPOSED Sept 2008		URANIUM REQUIRED 2008
	billion kWh	% e	No.	MWe	No.	MWe	No.	MWe	No.	MWe	tonnes U
Argentina	6.7	6.2	2	935	1	692	1	740	1	740	123
Armenia	2.35	43.5	1	376	0	0	0	0	1	1000	51
Bangladesh	0	0	0	0	0	0	0	0	2	2000	0
Belarus	0	0	0	0	0	0	2	2000	0	0	0
Belgium	46	54	7	5728	0	0	0	0	0	0	1011
Brazil	11.7	2.8	2	1901	0	0	1	1245	4	4000	303
Bulgaria	13.7	32	2	1906	0	0	2	1900	0	0	261
Canada*	88.2	14.7	18	12652	2	1500	3	3300	4	4400	1665
China	59.3	1.9	11	8587	7	6700	26	27620	76	62600	1396
Czech Republic	24.6	30.3	6	3472	0	0	0	0	2	3400	619
Egypt	0	0	0	0	0	0	0	0	1	1000	0
Finland	22.5	29	4	2696	1	1600	0	0	1	1000	1051
France	420.1	77	59	63473	1	1630	0	0	1	1600	10527
Germany	133.2	26	17	20339	0	0	0	0	0	0	3332
Hungary	13.9	37	4	1826	0	0	0	0	2	2000	271
India	15.8	2.5	17	3779	6	2976	10	8560	9	4800	978
Indonesia	0	0	0	0	0	0	2	2000	2	2000	0
Iran	0	0	0	0	1	915	2	1900	1	300	143
Israel	0	0	0	0	0	0	0	0	1	1200	0
Japan	267	27.5	55	47577	2	2285	11	14945	1	1100	7569
Kazakhstan	0	0	0	0	0	0	0	0	1	300	0
Korea DPR (North)	0	0	0	0	0	0	1	950	0	0	0
Korea RO (South)	136.6	35.3	20	17533	3	3000	5	6600	2	2700	3109
Lithuania	9.1	64.4	1	1185	0	0	0	0	2	3400	225
Mexico	9.95	4.6	2	1310	0	0	0	0	2	2000	246
Netherlands	4.0	4.1	1	485	0	0	0	0	0	0	98
Pakistan	2.3	2.34	2	400	1	300	2	600	2	2000	65
Romania	7.1	13	2	1310	0	0	2	1310	1	655	174
Russia	148	16	31	21743	7	4810	12	14340	25	22280	3365
Slovakia	14.2	54	5	2094	2	840	0	0	1	1200	313
Slovenia	5.4	42	1	696	0	0	0	0	1	1000	141
South Africa	12.6	5.5	2	1842	0	0	1	165	24	4000	303
Spain	52.7	17.4	8	7448	0	0	0	0	0	0	1398
Sweden	64.3	46	10	9016	0	0	0	0	0	0	1418
Switzerland	26.5	43	5	3220	0	0	0	0	3	4000	537
USA	806.6	19.4	104	100599	0	0	12	15000	20	26000	18918
Vietnam	0	0	0	0	0	0	0	0	2	2000	0
WORLD**	2608	16	439	373,247	36	29,848	97	105,075	221	198,575	64,615
	billion kWh	% e	No.	MWe	No.	MWe	No.	MWe	No.	MWe	tonnes U
	NUCLEAR ELECTRICITY GENERATION 2007		REACTORS OPERATING		REACTORS BUILDING		ON ORDER or PLANNED		PROPOSED		URANIUM REQUIRED

Sources:

Reactor data: WNA to 31/08/08.

(160)

Energy use in the United States

The United States is the largest energy consumer in terms of total use, using 100 quadrillion BTU (105 exajoules, or 29,000 million MWh) in 2005, equivalent to an (average) consumption rate of 3.3 million MW of the world's 15 million megawatts.

The U.S. ranks seventh in energy consumption per-capita after Canada and a number of small countries. (113) (115) The majority of this energy was derived from fossil fuels: in 2005, it was estimated that 40% of the nation's energy came from petroleum, 23% from coal, and 23% from natural gas. The remaining 14% was supplied by nuclear power, hydroelectric dams, and miscellaneous renewable energy sources. (115) From this listing it is obvious if oil is to be replaced by renewable energy, nuclear reactors or natural gas that there is a long way to go. We essentially have to generate 1.32 million MW of power to replace the loss of oil. That should be our planning. I estimate the world will be short of oil by the year 2037. If we take this as a target date we must find 1.32 million MW of power from solar power, nuclear power, biofuel power, wind power, geothermal power, and natural gas power to replace the loss of oil and to prevent any increase in the use of coal for power. These are all based on reducing the environmental contamination by carbon dioxide and other unhealthy contaminants that might be generated by added use of coal. I will show a plan of carbon containment that if successful will allow the use of more energy by fossil fuels to make up for the loss of oil.

The loss of oil will impact the transportation business more than anything else. Approximately thirty percent of the oil and its derivatives are used for transportation in the US. This would be equivalent to 1,680,000 MW of power required for transportation. This is the biggest issue to overcome that I see. Most of the remaining uses of oil and the other energy sources are used to produce electricity. Therefore their replacement by nuclear or renewable energy is fairly straightforward. However, this is not the case for transportation where the oil is converted to gasoline or diesel for automobiles, trucks, tractors, airplanes and mobile machines. Unless all means of transportation is converted to electrical capability I see no way to satisfy this application of oil derivatives. This is very doubtful at this time. Consider that by 2037 there may be three quarters of a billion cars in the world and approximately half of those will be in the United

States. There are approximately 250 million vehicles in the US at this time and the amount is increasing by approximately three million a year. Therefore, by the year 2037 there will be approximately 375 million vehicles in the US. Meanwhile the rest of the world is increasing at approximately double the rate of the US. The rest of the world will have approximately the same number of vehicles as the US by then for a total of three quarters of a billion cars in the world. Many of them will be over ten years old. There is no way the world's number of electrical or other power substitution vehicles will approach this number. Let's assume that five percent of the vehicles by 2037 are powered by electrical means, or liquefied natural gas, or biofuel. That would be 38 million vehicles of this nature and approximately 725 million of the kind that run on gasoline. Here is a dilemma that I see no way of fixing. Here we are today with around 375 million vehicles in the world running on gasoline or diesel and by 2037 they will double. We have a difficult time presently supplying half that many in he world. How will we handle this problem when there is double the number of vehicles? The engineers of the world are trying to convert the various vehicles to some other means of power. We presently use approximately 28% of the United States total oil for vehicle energy.

While this number is increasing to 375 million by the year 2037; the world's total increases to approximately 750 million. If we have no oil, how do we power these vehicles? The demand will double while the supply of oil is going down and could essentially reach zero by 2037. Then there's the other vehicles like airplanes that won't run on electricity or nuclear power and not on today's biofuel. There are the machines that presently run on gasoline or diesel from a huge source of fuel present today that won't be present in twenty nine or thirty or fifty years. This is the most serious of the energy issues.

Historic curve

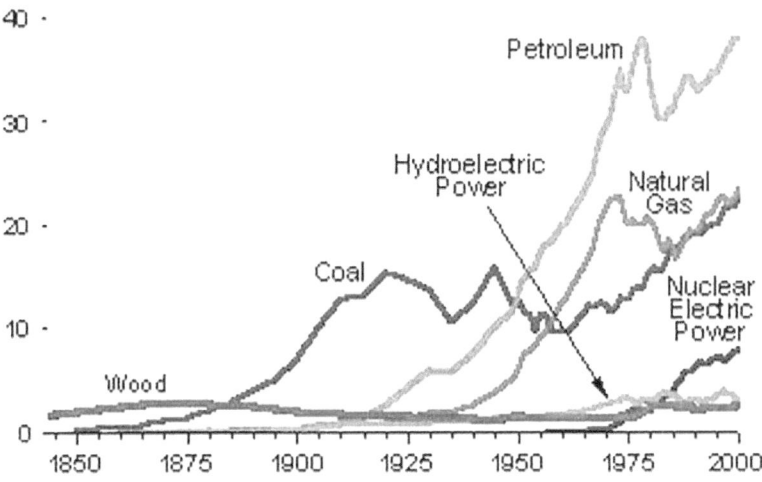

Figure 29 US energy consumption, by source, 1850-2000. Vertical axis is in quadrillion BTU (114)

The Historic curve tells the story all by itself. In the early years of our country the use of wood and other biomasses to fuel fire was the chief fuel. In the later quarter of the nineteenth century coal became the chief fuel and grew quite rapidly. This need for coal was increased by the use of steam engines for trains and river and ocean going ships. The first commercial oil was found in Titusville Pennsylvania in 1859 but didn't really take off till around 1910 when automobiles and airplanes began to provide the chief source of transportation. As oil became more plentiful and of lower cost it drove up its use. The low cost of oil and its derivatives began to sweep upward after World War I. By the time of World War II the use of petroleum and natural gas began to replace coal since they were cheap, easy to transport, and could be used in more applications. It was a mechanical engineer's dream. He invented machines and the machines he invented resulted in those machines began developing the next level of machines. There was a new age of aircraft that led to greater use of petroleum. In the early 70's the OPEC (Organization of petroleum exporting countries) community pulled a power play and essentially reduced the amount of petroleum they produced to raise the price of a barrel of oil. You can see the impact in the curves. Many countries, but especially the United States, moved to smaller cars and took other steps to reduce their use of petroleum and natural gas. At about the same time, the use of coal, which was competitive in price and was in abundant supply in various places of the world, but especially in the United States, turned up its production to offset some of the uses of petroleum. The use of coal was now directed toward the production of electricity rather than the past history where it was used in great abundance in the steel mills of the United States. Coal will continue to be used to provide electrical power by heating the steam that turns the turbines of the huge generating stations.

These moves to reduce the use of oil with more efficient cars and other vehicles resulted in a pressure on OPEC (Organization of petroleum exporting countries) and they turned their oil faucets back on and oil was again the inexpensive solution to many of the problems. However, in 2007 and on into 2008 the OPEC countries raised the price of a barrel of oil to almost $150.00 a barrel. It hovered around that level for several months, but then the reduced use by the countries in the world started to turn the market from a supply market to a demand market and the price of a barrel of oil has now gone below $100.00. This began another example of how inefficiently the world was using its oil. People, who had cars, drove the cars. They drove them for the fun of it rather than the necessity of it. People flew on airplane trips, until the price of tickets began to go up and then they stopped a good bit of their pleasure travel. The airlines were losing money since many times their scheduled flights were not full. So, the airlines took certain actions to ensure a higher loading by reducing the number of flights and eliminating some flights. It was like watching a game on television or on one's personal computer where there was a move by one group and a counter move by the other group, but the main thing it proved was that people had become careless with their use of their money and their use of their cars.

This may prove to be a very valuable lesson in the future. We can mentally plot what the curves will do in the next fifty or so years. As the reserves of petroleum are used up and become a little more difficult to extract (it only costs about a dollar a barrel to extract oil in 2008) the laws of supply and demand will come into play. The petroleum curve will bend downward while the demand curve will continue to rise. I assume a crossover point will be around the year 2020 when the flattened out curve of the supply is crossed by the demand curve. At this point there is going to be pressure exerted all over the world. The countries exporting oil will raise their price, but his time it will be a fundamental move. It will be made for the scarcity of the petroleum and the price pressure will increase as the years pass. Once this point is reached there will be no turning back. The laws of economics will prevail and the price will be an inverse function of the depleting supply. Countries that have oil will reach a point where they will not export this precious material. The countries fortunate enough to have an internal supply will take steps to maintain that supply within their country and will take steps to ration this supply. Eventually those countries will also run out of petroleum and if they made the proper steps to meet this crisis, they will be using renewable energy, or natural gas, or nuclear energy. The curve on petroleum will essentially bottom. There will be a continuous upturn of the curves that represent nuclear, natural gas, and renewable energy. Of course there will be a great pressure to use coal if coal is one of a country's natural resources. At this point the price of coal will start increasing because of the same scenario that prevailed when petroleum was in this position. The hope is that enough renewable energy supplies increased to the point where the use of coal flattens out as displayed by the curves at that time. If renewable supplies have reached a level where it has been able to offset the loss of petroleum and has grown to the point where there is no need for the coal to increase, the coal curve will be extended as a flat curve for at least one hundred years. The great hope is that the use of coal never is called upon to make up for the energy needs that can't be met by renewable energy and nuclear energy. Natural Gas will run out of steam in less than one hundred years and will start to be in short supply around the turn of the 21st to 22nd Century. It would have lasted longer but when oil supplies decreased there was an extra demand for natural gas, so its use expanded at a greater rate and therefore it started to reach a point of scarcity at an earlier date than most geologists and economists are projecting at this time. I provide this as an example of what I believe the model will be.

You will notice in the curves that there was also a surge in the use of nuclear energy around 1970 and it has grown in use at about the same rate as natural gas and petroleum. The key for the future is to keep the growth of nuclear energy along with natural gas on this slope because of their fairly clean power, while bringing on the supplies of the renewable fuels such as wind power, solar power, biofuel power, geothermal power and water wave power. We would like to increase the use of hydropower and biomass, but the natural resources are not there to increase them by much. Most of the hydropower increase will come in small local use hydropower, but this is part of the game. It will make the local communities energy independent except for the portable energy presently supplied by gasoline and diesel fuel.

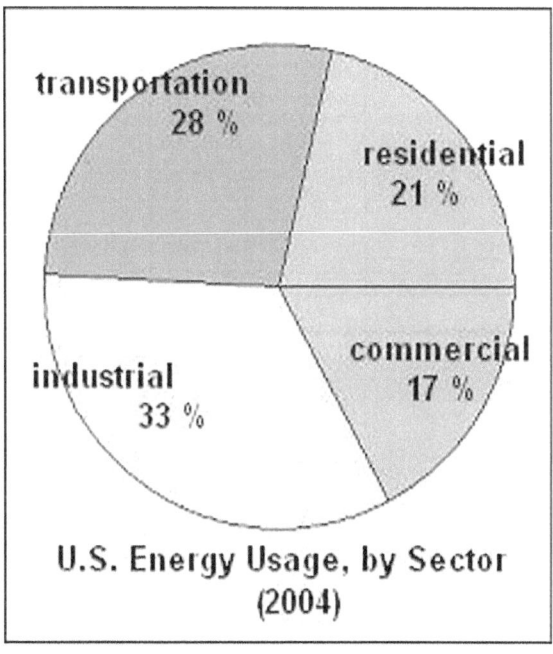

transportation
28 %

residential
21 %

industrial
33 %

commercial
17 %

U.S. Energy Usage, by Sector
(2004)

Figure 30 U.S. Energy use by sector (115)

U.S. Department of Energy tracks national energy consumption in four broad sectors: industrial, transportation, residential, and commercial. The industrial sector has long been the country's largest energy user, currently representing about 33% of the total. Next in importance is the transportation sector, followed by the residential and commercial sectors. The transportation sector's energy use is mainly diesel and gasoline derived from petroleum. This can be seen in the chart below which details the main uses in the various sectors. This is the section of the economy that will be under the biggest pressure as the demand curve for oil products exceeds the supply curve. The use of oil products is over 82% of the transportation's energy needs. This must be supplied by biofuels, hydrogen fuel cells later in the century, or there will be a major shift to cars driven electrically. This is beginning to happen this decade and will increase as battery technology improves and the ability to plug into standard110 ac volt systems. Probably over fifty percent of cars will be smaller and many will be two passenger cars to improve mileage with oil products or electricity. These small cars will be used for commuting to work and local travel.

Figure 31 Energy consumption by sector and major uses (115) (116)

Energy consumption by sector (116)

Sector Name	Description	Major uses
Industrial	Facilities and equipment used for producing and processing goods.	22% chemical production 16% petroleum refining 14% metal smelting/refining
Transportation	Vehicles which transport people/goods on ground, air or water.	61% gasoline fuel 21% diesel fuel 12% aviation
Residential	Living quarters for private households.	32% space heating 13% water heating 12% lighting 11% air conditioning 8% refrigeration 5% electronics 5% wet-clean (mostly clothes dryers)
Commercial	Service-providing facilities and equipment (businesses, government, other institutions).	25% lighting 13% heating 11% cooling 6% refrigeration 6% water heating 6% ventilation 6% electronics

The breakdown of energy consumption by source is given here:

Fuel type	2004 US consumption in TW [117]	2004 World consumption in TW [118]
Oil	1.34	5.6
Gas	0.77	3.5
Coal	0.77	3.8
Hydroelectric	0.09	0.9
Nuclear	0.27	0.9
Geothermal, wind, solar, wood	0.11	0.13
Total	3.35	15

Figure 32 U.S. consumption and world consumption in 2004 by fuel type.

The United States uses a little over 22 percent of the energy in the world at this time. The demand for fuel energy may not increase greatly in the next decade while the world demand will exceed 20 TW. Therefore the U.S. demand as a percentage will fall by about five percentage points to around 17 percent. The major increase worldwide will come from China and other Asian countries.

Figure 33 Regional variation within the United States (116)

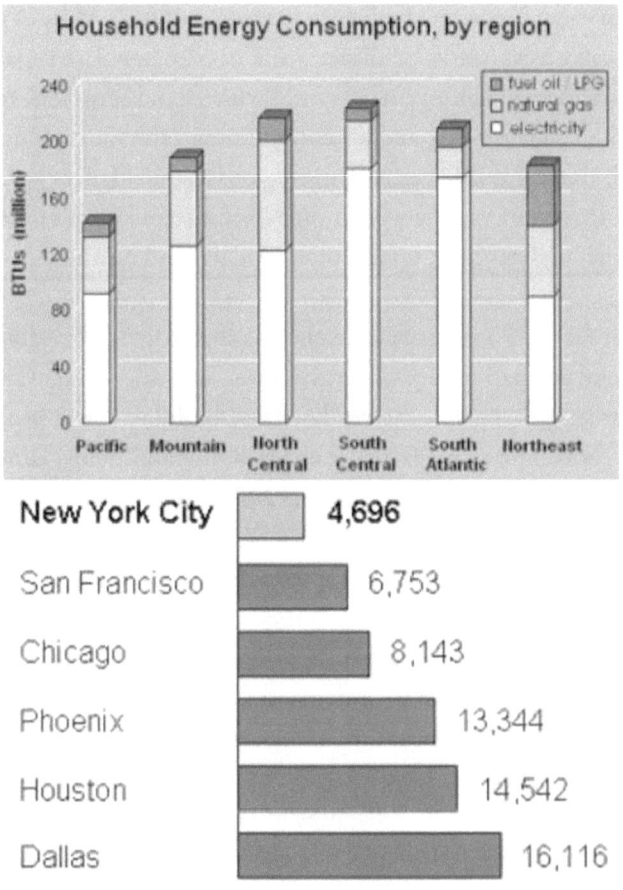

Figure 34 Average annual residential electricity usage by city, 2000-2005. Measured in Kilowatt hours per customer. (144) [10]

A review of the average electricity may come as a surprise to some. The New York City one shocked me. I believe this is due to the large percentage of townhouses and condominiums in the city which result in efficiencies due to each house essentially insulating the adjoining house in the case of townhouses. Household energy use varies significantly across the United States. An average home in the Pacific region (consisting of California,

Oregon, and Washington) consumes 35% less energy than a home in the South Central region. I believe that recent laws passed in California where newly built homes have to have improved insulation as well as an improved version of the roof wooden frame and that all new homes must have a plywood inner layer prior to dry walls to make the house more earthquake proof will also result in them being more efficient in the use of fuels Most of the regional differences can be explained by climate. The heavily populated coastal areas of the Pacific states experience generally mild winters and summers, reducing the need for both home heating and air conditioning. The warm, humid climates of the South Central and South Atlantic regions lead to higher electricity usage, while the cold winters experienced in the Northeast and North Central regions result in much higher consumption of natural gas and heating oil.

Another reason for regional differences is the variety of building codes and environmental regulations found at the local and state level. California has some of the strictest environmental laws and building codes in the country, which may contribute to the fact that its per-household energy consumption is lower than all other states except Hawaii. California building codes have gotten tougher in the last year which will result in improved insulation and improved efficiency in the use of power than it presently possesses. California uses a fair amount of air conditioning in their home for comfort that can be dispensed with if the supply of energy decreases. So, this state and probably others may be able to improve even more in their demand for home electricity.

Major U.S. cities also show significant variation in per capita energy consumption. In addition to differences in regional climates and variations in building code standards, factors affecting energy use in cities include population density and building design. Townhouses are more energy efficient than single-family homes because less heat, for example, is wasted per person. As California's population has increased the use of townhouses and condominiums have increased due to the high cost of single home housing and one would expect the efficiency to improve even farther.

U.S. oil consumption is approximately 21 million barrels/day, yet production is only 6 million barrels per day. Cost to import oil is approximately $630 billion dollars a year (at $115/barrel). While it costs the Arabian Peninsula just one U.S. dollar to extract a barrel of oil, the cost on the world market has varied up to $100/barrel in 2007 dollars and by mid 2008 oil was at $150/barrel. This inflationary price for a barrel of oil fell from this $150/barrel level to around $100/barrel in the third quarter of 2008 and economy slowdown in the world has caused the demand for oil to decrease and the price of oil has reduced to under $75 a barrel early in the fourth calendar quarter.

While U.S. oil usage increases by 2% per year, the economy has been growing at 3.3% per year. This is a significant point since it has been estimated that the United States demand would start flattening out while other countries like China and India would show a growth and keep the total world demand for oil increasing. The U.S. Strategic Petroleum Reserve currently holds about 640 million barrels (102,000,000 m³) of oil and is being filled to a level of 700 million barrels (1.1 x 10⁸ m³). Should, for example, oil production be stopped entirely, or becomes depleted, the U.S. would have only 32 to 35 days of resources to fall back upon. From a national security standpoint, such a situation is untenable. This is a very important point. Every time there is an increase in the price of a barrel of oil there are people and organizations that push for release of some of these reserves to cause the price of oil to drop. This is very risky. Consider the fact that the US is fighting a war in Iraq and Afghanistan and we decide to pull some oil from our reserves leaving us short of this backup for military purposes in case another source would start a war with the US. If the encounter would come from some country that is friendly with the OPEC countries and those countries decide to put an embargo on our oil supplies we could be put in a position of not having ample oil supplies to protect our country. It is not always obvious how an encounter will come and by what means it will be employed. It could be nuclear, weapons of mass destruction, political, economical or a combination of these. It is best to be cautious and retain our oil reserves. This is another reason why I am for drilling offshore in the United States. The installation of oil drilling equipment will take many years; some of which is just finding the right places to drill the most efficiently. I project it will take till 2020 to have these sources available. We need not use them if there are no world pressures to use them. However, world pressures normally result in price pressures on things like oil and are the source of pressures on the U.S. economy. To prevent this, we have to have a supply available that, along with the growth of our renewable energy sources is enough to prevent major blackmail type pressures from possible unfavorable sources toward the U.S.

During the Carter administration, in response to an energy crisis and hostile Iranian and Soviet Union relations, President Jimmy Carter announced the Carter Doctrine which declared that any interference with U. S. interests in the Persian Gulf would be considered an attack on U.S. vital interests.(119) This doctrine was expanded by Ronald Reagan.

Today, many scholars and politicians call for the immediate incubation of long term energy solutions prior to a 'peak oil' scenario which would force the economy to a grinding halt. Although additional drilling in areas such as continental shelf, the Gulf of Mexico, off the U.S. West Coast, Alaska, and the Great Lakes may stave off the inevitability of the problem, it would be only a temporary solution, and carries the risk of further polluting our environment. This is one argument against drilling offshore. However, **it takes about ten years from the initiation of offshore drilling to provide any energy from those sources. It is my opinion that we should begin drilling immediately so that by the time 2020 comes around we have the oil rigs in place and can decide whether to really draw from this supply.** There would not be any environmental danger using this scheme, but if we are endangered by the lack of an oil supply in the second decade of this century at a time when the worldwide oil supply has peaked, we at least have the alternative to produce oil from those offshore systems to provide our needs. What if we didn't prepare this way? What happens where we normally are running with a daily supply of 30 million barrels of oil a day (of which we would be supplying approximately 6 million barrels a day without the offshore sites and in fact the U.S. may be out of oil by the year 2020) and the faucet is turned off by OPEC because there is a world shortage versus demand. How do we handle that politically if we haven't handled the development of this alternate source to carry us till we produce enough renewable energy including nuclear, natural gas, and coal energies? Remember, none of these renewable supplies can provide the fuel to fly a plane unless we invent something between now and the second decade of this century. To my way of thinking the end of the second decade and the beginning of the third decade are significant. We need to be able to supply at least ten million barrels a day of our own source. I believe that this amount, plus the greatly installed solar power and other energy sources will find the United States in a strong position as the world leader in responsible control of the world's peace.

How many megawatts (MW) of power does a barrel of oil supply?

A million barrels of oil provides 73,000 MW of energy. In the third decade of this century the **United States will be using approximately thirty million barrels of oil a day which provides 2.1 million MW a day.** This is the energy, or a large percentage of it, we would have to produce to replace thirty million barrels a day. Meanwhile, in the third decade of this century the world will be using approximately 150 million barrels of oil per day with an energy capacity of 11 million MW of energy per day. This is just in the energy of oil and oil derivatives. To these you add the fossil energies, the renewable energy, and nuclear energy. (See the chart below. (120). There is no way we are going to get there in time if we continue our present stance on oil drilling off shore and applying more pressure to building up the renewable sources of energy.

2005 United States Electricity Production by Source shown in trillions of megawatt hours

This figure 35 chart is just for electrical use and is very revealing. The vertical axis is the use in trillions of megawatt hours and in 2005 the U.S. used 3000 trillion megawatt hours of power supplied by fossil fuels. That's the upper curve. You note the amount supplied by fossil fuels is enormous compared to the other sources. (115) This is a snap shot as of 2005. I extrapolated this curve for the fossil fuels such that if the world was capable of supplying (including our supply) fossil fuels the amount in 2037 would be exactly double or 6000 trillion megawatt hours of electrical power using fossil fuels. But, this would depend on obtaining oil from abroad. At some point, and I call it the year 2037, this curve would be in danger of dropping off and not reaching the 6000 trillion megawatt hours because of the shortage of oil. The key is that the bottom curves of renewable energy and nuclear energy would have to start turning up to intersect, or be close to intersecting this 6000 trillion megawatt hour point. I see good evidence that the curves have started up due to great improvements in solar and some indication that geothermal will be making a dramatic increase. The military is looking into ways of increasing the use of geothermal at certain locations to truncate the use of oil energy and to truncate the amount of money being sent out of the country to support this supply.

Figure 35 The United States electricity production by source (115)

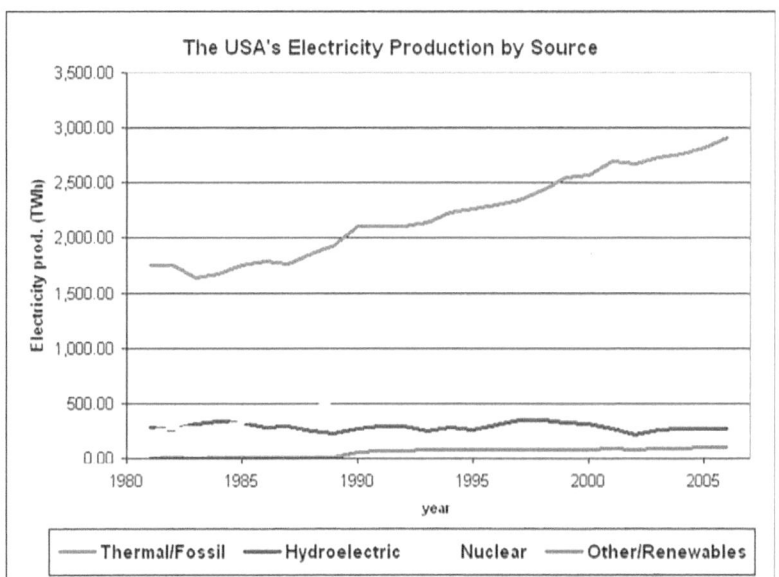

That United States has and continues to get most of its electrical production from conventional thermal power plants. Most of these are coal; however, the 1990s and 2000s have seen a disproportionate increase in natural gas and other kinds of gas powered plants.

From 1992 to 2005 some 270,000 MWe (Megawatt electric) of new gas-fired plant were built, but only 14,000 MWe of new nuclear and coal-fired capacity came on line, mostly coal, with 2,315 MWe of that being nuclear. Nuclear and coal are considerably capital intensive when compared to gas, and the great shift to gas plant construction is often attributed to deregulation and other political and economic factors. When I hear that I always remember that the highest cost is not having the resource. In this case, not having additional oil from off our shores, or not having a huge increase in renewable energy would be the highest cost.

As of 2007, there are a large number of new coal plants on order to keep up with fast increasing projected demand. This is in the United States, China, Germany and other countries of the world that have coal available. Keep in mind that the burning of coal is a greater contaminant of the atmosphere than gasoline or diesel. Therefore the environmentalists need to consider the cleanliness of nuclear and any other renewables and push for them over coal.

Incidentally the United States is the second biggest country in coal reserves after China. So, if need be, coal will be used to offset the lack of renewable or nuclear energy.

Hydroelectricity's contribution has been mostly constant throughout recent decades as has the contribution from new kinds of renewables including wind power and solar power, except for a sudden increase around 1990. Non-hydro renewable sources are also expected to increase in coming years. (121)

Figure 36 Electrical production in the United States for 2006 by all sources including renewable

Electrical Production in the United States for 2006 (144)

Power Source	Units in Operation	Total Nameplate Capacity (MW)	% of total Capacity	Annual Production (billion kWh)	% of annual production
Wind Power	341	11,603	1.08%	30.3	0.7%
Solar Energy	31	411	0.04%	2.1	0.1%
Petroleum Coke Fueled Boiler	31	1,754	0.16%	46.4	1.1%
Oil Fired Boiler	327	34,975	3.25%	7.8	0.2%
Nuclear Power	104	105,584	9.82%	787	19.4%
Natural Gas Fueled Boiler	776	97,632	9.08%	159	3.9%
Diesel Generators	4,514	8,563	0.8%	13.8	0.3%
Incinerators	96	2,671	0.25%	12.3	0.3%
Hydroelectric	4,138	96,988	9.02%	282	7.0%
Geothermal	215	3,170	0.29%	13.5	0.30%
Fuel Oil	13	956	0.09%	8.5	0.2%
Combustion Turbine Generators	2,882	155,227	14.4%	147	3.6%
Combined Cycle Natural Gas	1,686	216,269	20.1%	505	12.4%
Coal Fired Boilers	1,460	333,115	30.9%	1,995	49.1%
Biomass	270	6,256	0.58%	53.5	1.3%

My appraisal on the use of renewable energy and nuclear energy for the world's countries

Suppose you would be able to view what is going to happen relative to the energy requirements over the next fifty years and had to make certain strategic decisions on how the world should go and how the United States should go. What would you do? There is no doubt that oil will reach a peak in the next decade and by the year 2037, if there is still oil around, it would be used on a priority basis. The price will be enormous and there would be select areas around the world that would have some oil, but it would be tied to their own personal economy if they have the refinement capability. Let's assume this would be the scenario and when one looked back to this year he would then be able to determine whether his country made the right decisions on their energy path to energy freedom. If oil is gone the energy situation has settled down and there were only a few decisions that should have been made. One of them would have been to plan on a certain level of build up of nuclear energy. If they had the material that is required to provide a nuclear reactor with its fuel, they would have been in a fairly good position to have bargained for reciprocity; other country's nuclear material for reactors to keep them energy sufficient. All other countries would have had to make the decision early to provide a large part of their energy requirements on nuclear power. However, as you look back, you will see that it wasn't as easy as just making the decision. If the decision were to be made in 2009 or 2010 there would have been a chance to be in the critical queue of obtaining the materials including the Japanese Iron Works reactor shell. There would have been a queue of countries that made early commitments for nuclear energy and would have established their position in that queue by some comparable commitments to the countries that would supply them. This will have proven to be the right move. The queue by then would be quite long and there would be significant pressure by all countries to obtain this needed energy. Keep in mind the position Japan has because of its ability to supply the single shell main parts for a reactor.

United States

My position is that the United States should make that commitment by the year 2009 – 2010 to drill for offshore oil in order to have an early chance at a regular build up of these systems. Why? The main reason is energy independence. The United States will run out of its own domestic oil by the year 2020 and depend on oil from other countries. By the year 2037 the sources for energy for the United States has to come from the renewable energy sources to offset the loss of oil and its derivatives. If not, then coal will rear its ugly head. Why gamble when we know that nuclear energy is clean, long lasting, safe, and would allow us to offset the loss of oil. Why gamble when we know that the queue lining up for nuclear energy is getting longer and harder to enter.

Why gamble when we know if we decide five to ten years from now that we can make it without nuclear, we can sell the systems to the other countries that would not be as fortunate to have found their answers. Make a commitment now and ensure our energy independence by the end of the second decade of this century.

- Hydropower would have been flat for at least seventy years by 2037, therefore any growth in the population and the economic requirements to support them would not have come from hydropower.
- Natural gas would be in decent supply from the United States and probably Canada. Liquefied natural gas commitments would have been made to supply the US fairly heavily by the year 2020 from places like Australia. Use of these could help to allow the country to not have to use the large reserves we have on coal and its dirty contamination of the environment.
- Oil supplies will come from the offshore drilling and very little from the rest of the world. Oil will be dead as a big time supplier to the world. Fortunately the US will make commitments early enough (by 2010 -2011) to **drill offshore to be able to take advantage of their own supplies by 2020. It will take that long to have the oil rigs built and placed and to find the oil that is needed.** When I say offshore I mean as close as five miles, not the fifty miles that has just been approved. Too many people in this country believe that the push for drilling off shore is for money alone. This is the secondary issue. The establishment of those offshore sites is needed to be energy independent and be free of enormous pressure. Without this commitment the United States may lose their world power status in the second decade of this century. By 2037 the oil reserves under the United States will be low and will only be used for strategic purposes such as supplying the military, but the decision to drill off shore ha
- Coal could be there for the energy requirements. However, the coal will be under pressure not to be used because of its contamination issues. This will not be a huge problem if the United States made an early commitment to depend on a large amount of their energy from nuclear energy by 2037. It is possible that liquid coal will reach a point where it is less contaminating than the coal is today.

- Windmill supplies would have grown but are not expected to supply a significant amount of additional energy to the country. Windmills local use will help solve the problem for areas near their locations but windmill power will not play a large roll in the large major cities of the US.
- Solar energy will have built a large capacity supplied by private companies and some supplied by federal programs. PV solar for home use and business buildings will reduce the demand on the matrix suppliers and by those required by large thermal solar power systems and the large electrical generation plants. Private companies will play a major roll in supplying these systems. Thermal solar will supply the major portion of the US requirements for renewable energy. Solar will be the one renewable fuel that is spread through the southwest and several parts of the states to complement the supply of nuclear energy and natural gas energy. This is a huge bright spot in the energy picture; not only in the United States but in several parts of the world.

Other countries

Germany will be on solar, windmills, and natural gas for their supplies but may be in trouble for portable biofuels or other supplies for portable use. Natural gas will be supplied by Russia.

Norway, Sweden, Denmark, and Finland are a mixed bag. Several have large hydroelectric systems and there is a trend toward windmill farms. They probably will invest in wave and tidal water power. I don't believe they have ample solar energy resources since they are rather cold by nature. I would expect them to invest in nuclear to overcome any energy needs.

Spain and Portugal will be heavily involved with PV solar and Thermal solar as well as windmills to supply much of their energy. They will show an increase in nuclear energy.

France is a heavy user of nuclear and will see advances in PV solar and Thermal solar. This is a picture of what most of the countries in the southern part of Europe will portray. I expect Italy, Greece, and all the countries along the Mediterranean Sea will gain energy from PV solar, thermal solar, windmill farms and take on additional nuclear energy.

The U.K. will have nuclear, windmills, PV solar and some thermal solar. The U.K is one of the few countries that will not have significant contributions from solar power due to their weather and many days with fog and the lack of significant sunshine. They will invest in wave and tidal water power for certain locations in their country.

Russia will be pushing nuclear, natural gas, some oil energy in the third decade of the century, but will run out of oil energy early in the 2030 time frame. I wouldn't be surprised if they don't push for windmill farms on the large territory of their country. I also believe they would place a good bit of time on advances in geothermal energy.

China will be increasing their supply of hydropower, coal energy and they will probably be pushing their PV solar and thermal solar in some of the areas that are desert like such as the southwestern part of the United States has done. It's possible that China may also have a significant amount of geothermal energy located at various places in the country.

India This land of many people and only a little land may be in trouble except for coal. This country is about a third the size of the U.S. with about four times the people and very little arable land to feed its population. The main sources of energy are or will be hydroelectric, coal, and some PV solar and thermal solar. Clean water is a need.

Some of **the smaller countries along the Asian coasts** will be pushing water power as well as PV solar and thermal solar. Many of these small countries are along the equator and have excellent areas for the use of both PV solar and thermal solar. Some do not have enough land to place thermal solar in large systems as will be seen in other parts of the world. However, they can use roof top thermal solar for personal and business hot water systems.

South America has significant supplies of hydropower and they will have big increases in biofuel. Most of the countries should be in good positions to utilize PV solar power and thermal solar power. Biomass will continue to be of high usage and may find that they can pick up significant amounts of biomass from the refuge of the biofuels they generate. Certain of the countries would find windmill farms to their benefit.

Australia has large amounts of natural gas that can be use directly or converted to liquid natural gas for their own use and to sell worldwide. Australia would seem to be ideally situated for picking up large amounts of energy from PV solar and thermal solar. I would imagine they eventually will be using water power and windmill power that should be available at their location. I would take an educated guess that Australia would be affluent in biofuels to supply their country's requirements.

Africa is large and made up of many different climates. They will supply a great amount of biofuels for their use and should be in good shape with PV solar and thermal solar, especially along the northern coast. There are probably spots in various African countries that would have large amounts of geothermal energy, but that is to be proven. There are areas across this continent and along its long sea shores that would have locations for windmill farms. Still, in many of the countries the main source of energy will be biomass, as it has been since time began.

In summary, this provides the reader my thoughts on these spot areas around the world and I would expect that the countries that are adjacent or contiguous with these countries will act accordingly.

- Biofuels will play a minor part in the drive for energy, but it will play a significant part in the drive to replace gasoline and diesel fuel. It will be the major supplier of portable energy for the United States, Brazil and several other countries. The key is to use other materials besides food products, such as algae, wood chips, biomass refuge, and others that they have in ample supply for their basic energy for transportation. Over the next thirty years I would expect the world's scientists and engineers to find other means of supplying this energy. There will be chemical solutions that allow discarded material to be used to supplement the biofuel supply. Here's where I believe the consumer will play part savior for this country. They will continue their consumer ways and the large amount of material being sent to this country by China and others for consumer consumption will supplement the supply of discarded material to be used for generating biofuels. This would be a wondrous circle where the importing from other countries will end up supplying the United States the extraordinary amount of material that can be used for conversion to biofuels. I read a recent article where some college was reviewing the use of stink week for biofuel. This is a useless weed and a fast grower. Things of this nature will have a double impact since it will provide a fuel and it will help clean up many areas where weeds grow and there are many cast offs from consumer use that could be used as the fuel for supplying biofuel for portable energy.

- Geothermal energy would be able to supply a significant amount of the energy needed for supplying heat to turbines that generate electricity. In fact, it probably could supply it all if the decision were made to use the geothermal energy that is, or could be made, available. The study by MIT found that there is enough geothermal energy to supply the United States and probably the world if it selected to do so. My guess is that it won't be selected. The reason why is the one of the economics involved. There are no private companies that will go out on the limb to cultivate this resource and I believe the reason is because it can't be marketed like oil. There's no tangible product that can be marketed in the world economy and provide revenue like a standard product because it is too localized. Obtaining energy from a geothermal source is limited to the given area where found, more so than other renewable sources. It's a local source and therefore is only pushed locally. The fossil fuels and solar energy are examples of worldwide saleable products that have huge resources that can be marketed the world over. The initial investments are high due to the depth they may have to drill to reach the geothermal energy and the return on those investments would be a long time coming. This is hard for private companies to digest. A good comparison would be solar power where there are many private companies involved. Private companies know they can make money off this investment and the initial investment is not that high. PV Solar power is almost a "personal power the world over" where individuals can invest in solar for their home use without regard to what others are doing. It can come in small packages, medium packages, and large packages. The large packages can be supported by financial investors who can see a rapid return on their money. Geothermal is a different animal. There is no "personal use" tag that comes with this source of energy. It's like a myth that has been around for a long time and most of the world's people have not enjoyed its benefits. It's been around forever and no one has ever taken advantage of it because it's hard to quantify its resource value. It's viewed as a last resource that we can fall back on and these types never seem to happen. The key factor missing is not knowing how much energy one is going to obtain from a site and how long it will last. This will probably make it a local issue and there will be local geothermal sites appearing all over the world. It is a huge source that must be located – probably from satellites. Once located, it will be up to local governments to take advantage of the source.

For geothermal to get off the ground several things have to happen:

1. Someone of influence has to read this book, the MIT report, or something like these.
2. Or someone of influence has to get the word from some other means.
3. Someone of high visibility has to take it on and champion its value; probably take the MIT report and push the right buttons. Maybe take it on like Al Gore took on global warming. It needs a champion.
4. Someone really has to believe that there will be a significant drop in the supply of oil by the year 2037 (or there about) and must be in a position of influence to make that point with the top government officials to push programs like this.
5. Someone has to believe that the renewables will not be in position to supply the energy that is lost by the lost of oil, unless they turn to geothermal for their particular location.
6. Someone has to realize if we don't support the nuclear energy and/or the geothermal approach that we will not make it past the year 2037 without a major impact on the world economy and the world's way of life and life itself.
7. Many people must speak up against the use of coal as the fuel to carry the world till we find the renewable solutions. If there truly is a "Green world community" then they must not only push for resolving the exhaust of carbon dioxide by limiting the use of oil and its derivatives but to think of coal as a worse solution and stand up against it. They must not always create "negative waves" and use their massive influence with "positive waves" on the clean solutions of nuclear and especially geothermal in this case to carry us past coal as the solution.

8. Someone has to realize that the other renewable energy sources will not reach the level needed by the year 2037 or 2050 or 2070 when oil and its derivatives are gone.

9. Someone has to realize that some of the other renewable energy sources need to be used in particular applications and geothermal energy would give them the leeway needed to direct the other sources to their proper applications.

10. For some countries this may be the ultimate solution for their energy needs. The IEEE Spectrum of October 08 discussed a plan by the Navy to generate geothermal power in several of their bases. This is a program by the Navy to reduce the military costs of electrical power. Their plan is to prove feasibility at their White Sands New Mexico base and then to establish geothermal in many bases across the country. (145)

Energy trends in Europe

In Europe, the total consumption of energy is at a plateau and is almost stable until 2030, but then starts to increase (122) This is in a sense a statistical phenomenon arising from the high primary heat input of nuclear power. Renewable sources provide 22% and nuclear 30% of the European energy demand in 2050, bringing the share of fossil fuels to less than 50% on present day plans. Of course, I don't agree with this. I believe many countries will be forced to change their trends as soon as they realize the loss of a huge energy source such as oil.

Three quarters of power generation in Europe is based on nuclear and renewable sources and half of thermal power generation is in plants with CO_2 capture and storage. Germany has rejected farther use of nuclear power and will depend on renewables such as wind and solar. Natural Gas delivers a quantity of energy equivalent to 15% of that delivered by electricity. By 2050, half of the total building installed will be composed of low energy buildings and a quarter of very low energy buildings. More than half of vehicles are low emission or very low emission vehicles (e.g. electricity or hydrogen powered cars). These are the general plans I have read about, but since these plans were made things have changed. I don't believe the dramatic growth of PV solar and thermal solar was taken into account in those plans. It would have been too optimistic to predict that these areas would be growing this fast. I also believe that geothermal was not recognized to be as generous as it is around the world. This being the case, I believe there will be more renewable energy than is in those plans and less fossil fuel energy being used – especially coal.

Liquid fuels

There is another trend that has been occurring since the late 1980's till the present. This is the upward trend on the use of other liquid fuels besides oil and its derivatives. See the chart below. These are:

1. Gas conversion – There has been a trend in the liquefaction of natural gas to supply as a portable fuel. The natural gas is converted under pressure to liquid natural gas supplied in metal cylinders. There have been experimental programs in various parts of the world using this liquefied natural gas in buses and heavy equipment and it is expected to keep growing. The impact will be greater when lighter cylinders are found for holding this fuel.

2. Biofuel energy – We have already discussed this source of liquid fuel which is being used heavily in Brazil and has been trending upward in use in the United States. This approach is favorable in countries like Brazil that has large areas of arable land. There is also a trend toward converting other materials to biodiesel which could be a real help in reducing the worlds storage of garbage while providing a portable fuel.

3. Coal to liquids – This is an approach that is becoming more popular. The coal is liquefied through various methods and provides an easier means of transporting it than in the standard lump of coal form. Coal liquefaction could prove to be a very valuable process for supplying liquid energy when oil either becomes too scarce or becomes too costly. In some ways it limits the potential of oil becoming too expensive. However, it does put out more carbon dioxide than oil and resolving this issue would make it a very valuable source of liquid fuel for automobiles and other vehicles. Coal is the most plentiful fossil fuel on Earth. The United States contains one of the world's largest supplies of coal. It has been estimated that U.S. production of this liquid fuel becomes cost-competitive with oil priced at around $35.00 per barrel, (123) which is much lower than the present price of oil. China uses a large amount of coal and is probably looking into the use of this liquid

to replace oil, especially if they can find a way to reduce the CO_2 given off or provide CO_2 capture..

4. The Canadian Oil Sands have shown growth and continue to grow through the year 2030. This growth is in direct relationship to how hard it is to find more oil reserves in Canada. It is harder to process but becomes quite competitive with oil when the prices are running as high as they presently are.

5. The Ultra-Heavy Crudes again is a direct reflection of the difficulty in finding light oil in certain parts of the world today and a means of using them in easier fashion may come in time..

6. See the chart below on the growth of liquid fuels over time. Notice that the biofuel jumps up considerably by 2015 but then stays fairly constant. The liquid coal jumps up in 2015 and keep growing, showing a little over 2 billion barrels a day by 2030. The gas to liquids also takes off in 2015. This is a reflection of when the supply of oil starts to level off at about 120 million barrels a day and some of the smaller suppliers of oil drop out of the market and leave OPEC as not only the main supplier but one of the few. See complete report on web site - http://thefraserdomain.typepad.com/photos/uncategorized/2007/05 (124)

Figure 37 World production of unconventional liquids (including biofuels, coal-to-liquids, and gas-to-liquids), (left) which totaled only 2.6 million barrels per day in 2004, is projected to increase to 10.5 million barrels per day and account for 9 percent of total world liquids supply in 2030, on an oil equivalent basis, in the IEO2007 reference case.

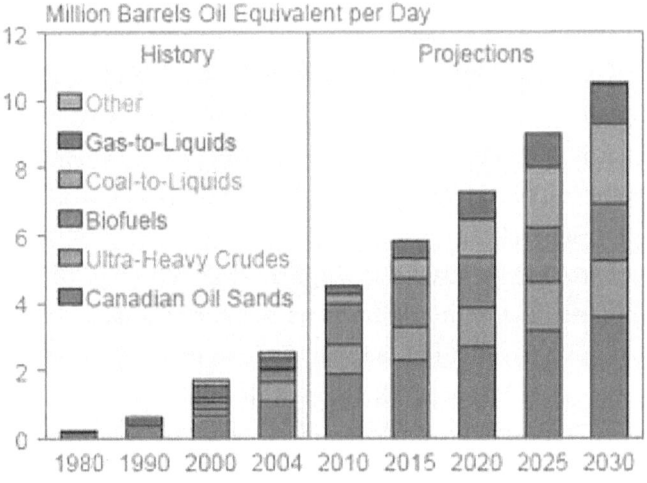

k.

Figure 37 World production of unconventional liquids (including biofuels, coal-to-liquids, and gas-to-liquids), (left) which totaled only 2.6 million barrels per day in 2004, is projected to increase to 10.5 million barrels per day and account for 9 percent of total world liquids supply in 2030, on an oil equivalent basis, in the IEO2007 reference case. (124)

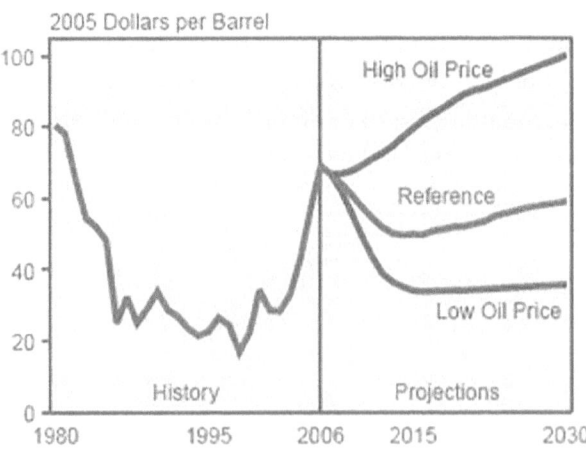

Figure 38 The world oil prices in the IEO2007 reference case— and in the high world oil price case—also are projected to make previously uneconomical, unconventional resources available. See web site – (125) (http://thefraserdomain.typepad.com/photos/uncategorized/2007/05/24/liquids

Reserve estimates for oil, natural gas, and coal are difficult to develop. EIA develops estimates of reserves for the United States but not for foreign countries. As a convenience to the public, EIA makes available global reserve estimates from the Oil & Gas Journal, World Oil, and BP's Statistical Review.

There is one very important point in the curves shown below. See the world total reserves of oil. They show the world total reserves as of 2007 being about 1,250 billion barrels of oil. This is 1.25 trillion barrels of oil reserve. Remember in my estimate of oil where I used one trillion barrels and then said if the price of oil goes up that they will probably find 2.0 trillion barrels. It was from these numbers that I extrapolated and determined that we would run out of oil in the year 2037 based on the use at present growing to the eventual 150 million barrels a day by the third decade. This would indicate that the reserves are not 2.0 trillion but 1.25 trillion. This makes the problem worse and indicates if we use the oil as I extrapolated that we will run out earlier. I still believe they will find more oil than this source indicates and will stick with my two trillion barrels to be found and 30 years and 2037 as the cut off date. of World Energy, shown.

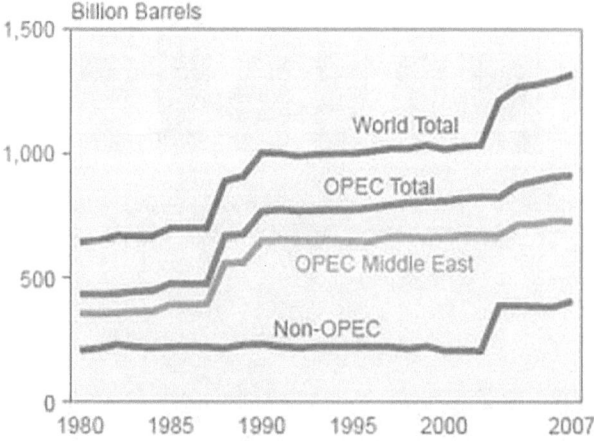

Figure 39 Chart of the billions of barrels of oil reserves in the worlds and under what control See web site for additional information (126)

Since 2000, the largest net increase in estimated proved oil reserves has been made in Canada, with the addition of 174 billion barrels of Canadian oil sands as a conventional reserve. Iranian oil reserves have increased by 46.6 billion barrels, or 52 percent, since 2000. Kazakhstan has had the third-largest increase, 24.6 billion barrels, since 2000.

World marketed energy consumption is projected to increase by 50 percent from 2005 to 2030. Total energy demand in the non-OECD countries increases by 85 percent, compared with an increase of 19 percent in the OECD countries. (OECD stands for Organization for Economic Cooperation and Development. **See figure 40 below – World Consumption (127)**

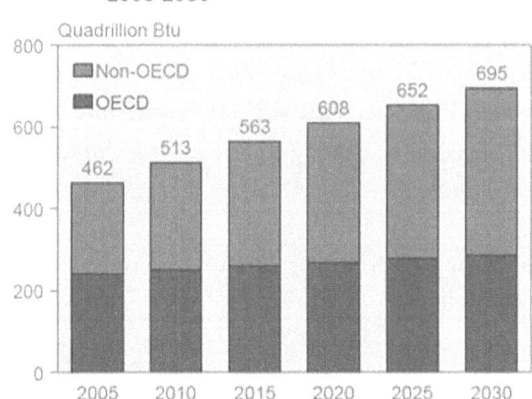

Figure 1. World Marketed Energy Consumption, 2005-2030

Sources: **2005:** Energy Information Administration (EIA), *International Energy Annual 2005* (June-October 2007), web site www.eia.doe.gov/iea. **Projections:** EIA, World Energy Projections Plus (2008).

Figure Data

IEO2009 Release Date: June 2008
(full report available August 2008)
WEB site www.eia.doe.gov/iea.

Other report highlights include:

- Coal consumption, which grows an average annual rate of 2.2 percent, is the fastest-growing energy source worldwide in the IEO2007 reference case projection, which assumes that existing laws and policies remain in effect through 2030 notwithstanding concerns related to the rising level of energy-related greenhouse gas emissions. World coal consumption increased sharply from 2003 to 2004, largely because of a 17-percent increase in non-OECD Asia (mainly China and India). With oil and natural gas prices expected to continue rising, coal is an attractive fuel for nations with access to ample coal resources, especially in coal-rich countries like China, India, and the United States. **These three countries combined account for 86 percent of the increment in world coal demand by 2030** in the referenced report. I don't want to see the coal rising that fast and this is the main issue for pushing for renewables as fast as we can put them into play and control them. We should think of coal as a last resort for energy needs.

• In the IEO2007 reference case, which does not include specific policies to limit greenhouse gas emissions, energy-related carbon dioxide emissions are projected to rise from 26.9 billion metric tons in 2004 to 33.9 billion metric tons in 2015 and 42.9 billion metric tons in 2030. From 2003 to 2004, carbon dioxide emissions from the non-OECD countries grew by almost 10 percent, while emissions in the OECD countries (grew by less than 2 percent. 2004 marked the first time in history that emissions from the non-OECD exceeded those from the OECD countries. Non-OECD countries will rely on fossil fuels of coal and oil to supply much of their future energy demand growth. Carbon dioxide emissions from the non-OECD countries in 2030 are projected to exceed those from the OECD by 57 percent. **(OECD stands for Organization for Economic Cooperation and Development and includes the highly developed countries of the world))128)**

The report described in this press release was prepared by the Energy Information Administration, the independent statistical and analytical agency within the U.S. Department of Energy. The information contained in the report and the press release should be attributed to the Energy Information Administration and should not be construed as advocating or reflecting any policy position of the Department of Energy or any other organization.

Source: National Energy Information Center (161)
Tags: alternative energy, Energy, Solar, solar energy, solar thermal

Crisis VI -
Population and Population Growth

Man's energy is given back to space via the 2,000 Calories per day that he consumes to help balance the indirect heat intake from the Sun. This energy does not just disappear. It is emitted as heat in the form of infrared wavelengths, water vapor from his sweat, and the moisture he breathes out. Carbon dioxide is expelled to provide the one necessary ingredient for plants to grow. Energy transfer occurs when he causes something to move. Man's blood delivers oxygen to all the cells in the body. In order to accomplish this task the oxygen that man breathes goes to his lungs. In the lungs there is blood that is being returned from making its flow around the body. This blood is returned through the veins, and is depleted of much of its oxygen. This blood has a look of a different color than the blood that leaves the heart, which is rather blue from acquiring the oxygen from the lungs. The blood coming back to the lungs comes via the blood that is depleted of its oxygen and is rich in iron. It is the iron in the blood that picks up the oxygen in the lungs. If the person is iron deficient he will not pick up enough oxygen in the lungs and will be weak, tire easily and be susceptible to sickness and disease.

It takes energy for the heart to keep beating and for the lungs to oxygenate the blood. It takes energy for the brain to tell the blood where to go. The body doesn't have enough blood to satisfy the body, so the blood needs prioritized as to where it is needed the most and where it should go. If a person eats food the brain is prioritizing the food digesting system to do its work and prioritizes the blood flow to the proper areas. It is for this reason that one is told not to eat and go swimming. If a person goes swimming after eating a meal, the energy used in swimming is prioritized by the brain to receive blood to ensure there is the proper amount of energy to handle the energy burned off by the swimming. This causes a conflict with the blood having been prioritized for the digestion of food. So, a person is likely to get a cramp while swimming because not enough blood is now reaching the digestive system and it could be fatal. These messages from the brain require energy. These are just a few of the body functions that require those 2000 Calories per day. Walking, running, physical jobs, eating, speaking, laughing, and crying, all require energy. One's eyes use considerable energy, again from the brain to interpret what one is seeing. If a person loses their sight there is more energy for other functions in the body. The person's other senses pick up and become more acute; hearing and smelling takes up energy.

When one walks outside on a spring day and looks about him/her and sees the sky and smells the air and takes a deep breath they are being rewarded with a taste in their mouth and a feeling of satisfaction throughout their body. This euphoric feeling is consuming some of the energy of the food taken in at some time in their lives. Man burns up energy while moving around objects that are part of Earth, which are not relative to energy that the Sun provides. It is just part of Earth that he moves around and man dissipates energy while doing this and his dissipation of energy results in heat given off to the atmosphere in addition to completing the task he is about. When man takes cement from the ground that is part of the Earth, and fabricates concrete to make roads, he is giving up body heat and energy while just moving around a part of Earth that is here as the planet is here. He is taking mass energy from Earth and returning it to Earth in a new form and that new form takes on a different energy than it had before this transaction. The wonderful thing is that, assuming the person takes in his Calories, these tasks are completed and he looks no less for the work accomplished. The wonderful thing is that not too many tens of thousands of years ago there were no humans on Earth, but in 2037 there will be an increase to 8.7 billion.

Any physical exertion requires energy that must be replaced. It is not important that it be replaced at exactly the time it is used but it must be replaced within days of use unless the person wants to lose weight. The same is true with water, only it doesn't contain any Calories, but man must have the water in order that the body retains enough fluid to carry his energy around and supplies fluid for critical functions. Man must return all the energy that was used to keep him alive. On an average, every day, he takes in and expels 2,000 Calories in some manner. The same is true of all the animals roaming the fields to supply man with Calories. Animals burn off energy, more than man in general, that is replaced by the plants they eat each day before man consumes them for one of his meals. The animals must emit heat in the form that man does, that is, heat is given off in infrared wavelengths. As a result, they give off more infrared energy back into space and they generate more carbon dioxide than man each day. Using this form of argument, man has taken this step to remain atop the food chain. He has improvised since the time he came on earth to ensure he is able to acquire the needed food to keep him alive. But I am repeating myself. I covered most of this in the section on global temperature cycling and possible global warming. Why am I repeating it again? It's because this section is on another crisis for this century. It is about the crisis on population growth of man and animals during the 21st century

Each day, throughout the world, this heat emission happens time after time by the 6.7 billion residents. But, keep in mind that these 6.7 billion residents depend completely on the Sun to provide the plants that grow on the Earth. They also depend on the food making its way to their tables at home or in a restaurant. A significant amount of energy is dissipated each day bringing that food to each of the 6.7 billion inhabitants of this planet.

Now think about the year 2037 and the population is approximately 8.7 billion people and there are more animals to help support their 2000 Calorie need along with more energy of the Sun being used to provide the plant food. Now think about the fact that I hypothesized that Earth would be without the portable high energy of gasoline or diesel. Is this a crisis? One would think it might be. We have two billion more people to feed here on Earth and we have less portable energy to provide the transportation to supply it. Remember, I even hypothesized that we might not have enough to fly airplanes. It might not be in the year 2037, but it could be. Maybe it's a little latter than 2037. That's fine, it gives us a little more time to prepare for this issue, this soon to be crisis. Whether the year is 2037 or a little beyond, the problem is the problem. Even if we develop renewable energy to take the place of the loss of oil, will we develop enough renewable energy to handle the significant number of people that have been added to Earth? Is the energy in a form that allows it to be portable and replace the function that gasoline has played in our lives? Keep in mind that this is only thirty years away. The possible crises I see that are a function of this increase in the human population:

1. The need for additional food for two billion people at 2000 Calories per person a day.

2. The added heat energy emanating from these additional two billion people could be the cause of any global warming. The 2000 Calories they take in each day are used up and this forms a constant expelling of the 2000 Calories times an additional two billion people.

3. The added vehicles needed in the world to transport these people around.

4. The added animals needed to provide food for these people assuming the diets of people remain the same and the demand for meat grows with the population growth.

5. The added heat energy emanating from these added animals.

6. The additional carbon dioxide being generated by the population growth and the animal growth; with the carbon dioxide generated by animals being much higher than from humans. If global warmth is due to excess carbon dioxide and proves to be the real problem with climate than this is a force that is increasing and a force to be reckoned with. Reduce the domestic animal population

7. The population growth in absolute numbers are greatest in China and India and Southeast Asia. The greatest growth in percent is in Africa. Do these areas have the resources food wise to support this growth? Will they be able to control the contamination of the atmosphere? I believe these are the countries where there is little arable land to provide plants for food. China in fact is using much of its land to provide energy via hydropower and the related dams and the related reservoirs and their use of the land.

8. Does the world possess the means of delivering this added food to the people of the world? Is there a replacement for gasoline that allows for transportation on a level that we see in today's transportation methods for providing food?

9. The Sun's energy continues to supply added sunlight energy to maintain the growth for photosynthesis rather than the energy of the Sun supplying its daily energy to Earth for other functions. The energy from the Sun is constant and added people means that part of this constant is being consumed by added people and added animals.

10. Contamination of the atmosphere must be restricted to a level that is tolerable for human life. Programs must go into effect as soon as

possible and beyond those that were in effect when there were 6.7 billion people on Earth.

11. Is there enough water for the increase needed to support added population growth of man and animals? Is there enough water to support both plants and the animals used for food? The amount of water supplied around the world from the hydrological cycle **is a constant.** Clouds retain water that is evaporated from the oceans and other waters of the world for nine days before that water is released. Clouds release water 45 times a year. The amount of fresh water derived from the hydrological cycle is a constant. If the water was allowed to remain on the surface of the earth from the rain each year it would provide fresh water at a depth of one meter across the surface of Earth. This is the constant. Fortunately it doesn't remain on the surface of Earth's land and oceans but is evaporated and this is followed by some form of precipitation, so the plants and Earth is cycled with this water and is used fairly efficiently. However, it precipitates at different places each year and results in floods in some areas and droughts in other areas. With the increase of population of people and animals, will there be water in the areas most needed each year, and will it be enough? Keep one thing in mind, the world is mostly water made up of oceans etc. This means that most of the precipitation falls on the oceans of the world, not on land where it can serve to supply man with drinking water. So, about 87% of the precipitation is lost before we have a chance to use it. Perhaps we can find a way to change that so that more is captured for drinking purposes or watering purposes. We need to do something or the big crisis in the 21ˢᵗ century will be the lack of water to serve 8.7 million people. We can plant more plants and hopefully find a way to deliver the results to the world's population; but water is different. We can't change what the Sun provides for us in the way of evaporation and precipitation. We can think about desalination, but where do we get the extra energy to provide the power to perform desalination?

12. Animals, per capita, consume more water than man and more calories from plants than man. Will decisions be made to restrict the population growth of animals and will it be an international agreement? We will need to depend more on plants for our food. A partial vegetarian diet is necessary. There is a conflict here. The more domestic animals are

reduced in number, the more water and plants for man. If we believe that a domesticated animal uses ten times more water and plant food than man, then for every reduction in the head count of domesticated animals there is room for more humans on earth. This is sad but true. This is in conflict with the economies of those who not only eat a great deal of meat but depend on its export to provide them a living. If we restrict the domesticated animal population growth, where do we get the leather needed to supply man's needs? We can't go to plastic because that takes even more energy to produce.

13. Population growth in general may have to be better controlled. An international committee on population growth should be formed that not only makes recommendations but is given the power to enforce them by some means. This population growth of 30% over the next thirty years that I estimate may need to be truncated to meet the international needs of all people. Its one thing to have a thirty percent growth in some countries that have natural resources to sustain the growth but there may be some countries where the natural resources do not exist and with the possibility of restrictions on transportation determined by the lack of the proper energy, there may not be the means to transport the resources for support of growth. Some countries population grows as a result of immigration. This growth within the country they immigrate to must be assessed to the country from which they immigrated. Otherwise there is a penalty on the country that is controlling birth but not on the other country that is not controlling birth. This is a difficult and sensitive issue that may not be popular but some restraint must be enforced or the world will suffer in general. This is an international problem and must be solved diplomatically. If it's not solved by the year 2037, then what year?

14. As the population of the world increases it displaces plants through the greater consumption of plants. Will this cause a balance between carbon dioxide and oxygen to exist? People and plants form a balance between the one giving off the carbon dioxide and the other the oxygen. The balance has been with the oxygen for about a billion years. We need to keep that balance.

15. Each person walks around the world giving off their mean temperature of 98.6 degrees Fahrenheit and with two billion more giving off this stable temperature, that doesn't include the energy expelled of using up

their 2000 Calories. Does this cause any problems with the stability that exists with the incoming energy from the sun and the increasing thermal energy that remains on Earth in the form of human beings and animals with their added heat? If not, how close it take us to a real fundamental problem? Can the world support additional population growth to the next century that may exceed ten billion human beings on the face of Earth?

16. Do you know what is even more dramatic? The population growth doesn't stop in 2037, it continues on and on. Data indicates that the population in 2050 will be around 9.2 billion; making it another half billion that must be served in one way or another.

Crisis VII -
Transportation energy needed to provide food for the population growth

With the growth of the world's population and the possible loss of our portable energy we may be impacted by the lack of proper transportation to carry the food around this globe day in and day out. It becomes a monumental task of planning. Whereas the governments of the world today have not had to plan the food supply because of each countries' economic requirements based on what they have and what they need and what the world economies need – i.e.; the need to have exports to balance out the countries' financial needs; this may not be true in the year 2037 or some later year. With the possible loss of portable energy and the increased population there will need to be a comprehensive global plan to determine where and when food supplies are shipped to on a daily basis. With these basic and fundamental conflicts of resources there will need to be a global plan.

There will be a mismatch between the countries that have an abundance of food supplies relative to their population and the lack of proper transportation to provide the countries that do not. There will be countries that have a good balance between their food supplies and their ability to transport food supplies to their people and to other countries. There will be countries that have neither the food nor the transportation to cope with their populations. This type of situation is one that has not existed to any extent in the past one hundred years. Sure, there have been undeveloped countries that didn't have enough food for their population in the past, but there was ample food elsewhere and good transportation means to handle this situation, but it has been difficult. As the years go on and we reach what I call the year 2037, this will only be handled with proper planning, proper diplomacy, and proper love for ones fellow man. And even when those are employed, there may not be the capability of transporting the food and water to the parts of the world that find themselves short.

The one key, besides the obvious, would be the resolution of the need for a portable fuel to replace gasoline. Perhaps the biofuels or the liquefied natural gas or the eventual fuel cell will prove to be a viable means of supplying the portable energy and be able to handle this fuel issue and transportation will not be an issue. Even so, it shows how close we are as a world body of people with needs that become closer to the reality of limiting the population on Earth. If we don't figure out a way, Mother Nature may solve the problem for us and we won't like the results.

Crisis VIII -
Logistics with renewable energy is different and needs solutions

Keep in mind the additional logistics that may be involved as the means of supplying energy shifts to renewable energy. We go from a world that is, and has been, one of a plethora of supplying man's needs. We will be going from a world that has oil in transit on a constant basis and therefore is usable on demand; to a world supplied by individual renewable energy that is not easily transferred worldwide. We will go to a system where the energy will be lost if not used the day of generation. We have never been in this type of situation before. Even if certain countries can generate renewable energy this is greater than their daily use, it will not be by a large margin and therefore there will not exist a supply that is greater than the demand.

During the nineteenth century the U.S. growth moved westward and the abundant open land of the Midwest and West was opened to large cattle farms and huge farms. This began the age of the great cattle runs and the spreading of the large open farm land of the Midwest and West. From this came the great wealth of natural resources from a land that was pristine and the population was scant. From a few came so much. Since the United States became a wealthy reality capable of supplying internal needs from a virginal supply of land and plants and eventually of domesticated food supplies during the nineteenth century; and when the 20th century arrived, so did the means of supplying this wonderful supply; oil was commercialized in the United States. Since the advent of the fuel to supply machines and to eventually supply all the transportation needs for their and other economies' needs, the problem of supplying the world's needs was a reality. Not that other countries didn't also supply the basic needs of the world, they did. But the one thing that helped was the use of an abundance of fuel and the inventions of the automobile and the airplane. With these findings and these inventions, many countries performed the functions needed to have the world move in a fairly healthy, robust condition. Where there were shortages of some things, they were supplied in a form of barter system of trade between countries. This system worked even better with money rather than trade goods. The world banking system allowed for a smooth transfer of the value of money from one country to the next and now there was this currency exchange to provide a smooth transfer of resources from one country to the next. The economies of the various countries found a way to value their goods so they could use money to buy the things they didn't have. What a wonderful century the 20th was.

But keep in mind what may occur in the year 2037 or some later time when the energy shifts toward the renewable energy supplies. There is wind energy we have discussed. There is the hydroelectric energy we have discussed. There are the different types of solar energy we have discussed. There is wave energy we have discussed. There is biofuel energy we have discussed. There is the liquefying of natural gas that we have discussed. There is geothermal energy we have discussed and there is nuclear energy we have discussed. All of these may end up as a form of electrical energy and providing the main source of energy for many countries. This isn't bad from the standpoint of shipping the energy around; in fact it may be ideal since electrical energy can be transmitted over long distances. However, there are the haves and the have-nots when it comes to the various countries around the world. There will be countries capable of supplying their own needs via any one or a combination of these renewable energies. There are countries where there are significant amounts of wind to help them derive their energy. There are countries we have discussed that have enormous amounts of hydroelectric power that can handle their needs. There are countries with a bright Sun capable of supplying them their needs through solar power. There are countries with significant amounts of natural gas supplying their needs from their natural resources and possibly being able to supply liquefied natural gas for transportation. There are countries with natural sources of geothermal power that can solve many of their issues. There are countries that are rich in agriculture and may be able to supply their needs with biofuels, but what about their ability to supply other countries? There are countries rich enough to be able to install a great amount of nuclear energy for their future use and they will not have a problem for most of their activities, but not for supplying fuel for airplanes to deliver food; this is not a solution. There are countries near ocean fronts that can supply significant amounts of energy via the use of water waves. But there will be some countries that have none of these capabilities or capacities. What problems might be created by all this?

The problem that could be created without proper communication between countries well in advance is how to handle the new logistics that these different supplies create. How to transfer this energy from one country to the next and on a timely basis? Where previously there existed the petroleum routes that were developed over a hundred years, these logistic routes may become outmoded through the loss of their petroleum resources and many of the pipes cannot handle some of the biofuels. The ships that used to carry millions of barrels of fuel around the world may be outmoded by the loss of significant petroleum supplies to propel them. But, in the mean time there will be the development of one or several of the renewable energy sources within countries graced with certain capabilities. This will require a shift to other means of supplying their energy needs.

The transporting of petroleum took years to develop to the levels that exist today. New logistics must be developed to handle the new energies to be supplied and they may be supplied to a completely different set of clients. Clients that had little or no oil resources might now be self efficient with renewable energy sources. There may be countries that were self sufficient with oil as their prime resource and when it runs out they may not have a renewable energy capability. Planning ahead is of super importance. International cooperation is of prime importance.

Do you see what now exists as this system of renewable energy takes on? We go from a world running fairly smoothly where currency is all that is needed to supply energy to a world of individual entities. It is a well oiled machine. It was almost a good thing that most of the world's supply of oil was located in only several places and in large quantities. This supply could be easily planned and transported using less energy than it was carrying. It was fortunate that there was a super abundance of oil from these few sources. It was like having huge banks with a lot of money that could be handled across the globe. For example, the large tankers carrying huge amounts of fuel only required a relatively small amount of energy that was an insignificant amount of the energy they were carrying. Huge tanker ships could be afforded to be built. Economically, they were a great resource and paid their way. The return on investment to build these large tankers was more than adequate.

And therefore, the world goes from one of few with large volume supplying many, to one of many with small volumes supplying a few with completely different logistical problems. This pertains to the energy used for transportation, but it also could relate to the food that is being transferred. What now with each country providing renewable energy that is in many cases what their country needs, but is not easily provided to others of the world? The world becomes a bunch of self providers and if they have any overages they may not be economical to transport to others, even in the form of electricity. There may be a bunch of "not so big" suppliers. Take biofuel for an example. Countries like Brazil may be quite happy with their supply of this ready means of fuel, but may not be in a good economical position to supply this form of portable energy to the world. In fact they won't. They may pick a few countries that are close and economically practical to supply their overages, but that will leave a lot to be desired. We go from a world of conglomerates to one of rather small independent suppliers scattered all over the globe – if we can call countries "small conglomerates".

Even though the common element may be electricity, how do you plan ahead to set up the optimum transfer routes to drop off some here and some there if the format of electricity is different at each place? It reminds me of when I was a kid and you got a train under the tree for Christmas, and only a few pieces of track to do anything with it. You could hardly wait till next Christmas to receive more tracks so you could really move your train around in a various number of routes. The same will be true of the logistics required to handle these rather small oversupplies of renewable energy that each country now has in this form that is not easy to transfer, except by electricity and that will be hard because of the multiplicity of suppliers and receivers of the renewable energy. Take a worse case where we have abundant electrical energy to handle most of our local needs and no airplanes are able to fly on electricity, or no large vehicles are developed that run off electricity.

Even if we develop vehicles to run off electricity, do we have the large battery capability to use them for mass transport? We obviously will have automobiles that run off electricity and have batteries now that can handle them for rather short runs. We don't want to have to sit around and wait till they recharge, so we probably will have to have an over abundance of battery packs that allow the batteries to be replaced at replacement centers rather than waiting for a charge. Another alternative is to have vehicles that belong to one country and have their electricity provided in that country and they drive up to the next country and drop off the material being transferred (including food) and that country picks it up and transports to a place in their country using their type of electricity for transportation – or drives to the next bordering country and drops it off for them to transport it farther. This may be a bad example but it gives you and idea of what it may be like with different forms of energy being used by countries based on what each has as its' means.

The various countries and the various renewable sources of energy that each is placing their bets on were viewed in great detail earlier in this book. If you look through these you will see obvious winners and obvious holes and you will have a view of where the logistics may play an important role in each of the countries of the world obtaining their energy; if not their energy, perhaps the next best thing; their food. Much depends on the planning well ahead of time. This may be a big problem since the world is so 'energy plenty' at this time that they will not be considering the need for different logistics to handle the new sources of energy from each in the not too distant future. You see, I go from source to sources. That is the indicator of the problem. The first thing is to plan the source and capacity of the renewable energy by each country. This takes time to implement. Once done, it takes more time to determine the logistics and how any overage of the energy will be transmitted across the global expanse of countries. Can you imagine the electrical transmission system when we are talking about the supplies coming from windmill farms, solar systems, water wave generators, biofuels, geothermal, fuel cells, hydropower, nuclear sites and perhaps others? We are talking about independent systems rather than a global system supplied by oil and the readily available currency as we have it today.

Most of the systems described will be individual systems rather than global ones. Most are systems that relate to a particular capability a country has rather than what it may need. So, this requires changes within the country itself. This is the easier part since each country can see what's coming. What can't be seen very easily is what is coming from other countries that a given country can tie into. When there are many individual small suppliers the logistics are much more difficult than when there are a few large suppliers with ample resources in oil to supply the world.

This sort of reminds me of the fact that areas near water have boats whereas areas near mountains have skis. Each of these areas can see what is in their best interests and their economy's move in that direction. The same thing can apply in countries that will build windmill farms, but find they do not have enough energy from these to match what they loss in the way of energy when oil was around. Now they have to lift their heads above the crowd and see what's available and are they in a position to accept what's available. Having done that, they now have to be fortunate enough that it will be delivered to them versus other countries and what method will be used for it be delivered; and what if it can't be delivered. If it can be delivered will it match what is used in that given country or must it be transformed. This reminds me of when the United States and the world were trying to determine whether to use ac power or dc power. DC power would be much easier to use, but it is harder to transport. Eventually ac power won out because it could be transferred over high voltage transmission lines and the receiving end used step down transformers to allow them to use the power at 110 volts or 220 volts. DC voltage is used for local or personal use.

Let me give you another example that relates somewhat to logistics and somewhat to the matching of resources. If we were to try to replace the energy provided by oil in 2004 of 5.6 million megawatts of power using solar power in the year 2037 as the source of energy, we would first have to take into account how much that demand for power would have increased by the year 2037. Let's assume with the growth of the world that the demand in 2037 increased to 10.6 million megawatts. However, since solar power is not readily addressable and transferable to the total global market because of the form factor that the energy is in, we probably need to have a supply of 20 million megawatts of solar power available around the globe. It may even be worse than that since some solar cells are produced for home use and do not participate to any great degree in the global supply. Because of this we may need a total of 30 million megawatts of power because of the loss of power due to inefficient methods of transfer from one type of source to another type of source. Today oil is carried by tankers that are very efficient in their transport and transfer of the energy into waiting systems that are also efficient. Each uses the same fuel it is transporting but not using much of it. The means of delivering it easily now becomes a major problem. Let's assume that the biggest supply of renewable power comes from PV solar cells and thermal solar cells. The PV solar comes in dc form and to convert it to ac results in losses. If it must be transmitted at 100 thousand ac volts it may lose a considerable amount of the power in the transfer from dc to ac and then in the stepping up of the voltage to what is needed for transmission. With thermal solar energy the problem will be considerably less since it transmits its energy through the conversion of water to steam and then the normal ac is generated by the large ac generation station that always worked off of steam. There is still considerable energy loss in the conversion of the solar energy to heat the water. In all cases where the renewable energy is provided in ac form the problems are much less than dc. Geothermal must convert its energy through the normal ac generator system of present day power systems. However, in many cases the heat off of the geothermal is not hot enough to provide steam. Therefore the geothermal must act as the first stage of a multiple heat transfer. The geothermal hot water would go into a heat exchanger where additional heat will be provided to bring it up to steam temperature. This extra heating must be supplied by another form of renewable energy such as ac or dc electricity from solar systems or ac from windmill farms. Therefore in using geothermal in this fashion there is lost energy in the double conversion but the ac generator delivers power in standard transformable form. In these scenarios the key difference is timing. When using oil for the energy there is no timing involved. You can use it when you need it. However, in the renewable energy functions that are dc or ac and the transfer is by electricity you must use it when its available. In most cases this can be handled if planned properly, but it is different with electricity now being transferred all around the world versus oil and its derivatives with extra energy available and being used when needed since it is transferred and then stored and used when needed.

How close can we come to meeting our renewable energy targets using PV solar and thermal solar?

Lets see how close we can come to achieving this supply using today's major builders of solar systems and what they see as the growth in the next five years. A recent article in a magazine I have received for about forty years (Solid State Technology) stated there was an explosive growth reshuffling the top ten solar suppliers in their rankings. A company named Q-Cells AG became the world's largest solar cell maker in 2007. They produced 400 MW of power. They passed Sharp which is a Japanese supplier of solar cells. The article went on to describe the world's top ten suppliers of solar cells and if I was to add them up they came to approximately 3000 MW of power being supplied per year. The article related that Sharp would pass 3,000 MW by 2010. Most of these cells only develop about six percent efficiency from the Sun's rays that hit them. To produce 500 MW per year a solar cell fab must produce as many as 400,000 silicon wafers a day, a much larger number than even the largest semiconductor plants presently produce. Much of the cost of the solar cells is in the cost of this material to make them. Several companies are working on thin film methods to supply the solar cells and these are the ones that have the lower efficiency but are less expensive to produce and the volume build up can be quite dramatic compared to using silicon cells. I expect someone to be creative and come up with thin film solar cells that are close to 20 percent efficient and very producible. This will be the bet on the future.

With this as background, let's see how long it will take to produce and install enough of these solar cells to handle the needs of the year 2037. Let's assume that the ten major suppliers mentioned total 6000 MW per year by the year 2010 and they stay flat at this capacity for thirty years. This would result in 180,000 MW being installed by 2037, well below the target of 10 million MW needed to replace the energy of oil. This would produce about two percent of what is needed. However, if we say that the PV solar is only to be supplied to the homes and the roofs of businesses of the world and the remaining would be supplied using thermal solar for industry, then it would only need to produce approximately two million megawatts for this PV solar application. Now the supply by these manufacturers if they held their capacity constant would be about ten percent of the required for this application in 2037. But in fact, neither the number of suppliers will stay constant nor will the amount each will supply per year stay constant. Both the number of suppliers and their amount each supplies will grow each year. I therefore expect that the PV solar will meet the goal of reaching a production and installation of between two million megawatts of PV solar capacity installed by the year 2037. This would find the homes and the business buildings being accommodated – world wide. There are limitations in each of these PV solar approaches. The standard method of using silicon wafers will be limited by the ability to produce enough silicon. Therefore this method which has the highest efficiency of turning solar rays into electricity will not meet the target. They can't produce enough silicon in the next twenty nine years to support the integrated circuit market and the solar cell market. I grant you that the production of silicon wafers for solar cells is a much less difficult task then making the integrated circuit wafers, even though the purity of the wafers produced for solar cells has to be better than those for integrated circuits. However, in order to meet either of these approaches one must be able to produce polysilicon which will limit this approach. There is not enough polysilicon producing capacity at this time and I don't believe it will come close to what is needed.

The thin film approach would seem to have the greater ability to build more plants to produce these cells and they won't be limited by silicon. However, it won't be able to reach the levels needed either if we used the thin film technology that is available today. It's going to require more plants building them and a more efficient conversion of the suns rays to electricity. Some other method of producing solar cells that are more efficient in converting solar rays to solar energy needs to be produced as well as a manufacturing method that is much faster and with greater capacity than that of silicon wafers. I believe that more efficient thin film technology will be found within five years; probably with efficiencies of approximately 15 to 20 percent. This improvement and the less expensive and easier to produce methods will make this achievable.

Now let's review the other 8 million megawatts of solar power that needs to be produced using solar thermal methods. In order to put into place 8 million megawatts of thermal solar capacity by the year 2037 we need to be installing large systems worldwide capable of building and supplying 16,000 steam driven generators with each supplying 500 MW of electrical power. The steam would be provided by one of the thermal solar methods already discussed like the ones in the Mojave Desert. If we built 500 generator systems world wide each year we would reach this goal by the year 2037. This is feasible but not practical. Let's see how we can reduce this number. Keep in mind that any renewable energy, natural gas, or nuclear energy put into place between now and 2037 would reduce the number of these thermal solar systems being installed.

Let's review the amount of power consumed by the United States and the World in 2004. We will use this as a reference for what is expected in 2037, using renewables, natural gas, and nuclear to replace the oil energy expected in 2037. Everything is in millions of megawatts consumed.

Figure 41 - Various energies for the future including my predictions by fuel type*

Fuel type	2004 US Consumed with oil	2004 World Consumed with oil	2037 US Consumed without oil	2037 World Consumed without oil	2037 US* Consumed	2037 World* Consumed
Oil	1.34	5.6	1.75	8.0	0.25	1.0
Nat Gas	0.77	3.5	0.96	5.25	1.5	6.5
Coal	0.77	3.8	0.96	5.05	1.0	6.1
Hydro- Electric	0.09	0.9	0.10	1.5	0.12	2.0
Nuclear	0.27	0.9	0.35	2.35	0.6	2.9
Wind mill	0.11	0.13	0.14	2.0	0.5	2.6
Geothermal						
Biomass						
Biofuel &						
Liquefied gas			0.75	1.5	1.0	2.0
Solar PV			1.0	2.0	1.0	2,0
Solar Thermal			2.0	3.0	2.0	3.0
Hydrogen/fuel cells						0.2
Total	3.35	15.0	7.96	30.5 7	.97	28.3

Consumption assumes the United States and the world countries would realize by 2010 that oil reserves are lower than expected and that oil will be scare and/or expensive and take pre-emptive steps to ensure that power is available in 2037 and the years after that. This being the case impacts the energy numbers for Biofuel, Solar PV and Solar Thermal shown. The strategy would be to then build renewables at a greater pace than originally expected. This causes the numbers to increase in several areas. The most dramatic increases are in biofuels, Solar PV and Solar Thermal. I believe these numbers will happen in these renewable energies, with or without oil being available at a reasonable price. This also finds that the consumption of this energy with or without oil will not be as high as listed above. I believe that the United States growth would be such that they would need 5.0 million MW instead of the 7.96 with or without oil. This is an ideal place to be since then the United States could determine if they want to reduce some of the energy such as coal to reduce environmental contamination. The alternative is to sell some of the oversupply since there will be countries in need of energy if oil is gone in 2037. **I believe the United States will meet their energy needs since they will not grow as dramatically as China, India, Africa and many countries of the world. The United States will run out of the domestic generated oil by the year 2022 unless we drill the offshore sites. Even then, we may not be able to extend the use beyond 2027. I believe the saving grace for some length of time will be supplies from Canada. When I say the U.S. will meet its energy needs I am considering the needs other than transportation. I believe the biofuels and biodiesel will help in the transportation area but not enough. We will need Canada for our transportation needs and the fact that many cars and machinery will be established in electrical instead of gas and diesel. Bottom-line we will probably not meet our transportation needs.**

The same scenario applies to the World demand. I believe the world's energy needs will be between 26.0 and 27.0 million MW instead of those numbers listed above for them with or without oil. However I don't believe that the world supply of energy will reach the numbers listed above for the World's overall needs. Unless there is a consensus of opinion among the world's leaders to bring on these renewable supplies as shown, I believe the numbers I have expressed will not be met. They will fall short on the renewables including hydroelectric power, nuclear power, windmill farms, geothermal, Solar PV and Solar Thermal. Without oil, the supply will fall short of the demand of 26.0 to 27.0 million MW. Europe may meet their needs since they are installing significant amounts of wind power, PV solar and Thermal solar. Europe's growth is such that it's GDP will not grow significantly by 2037 but begins to take off about that time. Therefore they need to meet their particular goals so they can be on a growth curve when its economy gains its second wind so to speak. I believe the World's demand can be met if oil is available at higher levels than I have listed. **This will be a significant miss by the world's countries and will get worse as the years pass.**

The key columns to review are those of the U.S. and the World with and without oil in 2037. Using the column where there is oil still available, it shows the U.S. using 1.75 million MW of oil energy and the total world, including the U.S., using 8.0 million MW of oil energy and the total world energy consumption would be 30.5 million MW. Without limitations on oil the World's demand would be close to 10 million MW for oil and the total energy used to be greater than 30.5 million MW.

These numbers would show the U.S. increasing its oil usage by 30% if oil is available in the year 2037. This coincides with their population growth. It would show the world increasing its oil usage by 43%. This is mainly due to a large increase in population in the Middle East and Africa; as well as a significant increase in the industrial use of energy by countries such as China, India and many of the other countries that will become more industrialized. However, the growth should be more like 65% for the World market since the population in many areas grows dramatically and is about double that for the United States. The U.S is expected to grow about 30% in its population and the Middle East and Africa are expected to grow by 65%. In actual fact the oil use would increase by more but there is not enough supply to permit that kind of growth as the oil reserves are much less, if any, in the year 2037. You notice I showed some oil energy for the Untied States and the World in the columns noted "without oil". This is based on my estimation that there will be this residual left in the oil reserves. I consider this as "no oil".

Now let's review the U.S. and World picture in 2037 if there was essentially no oil available for distribution in the world. This is the last column and that is what this book is about. I have put in 1.0 million MW of oil energy to be used by the Middle East and perhaps Russia in the last column and essentially none for distribution to the world. They still have some reserves and they will use those for their own consumption and some little amount to surrounding countries. This oil figure is about ten percent of what the world demand would be. To recover from this lack of oil there are increases in other energy supplies to make up for the lost and to keep contamination of the atmosphere down. To see the increases in the other supplies compare the last column with the World with oil column and it shows 8 million MW of oil energy used. This number could be as high as 10 million MW since the world's growth could demand that much. Therefore, even with oil available it falls 2.0 million MW short, even with a total of 30 million MW with oil shown in that column. There is an increase in the use of natural gas from 5.25 to 6.5 to make up for some of the oil energy loss. There is a restricted growth in coal (hopefully this can be accommodated by such countries as China) to prevent atmospheric contamination. It increases from 5.0 to 6.1 without oil.

Hydroelectric increases from 1.5 to 2.0. This increase is mainly in China and would require additional planning to achieve this amount of dammed water for this purpose. There will also be a fairly decent increase from the micro hydro systems around the world in places like Canada and other countries that have a high snow/ice levels in their country which normally can mean there are many streams and rivers that could provide micro hydro systems. These remind me of small businesses in the United States. The large businesses are high on the silhouette in the business news and therefore are obvious. However, there are so many small businesses in the U.S that one forgets about the fact that they make up the really big business of the United States. The same is true of micro hydro systems. They are all over the world and their energy accumulates to a high number when you sit down and add them up. With the cost of fuels going up the micro hydro systems will grow around the world. Nuclear would increase from 2.35 to 2.9 million MW if the countries around the world decide that this is their best source of energy for this century.. This definitely can be available if enough countries decide this is the easiest and maybe the only way they can increase their supply of needed energy.

Renewable is the big growth shown in both the world columns with and without oil. With oil; the renewable energy increases to 2.0 million MW from about 0.13 excluding the energy from biofuels and solar. Without oil the renewable energy increase to 2.6 million MW and this is shown in figure #4 below by energy source. Biofuels essentially go from nothing to 1.5 million MW with oil and increase to 2.0 million MW without oil. Most of these numbers are force fit, but I believe they are reasonable based on my research and what is happening in the third quarter of 2008. There has been a good jump start toward meeting these goals on biofuels, liquid natural gas, PV solar and Thermal solar. They are available if the world decides there will be a huge drop off of oil energy by the year 2037. There are natural gas reserves, coal reserves, and nuclear fuel available for these increases. There are biofuels available, but I have not seen any figures to show that they would grow by this amount. I have seen some figures for the United States and Brazil that I believe could reach 1.0 million MW but haven't seen any quantitative information concerning the world's commitments. Biofuels and liquid natural gas could be made available from many countries by the year 2037. Let's review the renewables and see where the energy is going to come from. Keep in mind that I consider nuclear as a renewable energy and I have considered natural gas as a cross-over energy source to complement the renewables.

Figure #42 My estimate of the world's added energy by type by 2037

Function	added power by 2037
Windmill farms	0.5 million MW added to 0.13 million MW
Hydroelectric	1 million MW added to 0.9 million MW
Biofuels/Biodiesel	1.0 to 2.0 million MW
Geothermal	0.5 million MW
Hydrogen fuel cells	.01 million MW
Biomass	0.5 million MW
PV Solar	2.0 million MW
Nuclear boilers	2.0 million MW to 2.4 million MW added to present 1.0 million MW
Thermal Solar	2.0 million MW to 3.0 million MW
Natural Gas Boilers	
Coal	Coal energy used in 2004 was 3.8 million MW which is second to oil and is the most plentiful of the fossil fuels. Its use could increase by anywhere between 3.0 to 4.0 million MW by 2037. This will happen if the other energy sources do not meet the listed goals.
Oil	<10 million MW> loss of oil energy
Total added energy	14.51 million MW to 17.01 counting fossil fuels added to present amount of 15.0 million MW less 5.6 million MW of oil Energy loss for a total of 23.91 to 26.41 million MW
	This is below target by 3.0 to 6,0 million MW based on expected growth by the year 2037.

It's important that the reader understands that I am projecting, on an optimistic basis, that the world will fall short of its needed energy in the year 2037 by 3.0 to 6.0 million megawatts (3.0 to 6.0 trillion watts. This is not insignificant. It is about 25% short of needed. If oil availability decreases as I project by the year 2037 the world will be running with only 75% of its needed energy. The problem is worse than this if you review the logistics discussed above. Because there is no oversupply, as exists with oil, and the logistics are much worse than those presented by the use of oil, the world will have to produce an additional twenty to thirty million megawatts of energy to result in having ten megawatts of real time use of this energy. Much of the energy generated will loss due to logistics.

The Solar impact on energy needs by the year 2037, assuming the batteries are there.

When you think of PV solar cell energy you have to consider it as displacement energy, or dislocated energy. It is not like oil which can be held for some length of time before actual use in the form of gasoline or other oil products, and oil doesn't have to be used "real time". PV Solar energy must be used as you obtain it or you have to store it in batteries. The problem at this time is several fold with batteries:

1. Building enough batteries to handle this problem worldwide.
2. Building different kinds of batteries that can hold charge longer, and provide a proven power for a longer time.
3. Building batteries that are rechargeable just by reversing the current flow.
4. There are technologies being developed using Lithium Ion batteries that are an improvement, but I don't know if they will be able to provide them in quantity early enough to solve this major problem. We need something beyond Lithium Ion batteries. I think the problem will be the same as the time problem indicated above for either silicon or thin film solar cells; you can't build the manufacturing capability fast enough and in high enough volume, due to a shortage in the materials to produce them.
5. There are no batteries to handle the major supplies of electricity that will be provided by wind, and solar PV that supply cities. Thermal solar must continue to find means of maintaining their supply of electricity during the nighttime. With these thoughts in mind, the multi attack approach must be used, i.e. the solar in parallel with the other sources of renewable energy must be able to reach the volume levels as a whole. The problem is that as long as we are not able to replace the energy of oil we will be stuck with using coal that is a worse contaminating source of the atmosphere than oil and will probably be expense by the year 2037. The good thing about many of these renewable energy sources is that they can provide this energy over long periods of time and the fuel is infinite as far as this world's energy is concerned.

Thermal Solar

Thermal solar is more forgiving than PV solar in that there are ways to store it without using batteries. It can be stored in salt and other materials in the form of heat. Go back and review the method being installed by Spain based on a technology developed by Sandia in this country. Since thermal solar is used like conventional fuel in that it uses its energy to heat water to steam and the steam energy turns the turbines of the big electrical generators of the world, it is quite readily applied to today's and the future economies of the world. The storing of the energy in the salt or other materials allows the heat energy to be used during the night when there is no sun.

I liken thermal solar to a mechanical method for using the sun's energy. It consists of panels that can be fabricated using today's sheet metal methods with some improvements. The key is to make a material that is quite reflective and easy to shape to focus the suns reflective beams on the heat exchanger.

To my way of thinking thermal solar is the great savior for the future without oil. The huge systems that were set up in Mojave Desert proved the viability and efficiency of this method of solar collection and utilization. You will note in the chart that shows the energy use for 2037 that this one is the one that jumps from nowhere in 2004 to the leader in 2037. The reason, it is straightforward and uses many of today's metal working methods. I would assume that as the years go by we will find even better material for use in these systems.

I show the thermal solar providing 2.0 to 3.0 million MW by 2037. I believe this number could be understated. If the world determines early enough that it must replace oil in the near future there should be nothing stopping this method from providing even more than the amount I have estimated. I can see this method being used throughout this century and into the next. The only limitation is finding the ideal spots for it in the world. If you go back and look at the maps for the United States, Europe, and the world it picks out the ideal spots for installation of this type of solar power. When you realize that Germany, which is not one of the areas ideal for solar, has made major moves in this direction, it gives you an idea how PV solar and thermal solar can even be worthy sources of energy in places that are not ideal.

The one ideal thing about thermal solar is its means of transmission. It provides electricity in the same format as those powered by the fossil fuels and with no contamination of the atmosphere. This transmission is ideal for providing energy to countries that have neither the ideal location nor the ideal economy to afford installation of almost any kind of renewable energy. High voltage transmission lines will be carrying this power to other country's matrix without any special equipment for use at 50 or 60 cycles per minute.

Timing

A lot depends on the conservation schemes that are employed to reduce the waste of the energy we have and extend the time so that changes can be made to accept the new energy. I projected the gasoline demise by 2037, however it was based on world use of 100 million barrels of petroleum being used each day and this expanding to 150 million barrels a day by the early or mid 20's. With this scenario being followed it would lead to a significant drop in oil reserves by the year 2037 and essentially the loss of gasoline as the portable fuel needed for transportation. Recent prices of the barrel of oil have reached levels where many countries of the world are reducing their use because of the expense involved. Countries are rapidly learning how to conserve and reduce their use with more efficient methods, moving away from 'just in time' methods which are efficient in supplying but not efficient in the use of transportation. Centers of transportation on land or in the air are waiting till they have a full load before dispensing their carriers. This reduction of use may carry through for some length of time and would be just what the doctor ordered. But, we shouldn't kid ourselves; conservation can only go on so long. The cut back in the use of gasoline because of cost can only go on for a short length of time and then countries, in order to remain economically solvent, must start back up using the supplies of oil until they are no longer available. The alternative is a drop in the world's productivity and a crash in some economies. Believe it or not, this is a population problem. The greater the population the greater the world's production must be to provide the capability and capacity to supply the world's needs.

However these conservation methods might reduce the use enough to carry over the oil supplies until the world reaches the point where we start producing a large amount of renewable energy and a number of automobiles that obtain a much higher 'miles per gallon' or are run on electricity. This would then stretch us to the point where the portable fuel called "gasoline" continues to be supplied in gracious quantities that allows the outage of the portable fuel to be put off for a significant number of years. To go along with this Boeing will be producing their new airplanes by 2009 and really delivering in quantity in the year 2011. These planes are expected to use twenty percent less fuel per mile of airway travel. This could be a significant step in the right direction to carry world supply of the portable fuels to somewhere around the 2075 time frame and give the world this extra time needed to increase their supply of renewable energy. The renewable energy, including hydroelectric power, would bring the world into a completely different scenario, a scenario that is a cleaner one and a world that does not depend on fossil fuels as the energy, but is just what it is called; renewable; renewable; year in and year out.

There are other problems with supplies and this time it is the transportation. Even if we develop electric cars the projection is to be able to provide only two million of them by the year 2037. Two million electric automobiles don't even begin to offset the billion gasoline and diesel running vehicles that will be on the roads of the world by the year 2037. Can you imagine a billion gasoline automobiles sitting around running on nothing? Neither can the world and the use of biofuel will definitely help this situation. However, it is also like a feather blowing in the wind. There will be cars running on biofuel in many of the countries, but then there will probably be 800 million gasoline cars sitting around not being used because there won't be nearly enough biofuel available and food available also. Here is one place where there is a collision between plants grown for fuel for cars versus plants grown for fuel for people and we know which will win. We also know that the soil will get depleted and start limiting the amount of plants that can be grown for either of these two needs. The fertilizers that have allowed the world to grow more plants by adding nutrients to the soil come from oil products. The sprays that were developed to kill the bugs and allow the plants to grow come from oil products. Many of the disinfectants that keep bacteria from killing plants or people come from the derivatives of oil.

But, what about the other fossil fuels? I have covered the decline of the petroleum age and there are still the other fossil fuels. One of the fossil fuels, natural gas, is the cleanest of the fossil fuels and maybe worth having around. As we mentioned previously, the use of liquefied natural gas may be a worthwhile substitute for gasoline, especially if the means of transportation are not as easily accomplished as one might believe. We may find that electric cars and electric use for other transportation doesn't pan out the way we would have wished. Keep in mind that for electric power use in transportation one doesn't just require electricity, it requires batteries that can be charged and hold that electricity and provide the stored energy in an efficient manner. So, the world must keep finding better means of providing more efficient and longer lasting batteries. We must find batteries capable of longer life so that, when charged, the vehicle can go a farther distance before requiring a recharge. We must find better means of replacement of the battery as it runs down. No one wants to use a vehicle and when it runs out of charge in its batteries to wait around while they are being charged. We must find a way of making the batteries easily exchanged. For example, instead of waiting for a charge there should be a means developed whereby the driver turns into a power station and the batteries are slipped out of the vehicle and new ones slipped back in and the vehicle is on its way in less than two minutes. The payment is automatic and the bill is forwarded to the user of the new battery. For this to be a factual event, there must be a standardized battery rack for all cars, and another for all trucks, and another for the large earth movers in the Midwest, Florida, California, and around the world. These are part of the logistics involved. It isn't only the renewable energy sources but all the peripheral gear that must allow this to be a step up from gasoline rather than a step down. If you have watched a car race like the Indy 500, you have seen how the cars pull in and have their tires changed and their fuel tanks filled. It is done in less than a minute. While we may not need this to be a race of this sort, it must be accomplished with ease. It may be developed to the point where the driver drives into a recharge station and the section of the vehicle automatically opens and the battery pack is discharged from the vehicle and a new battery pack is installed automatically and the driver is on his way.

This may take care of the battery pack but remember we may be using liquefied natural gas for fuel. This being the case there are several actions that must occur to make this a 'non event', that is, an event that is done automatically, safely, and with very little time involved. Probably the first thing that must be done to make the liquefied approach acceptable is to reduce the weight of the tank holding the liquefied natural gas. Present cylinders are too heavy and limit the amount that can be carried due to the weight. This limits the range of the vehicle with this approach. There must be considerable effort placed on the development of tanks of lighter material and of a size and shape that is easily inserted into a vehicle as automatically as the battery pack was. Remember, I am only mentioning the needs if the batteries do not reach the potential I suggested. The best of worlds would be the one where the battery pack doesn't require any liquid fuel to complement its use. However, if the batter packs prove to be as efficient as described above, then the work must go toward finding a way that the energy of the pack is increased to the point where its weight per energy derived is much improved over the present batteries being used. The lighter the weight per energy produced the farther the range of the vehicle.

So, you can see that the logistics with renewable energy are not only the supplying of the energy but the means of delivering it in a manner that is better than the present method of going to a gasoline station and filling your tank. Even if the new systems are able to be charged at home with the normal ac supply, they still need to be able to travel some viable distance before needing a recharge. There will be new batteries developed to accommodate the electricity that will be made available, but with each improved battery there will probably be a new means developed to deliver it to the vehicle. This reminds me of the coming of the personal computers. There could have been a long and involved time related to personal computers finding a common operating system and common presentation system. Microsoft solved these problems by coming up with the means and the volume capability of supplying the means. They got off to such a fast start that there was no second choice. Fortunately, they also provided enough volume that it became almost unnecessary for a second choice and the standard within the world market didn't have to go through the growing pains of trying various systems before there was standardization. Standardization became obvious because of the credible source, the credible volume and the fact that the personal computer suppliers wanted to run with it. Standardization was an "ad hoc" fact. But, this being the case; there were the improved new programs that were introduced by Microsoft that followed and had to be compatible with what had been done to date. Each new software change had to be a good fit. It had to be something the market desired. It had to have continuity. Obviously these things did follow and Microsoft remained the standard for the general PC marketplace.

We would need the same type of situation to occur with battery packs for electric vehicles of different types. There would need to be standardization for this to be an effective and efficient system and a system that allowed for change as better methods were introduced. Nothing should be introduced before its time and when introduced it must be flexible enough to match the demand and match the changes in demand as time passed. The world cannot deal with surprises. If someone came up with the best battery or best fuel without there being a great deal of anticipation ahead of time it would create a situation where there is no infrastructure to handle it. This being the case, there would be a great delay in this system taking off in the world. There is no panacea when it comes to the supply of energy or the logistics involved to properly and efficiently coping with the issue. There is a learning curve just like there always is with something new and especially when it involves many countries and many different approaches and a great volume is involved.

Just for effect

Just for the effect of what I am describing, let's assume we are in the middle of this century and there is no oil. We have none of the old ways of transporting energy around the world. We have turned on some renewable energy sources such as biofuels and liquefied natural gas in a few countries. We have turned on windmill farms at various locations around the world. We have turned on water wave energy as a source in certain outlying areas of the world. We have turned on solar energy in many homes, many businesses and isolated solar fields around the world. We have built some new nuclear energy plants and we have a lot more of them being built now that we know we can't reach the energy we need with what we have that I just listed. Meanwhile, we haven't built any windmill farms or solar farms in the Artic or the Antarctic as I recommended.

Let's next assume that in some of these energy sources that have been established that we have more energy than the local population needs for their quality of life and for their industries. But, how do these extra energies get transported to other places in the world? What are the logistics? Did we know well enough in time that this would happen and that we then set up some transmission capabilities for these countries to at least provide some of this over abundance to other countries? What did we use as a priority selection for supplying those particular clients versus others? Was it a wide choice? What about the other countries that did not have these logistics set up in time?

While considering these questions, from which type of energy source did this abundance arrive? If it was biofuels instead of some other energy source, how do we send the overage? If it was wind energy, is there enough overage to provide any really significant amount to others? Is it a fact that none of these is in excess enough to have provided a means of transmitting this local energy overage to anyone? You see, this could be the fact where we don't have anyone well endowed with a particular source of energy and the world saw it coming and built the proper infrastructure to take advantage of it.. All of these sources of energy are scattered around the globe and come from different sources and require different means for transmitting any overages.

North America as an example in 2037

Let's take an example where we consider North America and its supplies of energy in the year 2050. I am taking a blind stab at this with a somewhat educated guess. The purpose of this exercise is to show in general how North America would handle the various renewable energy supplies and to give a picture of what may happen in general throughout the world.

There is Canada with its hydropower which hadn't been expanded greatly during this century, some micro hydropower, some solar power, some windmill power, and some nuclear power. They have gone to liquefied natural gas to handle their large vehicles. They don't have a viable biofuel program to help supply automobiles. Let's assume they are close to being satisfied in their general power needs, but are questionable in being able to handle their transportation needs. There are no gas stations open.

There is the United States that we can assume has developed significant amounts of solar energy, but let's assume it is not equivalent to the amount of energy that had been supplied by oil where they were using about one quarter of the earth's amount in the early part of this century. They had a large amount of hydropower entering this century, but it hasn't been increased much in this century so that is no help at all. There has been micro hydropower systems developed at various parts of the country that supply local needs. They increased their windmill power along the coasts and parts of the states that receive a significant amount of wind to supply the local area. They have developed a significant amount of biofuel energy in the Midwest and Southwest. They have converted many of their large vehicles to run on liquefied natural gas. They were reticent to add much in the way of nuclear energy early in the century and then recently decided to expand the sites they already had to increase the volume output. This was an easy way out since these sites were originally qualified to be able to increase their output. So, they didn't have to fight the environmentalists and others that would try to stop nuclear expansion. They began to build some new ones that should come on in about 2060. They have a significant number of electric automobiles and they produce a large number of batteries.

The US probably will not be short of their overall needs, except there are many automobiles around that were produced early in the century and run on gasoline. There are no gas stations open.

There's Mexico and the Central America countries. Their oil supply ran out that mainly came from the Gulf of Mexico. They have developed biofuels to some extent. They have installed significant amounts of solar systems mainly in their industrial sites and in some open area territories. They began to increase their supply of nuclear power by installing new nuclear systems that are just coming on. They are using liquefied natural gas for buses and maybe for some large earth moving equipment to support their agriculture industry. The biofuels are being used in vehicles for transporting food. They have some vehicles that run on electricity and depend on other countries for their battery needs. They are in fairly good shape for supplying energy for general use but not for supplying portable energy. There are no gas stations open.

This is a picture of North America, an area that probably leads the world in technology, arable land, and has taken many steps to add renewable power and shifted to liquefied natural gas for large vehicles. They are short on supplies for everyday vehicles except those that run on electricity. However, they have not done enough to generate ample electricity for all the needs of the domestic portions of their population and their large industrial sites that ran heavily on oil and oil by products. But, let's take an optimistic view and say they are in good shape. But this is not enough. They are not in shape to provide any additional power to the rest of the world. They are caught in a logistic problem. They can't supply others and they are not set up to be supplied. They didn't know where there energy might be coming from. There are just too many "maybes" in the world of suppliers. And do you know another enormous problem – there may be no airplanes flying. Perhaps if the Arctic and Antarctic systems had been found a viable approach and they had invested in it they might have had ample power coming from these areas. To break the logistic issue world wide there must be a type of "Arctic/Antarctic" supplier somewhere in the world. A supplier that doesn't use its power generated and therefore is a supplier rather than a user. We need the equivalent of the Middle East and their oil which was well over there own use and therefore a viable supplier to the world.

Does this give you a picture of the possible and probable scenario for the world depending on renewable energy? The year 2050 is not too far off. Actions need to be initiated soon.

The one big supply that is available to solve most of the electricity problems world wide is nuclear power. There is a great deal of energy that can be generated from this source and solve most of the world's problems. The main problem here is the world is scared of having a Chernobyl (Russia) incident. As you review all the nuclear plants in the world, with France leading the way for their size of population and power needs, there are a large number of them and there are many that are going to be built between now and 2020. We will be sitting here with close to 500 plants around the world, so why should anyone be reticent to use nuclear power. If there is going to be a problem it probably will be with the ones that have been around for fifty years or so. Building another 500 won't create more danger than already exists and it would eliminate the logistic problem, the shortage of electrical power problem, the loss of oil as the major energy source issues, and give us another thousand years of power and time to invent new means of supplying power, maybe Hydrogen from the oceans waters – after which we can start turning the nuclear reactors off.

Renewable power is either the future or the future will be a tough one.

Conclusion on renewable energy sources for overcoming the shortage on oil energy

A review of the chart in figure #3 on the various energy supplies in 2004 and those available in 2037 shown on page 251 brings one to several conclusions.

1. There is a capability for the renewable energies listed along with nuclear and natural gas energy to be able to meet the total energy needs for the year 2037

2. In order to meet these goals the world's leaders must recognize very early that there will be this lack of energy due to the oil shortage by the year 2037 and take immediate actions.

3. In order for those actions to be effective they must complement the other countries renewable energy supplies.

4. For this to happen there must be a meeting of the countries under a specific charter to ensure that the world's needs are met. Each country that can supply energy in one form or another must take on that responsibility.

5. Even though the total energy that is needed may be available, it may not be available in the best form factor to meet the needs of transmission and use. See my section on logistics that follows.

6. Even though the total energy may be met it is obvious when reviewing the chart that there is a real big hole in the supply. Where the world growth would have demanded 10 million MW of oil energy and there is none, or very little. I have shown 8 million MW that might be available and that number therefore falls short by 2 million MW. In the case where I essentially declare there will be no oil energy available the world is in a really big hole. The only energy that can supplement this need for transportation is biofuels to replace gasoline and biodiesel to replace diesel and liquefied natural gas to supply large vehicles. In 2037 there will be approximately 1.0 billion automobiles that run on gasoline or diesel. Even though there will be a fairly large number of automobiles that run on electric power it will be a pittance compared to the ones on gasoline and diesel. This being the case, and one of the main reasons for this book, the world community must be made aware of this very possible situation. Besides automobiles, there are other vehicles and machines that run off gasoline or diesel. There are

    airplanes that require high energy liquid fuel that probably will not be satisfied by the biofuels that are available.

7. This one big hole in fuel for transportation results in many problems that I will cover as several of the major crises of the century.

8. The reader will see when reading the logistics section that meeting the ten million megawatt target is not sufficient because of the logistics involved. We will need to have thirty to forty million megawatts of power to offset the loss of oil's energy.

My suggestions on the Arctic and Antarctica areas for windmills and solar power!

I personally think about the North and South Poles when it comes to wind energy and solar power. Both of the Pole areas produce the greatest winds on Earth and for six months of the year either the North or the South Pole has daylight twenty four hours a day. In addition they are uninhabited and are not useful for agriculture or animal grazing.

We sometimes forget these areas since they are so far away and so cold and remote. But, when considering something like windmill farms they may be exactly what the doctor ordered. There is no doubt in my mind if we could find a way to construct windmill farms and solar farms in these areas they would solve most of the energy needs of the world. Since windmills have no problems that I know of in working in cold climates this may be a worthy consideration. The generators on these systems are closed systems and therefore no liquid to freeze. The lubricants may be a problem but I believe they can be solved by our chemists and chemical engineers and other scientists. One thing to keep in mind is that a certain amount of the electricity being produced by a windmill could be used to heat electrical heaters and keep the generators at a useable temperature.

The other advantage of having these systems in the Poles is that the electricity can be raised to high voltage levels for transmission to other parts of the world. In fact there may be a relay system set up whereby the energy is transmitted to countries that are about 1000 or more miles away to relay stations. From these stations the power could be transmitted at lower voltage levels (but still very high) to other countries that are thousands of miles away. There may be a method developed that is wireless and the energy can be transferred via this method.

The amount of energy a windmill generates is determined by the wind velocity and the radius of the blades. As the wind velocity goes up the design of the windmill can now use blades of a smaller radius. As the radius goes down the number of blades can be increased to insure better efficiency. By placing windmills in the North and South Pole regions the wind velocity is so high that the blades can be made quite small and therefore reduce the complexity of the structure, thus making it more feasible for installing windmill farms in these areas. Wouldn't that be a great use of the uninhabited and large areas of land that exist in these two parts of the world? Since windmills are not dependent on the light and heat of the sun, only the wind, these windmills could supply wind power during the all light times of the year as well as the all dark times of the year.

Now that I have broached the subject with windmills, how about with solar panels? Both of the pole regions have six months of daylight; when one turns off the other turns on so to speak. These are 24 hours solar energy for six months and when the six months is done on one there is six months of daylight on the other. Not only is there daylight but the areas are covered with snow and ice and the reflections off of these surfaces will add additional solar energy to the solar panels. In a sort of way we have natures form of reflectors built that essentially follow the sun. The designs of the panel tracking systems are also somewhat easier than systems that track the sun in other areas of the world. I see these two areas as fertile grounds for both wind and solar systems. The combination would put out a tremendous amount of power.

These systems when installed would be capable of providing power to the farther reaches of Earth. Plans would have to provide where and how the electricity would be transmitted. It may be possible to place both systems on the same stanchions. I don't believe the movements of the fan blades would interfere with the solar pickup. Both electrical systems could be directed into the same transmission systems. During the six months when there is light, the solar systems might be directed to keep the wind systems at an optimum temperature.

In order for this to be a feasible plan, assuming we were to agree that windmill farms and solar farms in these areas would be a fruitful adventure, it would have to be an international decision to support this approach. These two areas would be controlled by an international group with the sole purpose of supplying a huge amount of energy to the "world bank" for energy. I would think these compound systems would require international inputs and represent the world's international countries with proper diplomatic relations existing between countries that would enjoy their output. These countries might also be involved in the yearly operation and maintenance of these large fields of energy.

There is an important consideration to keep in mind if we decide to take this approach of adding windmill farms and solar collectors in the Artic and Antarctic lands; both of these systems do not put out a constant voltage and power. They put out peaks during certain times of the day. For example when the winds are blowing hard there is a different amount of energy being developed than when the winds are lower. The same is true of solar systems which put out more power during certain parts of the day. In all the other areas of the world where these systems are in place they have to take steps to correct for this and to put out a controllable amount of power. It must be decided to be fifty or sixty cycles per second and it must be able to take care of the peaks and valleys. For solar systems that are small like those that provide power for a home, the power is stored in a battery and released upon a programmed demand. When power exceeds that used by the home it is directed to the utility system's matrix to be used elsewhere. Windmill farms have a similar problem and it is being handled accordingly.

Now let's look at the system that might be in place in the two Polar areas of the world. They can't use a battery to handle the smoothing out of the power. In fact the power from the windmill farm is in ac power and there are several ways of storing their peaks to smooth out the power surges. The system might be programmed to supply via certain power plants at peak power and other power plants when that power is not at peak. These power plants might be set up to supply different parts of the world from each of the power plants. In this way one power plant may be able to handle peak power and the other the non peak power. These are issues that must be worked out. The solar systems would be huge and they supply ac power through the conversion of water to steam. This is converted to higher voltage ac for transmission and it would have a similar problem for supplying at peaks and non peaks of solar power. In many cases there is pumped storage facilities set up to handle these type of issues, but these systems would be too large to be handled by pumped storage. The key would be to have an overall control by computer that is directing this power scenario on a continuous basis. I believe our technical people would find a way to administer this power generation that would be so important for the world's use.

The one approach that comes to mind is to use the "salt storage" theory that is used in certain thermal solar systems. The units would put out the normal ac power and when the systems get hot the thermal energy would be supplied to a salt (or some other thermal battery) thermal pile and that would be used to heat water to steam and turn turbines for ac power during the night. Although this might not be the ideal method, it is food for thought and I believe that engineers and scientists that have worked on this problem for years would have better solutions than this. There has been considerable work done by Sandia Corporation in the United States on storage methods and some of them are being used in the Mojave Desert and in Spain.

Here we would have two huge areas for producing wind and solar power for the world's utilization and it would have to be under the direction of an international administration. Here is land that is essentially uninhabited and uninhibited that may prove to be a gold mine when it comes to supplying the world its power. I would hope that there are those of you reading this book who will take this into consideration. If it doesn't sound plausible I would like to hear from those readers. On the other hand I would like to hear from the people that might be advocates of this approach.

Crisis IX -
Food needed; grown and transported

But I am not done with logistics

While I have covered some of the issues related to logistics and how the world coordinates the total power needs and has the international community's needs at heart, I haven't covered the one major one; food for all the 9.2 billion people that will be around in 2050. The logistics of supplying the world's power needs as discussed is very difficult, but take that problem and combine it with the food requirements of the people of the world. During the twentieth century up to the present 2008 there has been an overage of power available and world wide enough food available for most if not all. But with the power of the future being renewable power and the logistics involved, the problem gets amplified when it comes to not only using the energy effectively but being able to transport the food supplies around the world for an additional 2.0 billion people over the 2008 population. Not only do we have to produce more food, but we must find a way of transporting it around the world 24 hours a day, seven days a week. This requires energy for the transportation, additional food from world sources, a new means of transporting food if there is not enough viable power for aircraft to fly, energy for refrigeration of food, energy for cooking the food, having enough vegetable plants to provide food while providing biofuel for transportation, and the issues go on.

This is exactly the opposite problem we had in the United States in the nineteenth and twentieth centuries. There were the resources and we could grow into them. By this I mean our population could grow to fit the overabundance of all our needs. This problem coming up finds us with already having the population and needing to develop the resources to provide this population their calories each day. There probably is enough food worldwide to handle this, but there will be restrictions on being able to move it. With renewable energy there will be enough energy to move a country's supplies within their own country or a very close neighbor but there will not be enough flexible energy to allow transportation of the needs across many miles on a continuous basis. It will help to have ample nuclear power to provide the electricity for these needs. If we have enough so that biofuels, liquefied natural gas, and electrical vehicles can be directed toward transportation and we find a way to fly airplanes without gasoline, we may get there. If not the population of the world may be truncated to a level that can be supplied. This population level will be at a saturated level.

The scenario I have described takes place in 2037 with a population of 8.7 billion people. From this year forward the problem becomes even more difficult if several things are not accomplished:

1. Provide the energy for world use
2. Provide a replacement for gasoline and diesel fuel so transportation is able to complete the cycle of delivering food to the world.
3. Population control is required unless the first two of this listing is not met.
4. Reduction of animal food with more nutrient supplied by plants so as to reduce the amount of inefficient energy consumed by the feeding of domesticated animals.
5. Improved control of the intake of calories by the people of the world so as to better supply the Earth's population.
6. Find a better means of transportation using electrical energy.
7. Invent a new means of transportation.

There is a terrible problem with the scenario I just covered. If there is not proper planning and execution to prevent this situation, there will probably be wars to settle it. When people can't get food through civilized means they will take the other approach to remain a viable entity in this world.

Crisis X -
Water water everywhere, but none to drink?

Will water be crisis VIX? This is both a rhetorical question and a scientific question.

Rhetorical

It is obvious as the population grows and the need for food grows the need for water also grows. In fact there are water shortages all over the world at present. While the countries of North America and the countries of Europe will remain stable it is because they do not grow rapidly in this century either in population or in industry demand. The growth in these countries people-wise and industry wise are fairly consistent with their resources. They have room for growth and arable land and water available to handle any growth they may have. The same is probably true of the continents of South America and Australia, and some other countries scattered across the world.

The places where there would seem to be a problem are the continents of Asia and Africa. Both of these grow in population and grow economically. Within these continents the countries of China, India, Malaysia, and several within Africa with their great economical growth are making increased demands on water. China and India already have the two largest populations in the world and very little arable land or bodies of fresh water to handle the growth that will be seen in these countries. There are programs in some of these countries to try to limit the population growth, seeing that there will be limitations for food and water. The problem for water may be the most drastic one. Food can be transported from various parts of the world unless the future finds us short of fuels to fly airplanes or energy to run trains, or energy to transport food by large ships. Water is a more difficult task since the countries that have enough, don't have an over supply that they can ship around the world.

How this problem can be solved I don't know. Perhaps there will be a way to extract large chunks of ice from the Antarctica or Arctic continents and float it to these countries. I can see that this may take an unusual amount of energy and fuel for this to occur but I can't think of another means of supplying water. However, I do know a way of freeing up more water for human consumption. The way is to go to more plant food for our needed nutrients and energy and reduce the amount of meat eaten around the world. I realize this may be wishing too much. But it is not too much in the United States. We have enough plant food and fish food and certain select food sources such as chicken and turkey to eat. If we moved in this direction, it would free up a tremendous amount of water in the United States. There are other countries in the world where there energy needs can be provided by plant and fish food. This would free up a tremendous amount of water for human consumption, including watering the huge fields of plant food.

Scientific

There may be ways that this will be solved scientifically. Keep in mind that if we have global warming and with the predicted warming it will result in additional water being evaporated and eventually result in additional rain falls. If this is the case, having global warming may have its benefits, especially this one of supplying more fresh water. It is a fact that most of the rain falls within a short distance of the equator. If this is the case, there may be added water in the regions of southern China, Malaysia, India and parts of Africa if this added rainfall is of some significance. Wouldn't that be something? Here we are trying to reduce global warming and it may in fact be what solves the water problem.

Another means might relate to such natural events as hurricanes. They provide huge amounts of fresh water. However, most of it is lost in run off from the land or is dropped directly in the oceans of the world. We should review how we can salvage that fresh water.

Another means is **desalination.** This is the method of taking sea water and removing the salt to make the water potable. Desalination is expensive and the

OPEC countries of the Middle East use it to provide much of their water, but they have the money from their sales of oil to allow them to afford it. We need to find a cheaper way to desalinate the oceans of the world. There is plenty of water there, so the scientists of the world need to find a way to convert a small portion of it to fresh water on a continuous basis without using a huge amount of energy. There have been major advances on reducing the cost of desalination of water and there are various methods used around the world. It is less expensive to desalinate the salty water than to filter water from a facility of "gray" water. This gray water is the water that comes out of a plant that filters the sewage water from a city. It is normally dumped into a nearby lake, bay, or ocean after the cleansing away the solids and minerals of the water. It is not potable for human consumption. However, this water can play an important role in providing potable water indirectly. When water is desalinated it ends up providing fresh water and brackish water that is left behind that is heavy with salts and minerals. This water needs to be discarded but it must be discarded in a way that it doesn't harm fish or animals. It is heavier in salt than the ocean salt water. Some desalination plants that are near the ocean and also have a water purification system near it combine the effluents prior to dropping the total into the ocean. This dilution is effective if the water purification system is larger than the desalination system. If not, the effluents are combined and fed into large pipes with holes in them the length of the pipes that go long distances along the ocean shore. In this way the combined effluent is distributed over a long distance and therefore improves the dilution as it combines with the ocean over this long distance. This has proved to be a working system in some places that are ideally fit for this means.

The main problem with desalination is the amount of energy required to bring this to fruition. In most cases it is done by boiling the salt water within a system that provides a vacuum and the water to be desalinated is heated.

Boiling takes place at a lower temperature at this reduced pressure and increased temperature of the salt laden water. It takes energy to provide the vacuum and to heat the water. In this method the vaporized water is allowed to condense in a separate tank as fresh water. This method is sort of like a small hurricane in that it takes the vaporized water that is salt free and dumps it into a separate container, leaving behind saltier water than it started with.

There are quite a few different methods all being very expensive, requiring considerable energy which is what we are trying to save in this book. A very popular method uses reverse osmosis. The pressure is increased through heating in a controlled vessel. As the temperature rises its pressure rises and this allows it to be forced through membranes or filters such as ceramic filters and separates out the salts and minerals and the water on the other side of the membrane or filters is fresh water. This is also costly because of the heat required to produce the pressure and the filters are costly and need to be cleaned or replaced fairly often. This is called reverse osmosis because in osmosis the opposite occurs. The liquid with the least solids moves through a membrane easily into liquids containing more solids via osmotic pressure.

I have read that there are countries and/or companies that are take advantage of the heat being generated in nuclear plants or geothermal plants and use this heat to raise the temperature in the desalination plants. This make sense since most nuclear plants are build near water sources so they can use the water as the cooling element of the nuclear reactors which create considerable heat while producing electricity. Instead of using the body of water to cool the piped water from the reactors the piped hot water heats the water to be desalinated, thus saving costs and energy.

There are other new methods being tried that I have heard about. One seems to be a natural since it sprays the salt water in a mist across moving hot air which causes it to be vaporized more readily because of the increased surface area around the molecules in the mist. As it is vaporized it leaves the solids behind and the vapor is condensed in a separate tank as fresh water. What I have heard about this method is that it is cheaper than the other methods since it combines the virtues of the two methods I described.

We need to find a way of conversion of the ice of the world into a readily available supply of fresh water. It turns out that there is more fresh water tied up in ice in the world than is available otherwise. There might be a method of establishing solar thermal power in the Arctic and Antarctic that is directed to melting the ice into piping systems that provide fresh water to designated areas of the world determined by an international committee that understands the total needs of the world and where the water would be best placed in a reservoir that is below the freezing lines of the Arctic and Antarctic.

I discussed the use of water in fuel cells where the water is split into hydrogen and oxygen and used in the fuel cells to provide electricity. The by-product of this is water, but of course less water than was used to begin with. If fuel cells become a solution to the portable electricity problem, it may cause an added problem in using up fresh water. Perhaps we can find a way to use the ions in salt water to provide the electricity in the fuel cells and come up with potable water as the by-product. The free ions in the oceans are Cl^- and Na^+. Perhaps we could attract the ions into the anode side of the fuel cell and the negative one provides the electricity after stripping the Cl and the positive one is stripped of the Sodium and leaves the positive charge which acts as the proton did in the description of the original fuel cell. When the electrons complete the circuit trip to the load and terminate in the cathode side of the cell it unites with the positive charge and the Oxygen to provide water that is potable. Wouldn't that be great?! We would provide electricity through the fuel cell and fresh water would be the by-product. We would kill two stones with one bird. The key would be using less power than this process provides – unless the available water makes up for the power loss.

One thing is a fact, if we don't plan on the providing of water for the increase in population, there will not be an increase in population. There will be considerable loss of life due to dehydration.

Why so much water and it's the thing that may be the shortest in supply?

It's a paradox that water is the most plentiful substance on Earth and yet it may be the substance that belies its true value. Most of Earth's water is salt water and that's where the rub lies. Man and animals cannot take in salt water and live more than a few hours. How come fish live in salt water and they don't have this problem. Let's start by stating that all animals and fish have salt in their blood. We humans have salt in our blood made up of salts of chlorine, sodium, and potassium as the main salts. They are required for certain muscle health and other body functions. Too much of any of these will cause a sickness and too little of potassium will cause ill health. While the same is true for chlorine and sodium they can stand less being in their blood. The normal healthy human has 0.9 percent salts in their blood (9000 parts per million).

Fish

Now let's look at fish and see if we can learn something from them. If you took the oceans salt level down to one fourth its salinity you would have the amount of salt in the fish's blood. Some fish have more or less of this amount of salt in their blood and others do not, but all are higher than humans. There are fresh water fish and salt water fish; and there are those that can live in either. The people that believe in evolution believe that fish were here on earth as one of the first living creatures. At first the water that fell on earth was fresh water and the fish lived in fresh water. But as the rain water ran off of the land into the oceans it picked up salts and eventually over a couple of billion years the salt content was approximately today's value. So, the original fish lived in fresh water but as the water of the oceans changed slowly over these billions of years the fish mutated to acclimate and become accustomed to this higher and higher salt content of the oceans. But they never really lost all their past completely. They never were and still aren't really salt fish as one would think of them. It is believed that some of these fish during evolution moved to the fresh waters to find food more readily and that's why you find fresh water fish.

Eventually the world had fish in both the salty and fresh water and some that lived in both. But in each case the fish's metabolism and the desires of its body needs provided a completely different answer for their environment. The fish living in salt water dispose of the water from their kidneys by urinating small amounts of diluted urine all day. They do this to rid the body of salt. They urinate a third of their body weight each day through urination. Some fish do this through their gills. Meanwhile there are the fresh water fish. They have the same problem. They take in food that has salt and they must rid themselves of this salt. These fresh water fish urinate less times a day but the urine is very concentrated with salts. So, they rid themselves of salts in large quantities each time they urinate.

Then there are the fish that live in both places. The salmon is a good example. The salmon eggs are hatched in fresh water and the fish remain in this fresh water for one to three years and are quite content. They urinate heavy amounts of salt a few times a day. However, there are certain salmon that like the salty water. After a couple of years in the fresh water they swim down the rivers to the oceans and become salt water fish. They stay there for the rest of their lives, quite content and they urinate all day with more dilute urine and their body salt content is about the same as when they were in fresh water. However the female does fight its way back up the rivers to the fresh water to lay their eggs. This would lead one to think the salmon and other species like it must have lived on Earth in fresh water when the Earth was young and then as time evolved they acclimated to the salt water but then later found that they could find food easier in fresh water and migrated in that direction. Over the course of thousands of years they became able to handle both extremes of fairly heavy salt water to water with no salt.

Why this discussion about fish? What does it have to do with the crises of this century? For one thing we may learn something about the fish's ability to rid them of salt and to be able to function with a certain amount of salt content. If this could be accomplished it could remove most of the issues with human's ability to live with salt water in all its abundance. Desalination would become easier. Reverse Osmotic action to relieve water of salt would become easier. The fish do both of these functions as well as disposing of the salt through normal urination. I don't know how much energy the fish use up to rid them of the salt. It may be that it is enormous for their body weight. If this proves to be true it may not be an acceptable process even if we found how to mutate to allow our bodies to take in salt water. It may result in the loss of a great amount of energy. I bring it up in this book so that someone reading it may come up with an answer on solving the world's eventual shortage of fresh water.

The need for more fresh water could be a huge crisis and may be the limiting factor here on Earth where humans find their homes. Like all problems that one knows can be solved, it needs to be solved. It is a matter of supply and demand. Where is supply is a given than the demand must be a given to meet the supply. In this case we can determine the supply by measurement and then make the hard decision of how to limit the demand. Not an easy chore.

Crisis XI - Economic issues

The 21ˢᵗ Century may find the world with many economic problems, many of which are related to the eleven Crises covered. As the world works to relieve the issues caused by a rise in temperature due to climate cycling or global warming and the issues related to energy, the population growth and the means of replacing fossil fuels with renewable energy there will be many opportunities for economical issues. A world under pressures of this sort only needs a spark to result in an economical crisis. We have recently been involved in this sort of situation with the cost of oil rising to one hundred and fifty dollars a barrel. With the world close to financial issues caused by the failures of the housing market in the United States and the related issues this caused with the investment banking business, it didn't take much for this to turn into an inferno; and the price of oil rising to non practical levels was that spark that caused a dramatic turmoil in the world. With the price of oil reaching these levels it initiated several severe reactions:

1. The cost of producing products of all nature went up due to their close tie to the cost of oil and oil derivatives.
2. The high cost of transportation resulted in a reduction of travel by people all over the world. This resulted in a reduction of the use of gasoline and diesel world wide.
3. The high cost of transportation resulted in the airlines cutting many of their flights to keep their costs down. This resulted in loss of revenue by the airlines.
4. There was a revenue reduction for all businesses due to the consumer holding back his spending since they had less to spend due to the cost of transportation increasing.
5. The reduction in business resulted in lay offs in many industries and more borrowing was required to get over the hurdles.

6. The "chicken and egg" effect. Which caused which first?
   A. The cost of oil and its affect on all business.
   B. The housing market collapse and its affect on the banks.
   C. The high losses by the investment banks causing some to go bankrupt and others to be bought out by banks that weren't hit as bad.
   D. The resulting credit crunch with the failure of the banks to loan money resulted in a monetary situation with high viscosity (lack of flow of money)
   E. The world wide effect which resulted in less import - export business and caused the downturn to be worldwide
   F. The end result also hurt the oil producing countries as the demand went down and the selling price went down and the margins began to disappear.

There is no doubt that the problem would have been less severe if the world wasn't being tied down by the high cost of oil crippling much of industry. The happens to be the first instance, but I feel that there will be many more chances for economic events such as this to occur several times in the near future as the crises I mentioned are met and governments take actions to evade the problems. I mentioned a listing previously of how many years certain key large economies had before they ran out of fuel to supply their own country. As these events happen they will cause consternation among countries – not of their own liking, but with little in the way of choices. This relates to fuel for transportation for one but it also relates to the supplies of food reaching parts of the world. If food doesn't reach areas it previously had no problem reaching it results in turmoil and turmoil can result in exacerbated turmoil. Like a snow ball rolling down a hill it picks up what is in its path and this may result in another set of problems. There will be mass migration of people to parts of the world that will accept them. The migration will be to find work or find food or find water. There will be a dislocation of world wide levels if all of these types of situations are not thought out well ahead of time and by the highest levels of governments.

In today's international community the financials of one country will have a bigger effect on other countries than they have in the past. The value of the dollar has an enormous impact on the import and export business of all the countries of world wide trade. It also has an impact on the visitors of one country to another and this is a big business. Can you imagine what will happen when the lost of oil or the high price of oil as it becomes less available results in less and less air travel? Do you realize the impact it will have on the tourist market? It will be bad enough as the second decade proceeds and several countries lose their own supply of oil but it will grow worse as the decade proceeds. By the year 2020 there will be a severe impact on all air travel as the countries I mentioned essentially will be out of their own supply and the supply is almost totally from the Middle East countries. If no suitable substitute is found for the products that are derived from oil and gasoline and diesel become scarce there may be a time when these two products are only used for military travel and military applications. If the U.S. decides to drill for oil just off the shores of the coasts of California, Florida, Texas, Louisiana, Alaska etc. and installs the drilling rigs beginning in the next two years then by 2020 the U.S. may have enough fuel to fly business flights and select flights during the third decade of this century. It's possible and probable that a trade agreement can be worked out with the Middle East countries such that a supply is sold to the U.S. There is also Canada with its significant oil reserves that might, because of a neighbor policy, work out a trade agreement with the U.S. to carry us through the third decade of this century.

It's important to keep in mind how much fuel is required to fly a commercial jet from New York to Los Angeles. First of all the jet fuel is high energy fuel. It takes ten gallons of crude oil to make one gallon of aircraft fuel. This is approximately a quarter of a barrel of oil to make one gallon of jet fuel. It takes 77 gallons of jet fuel to fly from New York to Los Angeles. This is equivalent to 770 gallons of crude oil or approximately 19 barrels of crude oil. Nineteen barrels of oil is equivalent to 1,387 kW of power and is approximately 2000 horsepower.

All things being equal, unless a proper substitute is found for gasoline and diesel, the flying of airplanes will be a rare occasion by the year 2037. Because of the price and scarcity of gasoline and diesel the use may be truncated over the second decade to the point where there will be fuel in 2037 but it will be expensive and be used on a priority basis. This will have the biggest impact on the economies of the world than any other phenomenon short of a world disaster. Although the lack of fuel to fly airplanes and other vehicles will have the biggest impact on the transportation industry, the other industries will be impacted due to three major elements:

1. Transportation is needed to ship parts and food to the world.
2. Oil and its derivatives are included in the finished products of many companies.
3. Gasoline and diesel are the primary sources of energy to run the machines of many industries.
4. Oil and gasoline are required from many remote/portable uses of energy that are not available by any other source of energy.

Isn't this scary? It's the prime reason for writing this book. People the world over should be aware of this issue. They can be a huge part of the solution, if there is a solution.

There is the hope that the biofuels can be refined to the point where they will be useful in the airline business. The biofuel industry is really in its infancy and there would be hope that with greater emphasis on pointing this source of energy toward use in aircraft that a solution will be forthcoming.

Experimental flights have been run with 30% biofuel mixture and have proven that more experiments need to be performed. I believe there will be experiments in 2009 with special biofuels made from algae biofuel and others. Even if they prove to work we are then talking about ten to fifteen years to prove viability and side effects. There are many safety features that must pass before a jet fuel is approved for commercial use. Even if this were to happen we are talking about the third decade of this century before it becomes practical and even then it needs to be proven that enough can be made to prove it can handle all the needs of fuel for other industries as well as the airline industry. It may be that only enough is available for military purposes. At this time the military uses approximately a billion barrels of jet fuel a year and that will increase in the future. I don't believe that biofuels that meet the requirements of aircraft will be available in the amounts required by the year 2037. If enough money is placed in this direction and if the government realizes the present status and the status of 2020 and they take the proper actions, it may come to fruition. But it may be limited by nature. We have to eat and if the biofuels require the same source as humans do for food, there will be a major issue.

Perhaps the use of the fuel cell toward the end of the third or fourth decade will open up options. It would have to be an option where the planes are flown via the use of electricity rather than gasoline. Keep in mind that the fuel cell requires hydrogen at its anode to produce electricity. Where would the hydrogen come from? If it came from pressurized metal bottles the weight of the bottles would preclude an efficient use of the fuel. Even if this problem could be solved it would take a tremendous amount of electrical energy to fly an airplane. A gallon of gasoline puts out 37 KWh of power and you know how much high grade fuel is used by a commercial airplane. A 737 uses approximately 6100 gallons of jet fuel to fly 3600 miles. That approaches 2 gallon per mile and therefore is not very fuel efficient, however based on gallons per passenger mile it is more efficient than an automobile that carries seven passengers. It would take a tremendous amount of electrical power to fly a motor driven commercial airplane with the motors powered by fuel cells. I estimate about 100,000 horsepower required to fly the commercial planes like the Boeing 737. This is equal to 74,600 kWe of electrical power based on 746 watts per horsepower. That would require a large electrical motor or motors and would probably be too heavy to make it practical for commercial flight. The same kind of scenario occurs if one tried to use nuclear fuel to fly an airplane. The system to provide the energy with the use of nuclear as its main source would be too heavy to be practical. Perhaps another approach using nuclear would prove to work but there would always be the danger of radiation if the plane ever failed.

Needless to say the loss of the energy of oil and its derivatives would be almost impossible to replace in some cases. There will be a major shift in all industries to convert to electrical power for all their functions. Electrical power provided by the other fossil fuels and the renewable energy sources would replace the functions of oil and its derivatives in industry, in the home, on land travel and probably ocean travel. I don't see a major fundamental impact in those cases. I do see a fundamental issue with the flight of airplanes and with this I see economical issues as well as political issues.

Conclusion on the Crises of the 21st Century

I have discussed what I believe to be major crises happening this century. There may be more but these I believe affect each and every person in the world and if we resolve these we can tackle many others as this century passes. I tried to cover them more or less in a chronological way, covering the ones that I believed would affect us first or the ones we could make headway on first. There's no sense in covering crises that you know need to be taken on but can be delayed beyond the solution of crises that stand in the way and you should take on first. However, the more I wrote the more I realized that most of these can and need to be taken on as soon as possible since they are inter-related. I named this book the crises of the 21st century, however most of these crises began in the first decade and all of them need to be addressed in the first three decades of this century. Some solutions may come in the second half of the century and they may come too late for some of the peoples of the world. Let's review the crises again and the actions required.

Crisis I. The increase in the global temperature; climate cycles or global warming?

Is the increase in Earth's average temperature due to climate cycling or global warming from human causes? The temperature increase is the problem, not which one is causing it. It will happen as I have shown and the world must acclimate to the increase. If the temperature increases one or two degrees in this century it will include five generations of people. Over five generations of people we can acclimate; humans mutate too. We should solve the contamination of the atmosphere no matter if it doesn't cause global warming. As you read on you will recognize problems that are more fundamental and need early resolution, more so than global temperature change. It will start to become colder, probably by the end of this century and in the 22nd century the people of the world will be trying to find a way to get warm.

Crisis II. The beginning of oil and the end of oil – an energy crisis.

The loss of oil energy by the year 2037 requires placing a focus on finding the various renewable energy sources that can be portable like oil and its derivatives. There are the biofuels for gasoline and biodiesel for use in transportation and other portable energy applications. This is a specific energy crisis and can't use most of the renewable energies we will exploit. No matter if there is a renewable source of portable fuel such as the biofuels, there won't be enough. Much of today's machines and transportation must be converted to electricity as supplied by renewable energy. But how do we fly the airplanes. Maybe biofuels will work but there won't be enough. We need approximately ten million megawatts of energy to replace the oil energy loss by the year 2037. However, with logistic issues the need may be as high as 40 million megawatts needed. Some renewable energy we will find that is portable, but not enough of a supply. Those not portable must be converted to electrical propulsion or natural gas for the many other uses. We don't want to use coal and its contamination when there is no oil or it is too costly to use. Renewables (where I also place nuclear) and natural gas will be our source of energy till we can develop enough renewable energy to allow us not to use coal. The energy is out there and it is up to the countries of the world to find a way to provide it so all countries and all people are advantaged. Most of the countries that supply oil will be out of oil by the year 2025. By the year 2037 if we aren't completely out, it's so close we might as well be out.

Crisis III. Understanding the fossil fuels and their limitations

Each of the fossil sources of energy have been reviewed to determine their major contributions to today's society and how many years of each are believed to be in the reserves; also which give off the most contaminants to the atmosphere and which are the cleanest. Natural gas stands out as the cleanest and there is a fairly large quantity of it already found and more will be found. In my solution for moving from the present fossil fuels to renewable energy I use natural gas as the "crossover" fuel since there is a large amount of it and it is much cleaner than coal and more efficient than coal. The strategy by the world's users and suppliers should be to move away from coal and toward natural gas while installing the renewable sources of energy. The Crisis here may be the need to find more natural gas and find more uses for liquefied natural gas. Natural gas can prevent a step backwards in reducing the contamination of the atmosphere that would happen with more coal use.

Crisis IV. The first priority is finding a renewable energy replacement for the portability of oil.

The review of the renewable energy sources as soon as possible to ascertain a strategy for which of these can overcome the huge loss of the energy as supplied by oil. This is a broader energy crisis than the others and it affects people worldwide. Oil energy is presently responsible for 38% of the world's use of energy and it will be gone by the year 2037. If not completely gone, it will be so scarce and so expensive that it might as well be gone. Liquefied natural gas is not the solution. It is too heavy in the cylinders required to be effective. It is too expensive for replacement parts in the vehicles being used. It has a high maintenance cost and is altogether too expensive for cars. It might be used in heavy equipment like the large farm equipment in the Midwest, California, Florida and the other states that are agricultural in nature. By the third decade of this century the only supply of oil will be from the Middle East. The United States may establish a fair trade agreement with its neighboring country of Canada who has both natural gas and oil that will carry us into the third decade of this century. This might be enough for the United States to resolve its renewable energy sources, but leaves many countries depending on the Middle East countries. However, my calculations show the Middle East Countries also running out of oil by 2037. If not completely out, it will not be available world wide and could result in exceedingly high international tension.

Crisis V. Understanding the renewable energy sources to replace functions that do not use gasoline or diesel. This is the resolution of the broader energy crisis.

I have provided a view of the various renewable energy sources and supplied information about certain countries that have these renewable energy sources. I have also tried to quantify those resources so the reader can have a picture of what is needed and when. It is important to focus on the various renewable energy sources with a worldwide strategy determined. Some countries can provide certain renewables due to their location while other countries are rather void in having natural resources related to renewable energy. There are countries with windpower locations that should be employed. There are countries where hydroelectric power should be employed. There are countries where geothermal energy should be employed. There are countries where tidal and wave energy from the oceans should be employed. There are countries where solar power is an ideal solution, either in the form of photovoltaic or thermal solar energy. Solar energy will be the biggest supplier of renewable energy for the first half and maybe all of this century. There will be worldwide use of this form of energy and its electrical output. The thermal solution is ideal for large power plants supplying energy in the 500 MW range. It is ideal since it will be used to heat water into steam to turn the turbines of the large electrical generation plants in the world. All of the equipment is available since it delivers power to systems that put out electricity just as our present systems do. The good news is that the energy is there ad infinitum and is inexpensive. We just have to get over the initial costs which are not much different than present methods using fossil fuels. The PV solar will be used in homes, business roof tops and in some industries worldwide. It is almost a personal source of energy since a person can buy it and put it on their roof and after the initial cost the energy is low cost. The world will see a dramatic shift to this personal energy supplier. When all else fails governments of countries should be installing nuclear power stations the world over. There are over 500 nuclear power stations scattered around the world. They have proven safe and the newer designs are more efficient and safer. Why worry about adding another couple of thousand of these reliable energy producers when we are living with 500 of them now. The initial cost is high but the costs after that are low. The biggest cost is not having the energy. The world cannot afford to overlook this energy source. There is enough nuclear fuel to last thousands of years.

Crisis VI. Population and Population Growth.

The growth of the world population may exceed the ability to provide food and water for the people of the world.

Today there are 6.7 billion people on Earth and by the year 2037 there will be 8.7 billion people. We must find more efficient means of growing plants and using renewable energy to provide the transportation to deliver it around the world. Keep in mind that we can't use this food for biofuel if there are no people around because they starved while we were making biofuel. Biofuel must come from what is not edible such as algae and other such plants. With renewable energy having to supply the means of providing the plant growth and the transportation, it must also find its "algae" to provide its own propulsion. Algae will be used since there is so much of it; however there will be many sources other than corn and sugar plants. There will be the garbage, wood shavings and sawdust, stinkweed and many more weeds or uneaten plants that will come to relieve this situation while giving entrepreneurs another source of income in the production.

Most of the world's population growth will be in China, India, and Africa. Their growth over the next thirty years is around 65%. Countries must take steps to control their growth to match their means as best is possible. Countries like China which is about the same size, area wise, as the United States has a population four times that of the United States and one fifth the arable land to grow food. This is completely out of balance. India which is about one third the size of the United States has a population almost four times that of the U.S. They are short on water and on arable land and must make some kind of accommodations to rectify this.

Africa is a large and fertile land with a population that is not out of step with its size, being about 990 million. It needs to find ways to take this huge land and have its people work the land and its resources to gain what is available there. The growth in population must be countered by a growth in production of food and other amenities. Africa has some physical problems that limit its growth, or should limit its growth. Africa stretches over many climate zones. Some of the countries are on the equator and Africa's climate stretches from this warm zone across the northern and southern temperate zones. Because of this it would have some areas with temperatures like the United States, some like Central America, and some like South America; however they lack the mountainous areas that are in Colorado and Chile and the areas that build up snow like some of these areas. It therefore lacks the precipitation and snow pack and the inherent ability to store water that is normally stored in these snow packs that provide runoff in the spring. Because of this it suffers from drought and lacks the capability to irrigate areas with run off that the countries with mountains have. The total lack of water in this continent that will have the greatest population growth of the next thirty years portrays a major problem.

Crisis VII Transportation energy needed to provide food for the population growth

The growth of food requires energy beyond what the Sun provides and, once grown, needs proper transportation world wide. This is an energy crisis related to the loss of oil energy more than any other form of energy. We must find new ways to fly airplanes since the loss of oil and its derivatives leaves a big hole in the energy bucket. Without the ability to fly airplanes to transport food and equipment around the world the battle will be lost. Here again, the entrepreneurs of the world will need to find new means of propelling the aircraft and delivering the food. With two billion more people the problem is greatly exacerbated and transportation becomes a monumental issue. This problem is exacerbated by the logistics problems associated with renewable energy.

Crisis VIII. Logistics with renewable energy is different and needs solutions.

Determining the new logistics required for supplying energy to the world with renewable energy replacing oil energy becomes a major assignment for the world's leaders of their countries

The renewable energy is a daily issue because it is located in different places than the fossil fuels and at lower quantities. There is not, nor will there be, an overabundance of renewable energy in any country. The renewable energy requires daily use of that energy which makes it quite different than oil energy which can be stored indefinitely. There are, country by country, sufficient energy for local use and the amounts in excess of internal use by these countries must be shipped or transmitted by some means that results in the energy being used. This results in a completely different solution for delivery. In many cases the food and energy for transporting it are not found in the same location. This dislocation of food and energy along with the means of transporting the food results in logistic issues that are different than those of oil and need to be internationally resolved early to benefit the peoples of the world. It took approximately 150 years to build the infrastructure we presently enjoy that provides us oil and its derivatives on a timely basis. Almost one hundred million barrels of oil are consumed worldwide each day. How many years will it take to install the use of renewable energy in the world? Keep in mind that renewable energy needs to build an infrastructure that is completely different than the one we presently enjoy. Instead of huge amounts of energy such as oil that is greater than the demand located in only a few places in the world, we will find renewable energy located around the world in many different forms and lower quantities in each location. This dispersion and shortness of supply will require greater planning and better execution with one reason being that it can't be stored. In many cases the countries having extra renewable energy will not enough toplan around. The extra energy may vary from day to day. The means of transporting it from the many locations just makes it more difficult and more imperative that the planning is worked out between countries beginning in the second decade of this century.

Crisis IX. Food needed; grown and transported

With the population increasing by two billion people by the year 2037 the world needs approximately thirty percent more food. Assuming we find a way to grow that much more food we need to transport it effectively worldwide and therefore must find replacement energy for this transportation. Much of the world's energy will be converted to electrical energy and this will change the way we presently transport it. We need to find a way to fly aircraft without the use of oil by the year 2037. We must review the use of plants versus meat for our daily diet since the animals that provide the meat require plants for their food and use much more energy than man. To conserve on plant food we must reduce the number of domestic animals used for our food. The use of domestic animals for our food results in inefficient use of energy which is in short supply. These animals also expel much more carbon dioxide than man or cars while eating ten times as much food as the people that are supplied this meat. The domestic animals also consume much more water than man and there will be a shortage of water during this century. We must also place restrictions on the diets of people. The average human being should be restricted to 1800 – 2000 calories per day. This is no problem in the countries of the world that are short on food, but here in the United States there are people eating 3000 to 3500 calories a day on a regular basis. The reduction will save food, energy, and will result in a healthier population of people.

In order to have an appreciation for the size of a country and its population see my listing below. The size of each country follows in order as you go down the list.

Country	Area (km²)	Population	percent of world area
Russia	17,098,242	141,377,752	11.5%
Canada	9,984,670	32,000,000	6.7%
U. S.	**9,629,091**	330,000,000	6.5%
China	9,568,094	1,400,000,000	6.4%
Brazil	8,514,877	190,010,647	5.75%
Australia	7,692,024	20,264,000	5.17
India	3,287,263	1,130,000,000	2.3%
Argentina	2,780,400	40,301,927	1.87
Mexico	1,964,375	108,700,891	1.32
France	551,500	61,083,916	0.37
Sweden	550,000	9,016,596	0.37
Spain	505,922	40,448,191	0.34
Iraq	438,317	27,499,638	0.29
California	**410,090**	**37,000,000**	**0.28**
Japan	377,915	127,467,972	0.25
Germany	357,022	82,400,996	0.24
Italy	301,318	58,147,733	0.19
U. K.	242,900	60,77f6,238	0.15
Romania	237,391	22,276,056	0.15
Israel	22,072	6,354,000	

It is obvious that the population doesn't follow the size of the country. Definitely out of order with the size is China, India, Russia, and Australia; with China and India having populations that are much higher than their size of land and Canada, Russia and Australia having populations much lower than their size would command. Some of these differences relate to the climate of those countries. Russia and Canada obviously have considerable amounts of their land covered by ice. This makes for interesting information relative to their food requirements and energy requirements. China has the fourth largest area in the world, just behind the United States, yet it has a population that is about four and a half times that of the United States and it has one fifth the arable land. China is definitely a country where food is a problem and will grow as a problem as the energy in the world has a problem losing gasoline and diesel. India is probably in worse problems as its population is huge for a country that is about one third the size of the United States and its arable land is probably one tenth that of the United States. Canada is unique in that its area is so big and its population so relatively small. It is also in a very good position relative to its energy since it acquires much of it from hydroelectric with big dams in the country. Likewise, it is rich in oil for the population size and should be one of the last countries to suffer from the loss of a portable fuel. Australia is unique in its population is much smaller than its area commands. This is due to large areas in the interior of the country being desert or uninhabitable for other reasons. Australia probably is in a position like that of Canada except it would gain its energy from solar and natural gas instead of oil.

I listed California to show how big it is and how big its population is. It is a shock that its population is bigger than that of Canada, Australia, Iraq, and Sweden and close to Argentina and Spain. California has more arable land than most, if not all, the countries listed above it. It's also a shock to me that it is bigger than Japan, Germany, Italy, the U.K. and most other countries in the world. The biggest problem with California and its food is if there is a lost of portable fuel to allow the land to be worked for all its food capacity. There are many countries smaller than California and with populations much bigger. These countries probably will suffer from the lack of food unless the transportation issue is solved before the 2037 date time.

The countries of the world are big and small and their populations don't equate to their size and stand a problem with supplying themselves with food if there is a transportation problem. Many of them with populations bigger than California will not have enough arable land to provide either food or biofuel if fuel becomes an issue.

Crisis X. Water, water everywhere, but none to drink?

With the population growth and the related increase in economical growth we need to find a way to provide the world more fresh water. Most methods of desalination of the ocean's water use considerable energy at a time when energy will be a need. We must find a way to use renewable energy to provide a method or methods to resolve the issue of fresh water requirements for a growing population. With renewable energy spread around the world, perhaps in lower volumes, the problem requires a local resolution. We cannot afford to ship water around the world, but we must find ways to store it that are better. Remember, each year it rains about the same amount and since the world is made up of 71% oceans, the oceans get most of the fresh rain water. There must be a way of recovering the rain water rather than desalinating the salt water of the oceans.

If we solve all the problems mentioned and don't solve the problem of supplying the people of the world with the water they require, we will lose.

Crisis XI - Economic issues

With the energy crises described, the growth in population, the transportation issues, the need for more food and other supplies, there is bound to be economic issues. Each of these crises will place a major burden and strain on the world's economies. As each comes to the forefront it comes with its bag of problems that are directly or indirectly related to the economic health of the world. We have had proof of that recently when the price of oil reached $150.00 a barrel. This resulted in all kinds of turmoil some of it disguised as another problem, but believe me; the price of oil caused other problems to be accentuated. This will be the way of the world in this century, but probably more so in the first five decades of this century. The economic health of the world depends on each country being strong enough to manage its resources well. All countries have resources, but there are only a few that have most of the resources needed and the United States is one of the fortunate ones. The countries must find a way to optimize the resources they have and find a way to bargain those resources for the ones they don't have, but need for a healthy economy. Most of the countries of the world have been able to do this using the fossil fuels in the past to provide them their energy needs. With renewable energy many of the countries will have some resources they gain from the Sun's energy. They must manage them well, but the world must realize the shortcomings of those countries that need other resources and take steps to provide them. Shortages of what it takes to live ends up with wars to acquire what they need. The world doesn't need this and must plan otherwise. We must help to make countries economically strong. We must make their wares mean something to all of us.

In the end, the strength of countries is determined by their economical strength. Anything that detracts from this economical strength takes something away, not only their own strength, but from the world's strength. Everything is connected one way or another. Anything done in this century to resolve the issues I have listed will help resolve any economic issues that would have occurred if they hadn't been solved. The economical strength of each country and the world is a measurement of how well we are doing on the list of crises I have brought forth. The crises of this century are all related and a failure in one will result in an impact on the others. A major impact caused by a failure of one may result in a snowballing effect because of how closely they are all related.

Final, final conclusion on the crises of the 21st century

While writing this book and bringing the various issues to the reader I began to think about some of the solutions to the energy problem. If the energy problem is solved, then clean air will be resolved and the world would be at peace with itself. So, within this book I discussed a possible solution to the energy crisis. The solution is found in the coldest parts of the world; the Arctic and Antarctic regions of the world. Here is a huge amount of land that has no inhabitants to speak of and appears to be of little use to the world. They serve a purpose by helping to balance the temperature of Earth as the heat from the equator tries to make its way to these coldest regions. This spreading of the heat as the Earth spins keeps the temperatures of the equator to a livable level, the temperate zones of the world at very livable level and the Arctic and Antarctic at reasonable levels. Evaporation of water from the ice of these regions provides some of the world's fresh water through the winds and jet streams of each.

But these areas provide very little in the way of proactive solutions for mankind. They are lands waiting to play an active role in the lives of the peoples of the world. They have the worse winds of the world and each has six months of daylight during different six months of the year. With these kinds of open land, unused and rather unproductive, I thought they would be ideal locations for a large part of the world's answer to the energy issues. We could install windmills on both of these continents to use the heavy winds. At the same time we could place PV solar systems and thermal solar power plants across the whole terrains of both to provide windmills and solar power combined to provide for the world. The windmill farms would generate electricity day and night the year around on both of these areas. The PV solar and thermal solar plants would provide six months of electrical power from the Arctic followed by six months of electrical power from the Antarctic. Keep in mind that PV solar doesn't depend on temperature but on the wave lengths of light. So, the cold climates are not an issue for PV solar. The thermal solar would work by using mirrors of metal or normal cold weather mirrors to focus the sun's light on tubes carrying water that would be converted to steam to turn the turbines of a normal large generator. There is a possibility that the white ice of the areas would also reflect sunlight to the water carrying tubes and provide additional heat. The output would go to high tension electrical lines (or underground conduits) to carry high voltage, high energy power for thousands of miles to power stations located around the world to transmit the power to the countries of the world. The windmill farms would operate in conjunction with the thermal solar power. With the high winds turning these windmills electrical controls would be employed to marry them to the same lines that carry the power from the solar systems. During the sunny six months the thermal solar might also apply some of this power to heat the windmills if it is determined that this would increase the capability of the windmill farms. During the dark six months the windmill farms might even exceed its sunlight months. During these dark periods some of the windmill energy could be used to heat the systems if it was determined that this would improve the electrical output and reduce any problems with the cold. The turbines of these systems are sealed and are able to operate at ery low temperatures. During the dark times the water involved in the thermal solar generator systems would be drained to prevent freezing. In the start up of the sunny half of the year the initial water would be warmed first by energy from the windmill farms and once this is done the continuous thermal solar during the six months of light would keep the water always hot and approaching the temperature of steam.

Assuming this is a feasible approach to supplying a huge amount of electrical power, the world would be required to establish a group of administrators from the countries around the world to overlook its output and transmission to qualified stations and countries. This would be an international committee selected by the countries of the world. Once the output of these systems was determined the planning would include how much is directed to which locations. This would truly be an international combined effort. I believe that each of these continents would be capable of supplying over two million MW of power to alleviate the loss of oil and eventually, along with the other renewable energy supplied by the countries of the world would eliminate the need for increasing the use of coal for energy purposes. Perhaps this won't be needed if a viable method of converting coal to a form that resulted in its energy being used with a significant reduction in the contamination of the atmosphere of the world. There is a huge amount of coal in the world and if it could be made less contaminating to the atmosphere it could resolve much of the energy issue and the need for this book.

Many problems of the world are materialistic, or due to religious differences, or due to an imbalance of some resource, or are economical in nature; these can be handled by man since they are of man's doing. The crises I picked out are problems relating to Mother Nature to a great degree – global warming, global temperature cycling, the lost of oil, the finding of renewable energy using the constant energy being supplied by the Sun, reaching energy requirements to replace the lost earth born energy, population growth beyond our capabilities or resources, food shortage, water shortage, and completely new logistics for transporting food and water using new sources of energy that have no infrastructure as existed with oil and its derivatives. These are monumental issues that require the world population to be involved, the leaders of countries to be involved and finding non partisan support for this worldwide list of taxing circumstances that must be overcome. This is not like running a business, or providing a religion where there are singular entities to look up to or lead us past these natural occurrences. There must be the leaders that shout out the technical and quantity insuffiencies that are to come; and be heard. There is no doubt that the leaders of the world's biggest economies must provide the mainframe for these global crises and spread the word.

With this conclusion, I hope enough readers of influence read this book. It can be a roadmap to bring into focus the problems and allow priorities to be set. I have not seen material that brings all of these crises to the forefront. I hopefully quantified the issues in a manner that it is easy to recognize possible solution. Not many people know how much energy oil supplies and how much energy is available from the various renewable energy sources. Not many people recognize the large amount of solar energy that is needed via either PV solar or thermal solar. Many people that see a plant being built that will supply 300 MW of solar energy don't realize that this isn't even scratching the surface of the energy needed to replace oil's energy. When I bring the number of 10 million megawatts needed to just replace the oil lost and believe it may need to be 30 million megawatts because of the inability to store it, many of the world's leaders will be surprised. When the logistic issues are weighed it will bring sense to the problems. As things are going we will fall quite short of the amount of energy needed by renewable energy to replace the loss of oil energy loss. This will result in increasing the use of coal which is the opposite direction we must go to reduce the contamination of the atmosphere. The Green World will not be what we want it to be. It won't be Green. Ask Japan and their suffering from the acid rain caused by the use of coal in China. The World Leaders must focus on these problems or they won't be resolved and our grandchildren and their children will suffer from the lack of attention to these issues. I wish the world resolves these issues in the first three decades of this century. I won't be around to see it, but my children, grandchildren, and great grandchildren will benefit by the solutions.

John Durbin Husher

Appendix

Appendix:
Item I – World Technology Outlook to 2050; as expressed by a memo from Brussels on January 8 2007 as denoted as WETO-H2 study (129)

Reference web site: http://europa.eu/rapid/pressRelesesAction.do?reference=MEMO/07/2

World Energy Technology Outlook to 2050

The following memo was released out of Brussels on 8 January 2007; it therefore represents a recent review of the energy distribution for the world and more specifically for Europe. For those interested in the details of this memo and others go to web site on the internet as follows: http://europa.eu/rapid/pressRelesesAction.do?reference=MEMO/07/2

World Energy Technology Outlook to 2050

MEMO/07/02

Brussels, 8 January 2007

The WETO-H2 study has developed a Reference projection of the world energy system and two variant scenarios, a carbon constraint case and a hydrogen case. These scenarios have been used to explore the options for technology and climate policies in the next half-century. All the projections to 2050 have been made with a world energy sector simulation model – the POLES model – that describes the development of the national and regional energy systems, and their interactions through international energy markets, under constraints on resources and climate policies.

The development of the world energy system in the reference projection

The reference projection

The Reference projection describes a continuation of existing economic and technological trends, including short-term constraints on the development of oil and gas production and moderate climate policies for which it is assumed that Europe keeps the lead.

World energy consumption

The total energy consumption in the world is expected to increase to 22 Gtoe per year in 2050, from the current 10 Gtoe per year. Fossil fuels provide 70% of this total (coal and oil 26% each, natural gas 18%) and non-fossil sources 30%; the non-fossil share is divided almost equally between renewable and nuclear energy.

Energy efficiency improvement

The size of the world economy in 2050 is four times as large as now, but world energy consumption only increases by a factor of 2.2. The significant improvement in energy efficiency arises partly from autonomous technological or structural changes in the economy, partly from energy efficiency policies and partly from the effects of much higher energy prices.

North-South balance in energy consumption

Energy demand grows strongly in the developing regions of the world, where basic energy needs are at present hardly satisfied. The consumption in these countries overtakes that of the industrialized world shortly after 2010 and accounts for two thirds of the world total in 2050.

Oil and gas production profiles

Conventional oil production levels off after 2025 at around 100 Mbl/d. The profile forms a plateau rather than the "peak" that is much discussed today. Non-conventional oils provide the increase in total liquids, to about 125 Mbl/d in 2050. Natural gas shows a similar pattern, with a delay of almost ten years.

Oil and gas prices

The prices of oil and natural gas on the international market increase steadily, and reach 110 $/bl for oil and 100 $/boe for gas in 2050 (130). The high prices mostly reflect the increasing resource scarcity. (I believe the price of oil will be much higher than this by 2050. If there is much oil around it will go for as much as $1000.00 a barrel)

Electricity: the comeback of coal, the take-off of renewable sources and the revival of nuclear energy

The growth in electricity consumption keeps pace with economic growth and in 2050, total electricity production is four times greater than today. Coal returns as an important source of electricity and is increasingly converted using new advanced technologies. The price of coal is expected to reach about 110 $/ ton in 2050 (130). The rapid increase of renewable sources and nuclear energy begins after 2020 and is massive after 2030; it implies a rapid deployment of new energy technologies, from large offshore wind farms to "Generation 4" nuclear power plants.

CO2 emissions

The deployment of non-fossil energy sources to some extent compensates for the comeback of coal in terms of CO_2 emissions, which increase almost proportionally to the total energy consumption. The resulting emission profile corresponds to a concentration of CO_2 in the atmospheric between 900 to 1000 ppmv in 2050. This value far exceeds what is considered today as an acceptable range for stabilization of the concentration.

The European energy system in the reference projection Energy demand trends

Total primary energy consumption in Europe increases only a little from 1.9 Gtoe / year today to 2.6 Gtoe / year in 2050. Until 2020, the primary fuel-mix is rather stable, except for a significant increase in natural gas consumption. Thereafter the development of renewable energy sources accelerates and nuclear energy revives. In 2050 non-fossil energy sources, nuclear and renewable provide 40% of the primary energy consumption, much above the present 20%. The consumption of electricity keeps pace with economic growth; the market for electricity remains dynamic because of new electricity uses, especially in the Information and Communication Technologies.

CO2 emissions

This combination of modest climate policies and new trends in electricity supply results in CO_2 emissions that are almost stable up to 2030 and then decrease until 2050. At that date CO_2 emissions in Europe are 10% lower than today.

Electricity production

Because of relatively strong climate policies, European electricity production is 70% decarbonized in 2050; renewable and nuclear sources provide 60% of the total generation of electricity and a quarter of thermal generation is equipped with CO2 capture and storage systems.

Hydrogen production

Hydrogen develops after 2030, with modest although not negligible results: it provides in 2050 the equivalent of 10% of final electricity consumption based on an optimistic estimate that invention will make fuel cells available as a commodity item.

The carbon constrained world energy system The carbon constraint case

This scenario explores the consequences of more ambitious carbon policies that aim at a long-term stabilization of the concentration of CO_2 in the atmosphere close to 500 ppmv by emerging and developing countries.

A "Factor 2" reduction in Europe

In this carbon constraint case, global emissions of CO_2 are stable between 2015 and 2030 (at about 40% above the 1990 level) and decrease thereafter; however, by 2050, they are still 25% higher than in 1990. In the EU-25, emissions in 2050 are half the 1990 level; on average they fall by 10% in each decade.

Appendix:

Item II – The world's largest hydroelectric plants and proposed plants

Location	Maximum Capacity	Country	Construction started	Scheduled completion	Comments (131)
Three Gorges Dam	22,500 MW	China	December 14, 1994	2009	Largest power plant in the world. First power in July 2003, with 12,600 MW installed by October 2007.
Xiluodu Dam	12,600 MW	China	December 26, 2005	2015	Construction once stopped due to lack of environmental impact study.
Xiangjiaba Dam	6,400 MW	China	November 26, 2006	2015	
Longtan Dam	6,300 MW	China	July 1, 2001	December 2009	
Nuozhadu Dam	5,850 MW	China	2006	2017	
Jinping 2 Hydropower Station	4,800 MW	China	January 30, 2007	2014	To build this dam, 23 families and 129 local residents need to be moved. It works with Jinping 1 Hydropower Station as a group.
Laxiwa Dam	4,200 MW	China	April 18, 2006	2010	
Xiaowan Dam	4,200 MW	China	January 1, 2002	December 2012	
Jinping 1 Hydropower Station	3,600 MW	China	November 11, 2005	2014	
Pubugou Dam	3,300 MW	China	March 30, 2004	2010	
Goupitan Dam	3,000 MW	China	November 8, 2003	2011	
Boguchan Dam	3,000 MW	Russia	1980	2012	

Chapetón	3,000 MW	Argentina			
Jinanqiao Dam	2,400 MW	China	December 2006	2010	
Guandi Dam	2,400 MW	China	November 11, 2007	2012	
Tocoma (Manuel Piar)	2,160 MW	Venezuela	2004	2014	This new power plant would be the last development in the Low Caroni Basin, bringing the total to six power plants on the same river, including the 10,000MW Guri Dam.
Bureya Dam	2,010 MW	Russia	1978	2009	
Ahai Dam	2,000 MW	China	July 27, 2006		
Lower Subansiri Dam	2,000 MW	India	2005	2009	

Proposed major hydroelectric projects (131)

Name	Maximum Capacity	Country	Construction starts	Scheduled completion	Comments (131)
Red Sea dam	50,000 MW	Middle East	Unknown	Unknown	Still in planning, would be largest dam in the world
Grand Inga	40,000 MW	Democratic Republic of the Congo	2010	Unknown	
Baihetan Dam	12,000 MW	China	2009	2015	Still in planning
Wudongde Dam	7,000 MW	China	2009	2015	Still in planning
Maji Dam	4,200 MW	China	2008	2013	
Songta Dam	4,200 MW	China	2008	2013	
Liangjiaren Dam	4,000 MW	China	2009	2015	Still in planning
Jirau Dam	3,300 MW	Brazil	2007	2012	
Pati Dam	3,300 MW	Argentina			
Santo Antônio Dam	3,150 MW	Brazil	2007	2012	

Guanyinyan Dam	3,000 MW	China	2009	2015	Still in planning
Lianghekou Dam	3,000 MW	China	2009	2015	
Lower Churchill	2,800 MW	Canada	2009	2014	
Liyuan Dam	2,400 MW	China	2008		
Dagangshan Dam	2,300 MW	China	2009	2015	
Changheba Dam	2,200 MW	China	2009	2015	
Ludila Dam	2,100 MW	China	2009	2015	

Appendix III - World's largest photovoltaic (PV) systems

World's largest photovoltaic (PV) systems (132)
See the listing of the world's top 500 PV systems.

The top fifty of the five hundred are displayed along with the power, the location, and the amount of carbon dioxide emissions that are reduced by each. The remaining four hundred and fifty can be reviewed by going on the web to

http://www.pvresources.com/en/top50pv.php

It is important to know that the top 500 systems result in Photovoltaic power (PV) in excess of <u>one million megawatts</u> against my goal of establishing ten million megawatts of renewable power by the year 2037 to replace the loss of oil energy. This is an extremely important step towards reaching the goal in the next twenty nine years. The bulk of the 1 million MW were attained over the last ten years. If we were to continue at this rate we would reach approximately three million additional megawatts (MW) for a total of 4 million MW against the goal of 10 million MW. This means we have to add PV energy at a greater rate than we have over the past ten years. Keep in mind that during these past ten years we have had a shot at some of the best places to install this energy of one million MW. There are still ideal places like the Mojave Dessert and the southwestern part of the U.S. to continue this expansion. There are also many places that are shown on the world map on page 144 to install this type of renewable energy.

It is also important to understand that many of the 500 listed were done within the past couple of years and the rate is climbing on installations. If we would continue to run at an installation rate like we have seen in 2007 and 2008 we would reach 5 to 6 million MW of solar installed and operating.

World's largest photovoltaic systems are presented in the table below. (132) The list is divided into tables - each table includes 50 plants. For each listed plant basic data is available (power, country, location, basic description etc.). Currently list with 1000 large photovoltaic plants is available (peak power > 230 kWp). In the table you may find different systems: standalone, hybrid, distributed, building integrated etc. But only systems (or system) which forms a unique photovoltaic power plant as a whole, are considered. If some power plants are missing and should be included in this table, or if some entries in the table should be modified, please keep in mind that this is a rapidly moving subject. It is also a politically active subject with some hyperbole involved:

Power	Location	Description	Constructed	MWh/GHG	Picture
24 MW (40 MW planned)	Germany, Brandis Picture courtesy: Juwi GmbH, Mainz	Solarpark "Waldpolenz" GM, GC	Juwi GmbH 2007 2008		
23,1 MW	Spain, Abertura (Caceres)	Parque Fotovoltaico Abertura Solar GM, GC, TRAC	Iberdrola 2008	47400 MWh 49800 tons CO$_2$ emission reduction annually	
23 MW	Spain, Hoya de Los Vincentes, Jumilla (Murcia)	Parque Solar Hoya de Los Vincentes, Jumilla GM, GC, TRAC	Luzentia January 2008	41600 MWh 42000 tons CO$_2$ emission reduction annually	
21,2 MW	Spain, Calavéron Picture source: EPURON GmbH, Hamburg	Solarpark Calaveron GM, GC, TRAC 100000 Conergy PowerPlus modules, 18 MW tracking arrays, 3 MW fixed arrays	EPURON GmbH 2008	40000 MWh	
20 MW	Spain, Trujillo (Cáceres)	Planta Solar La Magascona GM, GC, TRAC SunPower trackers 120,000 Atersa modules	Elecnor 2008	42,000 tons CO$_2$ emission reduction annually	
20 MW	Spain, Beneixama (Alicante) Picture courtesy/photo: City Solar AG Accener S.L.	Solarpark Beneixama GM, GC 200 x 100 kW Sinvert Master inverters 100000 City Solar PQ 200 modules	City Solar AG Accener S.L. September 2007	30000 MWh 30000 tons CO$_2$ emission reduction annually	
18 MW	Korea, SinAn Picture courtesy: Conergy	SinAn power plant GM, GC, TRAC 108,864 Sharp modules Conergy tracking structures	Conergy Ltd. SunTechnics Ltd. May 2008	27000 MWh 20000 tons CO$_2$ emission reduction annually	
14 MW	USA, Nellis, NV	Nellis Air Force Base GM, GC, TRAC SunPower T20 tracker, SunPower® tracker 70000 modules GT250 Xantrex inverters	SunPower Corp. December 2007	30000 MWh 24000 tons CO$_2$ emission reduction annually	
13,8 MW	Spain,	Planta Solar de Salamanca GM, GC	Avanzalia Solar, S.L. Kyocera Corp.		

	Salamanca Picture copyright: Kyocera Corp.	70000 Kyocera modules SMA inverters	September 2007		
12,7 MW	Spain, Lobosillo (Murcia) Picture courtesy: Ecostream	Solarpark Lobosillo, Murcia GM, GC 127 x 100 kW SolarMax inverters	Ecostream September 2007		
12 MW	Spain, Villafranca (Navarra)	Parque Solar Fotovoltaico Villafranca GM, GC, TRAC	Parques Solares de Navarra 2008		
12 MW	Germany, Erlasee/Arnstein	Solarpark Gut Erlasee GM, GC, TRAC 1408 SOLON movers used 8 kWp per mover, double axis tracking. 28000 Solon modules	Solon AG 2006	14000 MWh 7700 tons CO_2 emission reduction annually	
11 MW	Portugal, Serpa (Alentejo)	Serpa PV power plant GM, GC, TRAC 52000 SunPower, Sanyo, Sharp, Suntech modules PowerLight PowerTracker* Siemens inverters	PowerLight Corp. March 2007	30000 tons CO_2 emission reduction annually	
10,81 MW	Spain, Corella (Navarra)	Huerta Solar Corella GM, TRAC, GC	ACCIONA Energia 2008		
10,11 MW	Spain, Bardenas (Navarra)	Huerta Solar Bardenas GM, TRAC, GC	ACCIONA Energia 2008		
10 MW	Germany, Pocking Picture courtesy: Martin Bucher Projekt- entwicklungen	Solarpark Pocking GM, GC 57912 Shell Solar modules Siemens inverters 24 x 400 kVA 4 x 1600 kVA inverter units, 4 x 400 kVA MSSS each unit	Shell Solar GmbH Martin Butcher Projektentwicklungen part 1: December 2005 part 2: January 2006	10000 tons CO_2 emission reduction annually	
9,92 MW	Spain, Zuera (zaragoza)	Parque Solar de Zuera (under construction) GM, GC, TRAC 47000 modules	Elecnor 2008	14500 tons CO_2 emission reduction annually	
9,508 MW	Spain, Milagro Picture copyright: ACCIONA Energia	Huerta Solar Monte Alto GM, TRAC, GC 556 7 kWp units, 308 13 kWp units, most of them tracking Isofoton, BP Solar, Yingli Solar, Schott Solar, Sanyo Electric modules 889 units, 11 kW and 5 kW trackers	ACCIONA Solar S.A. 2006	14000 MWh 13400 tons CO_2 emission reduction annually	
9 MW	Spain, Villar de Cañas (Castilla-La Mancha)	Planta Solar Villar de Cañas GM, GC Yingli SOlar modules 90 x 100 kVA Siemens inverters	Control y Montajes Industriales, CYMI S.A. March 2008		
8,76 MW	Spain, Viana (Navarre)	Parque Fotovoltaico Arbinte, Viana GM, TRAC, GC 556 7 kWp units, 308 13 kWp units, most of them tracking 51410 ALEO, Scheuten modules 369 Ingeteam inverters	Solartia July 2007	11040 MWh 11670 tons CO_2, 32,7 tons SO_2 emission reduction annually	
8,4 MW	Spain, Isla Mayor (Sevilla)	Planta Solar Fotovoltaica "Isla Mayor" GM, TRAC, GC 41694 Sharp, PowerLight, Evergreen modulus Ingeteam, SMA inverters	SolarPack SunPower Corp. 2008	14200 MWh	
8,4 MW	Germany, Göttelborn Picture courtesy: City Solar AG	Solarpark Zeche Göttelborn GM, GC Part 1: 50000 modules, 23544 Phottowat A 165 P rest Asteria 175PX polycrystalline modules Part 2:.	City Solar AG EPURON GmbH Suntechnics GmbH Part 1: August 2004 Part 2: November 2007	8400 MWh 6500 tons CO_2 emission reduction annually	
8,22 MW	USA, San Luis Valley Alamosa, CO	Alamosa Photovoltaic Solar Plant GM, GC, TRAC Solon movers Xantrex inmverters 12 x GT 500 kW inverters, 288 x GT3.8 kW inverters	SunEdison LLC December 2007	17.000 MWh	
6,5 MW	Spain, La Solana (Ciudad Real)	Planta Solar La Solana GM, GC 40320 modules	Phoenix Solar AG April 2008	9800 MWh	

6,3 MW	Germany, Mühlhausen Picture courtesy: K&S Consulting GmbH	Solarpark Mühlhausen GM, GC part of 10 MW Bavaria Solarpark 15 x 340 MSS, 2 x 300 MSS Siemens Sinvert inverters	K&S Consulting GmbH & Co.KG PowerLight Corp. December 2004	6750 MWh 6200 tons CO_2 emission reduction annually
6,27 MW	Spain, Aldea del Conde (Extremadura)	Huerta solar de Aldea del Conde GM, GC, TRAC	Acciona Energia October 2007	
6 MW	Germany, Moorenweis (Bayern)	Solarpark Moorenweis GM, GC Ecostream 175 Wp modules Schletter mounting structures Siemens inverters	Ecostream December 2007	
6,2 MW	Spain, Crevillent (Alicante)	Huerta Solar El Realengo GM, TRAC, GC 556 7 kWp units, 308 13 kWp units, most of them tracking 27400 modules, 56 x 108 kW further 3,65 MW under construction	Enercoop Group January 2008	8000 MWh 7500 tons CO_2 emission reduction annually
6 MW	Spain, Olmedilla (Castilla La Mancha)	Huerta Solar de Olmedilla de Alarcón GM, GC, TRAC Part 1: 708 Degertrackers, 3,22 MWp Part 2: 720 Degertraker 5000 NT, 3,28 MWp	Solaer Energias Renovables November 2007	
6 MW	Germany, Doberschütz (Landkreis Delitzsch) Picture courtesy: juwi GmbH, Mainz	Solarpark "Rote Jahne" GM, GC 92880 solar modules First Solar FS-260, FS-262, FS-265 11 x Xantrex GT500E-FS9 inverters	juwi GmbH 2007	5700 MWh 3750 tons CO_2 emission reduction annually
5,8 MW	Germnay, Igling- Buchloe (Bayern)	Solarpark Igling-Buchloe GM, GC 78000 FirstSolar modules	EPURON GmbH 2008	6000 MWh
5,8 MW	Spain, Darro (Granada) Picture source: EPURON GmbH, Hamburg	Solarpark Darro GM, GC, TRAC 29964 Conergy C180M and SunPower STM210 modules 710 double axis trackers SolarOptimus by Conergy	EPURON GmbH SunTechnics GmbH July 2007	11600 MWh
5,568 MW	Germany, Oberottmarshausen (Bavaria) Picture courtesy: juwi GmbH, Mainz	Freiflächenanlage im Allgäu (Bayern) GM, GC	juwi GmbH 2007	
5,39 MW	Spain, Castuera (Badajoz)	Huerta Solar Castuera GM, TRAC, GC	ACCIONA Energia 2008	
5,27 MW	Germany, Miegersbach Picture courtesy: Phoenix Solar AG	Freiland SonnenStrom- Anlage Miegersbach GM, GC Part 1: 5824 PW 1650 175W modules, 5.792 PW 1650 165W modules (Photowatt) Part 2: 20412 Phoenix Solar PHX-160 162W modules Part 1: 2x SMA Sunny Central SC 1000MV Part 2: 3x SMA Sunny Central SC 1000MV 7 Habdank mounting structures	Phoenix Solar AG Part 1 June 2005 Part 2: December 2005	1877/3135 MWh 3150/5500 tons CO_2 emission reduction annually part 1/part 2
5,21 MW	Japan, Kameyama	Sharp plant, Kameyama BIPV, DIST, TRANS	2006	3400 tons CO_2 emission reduction annually
5,076 MW	Germany, Kleinaitingen (Bavaria) Picture courtesy: juwi GmbH, Mainz	Freiflächenanlage im Allgäu (Bayern) GM, GC	juwi GmbH 2007	
5,04 MW	Spain, Alvarado (Badajoz)	Planta de energia solar Girasol, Alvarado GM, GC, TRAC 25200 200 W modules	TUSSOL November 2007	
5 MW	Spain, La Puente de Piedra	Plataforma Solar Fotovoltaica La Puente de Piedra	Solarig January 2008	16000 MWh

	(Soria)	GM, GC 64000 modules when completed (11 MW)		11500 tons CO_2 emission reduction annually	
5 MW	Spain, Daimiel (Castilla-La Mancha)	Planta de energia solar Arsol 1 GM, GC	Aries Ingenieria March 2008	8500 tons CO_2 emission reduction annually	
5 MW	Spain, Abenójar (Ciudad Real)	Parque Fotovoltaico Abenójar GM, GC	Montebalito Energias Reovables February 2008		
5 MW	Spain, Bargas (Toledo)	Parque Fotovoltaico Bargas GM, GC	Montebalito Energias Reovables February 2008		
5 MW	Germany, Thierhaupten (Bayern)	Solarpark Thierhaupten GM, GC	City Solar AG December 2007		
5 MW	Spain, Bullas (Murcia)	Ecoparque Solar de Bullas, Murcia GM, GC, TF 73055 First Solar FS267, FS270 modules Habdank mounting structures 375 x SMA SMC 7000 HV inverters	Gehrlicher Umweltschoenende Energiesysteme GmbH 2007	7750 MWh 8155 tons CO_2 emission reduction annually	
5 MW	Germany, Bürstadt Picture courtesy: TAUBER-SOLAR Management GmbH, Tauberbischofsheim	Bürstadt plant BIPV, RM, GC BP Solar modules 3 x 340 MSS (3 units), 3 x 400 MSS (1 unit) Siemens Sinvert inverters	TAUBER-SOLAR Management GmbH, activ solar GmbH, Ralos Vertriebs Gmbh May 2005	4500 MWh 3200 tons CO_2 emission reduction annually	
5 MW	Germany, Espenhain Picture courtesy: GEOSOL Gesellschaft für Solarenergie mbH	Solarpark Leipziger Land GM, GC 32724 Shell Solar modules Serie SQ 150 (150Wp) 4 x MSS Siemens Sinvert inverters units (4 x 400 kW each) wooden mounting structure	Shell Solar GEOSOL Gesellschaft für Solarenergie mbH August 2004	5000 MWh 3700 tons CO_2 emission reduction annually	
4,8 MW	Spain, Llerena (Badajoz)	Planta Solar Fotovoltaica "Llerena 1" GM, TRAC, GC 20976 PowerLight, SunTech modules SMA inverters	SolarPack SunPower Corp. 2008	8500 MWh	
4,8 MW	Germany, Baar (Bayern) Picture source: EPURON GmbH, Hamburg	Solarpark Baar GM, GC, TF 66240 thin film modules SolarLineaa mounting structure by Conergy	EPURON GmbH SunTechnics GmbH December 2007	3600 tons CO_2 emission reduction annually	
4,59 MW	USA, Tucson, AZ Picture courtesy: Tucson Electric Power Tom Hansen	Springerville Generating Station GM, GC 34980 modules BP Solarex MST-43 ASE 300 DG/50 FIRST SOLAR FS-45 & FS-50	Global Solar Energy Inc. 2001-2004 additional arrays will be added	7732 MWh in 2005 minute peak performance 5113 kW AC	
4,4 MW	Spain, Herencia (Castilla La Mancha)	Parque fotovoltaico Herencia GM, GC	Montebalito Energias Renovables Invercartera Energia December 2007	5000 tons CO_2 emission reduction annually	

Proceed to: 51-100 > 101-150 > 151-200 > 200-250 > 251-300 > 301-350 > 351-400 ... by going to the web

http://www.pvresources.com/en/top50pv.php

Ausra and solar power panel production

Ausra built a new production facility for building thermal solar panels in April of this year. The factory, which the company also says is the first solar-thermal manufacturing plant in the United States, is equipped to produce up to 700 megawatts of solar-thermal equipment annually when it's fully ramped up. (162)

"This one factory will more than double the world output of thermal solar power capacity," Ausra Vice President John O'Donnell said. "Every year, we can fill 4 square miles with steel, or power half a million homes, from what's built out of this one plant."

A flurry of announcements in the last year, including solar-thermal parks from Israel's Solel Solar Systems and Spain's Acciona Energy, and an announcement that a consortium of southwestern states is looking to commission a 250-megawatt plant, indicate the market for a once-staid technology is growing. A report released by Emerging Energy Research on Tuesday forecast that up to $20 billion will be invested in concentrating solar power in the next five years.

"When you add up the global announcements for concentrated solar power, the market is in the thousands of megawatts," said Mike Taylor, a technical-services manager at the Solar Electric Power Association, who cautioned that many plants don't actually operate at their full capacity.

Solar-thermal power plants use the sun's heat, instead of its light, to produce electricity. In Ausra's case, the company is using fields of mirrors to heat water into steam, which can then be converted into electricity using a standard steam turbine.

Instead of expensive parabolic troughs, which are curved mirrors, and pricey evacuated tubes, Ausra's design uses fixed receivers that don't move and cheaper steel-backed troughs.

Systems such as Ausra's, which use what are called "compact linear Fresnel reflectors" with standard mirrors instead of parabolic troughs will cost less for the initial installation but may be less efficient.

But by replacing hand-built troughs with tractor-truck-sized modules that can be made on a production line and dropped into place with a forklift, Ausra claims its technology can cut solar-thermal costs to 10.4 cents per kilowatt-hour, from an estimated 16 to 18 cents per kilowatt-hour, right away and to 7.9 cents per kilowatt-hour -- less than the cost of coal-fired power -- in three years.

Ausra expects to be able to produce one module, which now takes two hours to make, every 10 minutes. The capacity far exceeds the requirements of the company's contract for a 177-megawatt power plant for PG&E located in California.

Ausra has been manufacturing for three years in Australia;. All the materials and process were developed for use in car manufacturing; bonding steel to glass such as car manufacturers do when manufacturing wind shields

Photovoltaic 'tree' in Styria, Austria

Appendix IV - Definition of terms

Definition of Energy Terms

With the different forms of energy and the various levels over wide ranges of energy, different measurement units had to be defined that made sense within the various industries for their level of energy being utilized. In order to understand the concept of energy within each of the various sciences and industries, it is important to recognize certain terms and how they relate to the overall function of energy. These units or terms are such things as joules, Calories, watts, kilowatt- hours, British thermal units (BTUs), Therms, horsepower, and other units used to express the use of energy within the various industries.

If you are interested at all in energy, then you should make a copy of this Appendix IV. It will come in handy.

Joule

The joule is the basic scientific term used to describe energy. In scientific terms, it is the energy required to move an electric charge of one coulomb through an electrical potential difference of one volt. If we moved the electric charge through a battery of 1.5 volts, it would require 1.5 joules of energy.

Watt

The watt is also the energy consumed to produce one joule continuously for one second, or one joule per second is called a watt. Because the joule and watt are too small a term for the power used in everyday life, the kilowatt-hour is used.

The watt is not a true international technical term for energy because it is a joule per second. This is a power measurement. However, the joule and second are recognized international terms of measurement. The watt as a unit of power is now accepted internationally as the means of measurement of energy; so most Americans recognize the watt and not the joule.

Watt-hour

The watt-hour (Wh) is a unit of energy most commonly used on household electricity meters in the form of kilowatt-hour (kWh). A watt has units of energy per time. An hour is a convenient time rather than seconds. When multiplied together, they produce a unit of energy called a watt-hour. The watt-hour is derived from the multiplication of an international unit (SI) of power (watt) and a non-SI unit of time (hour). This was discussed internationally for some time before this term was accepted.

One watt-hour is the amount of energy expended by a one-watt load, such as a small light bulb drawing power for one hour. For reasons of convenience and intuition, laymen and utilities tend to use watt-hours to measure energy rather than joules. The watt-hour is usually used in electrical terms, but it is also used in the measurements of Sun's heat input to Earth.

Kilowatt-hour

One kilowatt-hour is equal to the use of 1,000 watts for an hour, or 1,000 joules per hour. The kilowatt-hour is commonly used to measure electrical and natural gas energy. Many electric utility companies use the kilowatt-hour for billing their customers.

If one used a 100-watt light bulb for lighting, it would provide 100 watt-hours in an hour. If it was left on for twenty-four hours, it would use 2,400 watt-hours in a day or 2.4 KWhr. If it was left on for a month, multiply these daily Kilowatt- hours by the number of days in the month. That would result in an electric bill in kilowatt-hours.

For a monthly electric bill, one might see a bill for the use of several hundred kilowatt-hours. This would be the accumulation of the kilowatt-hours per day that adds up to that many kilowatt-hours accumulated over a month. This is much more convenient than using the term of joules per second of energy used for a month. For example, a bill for 200 kilowatt-hours in a month, if expressed in terms of joules, would be 720 million joules in a month on an electric bill.

This is not a reasonable unit to use. People would not comprehend the impact of the use of a 100-watt light bulb or other electrical equipment in their homes. Of course, industrial use is so high in a month that they even have to use units that work well within their systems.

Electron volt/Mega electron volt

The electron volt (eV) appears as a unit of measure at the other end of the energy spectrum. Scientists Use the electron volt to measure and define energy at the low-energy portion of the energy spectrum. It is equivalent to the energy required to move one electron through a potential difference of one volt. Physicists have found that a more useful unit of energy is the mega electron volt (MeV), or 106 electron volts. As the charge on the electron is -1.6 x 10-19 coulombs, it means there are 6.25 x 1018 eV in 1 joule. Conversely, 1 eV is 1.6 x 10-19 joules.

Calorie

A calorie (small calorie) is a unit of measurement for energy. In most fields, the joule has replaced it as the international standard unit. However, the calorie has been in common use for the amount of food energy one consumes and amount of energy one expends over a period of time. Therefore, the calorie retained its identifying feature of a measure of energy. However, there is one major difference.

There is a small calorie and a large kilocalorie, which is equivalent to 1,000 small calories. The calorie falls into two classes:

- The small calorie or gram calorie approximates the energy needed to increase the temperature of 1 gram of water by 1 degree Celsius (0.55 Fahrenheit) This is equal to 4.184 joules. The large calorie or kilocalorie is the table Calorie and equals 4,184 joules and approximates the energy needed to increase the temperature of 1 kilogram (2.2 pounds) of water by 1 degree C. (0.55 Fahrenheit). This is called the kilocalorie. In food content, it is marked by a large "C."
- This **large Calorie** is used in our definition of calories in food and food intake.

It is equal to the kilocalorie and is equal to 4,184 joules. One consumes the large calorie via exercising or just breathing. A person replaces the loss of Calories by taking on food Calories. **This unit is used throughout the discussions in the book and is marked with a capital C so one can relate to the everyday Calories that one eats. There is an interesting fact related to the table Calorie and the human consumption of energy. Not many people think of Calories and the amount of energy a human takes in when expressing it in Watts. Watts is an energy term that is familiar to the people in the United States.**

In general the average person consumes 2000 Calories per day. This is to replace the energy he/she burns off each day. In watts this is equivalent to approximately 8 million 400 thousand watts (8,400,000 watts) a day a person burns off in energy and must replace with food to maintain their weight. It is different for different people depending on how active one is and one's metabolism. Every time I mention to a person that they burn off approximately eight million four hundred thousand watts a day – they get shocked. The human body is a wondrous thing and burns off energy even while sleeping. If one normally consumes 2000 Calories a day and he cuts it to 1500 a day he will begin to lose weight at approximately 0.5 to 1.0 pounds a week.

British thermal unit (BTU)

The British thermal unit (BTU) describes the use of thermal energy. This term is used globally in the power, steam generation, heating, and air-conditioning industries as a measure of power. Although it is in common use in these industries, in scientific use, the joule and kilojoule have replaced it.

In North America, the BTU describes the heat value, that is, energy content, of fuels. It also describes the power of heating and cooling systems, such as furnaces, stoves, barbecue grills, and air conditioners, to state their energy capability.

Through early use of this term and the large number associated with its consumption, it was called out as MBtu to represent 1,000 Btu. This can be confused as a million BTU, but it remained to represent 1000 Btu's because of this historical character. Many industries have gone to MMBtu to represent one million BTU.

A BTU is defined as the amount of heat required to raise the temperature of 1 pound of water by 1 degree Fahrenheit. 143 BTU are required to melt 1 pound of ice at 32 degrees Fahrenheit. As is the case with the table Calorie, several different definitions of the BTU exist, which are based on different water temperatures. Therefore, it may vary by up to 0.5 percent. The value in joules is centered on 1,055 joules (or 1055 watts), which equals 1 BTU. One BTU is equal to 0.252 kilocalories, or about a quarter of a table Calorie.

Summary

Since different activities use different terms to measure their use of energy, we must review all these terms and see how they relate. In the end, they are all the uses of energy and when expressed over a time period they express power. One 170 Beyond Global Warming may have to convert from one type of unit measurement to another, depending on what one is trying to achieve. The basic measurement is in joules, but they are inconvenient to use at times. I think you will enjoy seeing conversions of all these terms on a few sheets of paper, and it will provide you with a reference for everyday use.

Appendix item V -
Conversions of Energy Units

Joules and Watts

1J = 1 joule = 1 watt for one second or watt-second = 1Ws

1 joule = amount of energy required to heat 1 gram of dry, cool air by 1 degree Celsius = 1W

1W = 1 watt = 1 joule per second

1MW = 1 megawatt = 10^6 watts =10^6 joules per second 1 gigawatt = 1GW = 1 x10^9 watts = one thousand MW 1 terawatt = 1 x 10^{12} watts = one million MW

1 watt-hour = 3,600 joules =3.6 x 10^3 joules = Wh =3.413 BTU

1 kilowatt-hour = 1 kWh =3.6 megajoules = 3.6 x 10^6 joules = 3.6 MJ

1 gigawatt-hour = 1 GWh = 1 x 10^9 watt-hours = 3.6 x 10^{12} joules = 3,600 MJ 1 terawatt-hour = 1 TWh = 1 x 10^{12} watt-hours = 3.6 x 10^{15} joules = one million MWh

1 petawatt-hour = 1 x 10^{15} watt-hours =1000 TWh = 1000 million MWh

1 joule = 6.242 x 10^{18} electron volts (eV)

1 EV = 1 electron volt = 1.6 x 10^{-19} joules

1 MeV = 10^6 eV = 10^6 electron volts = 1.6 x 10^{-13} joules

1 GJ = one gigajoule = 26.8 m^3 of natural gas at a defined temperature and pressure

1 TJ = 1 terajoule = 10^{12} joules = 31,710 watts = 31.71 kW

1 horsepower = 746 watts

1 horsepower-hour = 2.686 MJh= 746 Wh = 2.69 MW

1 ton of TNT = 4.2 x 10^9 joules = 4.2 x 10^9 watts

1 kT TNT = 1 kiloton of TNT = 4.2 x 10^{12} joules = 4.2 x 10^{12} watts= 4.2 million MW

15–20 kT TNT = 63 x 10^{12} W to 84 x 10^{12} W = 63 million MW to 84 million MW atomic bombs dropped in World War II

1MT TNT = 1 megaton of TNT = 4.2×10^{15} joules = 4.2×10^{15} watts = 4,200 million MW

Calories

1 calorie = 1 small calorie = 4.186 joules = 4.186 watts = energy to heat 1 gram of water by 1 degree Celsius

1 Calorie = 1 kilocalorie = 1 C = 1 table food calorie = 1,000 small calories = 4,1868 J = 4.1868×10^3 watts

1 C = kcal = energy to heat 1 kilogram of water by 1 degree Celsius or 2.2 pounds by 1 degree Celsius

38 C = 38 food calories = energy released by metabolism of 1 gram of fat 2,000 Calories = average intake of food Calories per day of man = average output of energy per day by a man

2,000 Calories = 8.1868×10^6 watts of energy consumed and burned by man per day =

8.187 megawatts per day = 8.187 MW/day = 8 million 187 thousand Watts per day

1,500 Calories = 1,500 C = average intake of food Calories per day of woman = average energy output a day for a woman = 6,140,250 Watts per day consumed by a woman

1,500 Calories = 6.28×10^6 watts of energy consumed and burned per day = 6.28

megawatts per day = 6.28 MW/day consumed by a woman on 1500 Calories per day

Converting Watts to Calories on Common Functions

Assume the average person consumes 2000 Calories per day and burns off 8.186 megawatts per day and there are 6.7×10^9 people in the world = 5.48×10^{16} watts per day

equal 13×10^{12} Calories per day = 54,800 million MW per day

5.0×10^4 W = energy released by combustion of one gram of gasoline = 11.94 C

5.0×10^7 W = energy released by combustion of 1 kilogram (2.2 pounds) of gasoline

= 11,940 C

200,000W to 500,000W= kinetic energy of a car at highway speeds = 47 to 119

C.= .2 to .5 MW = 2.4% to 6% of energy man burns off in a day.

7.2×10^{10} W = energy consumed by the average automobile in the United States

in 2000 = 17.197×10^6 Calories = 17.2 million Calories

1.74×10^{17}W= total energy from the sun that hits the Earth in one second=41.6 $\times 10^{12}$ C = 174,000 million MW per second

2.5×10^{17}W = energy release of Tsar Bomba, the largest nuclear weapon ever tested = 59.7 x 1012 C = little over the energy of the sun that hits earth in one second

1.04×10^{19}W= total energy from Sun that hits Earth in one minute=2.48 x 10^{15}

Calories = 10,400,000 million MW

1.339×10^{19} W = total production of electrical energy in the United States in 2001 = 3.198×10^{15} Calories which is just a little over the energy of the sun hitting the earth for one minute

1.05×10^{20}W= energy consumed by the United States in one year (2001) = 25.1

$\times 10^{15}$ C = 105,000,000 million MW

6.2×10^{20}W= energy from the sun that heats Earth in one hour =148.1 x 10^{15} C

= 148.1 PetaCalories

1.5×10^{22} W = energy from the Sun that heats Earth in one day =3.58×10^{18}C per day = 3.58 ExaCalories

6.0×10^{21} W = energy estimated natural gas reserves in world = 1433.0×10^{18} C

= 1433 ExaCalories

7.4×10^{21} W= energy estimated petroleum reserves in world = 1767.5×10^{18} C

=1,767.5 ExaCalories

BOE = Barrel of oil equivalent = 6.12×10^9 watts = 1.46×10^6 Calories = 1.46

MegaCalories

1 million barrel of oil per day = 73,000 MW per day

50 million barrels of oil per day = 3,650,000 MW per day

100 million barrels of oil per day = 73 million MW per day

British thermal unit (BTU

1 BTU = 1,055 joules = 1,055 watts = 1.055 kW

1 BTU = 253 small calories = 0.253 kilocalories = 0.253 Calories

1 BTU = 778 ft. lbf (foot pounds of force)

1 MMBtu = 1 million BTU in natural gas = 1,000 cubic feet (Mcf) natural gas

1 watt-hour = 1Wh = 3.41 BTU/h

1,000 BTU/h = 293 Wh

10,000 BTU/h = 2,930 Wh

1 horsepower hour = 2,540 BTU/hour = 746 W

12,000 BTU/h = 1 "ton of cooling" in air-conditioning = the amount of power needed to melt one short ton of ice in 24 hours

100,000 BTU = 1 therm (as used in heating and air-conditioning)

1 quad (energy) = 10^{15} BTU ≈ 1 exajoule (1.055×10^{18} J) = 33.5×10^9 W = 33,500 MW

Quads are occasionally used in the United States for representing the annual energy consumption of large economies; for example, the American economy used 99.75 quads per year in 2005 = 3.3 million MW per year

Appendix VI -
Powers of ten

Multiple	Name in watts	Symbol	Calories
10	watt	w	.00040C
10^3	Kilowatts	kW	.240C
10^6	Megawatts	MW	2.4×10^2
10^9	Gigawatts	GW	2.4×10^5
10^{12}	Terawatts	TW	2.4×10^8
10^{15}	Petawatts	PW	2.4×10^{11}
10^{18}	Exawatts	EW	2.4×10^{14}
10^{21}	Zettawatts	ZW	2.4×10^{17}
10^{24}	Yottawatts	YW	2.4×10^{20}

It is very important to understand that when you are converting any power of watts into Calories that the Calories are an energy value and not related to time whereas watts are a power term and is expressed in joules per second. So when converting a watt minute to Calories you must multiply the normal watts listed by 60 seconds to express the total joules in that minute and then convert the joules to the Calories in that minute (both joules and calories are pure energy terms). Remember one Calorie equals

4,186 joules, so to convert from joules to Calories one must divide the joules by 4.186×10^3 joules per Calorie to obtain the energy in Calories.

If the watts are expressed in hours then you must multiply the watt hours by 3600 seconds to convert to the total joules in those watt hours and then convert the joules to Calories.

Convert the total joules to calories by dividing by 4,186 joules per Calorie. When expressing watts per day, then you must multiple the watts by 3600 (seconds per hour) x 24 (hours per day) to obtain the total joules per day before converting to Calories per day by dividing by 4,186 joules per Calorie. When the watts are expressed in a year then you must multiply the watts by 3600 seconds per minute x 24 hours per day x 365 days a year to get the joules per year. Divide these joules by 4,186 joules per Calorie to obtain the Calories.

Many people get confused by this since scientists are use to expressing energy in terms of joules (energy) and the commercial world is used to expressing things in watts (power); like your electric bill each month is expressed in Kilowatt hours.

Many times the terms used are in kilowatts, megawatts, gigawatts, etc. and you need to convert to energy terms of joules, kilojoules, megajoules etc. before converting into Calories. In these cases you must convert to joules by using the same rules as I just indicated, taking the exponents into account and then converting into joules first and then converting into Calories by dividing by 4,186 joules per Calorie.

It is a good practice to keep in mind that there are 3600 seconds in an hour and 86,400 seconds in a day (8.64×10^4) and 31,536,000 seconds in a year.

Table of Contents

1. en.wikipedia.org/wiki/Solar_radiation;
2. okfirst.ocs.ou.edu/train/meteorology/EnergyBudget2.htm
3. Chart prepared by Climatologist Cliff Harris and Meteorologist Randy Mann
4. http://en.wikipedia.orog/wiki/Little_Ice_Age
5. http://en.wikipedia.orog/wiki/Little_Ice_Age
6. http://en.wikipedia.orog/wiki/Little_Ice_Age
7. physicalgeography.net/fundeamental/7j.htm
http://dev.nsta.org/ssc/moreinfo.asp?id=9471
8. physicalgeography.net/fundamentals/7j.html
http://okfirst.ocs.ou.edu/train/meteorology/EnergyBudget2.html
Solar constant 27.physicalgeography.net/fundamentals/7j.html
9. 31.en.wikipedia.org/wiki/Evaporation; In Semiconductor Devices: Physics and Technology by Simon M. Sze, there is an especially detailed discussion of film deposition by evaporation; Martin A. Silberberg, Chemistry, 4th ed. (New York: McGraw-Hill, 2006).
10. climatesci.colorado.edu/2007/04/05/
11. http://www.physicalgeography.net/fundamentals/7j.html
12. En.wikipedia.org/wiki/World_energy_resources_and _consumption; Energy
13. Space.com/searchforlife/life_origins_001205.html
14. En.wikipedia.org/widi/Cambrian; Stephen Jay Gould, Wonderful Life: the Burgess Shale and the Nature of Life (New York: Norton, 1989).
15. Chivilan and Epstein, Boston Globe April 10,1997
16. ABT Associates study
17. Chivilan and Epstein, Boston Globe, April 10, 1997
18. Department of Energy and Maryland Energy Administration
19. Matt Wald, The New York Times, August 11, 1997)
20. he Fund for Renewable Energy Everywhere)

21. http://www.dieoff.org/page136.htm
22. upc-online.org/slaughter/2000slaughter_stats.html en.wikipedia.org/wiki/Aquaculture; J. Hepburn, "Taking Aquaculture
23. Seriously," http://www.upc-online.org/slaughter/2000slaughter_stats.html
24. http://www.avma.org.onlnews/javma/aug02/020801a.asp
25. http://www.upc-online.org/slaughter/2000slaughter_stats.html
26. en.wikipedia.org/wiki/Aquaculture
27. NOAA atmospheric chemist Wouter Peters.
28. http://en.wikipedia.org/wiki/Carbon_ capture_and_storage//cite_note-20
29. http://www.dakotagas.com/Companyinfo/index.html
30. http://en.wikipedia.org/wiki/Carbon_capture_and_storage//cite_note 20
31. www.offshore-environment.com/facts.html134
32. Energy Innovations report) U.S. Department of Energy and Maryland Energy Administration)
33. U.S. Environmental Protection Agency and Alliance to Save Energy)
34. http://en.wikipedia.org/wiki/World_energy_resources_and_consumption#cite_ EIA-0
35. http://en.wikipedia.org/wiki/World_energy_resources_and_consumption#cite_ Renewables2006-2
36. http://en.wikipedia.org/wiki/World_energy_resources_and_consumption#cite_ 5
37. Source: California Energy Commission, Fuels Office, PIIRA database. Based on 2004 data. (42)
38. http://en.wikipedia.org/wiki/World_energy_resources_and_consumption#cite_ Renewables2006-2
39. http://www2.minambiente.it/Sito/Settori_azione/pia/docs/roundtable_09_12_2
40. http://en.wikipedia.org/wiki/World_energy_resources_and_consumption#cite_ 32
41. http://en.wikipedia.org/wiki/Wind_power#cite_note-gwec-0
42. http://en.wikipedia.org/wiki/Wind_power#cite_note-gwec-0
43. http://en.wikipedia.org/wiki/Wind_power#cite_note-gwec-0
44. http://en.wikipedia.org/wiki/World_energy_resources_and_consumption#cite_ 26

45. http://www.mlive.com/environment/index.ssf/2008/03/states_first_commercia

46. http://www.mlive.com/environment/index.ssf/2008/03/states_first_commercia

47. http://en.wikipedia.org/wiki/World_energy_resources_and_consumption#cite_ 67

48. International Commission on Large Dams. In 2000, there were over

49. 000 large dams around the world. (63)

50. http://en.wikipedia.org/wiki/Hydroelectricity#cite_note-11#cite_note-11

51. http://www.howstuffworks.com/framed.htm?parent=hydropower-plant.htm&url=http://www.nrel.gov/

52. http://www.erg.com.np/hydropower_global.php

53. http://ga.water.usgs.gov/edu/wuhy.html

54. http://www.hydrofoundation.org/hydropower/index.html

55. http://www.erg.com.np/hydropower_global.php 60http://en.wikipedia.org/wiki/Three_Gorges_Dam

56. http://en.wikipedia.org/wiki/Yangtze_River

57. http://en.wikipedia.org/wiki/Photovoltaics#cite_note-Smil-80

58. http://en.wikipedia.org/wiki/Solar_energy#cite_note-81#cite_note-81, 82, 83, 84, 85

59. http://en.wikipedia.org/wiki/World_energy_resources_and_consumption#cite_ Renewables2006-2

60. http://en.wikipedia.org/wiki/Solar_energy#cite_note-33#cite_note-33

61. http://en.wikipedia.org/wiki/Solar_energy#cite_note-Renewables_2007-36#cite_note-Renewables_2007-36

62. http://en.wikipedia.org/wiki/Solar_energy#cite_note-Renewables_2007-36#cite_note-Renewables_2007-36

63. http://www.wikinvest.com/industry/Solar_Power

64. http://www.wikinvest.com/image/RenewableGeneratingCosts.jpg

65. http://www.wikinvest.com/industry/Solar_Power#_note-11

66. http://www.wikinvest.com/images/d/db/RenewableGeneratingCosts.jpg

67. http://www.wikinvest.com/industry/Solar_Power

68. http://en.wikipedia.org/wiki/World_energy_resources_and_consumption#cite_ 29

69. http://en.wikipedia.org/wiki/Solar_energy#cite_note-8#cite_note-8

70. http://en.wikipedia.org/wiki/World_energy_resources_and_consumption#cite_ 30

71. http://en.wikipedia.org/wiki/Photovoltaics#cite_note-11 77 http://en.wikipedia.org/wiki/Photovoltaics#cite_note-75

72. Nomura Securities, Nikkei Microdevices as displayed in Solid State Technology magazine of October 08

73. http://en.wikipedia.org/wiki/Photovoltaics#cite_note-16

74. http://en.wikipedia.org/wiki/Photovoltaics#cite_note-62

75. http://en.wikipedia.org/wiki/Photovoltaics#cite_note-71

76. http://upload.wikimedia.org/wikipedia/en/c/c9/Usgs_mojave_desert.jpg

77. http://en.wikipedia.org/wiki/Solar_power_plants_in_the_Mojave_Desert# STS-0

78. http://en.wikipedia.org/wiki/Solar_power_plants_in_the_Mojave_Desert# conc-4

79. http://en.wikipedia.org/wiki/Solar_power_plants_in_the_Mojave_Desert# solel-3

80. http://en.wikipedia.org/wiki/Solar_power_plants_in_the_Mojave_Desert# STS-0

81. http://en.wikipedia.org/wiki/World_energy_resources_and_consumption# Tester_2005-56

82. Gavin Hudson summary on web site http://ecoworldly.com/2008/03/05/worlds-7-biggest-solar-energy-plants/

83. http://www.pvresources.com/en/top50pv.php

84. http://spectrum.ieee.org/oct08/6851 Article by Peter Fairley

85. http://en.wikipedia.org/wiki/World_energy_resources_and_consumption#cite_ Renewables2006-2

86. http://en.wikipedia.org/wiki/Wave_power#cite_note-11

87. http://www.energeninternational.com/

88. http://en.wikipedia.org/wiki/Wave_power#cite_note-14

89. http://en.wikipedia.org/wiki/Wave_power#cite_note-16

90. http://en.wikipedia.org/wiki/Wave_power#cite_note-22

91. http://en.wikipedia.org/wiki/World_energy_resources_and_consumption#cite_ Renewables2006-2

92. http://en.wikipedia.org/wiki/Geothermal_power#cite_note-12#cite_note-

93. http://en.wikipedia.org/wiki/Geothermal_power#cite_note-eere-13#cite_note-eere-13

94. http://en.wikipedia.org/wiki/Geothermal_power#cite_note-INEL-10#cite_note-INEL-10

95. http://en.wikipedia.org/wiki/World_energy_resources_and_consumption#cite_ INEL-31

96. http://en.wikipedia.org/wiki/Geothermal_power#cite_note-7#cite_note-7

97. http://en.wikipedia.org/wiki/World_energy_resources_and_consumption#cite_ ieakey2007-15

98. http://en.wikipedia.org/wiki/World_energy_resources_and_consumption#cite_UIC07-Italy-19

99. http://en.wikipedia.org/wiki/Nuclear_power#cite_note-38

100. http://en.wikipedia.org/wiki/Breeder_reactor#cite_note-5

101. http://en.wikipedia.org/wiki/Nuclear_power#cite_note-wna-thorium-45

102. http://en.wikipedia.org/wiki/Nuclear_power_plant#cite_note-55

103. http://en.wikipedia.org/wiki/Nuclear_power#cite_note-INL-27

104. http://en.wikipedia.org/wiki/Nuclear_power#cite_note-29

105. http://www.world-nuclear.org/info/reactors.html

106. http://www.world-nuclear.org/uploadedFiles/org/info/pdf/EconomicsNP.pdf

107. http://en.wikipedia.org/wiki/Energy_use_in_the_United_States#cite_note-1

108. http://en.wikipedia.org/wiki/Image:US_historical_energy_consumption.PNG

109. http://en.wikipedia.org/wiki/Image:USenergy2004

110. http://en.wikipedia.org/wiki/Energy_use_in_the_United_States#cite_note-5

111. http://en.wikipedia.org/wiki/Energy_use_in_the_United_States#cite_note-7

112. http://en.wikipedia.org/wiki/Energy_use_in_the_United_States#cite_note-EIA-8

113. http://en.wikipedia.org/wiki/Energy_use_in_the_United_States#cite_note-10

114. http://en.wikipedia.org/wiki/Energy_use_in_the_United_States#cite_note-12

115. http://www.eia.doe.gov/pub/international/iealf/tablee1c.xls
116. http://europa.eu/rapid/pressReleasesAction.do?reference=
117. MEMO/07/2#fn4
118. http://en.wikipedia.org/wiki/Coal#cite_note-13
119. http://thefraserdomain.typepad.com/photos/uncategorized/2007/
     05/24/liquid_consumption_2.jpg
120. http://thefraserdomain.typepad.com/photos/uncategorized/
     2007/05/24/liquids_prices.jpg
121. http://thefraserdomain.typepad.com/photos/uncategorized/
     2007/05/24/liquids_reserves.jpg
122. site www.eia.doe.gov/iea.
123. http://www.eia.doe.gov/oiaf/ieo/index.html
124. http://europa.eu/rapid/pressRelesesAction.do?
     reference=MEMO/07/2
125. http://europa.eu/rapid/pressReleasesAction.do?
     reference=MEMO/07/2#fn1
126. http://en.wikipedia.org/wiki/Hydroelectricity
127. http://www.pvresources.com/en/top50pv.php
128. http://en.wikipedia.org/wiki/World_energy_resources_and_
     consumption#cite_ EIA-0
129. http://en.wikipedia.org/wiki/World_energy_resources_and_
     consumption#cite_
130.

Renewables2006-2

131. http://en.wikipedia.org/wiki/Photovoltaics#cite_note-14
132. http://en.wikipedia.org/wiki/Photovoltaics#cite_note-75
133. http://en.wikipedia.org/wiki/Solar_power_plants_in_the_Mojave_
     Desert#cite_ ENS-1
134. http://en.wikipedia.org/wiki/Solar_power_tower
135. http://en.wikipedia.org/wiki/Image:SolarStirlingEngine.jpg
136. http://en.wikipedia.org/wiki/Portugal
137. http://en.wikipedia.org/wiki/World_energy_resources_and_
     consumption#cite_ Renewables2006-2
138. http://en.wikipedia.org/wiki/Plutonium
139. http://en.wikipedia.org/wiki/Japan_Steel_Works

140. http://en.wikipedia.org/wiki/Energy_use_in_the_United_States#cite_note-9

141. http://www.spectrum.ieee.org/oct08/6827

142. Article in San Jose Mercury News of 10/25/08

143. http://en.wikipedia.org/wiki/Oil_reserves

144.

145. Quotes from a memo from Elliot H Gue concerning Germany's windmill systems

146. http://en.wikipedia.org/wiki/Solar_power_plants_in_the_Mojave_Desert#cite_ STS-0.

147. http://en.wikipedia.org/wiki/Nevada_Solar_One

148. http://search.aol.com/aol/search?